The Canadian Book of Birthdays

The Canadian Book of Birthdays

Shane Sellar

BLUE BIKE BOOKS

© 2009 by Blue Bike Books
First printed in 2009 10 9 8 7 6 5 4 3 2 1
Printed in Canada

All rights reserved. No part of this work covered by the copyrights hereon may be reproduced or used in any form or by any means—graphic, electronic or mechanical—without the prior written permission of the publisher, except for reviewers, who may quote brief passages. Any request for photocopying, recording, taping or storage on information retrieval systems of any part of this work shall be directed in writing to the publisher.

The Publisher: Blue Bike Books

Website: www.bluebikebooks.com

Library and Archives Canada Cataloguing in Publication

Sellar, Shane, 1978–

    The Canadian book of birthdays / by Shane Sellar.

Includes bibliographical references.

ISBN 13: 978-1-897278-54-3

    1. Chronology, Historical. 2. Anniversaries.

3. Canada—Miscellanea. I. Title.

D11.5.S39 2009   902'.02   C2009-900196-9

Project Director: Nicholle Carrière
Project Editors: Nicholle Carrière and Kathy van Denderen
Cover Image: Courtesy of Dreamstime.com (© Jusabell | Dreamstime.com, 6977835; © Davinci | Dreamstime.com, 7188652).

We acknowledge the support of the Alberta Foundation for the Arts for our publishing program.

We acknowledge the financial support of the Government of Canada through the Book Publishing Industry Development Program (BPIDP) for our publishing activities.

 Canadian Heritage   Patrimoine canadien

PC: 1

DEDICATION

This book is dedicated to everyone who was ever born.

ACKNOWLEDGEMENTS

Thanks to Blue Bike Books for allowing me this great opportunity, my parents for their constant support, and my lady friend, who tried really hard not to bother me while I worked.

INTRODUCTION

How many times has this happened to you: you're walking down the street and someone asks you what today's date is.

If you're anything like me, you fake a heart attack in order to avoid answering the question.

Sure, I've owned calendars in the past, but besides my birthday, stat holidays and pending court dates, I could care less about the other dates of the year. Even on a friend's birthday, I was unable to mutter anything besides "Where's the cake?" I was a chump and I knew it. I couldn't even get the year right. In short, I was Date Dumb.

Fortunately, those awkward moments became a thing of the past when the good folks at Blue Bike Books bestowed this project on me. When originally asked to spearhead a birthdate book that would encompass all 365 days of the year, my first reaction was, "Don't you mean 265 months of the year?" Upon clarification of which ones were days and which were months, I accepted the challenge.

Wasting no time, I headed to the Spruce Grove Public Library and began referencing Canadian history books from the children's section. With supplementary information provided by the *Farmer's Almanac*, the magic computer box, Druid priests and personal tea readings, I compiled the book you currently hold in your hands.

Now, when asked the date or told of someone's birthday, I not only treat that person to the accurate date, but also to a listing of fun days, notable news items, an oddball factoid, the number one song, an astrological reading, lucky numbers and a list of notable people born on the day in question.

In fact, thanks to the date-to-date Canadian and world tidbits I've acquired, the people who once asked me for the date are now the ones faking heart attacks in order to get away from me and my Date Dominance.

So if you're sick of being Date Dumb and are interested in taking your calendar vocabulary from ignorance to irritation, then this book is for you. I hope you get as sweaty reading it, as I did writing it. Enjoy.

Peas out,

Shane Sellar

365 + 1
BIRTHDAYS

JANUARY 1
364 days until next year

In a Days

If you're a Babylonian, your New Year's resolution is to return borrowed farm equipment.

If you celebrate Kwanzaa, it ends today.

If your last name begins with the letter Z, you get to go first in line—it's "Z Day."

In the News

1876: St. Catharines, ON, was incorporated as a city.

1908: The first New Year's ball dropped in New York's Times Square.

1922: Motorists in BC began driving on the right-hand side of the road.

1929: Point Grey and South Vancouver amalgamated to form what is now Vancouver.

1965: Trans-Canada Airlines changed its name to Air Canada.

1970: Port Arthur and Fort William amalgamated to form what is now Thunder Bay.

1980: Canadian ski jumper Horst Bulau won the World Cup 90 m ski jump event.

2000: A 5.2-magnitude earthquake hit Lake Kipawa, ON.

2004: After much ballyhoo, Montréal-Dorval International Airport was renamed Montréal-Pierre Elliott Trudeau International Airport.

Capricorn

You are a charming and affectionate individual who has a tendency to be too trusting.
1, 2, 11

#1 Song

1959: "The Chipmunk Song" by The Chipmunks

Birth Friends Forever

Devin Setoguchi, Canadian hockey player, 1987

Becky Kellar, Canadian hockey player, 1975

Verne Troyer, actor (*Austin Powers*), 1969

Marcia Cross, actress (*Desperate Housewives*), 1961

Carol Alt, model, 1960

Grandmaster Flash, rapper, 1958

Jackie Burroughs, Canadian actress (*Road to Avonlea*), 1939

Alex Campbell, Canadian politician, 1933

J.D. Salinger, author (*Catcher in the Rye*), 1919

Frank Stack, Canadian speed skater, 1906

Harriet Brooks, Canadian physicist, 1876

Francis Bond Head, Canadian politician, 1793

Daily Oddity

On this date in 1947, the Canadian Citizenship Act went into effect. Until that point, Canadians were still considered "British subjects living in Canada."

JANUARY 2
363 days until next year

In a Days
Greetings, Earthling! It's "National Science Fiction Day."
Happy Meow Year! It's "Cat New Year's Day."

In the News

1808: The U.S. banned the importation of slaves.

1826: The Supreme Court of Newfoundland was founded.

1884: A railway accident near Humber, ON, killed 31 people.

1917: The Royal Bank of Canada took over the Québec Bank.

1929: World War I pilot Wop May began air-delivering diphtheria vaccine to Fort Vermilion, AB.

1929: Canada and the U.S. agreed to preserve Niagara Falls.

1935: Bruno Hauptmann went on trial for the kidnapping and murder of the Lindbergh baby.

1983: Joe Clark resigned as leader of Canada's Opposition Party.

2001: Sila Calderón became Puerto Rico's first female governor.

Capricorn
You are a creative and objective individual; however, you can sometimes place unrealistic demands on yourself.
2, 11, 20

#1 Song
2004: "Hey Ya!" by OutKast

Birth Friends Forever
Kate Bosworth, actress (*Blue Crush*), 1983

Taye Diggs, actor (*Chicago*), 1971

Christy Turlington, model, 1969

Cuba Gooding Jr., actor (*Jerry Maguire*), 1968

Tia Carrere, actress (*Wayne's World*), 1967

George Hungerford, Canadian rower, 1944

Avie Bennett, Canadian philanthropist, 1928

Glen Harmon, Canadian hockey player, 1921

Isaac Asimov, author (*I, Robot*), 1920

Barbara Lally Pentland, Canadian composer, 1912

Florence Lawrence, Canadian actress (*Confidence*), 1890

Frederick Horsman Varley, Canadian painter, 1881

Daily Oddity
Vulcan, AB, was named after the Roman god of fire.

JANUARY 3
362 days until next year

In a Days

If you are a chocolate-covered cherry, celebrate "Chocolate-Covered Cherry Day."

Purée the harvest and chug it back because it's "Drinking Straw Day."

If you're a Hobbit, an Orc or a Golum, celebrate "Tolkien Day."

In the News

1496: Leonardo da Vinci unsuccessfully attempted to fly.

1863: The first covered skating rink opened in Halifax, NS.

1870: Construction began on the Brooklyn Bridge.

1899: The word "automobile" was coined.

1938: The U.S. established the March of Dimes.

1956: The top of the Eiffel Tower caught fire.

1957: The electric watch was invented.

1961: The U.S. cut all ties with Cuba.

1977: Apple Computers was incorporated.

2003: New Brunswick was hit by an ice storm that left 60,000 people without power.

2008: A false bomb threat shut down Montréal's Victoria Bridge for 4 hours.

Capricorn

You are a persuasive and ambitious person whose drive to succeed sometimes overwhelms others.
2, 11, 13

#1 Song

1989: "Every Rose Has Its Thorn" by Poison

Birth Friends Forever

Alisen Down, Canadian actress (*The L Word*), 1976

Danica McKellar, actress (*Wonder Years*), 1975

Cory Cross, Canadian hockey player, 1971

Mel Gibson, actor (*Lethal Weapon*) 1956

Dean Hart, Canadian wrestler, 1954

John Paul Jones, musician (*Led Zeppelin*), 1946

Bobby Hull, Canadian hockey player, 1939

Marcel Dubé, Canadian playwright, 1930

Robert Loggia, actor (*Scarface*), 1930

Renaude Lapointe, Canadian journalist, 1912

Victor Borge, pianist/comedian, 1909

J.R.R. Tolkien, author (*The Hobbit*), 1892

Daily Oddity

The number of days in a year is based on the Sun.

JANUARY 4
361 days until next year

In a Days

If you are a spermologist, you should know that today is "Trivia Day"—you should also know that spermology is the study of trivia.

If you're blind, I'm proud of you for reading this book. It's "World Braille Day."

If you are susceptible to becoming a chicken, be warned that it's "World Hypnotism Day."

In the News

1817: Stagecoach service commenced between York and Kingston, ON.

1847: Samuel Colt sold his first revolver to the U.S. government.

1883: The Ontario Rugby Football Union, the forerunner of the CFL, was founded.

1885: The first successful appendectomy was performed.

1910: The kitchen blender was first introduced.

1990: Canada defeated Czechoslovakia for the World Junior Hockey Cup Championship title.

1999: Retired professional wrestler and radio talk-show host Jesse Ventura was sworn in as governor of Minnesota; he served until January 2003.

2005: Canada defeated Russia for the World Junior Hockey Cup Championship title.

Capricorn

You are determined, with a can-do personality, which sometimes causes you to overlook other people's opinions.
2, 4, 13

#1 Song

1985: "Like a Virgin" by Madonna

Birth Friends Forever

Marina Orsini, Canadian actress (*Eddie & the Cruisers*), 1967

Benjamin Darvill, Canadian musician (Crash Test Dummies), 1967

Julia Ormond, actress (*Sabrina*), 1965

Dave Foley, Canadian comedian (*The Kids in the Hall*), 1963

Michael Stipe, singer (R.E.M.), 1960

Matt Frewer, Canadian actor (*Max Headroom*), 1958

Patty Loveless, country singer, 1957

Paul Desmarais, Canadian businessman, 1927

Arthur Villeneuve, Canadian painter, 1910

Charles "Tom Thumb" Stratton, circus performer, 1838

Louis Braille, inventor of Braille, 1809

Jakob Grimm, author (*Grimms' Fairy Tales*), 1785

Daily Oddity

The odds of getting a hole-in-one are 1 in 15,000.

JANUARY 5
360 days until next year

In a Days

Look out for 12 lords a-leaping. It's "Twelfth Night."

If you are a bird, you should celebrate "Bird Day."

If you are a younger sibling, you'll be happy to know that today is "National Second-Hand Wardrobe Day."

If you are a fruitcake, be warned—today is "National Fruitcake Toss Day."

In the News

1914: Ford Motors doubled its day wage and cut back to an 8-hour workday.

1933: Construction began on San Francisco's Golden Gate Bridge.

1940: FM radio was first demonstrated before the Federal Communications Commission.

1967: A federal proclamation was made to observe Sir John A. Macdonald's birthday; three decades later, January 11 is still not a recognized holiday in Canada.

1993: The first hanging since 1965 occurred in the U.S.

1998: Between January 5 and January 10, Eastern Canada was hit by an ice storm that dumped 100 mm of freezing rain; 25 people died.

2005: Eris, the largest known dwarf planet in the solar system, was discovered.

2007: The roof of Vancouver's BC Place Stadium collapsed.

Capricorn

You are imaginative and independent, but at times you may be too self-reliant. 5, 8, 23

#1 Song

1967: "I'm a Believer" by The Monkees

Birth Friends Forever

Kyle Calder, Canadian hockey player, 1979

Rick "The Temp" Campanelli, Canadian TV personality, 1970

Marilyn Manson, singer, 1969

Vinnie Jones, soccer player/actor (*Snatch*), 1965

John Manley, Canadian politician, 1950

Charlie Richmond, Canadian entrepreneur, 1950

Diane Keaton, actress (*Annie Hall*), 1946

Roger Spottiswoode, Canadian director (*Tomorrow Never Dies*), 1945

Robert Duvall, actor (*The Godfather*), 1931

Arthur H. Robinson, Canadian cartographer, 1915

George Reeves, actor (*Superman*), 1914

King Camp Gillette, inventor of the safety razor, 1855

Sam Steele, famed RCMP officer, 1849

Daily Oddity

Vikings thought the northern lights were the reflections of dead maidens.

JANUARY 6
359 days until next year

In a Days
If you are one of the Magi, today you visit the baby Jesus. It's "Epiphany."
If you are a Christmas tree, today you must be taken down.

In the News
1910: The Montréal Canadiens played their first game.

1918: The Free Committee for a German Workers' Peace, a forerunner to the Nazi Party, was founded.

1931: Inventor Thomas Edison filed his final patent.

1942: Pan American Airlines became the first commercial airline to schedule a flight around the world.

1974: Because of an energy crisis, the U.S. started daylight saving time 4 months early.

1987: Margaret Laurence, Canadian author of *The Stone Angel*, died at the age of 60.

1994: A masked assailant clubbed figure skater Nancy Kerrigan in the knee.

2005: Lois Hole, bestselling author and Alberta lieutenant-governor, passed away at the age of 71.

2006: Canada won gold at the 2006 World Junior Hockey Championship.

Capricorn
You are inspiring and moralistic; however, you may become too obsessed with achieving your goals.
1, 7, 15

#1 Song
1974: "The Joker" by The Steve Miller Band

Birth Friends Forever
Canada's first sextuplets, four boys and two girls, 2007

Tara Spencer-Nairn, Canadian actress (*Corner Gas*), 1978

Nikki Einfeld, Canadian opera singer, 1978

Scott Ferguson, Canadian hockey player, 1973

Rowan Atkinson, comedian (*Mr. Bean*) 1955

Anthony Minghella, director (*The English Patient*), 1954

Malcolm Young, musician (AC/DC), 1953

Syd Barrett, musician (Pink Floyd), 1946

Dickie Moore, Canadian hockey player, 1931

Tom Mix, cowboy actor, 1880

Joan of Arc, Catholic saint, 1412

Richard II, King of England, 1367

Daily Oddity
Before the name Canada was chosen, another name being discussed for the country was Albertsland.

JANUARY 7
358 days until next year

In a Days
Even though Mondays are the work of the Devil, today is "Thank God It's Monday Day."

In the News
1610: Galileo Galilei discovered the 4 moons of Jupiter, which he named after himself.

1797: The Italian flag was unveiled for the first time.

1811: The first time a non–Native American sighted Bigfoot.

1859: The first Canadian silver coins were issued.

1955: The first TV cameras were allowed into Canadian Parliament.

1990: The Leaning Tower of Pisa was closed to the public because of safety concerns and would not open again until December 2001.

1991: Operation Desert Storm began.

2003: Calgary, AB, hit 17°C, the hottest recorded temperature for January.

2004: The NHL suspended Toronto Maple Leaf Mats Sundin after he threw a broken hockey stick into the stands.

2004: Curler Randy Ferbey of Sherwood Park, AB, won the Canada Cup.

Capricorn
You are empathetic and open-minded, but you tend to suppress your opinion in order to please others.
1, 7, 16

#1 Song
1987: "Walk Like an Egyptian" by The Bangles

Birth Friends Forever
Max Morrow, Canadian actor (*Monk*), 1991

Alex Auld, Canadian hockey player, 1981

Dustin Diamond, actor (*Saved by the Bell*), 1977

Éric Gagné, Canadian baseball player, 1976

Nicolas Cage, actor (*Face/Off*), 1964

Katie Couric, news anchor, 1957

Mike Liut, Canadian hockey player, 1956

David Caruso, actor (*CSI: Miami*), 1956

Kenny Loggins, musician, 1948

Jean Corbeil, Canadian politician, 1934

Charles Addams, cartoonist (*Addams Family*), 1912

Sandford Fleming, Canadian inventor of the time zones, 1827

Daily Oddity
Heinz ketchup leaves the bottle at 40 km/h.

JANUARY 8
357 days until next year

In a Days

If you are contagious with joy germs, spread 'em around. It's "National Joy Germ Day."

If you have a good dental plan, celebrate "National English Toffee Day."

If you are employed and own a stuffed animal, bring it to "Show and Tell Day at Work."

In the News

1869: The first suspension bridge over the Niagara Gorge at Niagara Falls opened.

1877: Crazy Horse fought his last battle against the U.S. Cavalry at Wolf Mountain, MT.

1940: Britain introduced food rationing during World War II.

1941: The Federal Minister of BC announced that all Japanese Canadians in BC would be registered under the War Measures Act. They were later moved inland and put in detention camps.

1947: Toronto Maple Leaf Howie Meeker scored five goals in one game.

1948: Canada's 10th prime minister, Mackenzie King, became the longest-serving PM in the Commonwealth, serving 7825 days in office.

2006: An 6.9-magnitude earthquake hit the Mediterranean.

Capricorn

You are motivated and self-disciplined; however, sometimes you to take yourself too seriously.
8, 17, 26

#1 Song

1970: "Raindrops Keep Falling on My Head" by B.J. Thomas

Birth Friends Forever

Jeff Francis, Canadian baseball player, 1981

Sarah Polley, Canadian actress/director (*Road to Avonlea*), 1979

Ron Pederson, Canadian actor, 1977

Brad Snyder, Canadian shot putter, 1976

Jenny Lewis, musician (Rilo Kiley), 1976

R. Kelly, musician, 1967

Mike Reno, Canadian musician (Loverboy), 1955

David Bowie, musician, 1947

Stephen Hawking, physicist/author, 1942

Bob Eubanks, game-show host, 1938

Elvis Presley, the king of rock 'n' roll, 1935

Soupy Sales, comedian, 1926

Daily Oddity

Beer is the 4th most popular beverage in Canada after water, coffee and milk.

JANUARY 9
356 days until next year

In a Days

If you are a conduit, keep your hat on and don't touch anything metal—today is "National Static Electricity Day."

If you are an apricot, you should be proud—today is "National Apricot Day."

In the News

1889: The Niagara Suspension Bridge collapsed during a winter storm.

1899: It was −52°C in Norway House, MB.

1923: The first autogyro flight took place.

1951: The United Nations headquarters opened in New York City.

1965: An avalanche killed 4 drivers on a highway near Hope, BC.

1968: The only known snowfall occurred in Mexico City.

2001: Apple announced iTunes.

2005: Rawhi Fattouh was elected head of the Palestine Liberation Organization following the death of Yasser Arafat.

2007: Apple announced the iPhone.

Capricorn

You are tenacious and driven; however, this may deprive you of life's simple pleasures.

9, 18, 27

#1 Song

1980: "Escape (The Piña Colada Song)" by Rupert Holmes

Birth Friends Forever

Mathieu Garon, Canadian hockey player, 1978

AJ McLean, singer (Backstreet Boys), 1978

Dave Matthews, musician, 1967

Crystal Gayle, country singer, 1951

Buster Poindexter, singer, 1950

Jimmy Page, musician (Led Zeppelin), 1944

Joan Baez, singer, 1941

Bob Denver, actor (*Gilligan's Island*), 1935

Jean-Pierre Côté, Canadian politician, 1926

Lee Van Cleef, actor (*The Good, the Bad and the Ugly*), 1925

Lister Sinclair, Canadian broadcaster, 1921

Richard Nixon, U.S. president, 1913

Irene Parlby, Canadian member of the Famous Five, 1868

Daily Oddity

Rain is measured in millimetres, while snow is measured in centimetres.

JANUARY 10
355 days until next year

In a Days
Start a bonfire and enjoy "National Cut Your Energy Costs Day."
If the bonfire gets out of control, celebrate "Volunteer Fireman's Day."

In the News
1810: Napoleon Bonaparte annulled his marriage to Josephine.

1815: The British government banned Americans from settling in Canada.

1920: The League of Nations held its first meeting and ratified the Treaty of Versailles, which ended World War I.

1931: The Philadelphia Quakers ended the Montréal Maroons' 15-game winning streak, which remains the longest consecutive winning streak in NHL history.

1971: *Masterpiece Theater* premiered.

1990: Time Inc. and Warner Communications merged to become Time Warner.

2001: A chunk of the chalk cliff in Beachy Head, England, fell off.

2005: A mudslide in California killed 10 people and shut down the San Francisco to Los Angeles highway for 2 weeks.

Capricorn
You are a positive and confident individual, but you must be careful not to use those attributes to manipulate others.
2, 8, 19

#1 Song
1954: "Oh! My Pa-Pa (O Mein Papa)" by Eddie Fisher

Birth Friends Forever
Brad Roberts, Canadian singer (Crash Test Dummies), 1964
Benoît Pelletier, Canadian politician, 1960
Pat Benatar, singer, 1953
Rod Stewart, singer, 1945
Bernard Derome, Canadian news anchor, 1944
Jim Croce, singer, 1943
Frank Mahovlich, Canadian hockey player, 1938
Ronnie Hawkins, honorary Canadian musician, 1935
Gisele MacKenzie, Canadian singer, 1927
Ludmilla Chiriaeff, Canadian ballet dancer, 1924
Don Metz, Canadian hockey player, 1916
Ray Bolger, actor (*Wizard of Oz*), 1904
Frank James, outlaw, 1843

Daily Oddity
Every minute 160 babies are born.

JANUARY 11
354 days until next year

In a Days
If you are looking to end a friendship, celebrate "National Step in a Puddle and Splash Your Friend Day."

Although you should always say it, today is "International Thank You Day."

In the News

1569: The first-ever recorded lottery was held in London, England.

1787: Uranus' 2 moons—Titania and Oberon—were discovered.

1878: Milk was delivered in glass bottles for the first time.

1911: It was −61°C in Fort Vermillion, AB.

1922: A 14-year-old Canadian became the first person to be successfully treated for diabetes with insulin, which was discovered by 2 Canadians.

1935: Amelia Earhart became the first woman to fly solo from Hawaii to California.

1949: Los Angeles had its first recorded snowfall.

1972: East Pakistan was renamed Bangladesh.

1995: A 103-day National Hockey League lockout ended.

2007: Saskatchewan was hit by a severe winter blizzard.

Capricorn
You are logical and reliable; however, these attributes may make you seem arrogant.
2, 11, 13

#1 Song
1983: "Down Under" by Men at Work

Birth Friends Forever
Matthew Palleschi, Canadian soccer player, 1983

Cody McKay, Canadian baseball player, 1974

Amanda Peet, actress (*The Whole Nine Yards*), 1972

Mary J. Blige, singer, 1971

Kelley Law, Canadian curler, 1966

Rob Ramage, Canadian hockey player, 1959

Naomi Judd, country singer (The Judds), 1946

Anne Heggtveit, Canadian alpine skier, 1939

Jean Chrétien, Canadian prime minister, 1934

John Robarts, premier of Ontario, 1917

John Alexander Macdonald, Canadian prime minister, 1815

Daily Oddity
The average person walks 185,074 km (115,000 mi) in his or her lifetime.

JANUARY 12
353 days until next year

In a Days
Put on your tuxedo and enjoy some frozen fish. It's "Penguin Awareness Day." Indulge your cavities. It's "National Marzipan Day."

In the News
1842: The first issue of Charlottetown, PEI's *The Islander* newspaper was published.

1907: *The Financial Post* was first published.

1908: For the first time, a long-distance radio message was transmitted from the Eiffel Tower.

1977: Canadian ballet dancers Karen Kain and Frank Augustyn performed with the Bolshoi Ballet in Moscow.

1991: The Gulf War conflict began.

1995: Canadian musician Neil Young was inducted into the Rock and Roll Hall of Fame.

1998: Nineteen European nations agreed to ban human cloning.

2004: Stephen Harper entered the leadership race for Canada's Conservative Party.

2008: Eight members of New Brunswick's Bathurst High School basketball team were killed in a highway accident.

Capricorn
You are a quick-witted and confident individual who can sometimes be construed as being sarcastic.
3, 8, 21

#1 Song
1923: "Toot Toot Tootsie (Goo'bye)" by Al Jolson

Birth Friends Forever
Jocelyn Thibault, Canadian hockey player, 1975

Heather Mills, Paul McCartney's ex, 1968

Rob Zombie, musician, 1965

François Girard, Canadian director (*The Red Violin*), 1963

Oliver Platt, Canadian actor (*Simon Birch*), 1960

John Lasseter, Pixar animation director, 1957

Howard Stern, talk-radio host, 1954

Kirstie Alley, actress (*Cheers*), 1951

Joe "Smokin' Joe" Frazier, boxer, 1944

Tim Horton, Canadian hockey player/doughnut king, 1930

Jimmy Skinner, Canadian hockey coach, 1917

Jack London, author (*White Fang*), 1876

Daily Oddity
The international weather symbol for drizzle is a comma (,), while the international weather symbol for snow is an asterisk (*).

JANUARY 13
352 days until next year

In a Days
If you live in Sweden, Finland or are just extremely lazy, take down your Christmas tree. It's "St. Knut's Day."

In the News
- **1837:** A fiery blaze destroyed the Saint John, NB, business district.
- **1915:** An earthquake in Italy killed over 29,000 people.
- **1938:** The Church of England accepted the theory of evolution.
- **1942:** Henry Ford patented a plastic car.
- **1942:** A German test pilot first used an ejection seat.
- **1949:** To protect the dairy industry, PEI banned the manufacture and sale of margarine.
- **1968:** Country singer Johnny Cash performed live at Folsom Prison.
- **1982:** Ann Cools was appointed to the Senate and became the first African Canadian to serve in the Upper Chamber.
- **1992:** Japan apologized for forcing Korean women into sexual slavery during World War II.
- **2001:** Eight hundred people died in an earthquake in El Salvador.

Capricorn
You are a determined individual, bordering on obsessive. It is that insatiable drive that may cause you to alienate others.
4, 13, 14

#1 Song
2003: "Lose Yourself" by Eminem

Birth Friends Forever
Tania Vicent, Canadian short track speed skater, 1976
Patrick Dempsey, actor (*Grey's Anatomy*), 1966
Paul Higgins, Canadian hockey player, 1962
Julia Louis-Dreyfus, actress (*Seinfeld*), 1961
Richard Moll, actor (*Night Court*), 1943
Cesare Maniago, Canadian hockey player, 1939
William B. Davis, Canadian actor (*The X-Files*), 1938
Rip Taylor, comedian (*The Gong Show*), 1934
Charles Nelson Reilly, comedian (*Match Game*), 1931
Robert Stack, actor (*Unsolved Mysteries*), 1919
Art Ross, Canadian hockey player, 1886
Lionel Groulx, Canadian nationalist, 1878

Daily Oddity
No new animals have been domesticated in over 4000 years.

JANUARY 14
351 days until next year

In a Days
If you are a slob, celebrate "National Clean Off Your Desk Day."
If you are a hoarder, celebrate "Organize Your Home Day."
If you are hungry, celebrate "National Hot Pastrami Sandwich Day."
If you are lonely, celebrate "National Dress Up Your Pet Day."

In the News
1539: Spain annexed Cuba.

1942: The Canadian government ordered Japanese Canadians out of BC's coastal region.

1949: The first nonstop trans-Canada flight from Halifax to Vancouver took place.

1967: In San Francisco, 30,000 people took part in "The Human Be-In," which kick-started the "Summer of Love."

1974: Jules Léger was sworn in as Canada's 21st governor general.

1976: Eaton's department store ceased publication of its catalogue, which had been a staple of Canadian homes since 1884.

1998: Researchers presented findings on an enzyme that has the power to slow the aging process.

2005: The *Huygens* probe landed on Titan, one of Saturn's moons.

Capricorn
You are a strong-willed individual; however, that quality may cause you to disregard other people's opinions.
4, 13, 14

#1 Song
1988: "Got My Mind Set on You" by George Harrison

Birth Friends Forever
Kevin Durand, Canadian actor (*Lost*), 1974

Jason Bateman, actor (*Arrested Development*), 1969

LL Cool J, rapper, 1968

Emily Watson, actress (*Gosford Park*), 1967

Bob Essensa, Canadian hockey player, 1965

Steven Soderbergh, director (*Ocean's Eleven*), 1963

Ben Heppner, Canadian singer, 1956

Carl Weathers, actor (*Rocky*), 1948

Bill Werbeniuk, Canadian snooker player, 1947

Faye Dunaway, actress (*Bonnie & Clyde*), 1941

Louis Quilico, Canadian baritone, 1925

Henry Charles Keith Petty-Fitzmaurice, governor general of Canada, 1845

Daily Oddity
In the olden days, street-hockey players used Eaton's catalogues for shin pads.

JANUARY 15
350 days until next year

In a Days

If you are a mean person—stay home. Today is "Humanitarian Day."

If you are Neapolitan ice cream, there may be animosity in the freezer. Today is "National Strawberry Ice Cream Day."

If you are bald, or just have a bad hairdo, you'll be happy to know that today is "Hat Day."

In the News

1559: Queen Elizabeth I was crowned Queen of England.

1759: The British Museum opened.

1835: The sale of liquor to Native Americans in Upper Canada was banned.

1889: The Coca-Cola Company was incorporated.

1892: Canadian James Naismith published the first set of rules for the game of basketball, which he invented in December 1891.

1943: The Pentagon was dedicated.

1967: The first Super Bowl was played.

2001: The *Wikipedia* website was unveiled.

2005: Solar flare blasts emitted x-rays throughout the solar system.

2005: The elements calcium, aluminum, silicon and iron were discovered on the moon.

Capricorn

You are a person of unshakable conviction, which may cause you to be too idealistic.

2, 15, 24

#1 Song

1979: "Le Freak" by Chic

Birth Friends Forever

Michael Seater, Canadian actor (*Life with Derek*), 1987

Regina King, actress (*Jerry Maguire*), 1971

Shane McMahon, pro wrestler, 1970

Chad Lowe, actor (*24*), 1968

Yves P. Pelletier, Canadian film director (*Karmina*), 1961

Mario Van Peebles, actor (*Ali*), 1957

Andrea Martin, Canadian actress (*SCTV*), 1947

Martin Luther King Jr., civil rights leader, 1929

Édouard Gagnon, Canadian cardinal, 1918

Lloyd Bridges, actor (*Sea Hunt*), 1913

Mazo de la Roche, Canadian author (*Jalna*), 1879

Frederick Stanley, governor general of Canada, 1841

Daily Oddity

If you dream of polar bears, you will have good fortune.

JANUARY 16
349 days until next year

In a Days
If you are a nihilist, enjoy "Nothing Day."
If you have beliefs, allow others to as well. Today is "Religious Freedom Day."
If you still live in your parents' basement, celebrate "Appreciate a Dragon Day."

In the News
1800: John Murray Bliss fought the first duel in New Brunswick against Samuel D. Stuart.

1847: Colin Campbell Ferrie was elected the first mayor of Hamilton, ON.

1909: Explorer Ernest Shackleton reached the South Pole.

1920: Prohibition went into effect in the U.S.

1939: Canadian-born Joe Schuster and his partner Jerry Siegel published their first *Superman* comic strip.

1965: Winnipeg band Chad Allen and the Expressions re-released their hit single "Shakin' All Over" under their new moniker, The Guess Who.

1986: The Internet Engineering Task Force met for the first time.

2006: Ellen Johnson-Sirleaf of Liberia was sworn in as Africa's first female elected head of state.

Capricorn
You are a sensitive and intuitive individual; however, those attributes may cause you to suffer bouts of depression.
1, 6, 24

#1 Song
1986: "That's What Friends Are For" by Dionne Warwick & Friends

Birth Friends Forever
Jared Slingerland, Canadian musician, 1984

Brenden Morrow, Canadian hockey player, 1979

Kate Moss, model, 1974

Dameon Clarke, Canadian actor (*Prison Break*), 1972

Garth Ennis, comic book author (*Preacher*), 1970

Sade, singer, 1959

Jennifer Dale, Canadian actress (*Whale Music*), 1956

Cliff Thorburn, Canadian snooker player, 1948

John Carpenter, director (*The Thing*), 1948

Dian Fossey, zoologist, 1932

Ethel Merman, singer, 1908

Frank Zamboni, inventor of the Zamboni, 1901

Robert W. Service, Canadian poet, 1874

Daily Oddity
Manitoba has the highest rate of car theft.

JANUARY 17
348 days until next year

In a Days
Go harass someone wearing a nametag. It's "Customer Service Day."
Ask your customers their bra size. It's "Get to Know Your Customers Day."
Kiss your ass goodbye—it's "Judgment Day."

In the News

1605: *Don Quixote* was first published.

1929: Popeye the Sailor Man made his first appearance.

1964: The Winnipeg International Airport opened.

1972: Canadian air traffic controllers began a 12-day strike, grounding most commercial flights.

1994: A 6.7-magnitude earthquake hit California.

1995: A 7.3-magnitude earthquake hit Japan, killing 6434 people.

1996: Canadian-born NHL player Steve Yzerman scored his 500th goal.

1998: Paula Jones accused President Bill Clinton of sexual harassment.

2001: Canada's new, security-enhanced $20 bill was unveiled.

2007: Nuclear testing in North Korea caused the Doomsday Clock to move to 5 minutes before midnight.

Capricorn
You are confident and tenacious, which can make you domineering at times.
8, 17, 35

#1 Song
1982: "Physical" by Olivia Newton-John

Birth Friends Forever

Amanda Wilkinson, Canadian singer (The Wilkinsons), 1982

Aaron Ward, Canadian hockey player, 1973

Kid Rock, singer, 1971

Sylvain Turgeon, Canadian hockey player, 1965

Jim Carrey, Canadian actor (*Ace Ventura*), 1962

Andy Kaufman, comedian, 1949

Muhammad Ali, boxer, 1942

James Earl Jones, actor (*Star Wars*), 1931

Jacques Plante, Canadian hockey player, 1929

Vidal Sassoon, cosmetologist, 1928

Eartha Kitt, actress (*Batman*), 1927

Betty White, actress (*The Golden Girls*), 1922

Al Capone, gangster, 1899

Benjamin Franklin, inventor and statesman, 1706

Daily Oddity
The black box on an aircraft is actually orange.

JANUARY 18
347 days until next year

In a Days
Warm up your jazz hands. It's "Jazz Day."
Don't forget to wipe—it's "Pooh Day." Oops, I mean "Winnie-the-Pooh Day."

In the News

1778: James Cook discovered the Hawaiian Islands, which he deliciously named the Sandwich Islands.

1839: A group of rebels were hanged following the rebellion in Lower Canada

1896: The x-ray machine was demonstrated for the first time.

1958: Willie O'Ree of the Boston Bruins became the first African Canadian hockey player in the NHL.

1967: Yellowknife became the capital of the Northwest Territories.

2002: The Walkerton Report, pertaining to the *E. coli* bacteria outbreak in 2000 in Walkerton, ON, which caused thousands of residents to become ill, was released.

2002: The civil war in Sierra Leone ended.

2003: A bushfire in Australia killed 4 people and destroyed 500 homes.

2007: One of the worst storms in UK history killed 14 people.

Capricorn
You are a curious and intelligent individual; however, you easily become bored and frustrated.
2, 7, 9, 27

#1 Song
1953: "Don't Let the Stars Get in Your Eyes" by Perry Como

Birth Friends Forever

Jason Segel, actor (*Forgetting Sarah Marshall*), 1980

Seamus O'Regan, Canadian broadcaster, 1971

Jesse L. Martin, actor (*Law & Order*), 1969

Maxime Bernier, Canadian politician, 1963

Mark Messier, Canadian hockey player, 1961

Kevin Costner, actor (*Field of Dreams*), 1955

Gilles Villeneuve, Canadian racecar driver, 1950

Gustave Gingras, Canadian physician, 1918

Danny Kaye, actor (*Hans Christian Andersen*), 1913

Cary Grant, actor (*To Catch a Thief*), 1904

Oliver Hardy, comedian (Laurel and Hardy) 1892

A.A. Milne, author (*Winnie-the-Pooh*), 1882

Daily Oddity
Shirley Temple had 56 curls in her hair all the time.

JANUARY 19
346 days until next year

In a Days
Drench yourself in hot butter. It's "National Popcorn Day."
Go hug a bald eagle or Joe Walsh, because it's "Eagles Day."
Look out! It's "Archery Day."

In the News
1935: Coopers Inc., later Jockey, sold the world's first pair of men's briefs.

1937: Howard Hughes flew from Los Angeles to New York City in 7 hours, 28 minutes, 25 seconds—a new world record.

1950: The Avro Canada CF-100 military jet (a.k.a. *The Clunk*) took its maiden flight.

1953: Lucille Ball gave birth live on her show *I Love Lucy*.

1958: The Canadian Football Council was renamed the Canadian Football League.

1977: Snow fell in Miami, FL, for the first and only time in history.

1978: The last Volkswagen Beetle was made in Germany.

1993: IBM announced the largest single-year corporate loss in U.S. history—$4.97 billion.

2006: The first mission to Pluto was launched.

Capricorn
You are a very focused individual with a lot of drive; however, you have a tendency to lose your focus.
1, 2, 8, 37

#1 Song
1994: "All for Love" by Bryan Adams, Rod Stewart and Sting

Birth Friends Forever
Shawn Johnson, gymnast, 1992

Jodie Sweetin, actress (*Full House*), 1982

Ian Laperrière, Canadian hockey player, 1974

Katey Sagal, actress (*Married with Children*), 1954

Grant Nordman, Canadian politician, 1950

Robert Palmer, singer, 1949

Frank McKenna, Canadian politician, 1948

Dolly Parton, country singer, 1946

Janis Joplin, singer, 1943

Pat Patterson, Canadian wrestler, 1941

Robert MacNeil, Canadian journalist, 1931

Edgar Allan Poe, author ("The Raven"), 1809

Daily Oddity
The word "toboggan" is Algonquin for sled.

JANUARY 20
345 days until next year

In a Days
Today we celebrate "World Religion Day," which includes Scientology, Kabala and all other fad religions.

It's "Basketball Day." Please don't pick me last.

Don't answer the phone. It's "National Disc Jockey Day."

Speaking of disc jockeys, it's also "Cheese Day."

In the News
1885: The roller coaster was patented.

1892: The first-ever basketball game was played.

1986: "Martin Luther King Jr. Day" was observed as a U.S. holiday for the first time.

1994: Canadian comedic actress Beatrice Lillie (*Auntie Mame*) died at the age of 94.

1994: Solar activity knocked out 2 Canadian satellites, affecting TV, radio and phone lines throughout the country.

1995: After a lengthy strike, the 1994–95 NHL season started up.

2003: An avalanche in eastern BC killed eight skiers.

2008: The controversial movie *Karla*, about Canadian serial killer Karla Homolka, was released.

Aquarius
You are energetic, inquisitive and the centre of attention; however, you are prone to arrogance.
2, 8, 11

#1 Song
1973: "You're So Vain" by Carly Simon

Birth Friends Forever
Daniel Cudmore, Canadian actor (*X-Men*), 1981

Rainn Wilson, actor (*The Office*), 1968

Bill Maher, comedian, 1956

Paul Stanley, musician (Kiss), 1952

Chuck Lefley, Canadian hockey player, 1950

David Lynch, director (*Twin Peaks*), 1946

Lou Fontinato, Canadian hockey player, 1932

Buzz Aldrin, astronaut, 1930

Slim Whitman, singer, 1924

DeForest Kelley, actor (*Star Trek*), 1920

Federico Fellini, director (*8½*), 1920

George Burns, comedian, 1896

Samuel Keefer, Canadian engineer, 1811

Daily Oddity
You would die quicker from sleep deprivation than you would from starvation.

JANUARY 21
344 days until next year

In a Days
Put on your deodorant. It's "National Hugging Day."
Hide your nuts. It's "Squirrel Appreciation Day."

In the News

1891: Calixa Lavallée, the composer of "O Canada," died at the age 48.

1907: The Kenora Thistles beat the Montréal Wanderers to win the Stanley Cup.

1911: The first-ever Monte Carlo Rally was held.

1924: Russian leader Vladimir Lenin died.

1976: The Concorde aircraft began commercial service.

1977: U.S. President Jimmy Carter pardoned American draft dodgers, who fled to Canada to avoid conscription during the Vietnam War.

2002: The Canadian dollar reached an all-time low against the U.S. dollar.

2005: China permitted its residents to travel to Canada.

2007: The long-thought-extinct frilled shark was discovered near Japan.

2008: Black Monday—worldwide stock markets had their worst results since 9/11.

2008: The ancient Alaskan language Eyak became extinct.

Aquarius
You are an emotional free spirit, but at times you are indecisive.
3, 8, 21

#1 Song
1971: "Knock Three Times" by Tony Orlando and Dawn

Birth Friends Forever
Maryse Ouellet, Canadian model, 1983

Dany Heatley, Canadian hockey player, 1981

Emma Bunton, singer (Spice Girls), 1976

Michael Wincott, Canadian actor (*The Crow*), 1958

Geena Davis, actress (*The Fly*), 1956

Plácido Domingo, tenor, 1941

Jack Nicklaus, golfer, 1940

Wolfman Jack, disc jockey, 1938

Telly Savalas, actor (*The Dirty Dozen*), 1922

Christian Dior, fashion designer, 1905

Georges Vézina, Canadian hockey player, 1887

Daily Oddity
Couples married in January, February and March have the highest divorce rate.

JANUARY 22
343 days until next year

In a Days
If you're a crazy cat lady, celebrate "Answer Your Cat's Question Day."
If you are meek, celebrate "National Speak Up and Succeed Day."
Stop fighting and celebrate "International Day of Radiant Peace."
If you are on a low-carb, no-carb, all-chewing-gum diet, celebrate "Rid the World of Fad Diets and Gimmicks Day."

In the News
1874: Louis Riel was elected MP for Provencher, MB, but was unable to take the position because of an outstanding warrant for his arrest.

1901: Queen Victoria died at at the age of 82, ending the longest reign in British history—64 years.

1906: More than 130 people died when the SS *Valencia* ran aground near Vancouver Island.

1946: The Central Intelligence Group (later the CIA) was formed.

1968: *Rowen and Martin's Laugh-In* premiered.

1975: Pierre Trudeau declared 1975 as "International Women's Year."

1984: The landmark "1984" Apple Macintosh commercial aired.

1992: Roberta Bondar became the first Canadian woman in space.

2002: Kmart filed for bankruptcy protection.

2007: The jury portion of serial killer Robert Pickton's trial began in BC.

Aquarius
You are versatile and multifaceted, but you do have a short temper.
1, 4, 22

#1 Song
1966: "The Sounds of Silence" by Simon & Garfunkel

Birth Friends Forever
Ben Eager, Canadian hockey player, 1984

Diane Lane, actress (*Unfaithful*), 1965

DJ Jazzy Jeff, DJ for the Fresh Prince, 1965

Michael Hutchence, singer (INXS), 1960

Mike Bossy, Canadian hockey player, 1957

Serge Savard, Canadian hockey player, 1946

J.C. Tremblay, Canadian hockey player, 1939

Bill Bixby, actor (*The Incredible Hulk*), 1934

Robert E. Howard, author (*Conan the Barbarian*), 1906

Grigori Rasputin, monk, 1869

Ludger Duvernay, Canadian publisher, 1799

Francis Bacon, philosopher, 1561

Daily Oddity
On average, women shoplift more than men do.

JANUARY 23
342 days until next year

In a Days
Put a jockstrap on your mailbox; today is "Snowplow Mailbox Hockey Day."
If you write like a chicken, celebrate "National Handwriting Day."
Cover your face. It's "National Pie Day."
Fake an illness. It's "School Nurse Day."

In the News
- **1556:** China experienced its worst recorded earthquake; 830,000 people died.
- **1883:** Montréal celebrated its first ice palace carnival.
- **1935:** The temperature in Iroquois Falls was –60°C, the lowest temperature in Ontario history.
- **1949:** A fire destroyed the Regina transit storage facility.
- **1978:** Sweden banned aerosol spray cans.
- **1985:** O.J. Simpson was elected to the Football Hall of Fame.
- **1986:** Chuck Berry, James Brown, Ray Charles, Fats Domino, the Everly Brothers, Buddy Holly, Jerry Lee Lewis and Elvis Presley were all inducted into the Rock and Roll Hall of Fame.
- **1995:** The Canadian Airborne Regiment was disbanded after hazing resulted in the death of a Somali boy.
- **1997:** Madeleine Albright became the first female U.S. Secretary of State.

Aquarius
You are an original thinker, a true individual; however, you are uneasy when put in a leadership role.
7, 14, 23

#1 Song
1965: "Downtown" by Petula Clark

Birth Friends Forever
Rob Friend, Canadian soccer player, 1981
Tito Ortiz, UFC fighter, 1975
Tiffani Amber Thiessen, actress (*Saved by the Bell*), 1974
Brendan Shanahan, Canadian hockey player, 1969
Mariska Hargitay, actress (*Law & Oder: SVU*), 1964
Jean-François Sauvé, Canadian hockey player, 1960
Richard Dean Anderson, actor (*MacGyver*), 1950
Mike Harris, premier of Ontario, 1945
Rutger Hauer, actor (*Blade Runner*), 1944
John Charles Polanyi, Canadian chemist, 1929
Ernie Kovacs, comedian, 1919
Peggy Seller, Canadian synchronized swimmer, 1904
William Samuel Stephenson, Canadian soldier and inspiration for James Bond, 1897

Daily Oddity
The average North American knows 10,000 words.

JANUARY 24
341 days until next year

In a Days

To avoid a black eye, remember that today is "Belly Laugh Day" and not "Laugh at a Belly Day."

Ladies, feel free to wear your denim pantsuits to work. It's "Women in Blue Jeans Day."

Why thank you. It's "National Compliment Day."

In the News

1885: The CPR telegraph connected Vancouver to Halifax.

1927: Alfred Hitchcock made his directorial debut.

1952: Vincent Massey was sworn in as the first Canadian-born governor general of Canada.

1955: Canada's first nuclear power plant went on line in Des Joachims, ON.

1978: Debris from a burned-up Soviet satellite landed in the Northwest Territories.

1984: The ABC network paid $386 million for U.S. TV rights to the 1988 Calgary Winter Olympics.

1984: The first Apple Macintosh computer went on sale.

1986: Canadian hockey player Mike Bossy scored his 1000th point.

1986: *Voyager 2* sent photos of Uranus back to Earth.

2003: The U.S Department of Homeland Security was formed.

Aquarius

You are a sensitive individual who is attracted to the obscure; however, you have a tendency to be oversensitive at times.
1, 15, 24

#1 Song

1973: "Superstition" by Stevie Wonder

Birth Friends Forever

Mischa Barton, actress (*The OC*), 1986

Tom Kostopoulos, Canadian hockey player, 1979

Shae-Lynn Bourne, Canadian ice dancer, 1976

Ed Helms, actor (*The Office*), 1974

Mary Lou Retton, gymnast, 1968

John Belushi, actor (*Blues Brothers*), 1949

Michael Ontkean, Canadian actor (*Slapshot*), 1946

Jack Scott, Canadian singer, 1936

Ernest Borgnine, actor (*Marty*), 1917

Daily Oddity

The average shower uses 100 L of water.

JANUARY 25
340 days until next year

In a Days
Check into an asylum. It's "A Room of One's Own Day."
Accuse your co-workers of theft. It's "Fun at Work Day."
Shove a sheep's heart, lungs and liver into its stomach to make haggis for "Robbie Burns Day."

In the News
1791: Québec was split into Upper and Lower Canada.

1858: Mendelssohn's "Wedding March" was played for the first time.

1881: Canadian Alexander Graham Bell and U.S. inventor Thomas Edison formed the Oriental Telephone Company.

1915: Alexander Graham Bell launched the U.S.'s transcontinental telephone service.

1919: The League of Nations was founded.

1924: The first Winter Olympics were held in Chamonix, France.

1949: The first Emmy Awards were held.

1971: Charles Manson was found guilty for his involvement in the Tate murders.

1973: An Irish freighter spilled 378,000 litres of oil when it ran aground near Vancouver Island.

1996: Thirty-six years after she was wrongly diagnosed as mentally disabled and sterilized by the Albertan Eugenics Board, Red Deer, AB, resident Leilani Muir was awarded $750,000.

Aquarius
You are a dynamic individual with an insatiable love for variety; however, at times you are prone to anxiety.
1, 25, 34

#1 Song
1999: "Hit Me Baby One More Time" by Britney Spears

Birth Friends Forever
Andrée Watters, Canadian singer, 1983
Alicia Keys, singer, 1981
Mia Kirshner, Canadian actress (*The L Word*), 1975
Randy McKay, Canadian hockey player, 1967
Chris Chelios, hockey player, 1962
Steve Prefontaine, runner, 1951
Etta James, singer, 1938
Jérôme Choquette, Canadian politician, 1928
Paul Rowe, Canadian football player, 1917
Maurice Roy, Canadian cardinal, 1905
Virginia Woolf, writer (*A Room of One's Own*), 1882
Robert Burns, Scottish poet, 1759

Daily Oddity
The most tattooed woman in the world is a Canadian stripper named Krystyne Kolorful.

JANUARY 26
339 days until next year

In a Days

Call your grandmother and tell her it's "National Peanut Brittle Day."

Hey, you're doing a great job. It's "Toad Hollow Day of Encouragement."

If you are a swinger, don't get too excited. "National Seed Swap Day" pertains to horticulture, not sexual relations.

In the News

1911: The first seaplane was flown.

1965: Hindi became India's official language.

1980: Prime Minister Joe Clark gave the USSR an ultimatum: "Remove troops from Afghanistan by February 20 or Canada will boycott the Summer Olympics." They did not comply, so Canada did not compete.

1985: Wayne Gretzky scored his 50th goal in the 49th game of the season.

1988: *The Phantom of the Opera* began its Broadway run.

1992: Russian president Boris Yeltsin stated that Russia would cease to target U.S. cities with nuclear weapons.

1998: Bill Clinton denied having "sexual relations" with Monica Lewinsky.

2004: In Taiwan, a buildup of gas inside a beached, decomposing sperm whale caused it to explode.

2006: Western Union ceased all telegram service.

Aquarius

You are quick-witted and confident, which at times can make you intimidating to others.
7, 8, 26

#1 Song

1992: "Don't Let the Sun Go Down on Me" by George Michael and Elton John

Birth Friends Forever

Cameron Bright, Canadian actor (*X-Men: The Last Stand*), 1993

Shantelle Taylor, Canadian pro wrestler, 1986

Vince Carter, former Toronto Raptor, 1977

Wayne Gretzky, Canadian hockey player, 1961

Ellen DeGeneres, comedian, 1958

Eddie Van Halen, musician (Van Halen), 1955

Gene Siskel, film critic, 1946

Roger Landry, Canadian newspaper publisher, 1934

Claude Ryan, Canadian newspaper editor, 1925

Paul Newman, actor (*The Hustler*), 1925

Wilder Penfield, Canadian neurosurgeon, 1891

Frank Costello, gangster, 1891

Daily Oddity

If you add up all the numbers on a roulette wheel, from 1 to 36, they total 666.

JANUARY 27
338 days until next year

In a Days
Lest we forget, it's "International Holocaust Remembrance Day."
Take a seat and relieve yourself. It's "Thomas Crapper Day."

In the News
1606: The trial of Guy Fawkes, a conspirator who tried to blow up British Parliament, began.

1721: The first mail coach service between Québec and Montréal began.

1888: The National Geographic Society was founded.

1916: Manitoba became the first province to grant women the right to vote.

1938: Honeymoon Bridge at Niagara Falls collapsed because of an ice jam.

1951: Nuclear testing began in Nevada.

1967: More than 60 nations agreed to ban nuclear weapons in space.

1967: The Doors released their debut album.

1996: Germany observed International Holocaust Remembrance Day for the first time.

2006: Western Union discontinued its telegram messaging service.

Aquarius
You are a person who rises to the occasion and loves a challenge; however, you are constantly in search of new sensations and physical indulgences.
2, 7, 9, 36

#1 Song
1981: "The Tide Is High" by Blondie

Birth Friends Forever
Pete Laforest, Canadian baseball player, 1978

Patrice Brisebois, Canadian hockey player, 1971

Michael Kulas, Canadian singer (James), 1969

Susan Aglukark, Inuit singer, 1967

Margo Timmins, Canadian singer (Cowboy Junkies), 1961

Frank Miller, comic book author (*Sin City*), 1957

Brian Engblom, Canadian hockey player, 1955

Harold Cardinal, Canadian Native rights activist, 1945

Nick Mason, drummer (Pink Floyd), 1944

Mordecai Richler, Canadian author (*Jacob Two-Two*), 1931

Donna Reed, actress (*It's a Wonderful Life*), 1921

Lewis Carroll, author (*Alice in Wonderland*), 1832

Wolfgang Amadeus Mozart, composer, 1756

Daily Oddity
Birds do not pee; they excrete both feces and urine simultaneously.

JANUARY 28
337 days until next year

In a Days
Get the maple syrup. It's "National Blueberry Pancake Day."

As along as you aren't pushing them up, you should celebrate "Daisy Day."

Get ready to doubly annoy friends and co-workers. It's both "National Kazoo Day" and "Bubble Wrap Appreciation Day."

In the News
1754: The word "serendipity" was coined.

1813: Jane Austen's *Pride and Prejudice* was first published.

1914: Nellie McClung staged a mock Parliament in Regina in which actors debated if men should be allowed to vote.

1918: John McCrae, author of "In Flanders Fields," died.

1958: Lego patented the design of its bricks.

1986: The *Challenger* space shuttle exploded, killing all seven astronauts aboard.

1988: Supreme Court of Canada ruled that Canada's anti-abortion law violated pregnant women's right to "security of the person" under the Charter of Rights and Freedoms.

1998: Wayne Gretzky received the Order of Canada.

2002: Over 90 passengers died when a Boeing 727-100 crashed into the Andes.

Aquarius
You are a compassionate and realistic individual who, at times, may become overwhelmed by empathy.

1, 19, 28

#1 Song
1976: "Love Rollercoaster" by The Ohio Players

Birth Friends Forever
Elijah Wood, actor (*The Lord of the Rings*), 1981

Nick Carter, singer (Backstreet Boys), 1980

Joey Fatone, singer ('N Sync), 1977

Anne Montminy, Canadian diver, 1975

Sarah McLachlan, Canadian singer, 1968

Normand Rochefort, Canadian hockey player, 1961

Frank Darabont, director (*The Shawshank Redemption*), 1959

Mark Napier, Canadian hockey player, 1957

Paul Henderson, Canadian hockey player, 1943

Alan Alda, actor (*M*A*S*H*), 1936

Jackson Pollock, painter, 1912

Alexander Mackenzie, prime minister of Canada, 1822

Daily Oddity
This is the time of year that raccoons begin to mate.

JANUARY 29
336 days until next year

In a Days
Feel free to ponder all you can. It's "Free Thinkers Day."
If someone offers you a hand today, watch out! It's "World Leprosy Day."

In the News
1595: Shakespeare's *Romeo and Juliet* was first performed.

1796: Toronto's Yonge Street, originally a portage route from York to Lake Simcoe, officially opened.

1829: McGill University opened in Montréal.

1845: Edgar Allan Poe's "The Raven" was first published.

1856: The Victoria Cross was created.

1886: The first automobile powered by gasoline was patented.

1916: German Zeppelins bombed Paris.

1946: The Canadian racing schooner *The Bluenose* sank off Haiti.

1959: The Walt Disney animated film *Sleeping Beauty* premiered.

1990: Ray Hnatyshyn was sworn in as Canada's 24th governor general

2005: For the first time since 1949, a direct commercial flight from China to Taiwan departed.

Aquarius
You are a bright individual who always likes to right the wrongs; however, this may cause you to take on more than you can handle.
1, 2, 29, 36

#1 Song
1990: "How Am I Supposed to Live Without You" by Michael Bolton

Birth Friends Forever
Jonny Lang, musician, 1981
Sara Gilbert, actress (*Roseanne*), 1975
Heather Graham, actress (*Boogie Nights*), 1970
Edward Burns, actor (*27 Dresses*), 1968
Greg Louganis, diver, 1960
Doug Risebrough, Canadian hockey player, 1954
Oprah Winfrey, talk-show host, 1954
Marc Singer, Canadian-born actor (*V*), 1948
Tom Selleck, actor (*Magnum, P.I.*), 1945
Marcelle Ferron, Canadian painter, 1924
John Forsythe, actor (*Dynasty*), 1918
Joe Primeau, Canadian hockey player, 1906
John D. Rockefeller Jr., entrepreneur, 1874

Daily Oddity
Yonge Street was once the world's longest street, running nearly 1900 km.

JANUARY 30
335 days until next year

In a Days
Hello, I'm not here right now because I'm out celebrating "Inane Answering Machine Message Day."

As long as you don't include any death threats, then today you should celebrate "National Write to Parliament Day."

In the News
1649: King Charles I was beheaded.

1835: The first assassination attempt was made on a U.S. president (Andrew Jackson).

1847: Yerba Buena, CA, was renamed San Francisco.

1911: The Canadian Naval Service became the Royal Canadian Navy.

1923: The Canadian National Railway Company took over the Grand Trunk Railway, which laid the rails for CN Rail.

1933: Hitler was sworn in as chancellor of Germany.

1948: Mahatma Gandhi was assassinated.

1962: Two members of the Flying Wallendas high-wire troupe were killed when their 7-person pyramid collapsed during a performance in Detroit, MI.

1982: Hacker Richard Skrenta wrote the first virus code for a PC.

2003: Belgium legalized same-sex marriage.

Aquarius
You are a natural-born leader who is extremely persuasive; however, you may become a victim of your own vanity.
7, 21, 30

#1 Song
1974: "The Way We Were" by Barbra Streisand

Birth Friends Forever
Christian Bale, actor (*Dark Knight*), 1974

Chris Simon, Canadian hockey player, 1972

Danielle Goyette, Canadian female hockey player, 1966

Doug Falconer, Canadian football player, 1952

Phil Collins, musician, 1951

Vanessa Redgrave, actress (*Howard's End*), 1937

John Crosbie, Canadian politician, 1931

Gene Hackman, actor (*The French Connection*), 1930

Lucille Teasdale-Corti, Canadian surgeon, 1929

John Ireland, Canadian actor (*Red River*), 1914

Franklin D. Roosevelt, U.S. president, 1882

Daily Oddity
The grass at Wimbledon is cut to a height of exactly 8 mm.

JANUARY 31
334 days until next year

In a Days
Go stare at *Dogs Playing Poker*. Today is "Inspire Your Heart with Art Day." Honour Manitoba's provincial bird. It's "Mosquito Appreciation Day."

In the News

1606: Conspirator Guy Fawkes was executed for his attempt to blow up British Parliament.

1747: The first VD clinic opened in London.

1876: The U.S. government ordered all Native Americans onto reservations.

1929: The Soviet Union exiled Leon Trotsky.

1930: Scotch Tape was introduced by 3M.

1936: *The Green Hornet* premiered on the radio.

1957: The Canadian government declared the second Monday in October to be Thanksgiving Day.

1958: James Gladstone became Canada's first Native senator.

1970: A Saskatchewan Court convicted David Milgaard of murder. He spent 23 years behind bars until DNA evidence proved his innocence.

1990: The first McDonald's opened in Moscow, Russia.

1999: *Family Guy* made its TV debut.

Aquarius
You are an idealistic and empathetic person; however, you are oversensitive at times.
1, 4, 22, 31

#1 Song
1984: "Karma Chameleon" by Culture Club

Birth Friends Forever

Justin Timberlake, singer, 1981

Portia de Rossi, actress (*Arrested Development*), 1973

Minnie Driver, actress (*Good Will Hunting*), 1970

Fat Mike, musician (NOFX), 1967

Sylvie Bernier, Canadian diver, 1964

Johnny Rotten, singer (Sex Pistols), 1956

Claude Gauthier, Canadian singer, 1939

Queen Beatrix of the Netherlands, 1938

Andrée Boucher, Canadian politician, 1937

Philip Glass, composer, 1937

Suzanne Pleshette, actress (*The Bob Newhart Show*), 1937

Bob Turner, Canadian hockey player, 1934

Norman Mailer, author (*The Naked and the Dead*), 1923

Zane Grey, author (*The Thundering Herd*), 1872

Daily Oddity
The word *igloo* means "house" in Inuit.

FEBRUARY 1
333 days until next year

In a Days
Be it on your shoe or in your hair, celebrate "Bubble Gum Day."
Get shipwrecked. It's "Robinson Crusoe Day."
Plan to outlive your husband. It's "Women's Heart Health Day."

In the News
1796: The capital of Upper Canada moved from Newark to York.

1884: *The Oxford English Dictionary* was first published.

1893: It was −56°C in Prince Albert, SK.

1912: Edmonton and Strathcona amalgamated to form what is now the city of Edmonton.

1920: The Royal North-West Mounted Police became the Royal Canadian Mounted Police.

1948: Snowdrifts across the Prairies reached the tops of telephone poles.

1963: A 17-year-old Neil Young made his singing debut at a Winnipeg country club.

1969: Canada Post cancelled Saturday mail delivery.

2004: Janet Jackson's breast was exposed during the Super Bowl half-time show.

2006: The final Gomery Report investigating the federal sponsorship scandal was released.

Aquarius
You are compassionate and multi-talented, yet you can be stubborn at times.
1, 7, 19, 28

#1 Song
1968: "Green Tambourine" by The Lemon Pipers

Birth Friends Forever
Big Boi, musician (Outkast), 1975
Michael C. Hall, actor (*Dexter*), 1971
Mark Recchi, Canadian hockey player, 1968
Lisa Marie Presley, singer, 1968
Princess Stéphanie of Monaco, 1965
Mike Kitchen, Canadian hockey coach, 1956
Serge Joyal, Canadian politician, 1945
Hervé Filion, Canadian harness racer, 1940
Boris Yeltsin, Russian president, 1931
Ben Weider, Canadian fitness guru, 1924
Clark Gable, actor (*Gone with the Wind*), 1901
Conn Smythe, Canadian father of the NHL, 1895
Louis Stephen St. Laurent, Canadian prime minister, 1882

Daily Oddity
On this day in 1851, Mary Shelley, the author of *Frankenstein*, died… or did she?

FEBRUARY 2
332 days until next year

In a Days
It's "Groundhog Day." If you are Wiarton Willie, Balzac Billy or Brandon Bob, you'd better not see your shadow today, or else.

If you are Gaelic, then today you celebrate Imbolc, a spring festival.

If you are Christian, then today you celebrate Candlemas, the Purification of the Blessed Virgin.

Don't be embarrassed. It's "Wear Red Day."

In the News
1887: The first Groundhog Day was observed in Punxsutawney, PA.

1901: Queen Victoria's funeral took place.

1913: Grand Central Station opened in New York City.

1940: Frank Sinatra made his singing debut with the Tommy Dorsey orchestra.

1955: The temperature was −47°C in Sisson Dam, NB.

1974: Canada finished third in the 10th Commonwealth Games in New Zealand with 25 gold medals, 19 silver and 18 bronze.

1976: A severe winter storm hit southeastern Canada.

2001: Canada banned the importation of beef from Brazil because of mad cow disease.

2003: An avalanche in Glacier National Park, BC, killed 7 people.

Aquarius
You are a driven individual and a straight shooter; however, you may be perceived as cold at times.
2, 7, 11, 20

#1 Song
1992: "I'm Too Sexy" by Right Said Fred

Birth Friends Forever
Jordin Tootoo, Canadian hockey player, 1983

Teddy Hart, Canadian pro wrestler, 1980

Shakira, singer, 1977

Todd Bertuzzi, Canadian hockey player, 1975

C. Ernst Harth, Canadian actor (*The X-Files*), 1970

Michel Marc Bouchard, Canadian playwright, 1958

Duane "Dog" Chapman, bounty hunter, 1953

Brent Spiner, actor (*Star Trek: TNG*), 1949

Farrah Fawcett, actress (*Charlie's Angels*), 1947

Eric Kierans, Canadian politician, 1914

Ayn Rand, author (*Atlas Shrugged*), 1905

James Joyce, author (*Ulysses*), 1882

Daily Oddity
Groundhogs are accurate about 28 percent of the time.

FEBRUARY 3
331 days until next year

In a Days
If you are a rabbit, you'll be happy to know that today is "National Carrot Day." If you are a bachelorette, you'll be happy to know that today is "Wedding Ring Day."

In the News

1916: The Parliament Buildings in Ottawa burned to the ground.

1947: The temperature in Snag, Yukon, was −63°C, the coldest recorded temperature in North American history.

1959: Buddy Holly, Ritchie Valens, the Big Bopper and Roger Peterson died in a plane crash near Clear Lake, Iowa. The day was immortalized in the Don McLean song "American Pie," which christened February 3 as "The Day the Music Died."

1967: The last person to be executed in Australia was hanged.

1971: New York police officer Frank Serpico was allegedly shot by fellow officers, leading to him testifying against police corruption.

1998: The first woman since 1984 was executed in the U.S.

2007: During a Calgary Flames hockey game, Cree singer Akina Shirt became the first individual to sing "O Canada" in an Aboriginal language at a major sporting event.

Aquarius
You are charming and adventurous, but at times you can be unreliable.
3, 7, 21

#1 Song
1972: "American Pie" by Don McLean

Birth Friends Forever
Sean Kingston, singer, 1990
Mathieu Dandenault, Canadian hockey player, 1976
Isla Fisher, actress (*Wedding Crashers*), 1976
Warwick Davis, actor (*Leprechaun*), 1970
Maura Tierney, actress (*E.R.*), 1965
Nathan Lane, actor (*The Birdcage*), 1956
Tiger Williams, Canadian hockey player, 1954
Morgan Fairchild, actress (*Dallas*), 1950
Stephen McHattie, Canadian actor (*The Rocket*), 1947
Martial Asselin, Canadian politician, 1924
Pretty Boy Floyd, gangster, 1904
Norman Rockwell, artist, 1894
Ranald MacDonald, Canadian educator, 1824

Daily Oddity
Over 8 minutes long, "American Pie" set a record as the longest running number one hit song.

FEBRUARY 4
330 days until next year

In a Days
If you never remember to put down the toilet seat—watch out! Today is "Dump Your Significant Jerk Day."

If you are dumped today, drown your sorrows in "National Stuffed Mushroom Day."

In the News

1703: Forty-six of the Forty-Seven Ronin committed ritual suicide after they avenged their master's murder.

1789: George Washington was elected the first U.S. president.

1858: Gold was first discovered in BC's Fraser River, starting the gold rush.

1873: Winnipeg officially became a city.

1924: The Toronto Granite Club hockey team brought home gold for Canada at the first-ever Winter Olympics, which were held in Chamonix, France.

1969: Yasser Arafat became chairman of the Palestine Liberation Organization.

1974: The Symbionese Liberation Army kidnapped heiress Patty Hearst.

1982: Canada signed a UN declaration against "torture and other cruel treatment."

2004: The website *Facebook* went online.

Aquarius
You are quick-witted and inquisitive; however, these attributes can cause you to be impulsive.
1, 4, 13, 22

#1 Song
2001: "It Wasn't Me" by Shaggy

Birth Friends Forever
Oscar de la Hoya, boxer, 1973

Duncan Coutts, Canadian musician (Our Lady Peace), 1969

Michael Riley, Canadian actor (*This is Wonderland*), 1962

Denis Savard, Canadian hockey player, 1961

Alice Cooper, musician, 1948

George A. Romero, director (*Night of the Living Dead*), 1940

Conrad Bain, Canadian actor (*Diff'rent Strokes*), 1923

Ida Lupino, female filmmaker (*The Hitch-Hiker*), 1918

Rosa Parks, civil rights activist, 1913

Charles Lindbergh, pilot, 1902

Cairine Ray Wilson, Canadian senator, 1885

Étienne Desmarteau, Canadian athlete, 1873

Daily Oddity
During the BC gold rush, camels were used to carry supplies. However, the rocky terrain proved too difficult for the creatures, which were released into the Canadian wild 4 months later.

FEBRUARY 5
329 days until next year

In a Days
There is a 75 percent chance that today is "Weatherman's Day."

In the News

1846: *The Oregon Spectator* became the first U.S. newspaper published.

1919: Canadian-born silent film actress Mary Pickford, along with Charlie Chaplin, Douglas Fairbanks and D.W. Griffith, established United Artists film studio.

1973: Construction of the CN Tower in Toronto began.

1980: Winnipeg-born William Stephenson—the inspiration behind James Bond—was awarded the Order of Canada.

1981: Canadian singer Joni Mitchell was inducted into the Juno Hall of Fame.

1989: Banff-native Karen Percy won a silver medal in the Women's World Alpine Ski Championship.

2001: Canadian Prime Minister Jean Chrétien became the first world leader to visit newly elected U.S. President George W. Bush.

2008: Over 50 people died during a tornado outbreak in the southern U.S.

Aquarius
You are self-disciplined and competent, but can sometimes come off as superior.
5, 7, 14, 23

#1 Song
1979: "Do You Think I'm Sexy?" by Rod Stewart

Birth Friends Forever

Richard Matvichuk, Canadian hockey player, 1973

Bobby Brown, singer, 1969

Chris Parnell, actor (*SNL*), 1967

Laura Linney, actress (*You Can Count on Me*), 1964

Jennifer Jason Leigh, actress (*Rush*), 1962

Barbara Hershey, actress (*Beaches*), 1948

Christopher Guest, actor (*Spinal Tap*), 1948

Michael Mann, director (*Heat*), 1943

H.R. Giger, artist, 1940

Don "Grapes" Cherry, Canadian hockey commentator, 1934

Hank Aaron, baseball player, 1934

Red Buttons, comedian, 1919

William S. Burroughs, author (*Naked Lunch*), 1914

Charles Leblond, Canadian biologist, 1910

Daisy and Violet Hilton, conjoined twins, 1908

Daily Oddity
The CN Tower is considered to be one of the Seven Wonders of the Modern World.

FEBRUARY 6
328 days until next year

In a Days
If you are an African American or African Canadian coach, take a lap. It's "National African American/Canadian Coaches Day."

To enjoy "National Frozen Yogurt Day" in Canada, leave your regular yogurt outside for 2 seconds.

You're really not that ugly. It's "Pay a Compliment Day."

In the News
1932: A Canadian team presented dogsled racing as a demonstration sport at the Lake Placid Winter Olympic Games.

1952: The King of England George VI, the father of Elizabeth II, died.

1959: The first microchip was patented.

1971: Astronaut Allan Sheppard became the first man to hit a golf ball on the moon.

1975: With personal income tax cut by 28 percent, Albertans became the lowest-taxed Canadians.

1990: Brett Hull became the first NHL player to score 50 goals like his father.

2000: A shrunken head worth $20,000 was stolen from a museum in Niagara Falls.

2002: The Golden Jubilee of Elizabeth II's accession to the throne of England was celebrated.

2004: CBC announced a time delay during "Coaches Corner" because of anti-French remarks made earlier by host Don Cherry while on air.

Aquarius
You are an intelligent and curious person, but you may become bored if not stimulated.
1, 6, 15, 24

#1 Song
1965: "You've Lost that Lovin' Feelin'" by The Righteous Brothers

Birth Friends Forever
Myron Wolf Child, Canadian politician, 1983

Kim Poirier, Canadian actress (*Breaker High*), 1980

Rick Astley, singer, 1966

Axl Rose, singer (Guns N' Roses), 1962

Kate McGarrigle, Canadian singer, 1946

Bob Marley, musician, 1945

Tom Brokaw, news anchorman, 1940

Kent Douglas, Canadian hockey player, 1939

Zsa Zsa Gabor, actress (*The Naked Gun 2½*), 1917

Ronald Reagan, U.S. president, 1911

Babe Ruth, baseball player, 1895

Daily Oddity
On average, this is the coldest day of the year in Canada.

FEBRUARY 7
327 days until next year

In a Days

If you are a female athlete, take a lap to celebrate "National Girls and Women in Sports Day."

If you haven't lost your fingers in a tragic snowblower accident, enjoy "Wave All your Fingers at Your Neighbour Day."

In the News

1882: The last heavyweight boxing championship bare-knuckle fight took place in the U.S.

1891: John A. Macdonald declared, "A British subject I was born, a British subject I will die," before entering his final election.

1922: Manitoba-born Lila Acheson Wallace and her husband sold the first 5000 copies of their magazine, *Reader's Digest*.

1926: The gold rush began in Red Bank, ON.

1964: The Beatles arrived in the U.S. for the first time.

1971: Switzerland gave women the vote.

1976: Toronto Maple Leaf Darryl Sittler got an all-time NHL points record when he made 4 assists and scored 6 goals in the same game.

Aquarius

You are an optimistic and energetic individual; however, you are sometimes a tad cynical.
7, 25, 43

#1 Song

1960: "Teen Angel" by Mark Dinning

Birth Friends Forever

Steven Stamkos, Canadian hockey player, 1990

Deanna Casaluce, Canadian actress (*Degrassi: TNG*), 1986

Ashton Kutcher, actor (*That '70s Show*), 1978

Paul Comrie, Canadian hockey player, 1977

Steve Nash, Canadian basketball player, 1974

Chris Rock, comedian (*SNL*), 1965

Garth Brooks, country singer, 1962

James Spader, actor (*Boston Public*), 1960

Arthur Ozolins, Canadian pianist, 1946

Oscar Brand, Canadian singer, 1920

Laura Ingalls Wilder, author (*Little House on the Prairie*), 1867

Charles Dickens, author (*A Christmas Carol*), 1812

John Deere, tractor manufacturer, 1804

Daily Oddity

Chinese New Year is associated with animals because when Buddha asked all the animals in the world to visit with him on New Year's Day, only 12 showed up, so he gave each one its own year.

FEBRUARY 8
326 days until next year

In a Days
If you're helping an old lady across the street, leave her there and go celebrate "Boy Scout Anniversary Day."

Pipe nitrous oxide into your home or office. It's "Laugh and Get Rich Day."

Sail your leadership to success. Today is "Leadership Success Day."

In the News

1587: Mary, Queen of Scots, was beheaded.

1692: A doctor in Salem, MA, suggested that 4 girls might be bewitched; the Salem witch trials followed.

1879: Canadian engineer Sanford Fleming proposed adopting Universal Standard Time.

1910: The Boy Scouts of America was incorporated.

1926: Walt Disney Studios was founded.

1952: Elizabeth II was proclaimed Queen of England, following the death of her father George VI.

1983: Wayne Gretzky scored 4 goals in the last period of game play.

1986: A VIA Rail train collided with a CN freight train near Hinton, AB, killing 29 people.

1995: Romeo LeBlanc was appointed governor general of Canada.

2008: A third severed foot inside a running shoe washed up off the coast of BC.

Aquarius
You are creative and intuitive, though you feel anxious when you're not in control.
7, 26, 44

#1 Song
1898: "My Old Kentucky Home" by Edison Male Quartette

Birth Friends Forever

Jordan Todosey, Canadian actress (*Life with Derek*), 1995

Mathieu Turcotte, Canadian short-track speed skater, 1977

Seth Green, actor (*Austin Powers*), 1974

Gary Coleman, actor (*Diff'rent Strokes*), 1968

Vince Neil, singer (Mötley Crüe), 1961

Dino Ciccarelli, Canadian hockey player, 1960

John Grisham, author (*The Firm*), 1955

Nick Nolte, actor (*48 Hours*), 1941

Ted Koppel, news anchor, 1940

James Dean, actor (*East of Eden*), 1931

Jack Lemmon, actor (*The Odd Couple*), 1925

Billy Bishop, Canadian pilot, 1894

Jules Verne, author (*20,000 Leagues Under the Sea*), 1828

Daily Oddity
Canadian World War I hero Billy Bishop shot down 25 enemy aircraft in a 10-day period.

FEBRUARY 9
325 days until next year

In a Days
Hope you have a good dental plan. Today is "Toothache Day."
Oy vay! It's "National Bagels and Lox Day."

In the News
1883: The first public library opened in Ontario.

1895: Volleyball was invented.

1964: The Beatles appeared on the *Ed Sullivan Show*, where they performed "She Loves You" and "I Want to Hold Your Hand."

1966: The NHL announced the West Division and 6 new teams: California Seals, Los Angeles Kings, Minnesota North Stars, Philadelphia Flyers, Pittsburgh Penguins and St. Louis Blues.

1969: The Boeing 747 made its first commercial flight.

1974: Canadian journalist Gordon Sinclair's radio commentary "The Americans (A Canadian's Opinion)" peaked on the pop charts at number 24.

1995: Astronaut Bernard A. Harris Jr. became the first African American to perform a spacewalk.

1996: Canadian runner Donovan Bailey set a new world record for the 50-metre dash—5.56 seconds.

Aquarius
You are sympathetic as well as empathic; however, those qualities can sometimes cause you to be exploited by others.
9, 26, 36

#1 Song
1964: "I Want to Hold Your Hand" by The Beatles

Birth Friends Forever
Avan Jogia, Canadian actor (*Caprica*), 1992

Travis Tritt, country singer, 1963

Anik Bissonnette, Canadian ballet dancer, 1962

Judith Light, actress (*Ugly Betty*), 1949

Mia Farrow, actress (*Rosemary's Baby*), 1945

Joe Pesci, actor (*Goodfellas*), 1943

Carole King, singer, 1942

Stompin' Tom Connors, Canadian country singer, 1936

John Ziegler, former hockey commissioner, 1934

Frank Frazetta, fantasy illustrator, 1928

Gypsy Rose Lee, dancer, 1914

Daily Oddity
Canadian rock band Klaatu gained national recognition when it was rumoured the band was really The Beatles in disguise.

FEBRUARY 10
324 days until next year

In a Days
Boo, hiss! It's "School Day."
Put a cocktail umbrella in your piña colada today. It's "Umbrella Day."
If you are a trophy wife, be sure to celebrate "Pro-Sports Wives Day."

In the News

1840: Queen Victoria of the United Kingdom married Prince Albert of Saxe-Coburg-Gotha.

1863: Tom Thumb married fellow dwarf Lavinia Warren.

1870: The YWCA was founded.

1929: The Vatican became an independent state within Rome.

1931: New Delhi became the capital of India.

1975: Margaret Thatcher became the first female leader of a British political party.

1981: Eight people died and 198 were injured in a fire at the Las Vegas Hilton hotel and casino.

1982: Twenty-eight Canadian skiers entered the *Guinness World Records* after they simultaneously performed back-flips while holding hands.

1996: An IBM supercomputer named Deep Blue beat Russian chess master Garry Kasparov.

2008: The *Namdaemun*, a historical gate in South Korea, was severely damaged by fire.

Aquarius
You are a clear-sighted and multi-talented individual, but at times those attributes may cause you to become obsessive.
1, 19, 37

#1 Song
1969: "Everyday People" by Sly & the Family Stone

Birth Friends Forever
Emma Roberts, actress (*Unfabulous*), 1991
Natasha St-Pier, Canadian singer, 1981
Mike Ribeiro, Canadian hockey player, 1980
Laura Dern, actress (*Jurassic Park*), 1967
Victor Davis, Canadian swimmer, 1964
Mark Spitz, swimmer, 1950
Jim Corcoran, Canadian singer, 1949
Louise Arbour, Canadian judge, 1947
Adrienne Clarkson, governor general of Canada, 1939
Roberta Flack, singer, 1937
Robert Wagner, actor (*Austin Powers*), 1930
Bud Poile, Canadian hockey player, 1924
Lon Chaney Jr., actor (*The Wolf Man*), 1906
Jimmy Durante, singer/comedian, 1893

Daily Oddity
Ash Wednesday can occur as early as February 4 or as late as March 10.

FEBRUARY 11
323 days until next year

In a Days
Release some gas. It's "Man Day."
Enjoy having the bed to yourself. It's "Satisfied Staying Single Day."
Until you stain it with coffee, enjoy "White T-shirt Day."
Wear a hard hat. It's "World Safety Day."

In the News
1531: Henry VIII became head of the Church of England
1897: A fire destroyed the west wing of Canada's Parliament Buildings.
1907: The Supreme Court of Alberta was founded.
1922: Canadian scientist Frederick Banting and his assistant, Charles Best, announced the discovery of insulin.
1923: Winnifred Blair became the first Miss Canada.
1941: Glenn Miller received the first-ever gold record.
1963: Author Sylvia Plath (*The Bell Jar*) committed suicide.
1977: A Nova Scotia fisherman caught the world's heaviest lobster, weighing 20.2 kg.
1990: Nelson Mandela was released after 27 years in prison.
1999: Tahtsa Lake, BC, had its greatest one-day snowfall—145 cm.
2006: Former U.S. VP Dick Cheney shot his friend in the face while hunting.

Aquarius
You are a charming and eccentric person who, at times, neglects personal relationships.
2, 7, 38

#1 Song
1987: "Livin' on a Prayer" by Bon Jovi

Birth Friends Forever
Mike Richards, Canadian hockey player, 1985
Nicki Clyne, Canadian actress (*Battlestar Galactica*), 1983
Matthew Lawrence, actor (*Boy Meets World*), 1980
Brandy, singer, 1979
Jennifer Aniston, actress (*Friends*), 1969
Sheryl Crow, musician, 1962
Abby Hoffman, Canadian runner, 1945
Sergio Mendes, musician, 1941
Eddie Shack, Canadian hockey player, 1937
Burt Reynolds, actor (*Smokey and the Bandit*), 1936
Leslie Nielsen, Canadian actor (*The Naked Gun*), 1926
Eva Gabor, actress (*Green Acres*), 1919

Daily Oddity
Mohammed is the most common name in the world.

FEBRUARY 12
322 days until next year

In a Days
Time to evolve. It's "Darwin Day."
If they were worth more, we wouldn't have to celebrate "Lost Penny Day."
Put a hockey helmet on your dog. It's "Safety Pup Day."

In the News

1800: The College of New Brunswick was founded.

1816: A fire nearly destroyed St. John's, NL.

1839: The first curling bonspiel was held on the Don River in Toronto.

1970: In a Montréal hospital, a 3-month-old baby was Canada's first successful liver transplant recipient.

1989: Wayne Gretzky scored his 45th hat trick.

1990: Teenagers in Hagersville, ON, lit a tire dump on fire. Smoke from the blaze forced the evacuation of hundreds of residents.

2004: A Saskatchewan woman—left quadriplegic after an accident—was awarded $12 million in a lawsuit against the driver of the vehicle, the City of Moose Jaw and the former police chief, the largest lawsuit ever awarded in Saskatchewan history.

Aquarius
You are an objective person with strong convictions; however, you have a difficult time compromising your values.
1, 7, 12, 32

#1 Song
1971: "One Bad Apple" by The Osmonds

Birth Friends Forever

Christina Ricci, actress (*The Addams Family*), 1980

Tara Strong, Canadian voice actress (*Powerpuff Girls*), 1973

Owen Nolan, Canadian hockey player, 1972

Jim Creeggan, Canadian musician (Barenaked Ladies), 1970

Josh Brolin, actor (*No Country for Old Men*), 1968

Jim Harris, Canadian politician, 1961

Michael Ironside, Canadian actor (*The Perfect Storm*), 1950

Mike Robitaille, Canadian hockey player, 1948

Judy Blume, author (*Harriet the Spy*), 1938

Lorne Greene, Canadian actor (*Bonanza*), 1915

Abraham Lincoln, U.S. president, 1809

Charles Darwin, naturalist, 1809

Daily Oddity
The zodiac sign Aquarius is believed to have influence over the feet.

FEBRUARY 13
321 days until next year

In a Days
Put on some Barry White. It's "Black Love Day."
Don't tell your boss, but it's "Employee Legal Awareness Day."
Change your name to Percival or Humperdinck. It's "Get a Different Name Day."

In the News
1833: Hamilton, ON, was incorporated as a city.

1866: Jesse James and his gang pulled off the first bank robbery in U.S. history.

1907: Portage la Prairie, MB, was incorporated as a city.

1937: Halifax native Harold Foster published his first *Prince Valiant* comic strip.

1947: Oil was discovered near Leduc, sparking Alberta's oil boom.

1969: A terrorist bomb exploded at the Montréal Stock Exchange, injuring 27 people.

1973: The temperature in Shepard Bay, NWT, was –57°C.

1988: The Winter Olympic Games opened in Calgary.

2000: The last original *Peanuts* comic strip appeared a day after its creator, Charles Schulz, died.

2008: Arson was the cause of an explosion at a Taco del Mar restaurant on Broadway in Vancouver.

Aquarius
You are a unique and exuberant individual; however, you may be prone to erratic behaviour.
1, 4, 22, 31

#1 Song
1962: "Duke of Earl" by Gene Chandler

Birth Friends Forever
Carly McKillip, Canadian actress (*Alice, I Think*), 1989

Feist, Canadian singer, 1976

Dave Padden, Canadian musician (Annihilator), 1976

Mats Sundin, Canadian hockey player, 1971

Jeff Waters, Canadian musician (Annihilator), 1966

Marc Crawford, Canadian hockey player, 1961

Henry Rollins, musician (Black Flag), 1961

Marc Emery, Canadian cannabis activist, 1958

Peter Gabriel, musician, 1950

Stockard Channing, actress (*Grease*), 1944

Kim Novak, actress (*Vertigo*), 1933

Robert Fulford, Canadian journalist, 1932

Daily Oddity
Some believe that the ring finger is connected to the heart by the "vein of love."

FEBRUARY 14
320 days until next year

In a Days
Roses are 3 times more expensive than they were yesterday. It's "Valentines Day."
Don't throw up. It's "Ferris Wheel Day."
Feel free to love yourself—but not in public. It's "Quirkyalone Day."
If you do not have a heart, get one. It's "National Have a Heart Day."

In the News
1876: Canadian inventor Alexander Graham Bell applied for a patent on the telephone.

1918: Sixty-four children died in a fire at a Grey Nuns orphanage in Montréal.

1927: Conn Smythe took over the Toronto St. Patricks and renamed them the Toronto Maple Leafs.

1929: Al Capone's men mowed down 6 rival gang members during the St. Valentine's Day Massacre.

1999: Over 1500 people in Sarnia, ON, made it into the *Guinness World Records* for kissing at the same time, in the same place.

2004: More than 25 people died when the roof of a waterpark in Russia collapsed.

2008: Twenty-four students were killed at a university shooting in northern Illinois.

Aquarius
You are a sensual individual with exceptional communication skills; however, you are liable to lose your temper easily.
5, 14, 23

#1 Song
1998: "Nice & Slow" by Usher

Birth Friends Forever
Brandon Sutter, Canadian hockey player, 1989

Rob Thomas, musician (Matchbox Twenty), 1972

Simon Pegg, actor (*Shaun of the Dead*), 1970

Enrico Colantoni, Canadian actor (*FlashPoint*), 1963

Meg Tilly, Canadian actress (*The Big Chill*), 1960

Raymond Teller, magician (Penn and Teller), 1948

Gregory Hines, tap dancer, 1946

Florence Henderson, actress (*The Brady Bunch*), 1934

Bernie "Boom Boom" Geoffrion, Canadian hockey player, 1931

Lois Maxwell, Canadian actress (Miss Moneypenny, *James Bond*), 1927

Jimmy Hoffa, missing labour union leader, 1913

Jack Benny, comedian/violinist, 1894

Daily Oddity
Fifteen percent of women send themselves flowers on Valentines Day.

FEBRUARY 15
319 days until next year

In a Days
If you are Canadian, salute the flag. It's "Canadian Flag Day."
If you are a woman, let's hear you roar. It's "Susan B. Anthony Day."
If you have a good dental plan, enjoy "National Gum Drop Day."

In the News
1946: ENIAC, the first computer, was unveiled.

1965: Canada adopted the red-and-white maple leaf emblem as its national flag.

1968: Canadian skier Nancy Greene won gold at the Winter Olympics in Grenoble.

1979: Canadian singer Anne Murray and Canadian pianist Oscar Peterson both won Grammy Awards.

1980: Wayne Gretzky tied the NHL record with 7 assists in a single game.

2001: The complete human genome was first published.

2003: A number of homes in Badger, NL, were flooded when 3 rivers in the area overflowed.

2005: The website *YouTube* was launched.

Aquarius
You are a charming individual who has the ability to bring about humanitarian improvements; however, you lack discipline.
1, 6, 15, 33

#1 Song
1978: "Staying Alive" by The Bee Gees

Birth Friends Forever
Russell Martin, Canadian baseball player, 1983

Shane Sellar, Canadian author (this book), 1978

Seattle Slew, racehorse, 1974

Jane Child, Canadian musician, 1967

Brian Propp, Canadian hockey player, 1959

Christopher McDonald, actor (*Happy Gilmore*), 1955

Matt Groening, creator of *The Simpsons*, 1954

Jane Seymour, actress (*Dr. Quinn, Medicine Woman*), 1951

Harvey Korman, comedian, 1927

Cesar Romero, actor (*Batman*), 1907

Susan B. Anthony, women's rights advocate, 1820

Charles Tiffany, jeweller, 1812

Galileo Galilei, astronomer, 1564

Daily Oddity
In 1994, Clayton Simko of Windsor, ON, followed in his sister's, mother's and grandmother's footsteps, becoming the 4th person in his family to be born on February 15.

FEBRUARY 16
318 days until next year

In a Days
Smoke, salt and seal yourself in a tiny little package and distribute yourself on an aircraft. It's "National Almond Day."

If you are sick or giving birth today, rejoice. It's the "Feast of St. Juliana of Nicomedia," the patron saint of childbirth and sickness.

In the News
1857: An early winter thaw flooded much of Ontario.

1923: Howard Carter discovered the tomb of Tutankhamun.

1937: Nylon was patented.

1947: After 80 years of being British subjects, the people of Canada were granted Canadian citizenship.

1959: Fidel Castro became president of Cuba.

1970: Canada's Betsy Clifford won the gold medal in giant slalom at the World Alpine Ski Championship.

1972: Britain abolished the death penalty.

1984: Canadian ice skater Brian Orser won a silver medal at the Winter Olympic Games in Sarajevo.

1985: The political organization Hezbollah was founded.

2005: The NHL cancelled the entire 2004–05 season because of a labour dispute.

Aquarius
You are an empathic and sensitive individual; however, these qualities may cause feelings of pessimism.
7, 25, 34

#1 Song
1960: "Theme from A Summer Place" by Percy Faith

Birth Friends Forever
Keith Gretzky, Canadian hockey player, 1967

John McEnroe, tennis player, 1959

Ice-T, rapper, 1958

LeVar Burton, actor (*Roots*), 1957

Lanny McDonald, Canadian hockey player, 1953

Eckhart Tolle, Canada-based spiritual teacher, 1948

Sonny Bono, singer (Sonny & Cher), 1935

George-Henri Lévesque, Canadian priest, 1903

Edgar Bergen, ventriloquist, 1903

Daily Oddity
Prime Minister Mackenzie King became the first Canadian citizen. He was also the longest serving prime minister in the British Commonwealth, with 21 years under his belt.

FEBRUARY 17
317 days until next year

In a Days
Put on some Frank Sinatra. It's "My Way Day."
If you're a parent or a teacher, celebrate "National PTA Founders Day."
Experiment with a new identity. It's "Who Shall I Be Day?"

In the News
1904: Puccini's *Madame Butterfly* premiered.

1919: Former prime minister Wilfrid Laurier died of a stroke at the age of 77.

1932: RCMP killed Albert Johnson, the "Mad Trapper of Rat River," after a 48-day manhunt. Johnson had killed one Mountie and wounded 2 others.

1933: *Newsweek* was first published.

1936: The purple-clad jungle hero, the Phantom, made his debut.

1972: The Progressive Conservative Party of Canada was registered.

1973: The temperature in Labrador, NL, was −51°C.

1992: Serial killer Jeffrey Dahmer was sentenced to life in prison.

2003: Forty Edmontonians set a world record for playing the longest outdoor hockey game.

2008: Kosovo declared its independence.

Aquarius
You are a compassionate and determined individual; however, this may cause you to set unrealistic goals for yourself.
8, 26, 35

#1 Song
1965: "This Diamond Ring" by Gary Lewis & the Playboys

Birth Friends Forever
Paris Hilton, heiress, 1981

Todd Harvey, Canadian hockey player, 1975

Jerry O'Connell, actor (*Stand By Me*), 1974

Billie Joe Armstrong, musician (Green Day), 1972

Martyn Bennett, Canadian composer, 1971

Denise Richards, actress (*Wild Things*), 1971

Luc Robitaille, Canadian hockey player, 1966

Larry the Cable Guy, comedian, 1963

Lou Diamond Phillips, actor (*La Bamba*), 1962

Michael "Air" Jordan, basketball player, 1961

Loreena McKennitt, Canadian musician, 1957

Rene Russo, actress (*Get Shorty*), 1954

Paul Meger, Canadian hockey player, 1929

Daily Oddity
Nothing rhymes with the word "diamond."

FEBRUARY 18
316 days until next year

In a Days
If you're a crab, cram yourself into a flounder and get ready to be eaten. It's "National Crab-Stuffed Flounder Day."

In the News
1885: Mark Twain's *The Adventures of Huckleberry Finn* was first published.

1930: The planet Pluto was discovered.

1930: Ollie the Cow became the first bovine to be milked in an aircraft.

1954: The Church of Scientology was established.

1965: An avalanche in Stewart, BC, killed 18 copper miners.

1972: A record 112 cm of snow fell on Kitimat, BC.

1979: Snow fell in the Sahara Desert for the first and only time in history.

1981: Wayne Gretzky scored 5 goals and made 2 assists in one game.

2008: "Family Day" was declared in Ontario, while "Louis Riel Day" was declared in Manitoba.

Aquarius
You are an eccentric and progressive individual who, at times, may alienate others.
9, 27, 36

#1 Song
1973: "Killing Me Softly with His Song" by Roberta Flack

Birth Friends Forever
Ruby Dhalla, Canadian politician, 1974

Raine Maida, Canadian musician (Our Lady Peace), 1970

Dr. Dre, rapper, 1965

Matt Dillon, actor (*The Outsiders*), 1964

Andy Moog, Canadian hockey player, 1960

Raymond Rougeau, Canadian pro wrestler, 1955

John Travolta, actor (*Pulp Fiction*), 1954

Robbie Bachman, Canadian musician (BTO), 1953

Cybill Shepherd, actress (*Moonlighting*), 1950

Dick Duff, Canadian hockey player, 1936

Yoko Ono, artist/wife of John Lennon, 1933

André Mathieu, Canadian composer, 1929

George Kennedy, actor (*Cool Hand Luke*), 1925

Jean Drapeau, Montréal mayor, 1916

Queen Mary I of England (Bloody Mary), 1516

Daily Oddity
Five hundred North Americans freeze to death every year.

FEBRUARY 19
315 days until next year

In a Days
If you have horrible taste in candy, celebrate "Chocolate Mint Day."
If you are a woman over the age of 65, celebrate "Spunky Old Broads Day."

In the News

1674: New Amsterdam was renamed New York.

1847: The uneaten members of the Donner Party were rescued.

1878: Thomas Edison patented the phonograph.

1927: Canadian business magnate Ted Rogers founded CFRB radio.

1930: Quebec rejected a bill to allow women to practice law.

1983: Joe Clark resigned as Progressive Conservative Party leader.

1985: The first recipient of an artificial heart was released from hospital.

1986: The Soviet Union launched the *Mir* space station.

1996: The Canadian $2 coin, a.k.a. "The Toonie," was introduced.

2002: The *Mars Odyssey* probe began mapping the surface of Mars.

2008: HD DVD joined Beta in the annals of dead home video formats.

Pisces
You are a perceptive problem solver who has a habit of suppressing your instincts.
1, 19, 28

#1 Song
1981: "9 to 5" by Dolly Parton

Birth Friends Forever

Kyle Chipchura, Canadian hockey player, 1986

Haylie Duff, actress (*Napoleon Dynamite*), 1985

Ronnie Arniell, Canadian pro wrestler, 1981

Benicio del Toro, actor (*Traffic*), 1967

Justine Bateman, actress (*Family Ties*), 1966

Seal, singer, 1963

Laurell K. Hamilton, author (*Anita Blake: Vampire Hunter*), 1963

Ray Winstone, actor (*Beowulf*), 1957

Jeff Daniels, actor (*Dumb and Dumber*), 1955

Paul Dean, Canadian musician (Loverboy), 1946

Smokey Robinson, singer, 1940

Lee Marvin, actor (*The Dirty Dozen*), 1924

Daily Oddity
Two proposed nicknames for the Canadian $2 coin were the "Doozie" and the "Doubloon."

FEBRUARY 20
314 days until next year

In a Days
Cover yourself in maple syrup. It's "International Pancake Day."

It's "Northern Hemisphere Hoodie-Hoo Day." If you want to scare away winter, go outside and yell "Hoodie-hoo"; spring will arrive a month later.

In the News
1930: Montréal Maroons goalie Clint Benedict wore the first goalie mask.

1945: The Canadian government issued the first Family Allowance cheques.

1959: Prime Minister Diefenbaker cancelled the Avro Arrow project to save money; 14,000 people lost their jobs.

1985: Ireland legalized the sale of contraceptives.

1992: Canadian painter A.J. Casson, the last surviving member of the Group of Seven, died at age 93.

1998: U.S. figure skater Tara Lipinski became the youngest gold medallist at the Winter Olympics in Nagano.

2003: A hundred people died during a Great White concert when the pyrotechnics display set the club on fire.

Pisces
You are a charismatic and ambitious individual, but you are sometimes too single-minded.
6, 11, 20

#1 Song
1966: "These Boots Are Made for Walkin'" by Nancy Sinatra

Birth Friends Forever
Melanie Leishman, Canadian actress (*Darcy's Wild Life*), 1989

Rihanna, singer, 1988

Gail Kim, Canadian pro wrestler, 1976

K-OS, Canadian musician, 1972

Kurt Cobain, musician (Nirvana), 1967

Cindy Crawford, model, 1966

Charles Barkley, basketball player, 1963

Pierre Bouchard, Canadian hockey player, 1948

Phil Esposito, Canadian hockey player, 1942

Buffy Sainte-Marie, Canadian singer, 1941

Sidney Poitier, actor (*In the Heat of the Night*), 1927

Robert Altman, director (*M*A*S*H*), 1925

Gloria Vanderbilt, fashion designer, 1924

Ansel Adams, photographer, 1902

Vincent Massey, governor general of Canada, 1887

Joshua Slocum, Canadian adventurer, 1844

Daily Oddity
Six members of the "Group of Seven," including Casson, are buried on the grounds of the McMichael Canadian Art Collection in Kleinburg, ON.

FEBRUARY 21
313 days until next year

In a Days
No wonder kids refuse to listen to their mothers—they speak a different language. It's "International Mother Language Day."

If you are a mother, "Single-Tasking Day" does not apply to you.

In the News
1824: An 18-year-old boy in Saint John, NB, was hanged for stealing 25 cents.

1842: The sewing machine was patented.

1848: *The Communist Manifesto* was first published.

1878: The first telephone book was issued in the U.S.

1891: A coal gas explosion in Springhill, NS, killed 129 miners.

1941: The Canadian co-inventor of insulin, Frederick Banting, died in plane crash near Newfoundland.

1958: The Peace sign was unveiled.

1961: The Ontario Royal Commission endorsed putting fluoride into drinking water.

1965: Malcolm X was assassinated.

1995: Adventurer Steve Fossett became the first person to make a solo flight across the Pacific Ocean in a balloon when he landed safely in Leader, SK.

Pisces
You are a caring, intuitive person who sometimes shields yourself from others.
3, 12, 21

#1 Song
1984: "Jump" by Van Halen

Birth Friends Forever
Ellen Page, Canadian actress (*Juno*), 1987

Charlotte Church, singer, 1986

Jim Vandermeer, Canadian hockey player, 1980

Jennifer Love Hewitt, actress (*Ghost Whisperer*), 1979

Ryan Smyth, Canadian hockey player, 1976

Kelsey Grammer, actor (*Frasier*), 1955

Anthony Daniels, actor (*Star Wars*), 1946

Alan Rickman, actor (*Harry Potter* movies), 1946

Jean Pelletier, Canadian politician, 1935

Rue McClanahan, actress (*Golden Girls*), 1934

Pierre Mercure, Canadian musician, 1927

Robert Campbell, Canadian fur trader, 1808

Daily Oddity
The Peace sign was originally commissioned by a campaign for nuclear disarmament.

FEBRUARY 22
312 days until next year

In a Days
Too bad, Pete, today is "For the Love of Mike Day."

Even if you don't consider yourself a matchmaker, it's "Introduce a Girl to Engineering Day" today.

Taks some Beano and hold your nose. It's "National Chili Day."

In the News
1879: The first Woolworth's store opened.

1974: An assassination attempt was made on U.S. president Richard Nixon.

1980: The Miracle on Ice—the U.S. hockey team defeated the Soviet Union team 4–3.

1990: Albertan country singer k.d. lang won top honours at the Grammy Awards.

1995: Bloc Québécois leader Lucien Bouchard returned to the House of Commons after having lost his leg to flesh-eating disease.

1997: Scientists in Scotland announced they had cloned a sheep, whom they named Dolly, from an adult sheep.

1998: The Winter Olympic Games in Nagano, Japan, closed; Canada took home a record number of medals.

2005: Musical group Blink-182 broke up.

2006: The biggest robbery in Britain's history took place—$92.5 million was stolen.

Pisces
You are a focused person with good moral integrity; however, sometimes you take on too much responsibility.
4, 13, 31

#1 Song
1989: "Straight Up" by Paula Abdul

Birth Friends Forever
Drew Barrymore, actress (*E.T.*), 1975

James Blunt, musician, 1974

Dominic Roussel, Canadian hockey player, 1970

Steve Irwin, the Crocodile Hunter, 1962

Pierre Vallières, Canadian politician, 1938

Edward Gorey, artist, 1925

Sid Abel, Canadian hockey player, 1918

Don Pardo, television announcer, 1918

Robert Wadlow, tallest human ever (2.72 m), 1918

Morley Callaghan, Canadian author (*That Summer in Paris*), 1903

Robert Baden-Powell, founder of the Boy Scouts, 1857

George Washington, U.S. president, 1732

Daily Oddity
"Whiskey" is spelled with an "e" in England and the U.S., but in Ireland and Canada, "whisky" is spelled without the "e."

FEBRUARY 23
311 days until next year

In a Days
If you love shuffleboard, you'll love "Curling is Cool Day."

How does a fruit become a grain—we'll never know. It's "National Banana Bread Day."

They don't taste as bad as you'd think. It's "National Dog Biscuit Day."

In the News
1836: The Battle of the Alamo began.

1906: Canadian boxer Tommy Burns became the world heavyweight boxing champion.

1909: The AEA Silver Dart aircraft made its first flight in Canada.

1914: A rockslide in Fraser River, BC, almost destroyed the area's salmon-fishing industry.

1919: Benito Mussolini formed the Fascist Party.

1941: Plutonium was first isolated.

1945: Pulitzer Prize–winning photo of the raising of the American flag on Iwo Jima was taken.

1975: Daylight saving time started 2 months early in the U.S. because of an energy crisis.

1997: A fire broke out on the *Mir* space station.

2008: A U.S. Air Force B-2 Spirit worth $1.2 billion crashed on Guam. It was the most expensive airplane crash in history.

Pisces
You are a rational and determined individual; however, at times, you are prone to being a martyr.
6, 14, 23

#1 Song
1930: "Puttin' On the Ritz" by Harry Richman

Birth Friends Forever
Dakota Fanning, actress (*I Am Sam*), 1994

Emily Blunt, actress (*The Devil Wears Prada*), 1983

Dan Snyder, Canadian hockey player, 1978

Don Maxwell, Canadian cricket player, 1971

Kristin Davis, actress (*Sex and the City*), 1965

Marc Garneau, Canadian astronaut, 1949

Peter Fonda, actor (*Easy Rider*), 1940

Paul Gérin-Lajoie, Canadian politician, 1920

Victor Fleming, director (*The Wizard of Oz*), 1889

César Ritz, hotelier, 1850

Daily Oddity
The National Film Board of Canada was created to assist in the war effort by showing Canadians the atrocities being committed by the Nazis.

FEBRUARY 24
310 days until next year

In a Days
As long as you're not underage, in AA or a buzzkill, celebrate "Open that Bottle Night."

In the News
1905: The Stanley Cup was tossed onto the frozen Rideau Canal.

1920: The Nazi Party was founded.

1956: Queen Elizabeth authorized the coats of arms of the Yukon and North West Territories.

1963: New Brunswick proclaimed its official flag.

1981: The engagement of Prince Charles and Lady Diana was announced.

1982: Wayne Gretzky scored his 77th goal of the season, breaking Phil Esposito's previous record.

1986: Tommy Douglas, the father of health care, died.

1993: Brian Mulroney announced he would be stepping down as prime minister of Canada.

2008: After nearly 50 years, Fidel Castro retired as president of Cuba.

Pisces
You help others and can easily achieve the goals you set for yourself; however, you tend to see things only in black and white.
6, 17, 24

#1 Song
1997: "Wannabe" by Spice Girls

Birth Friends Forever
Ashley MacIsaac, Canadian fiddler, 1975

Richard Clapp, Canadian baseball player, 1973

Manon Rhéaume, Canadian hockey player, 1972

The Kienast quintuplets, 1970

Billy Zane, actor (*Zoolander*), 1966

Mike Vernon, Canadian hockey player, 1963

Steve Jobs, CEO of Apple Computers, 1955

Helen Shaver, Canadian actress (*The Color of Money*), 1951

George Thorogood, musician, 1950

Edward James Olmos, actor (*Battlestar Galactica*), 1947

John Vernon, Canadian actor (*Animal House*), 1932

Abe Vigoda, actor (*Barney Miller*), 1921

Daily Oddity
Sleeping with a spoon under your pillow guarantees a snow day. Wearing your PJs inside out increases those odds.

FEBRUARY 25
309 days until next year

In a Days
If you travel to the Philippines today, you won't have to work, because it's the national holiday "People Power Day."

In the News
1836: The Colt revolver was patented.

1880: Fire destroyed the Parliament Buildings in Fredericton, NB.

1908: St. Boniface, MB, was incorporated as a city.

1940: The first-ever hockey game was televised.

1951: The first Pan American Games were held in Buenos Aires.

1971: The first commercial nuclear power station in Canada went on line.

1981: The Calgary Flames scored 11 goals against the New York Islanders.

1983: Playwright Tennessee Williams (*A Streetcar Named Desire*) died after choking on a bottle cap.

1986: The People Power Revolution took place in the Philippines.

1991: Wayne Gretzky, Bruce McNall and John Candy jointly purchased the Toronto Argonauts football team.

2008: Kosovo declared its independence from Serbia.

Pisces
You are an energetic and idealistic person; however, sometimes you don't plan ahead.
7, 17, 27

#1 Song
1992: "To Be with You" by Mr. Big

Birth Friends Forever
Eva Avila, *Canadian Idol* winner, 1987

Tara Wilson, Canadian actress (*Smallville*), 1982

Daniel Powter, Canadian musician (Bad Day), 1971

Sean Astin, actor (*The Lord of the Rings*), 1971

Carrot Top, prop comic, 1965

Carl Marotte, Canadian actor (*Street Legal*), 1959

Ric "Nature Boy" Flair, pro wrestler, 1949

Sally Jessy Raphael, talk-show host, 1935

Pierre Laporte, Canadian politician, 1921

King Clancy, Canadian hockey player, 1903

Zeppo Marx, comic (The Marx Brothers), 1901

John Graves Simcoe, first lieutenant-governor of Upper Canada, 1752

Daily Oddity
Ash Wednesday occurs 40 days before Easter and marks the first day of Lent.

FEBRUARY 26
308 days until next year

In a Days
Too bad, Mike. Today is "For Pete's Sake Day."
Go nuts, it's "National Pistachio Day."

In the News
1798: Explorer David Thompson set off on the Red River to explore the Mississippi.

1857: The Province of Canada asked Queen Victoria to choose a new capital for the country.

1917: The first jazz recording was made.

1933: The groundbreaking ceremony for the Golden Gate Bridge was held.

1936: Hitler opened the first Volkswagen factory.

1952: The UK announced that it had an atomic bomb.

1979: A total solar eclipse covered much of western Canada with a shadow that spanned 250 km.

1981: The Boston Bruins and Minnesota North Stars played the most penalty-filled NHL game on record, totalling 406 minutes.

1993: A terrorist bomb exploded at the World Trade Center, killing six people and injuring 1000.

2003: The war in Darfur began.

Pisces
You are an independent thinker who is filled with compassion; however, you may be too morally rigid at times.
8, 17, 35

#1 Song
1983: "Billie Jean" by Michael Jackson

Birth Friends Forever
Currie Graham, Canadian actor (*NYPD Blue*), 1967

Jim Crichton, Canadian musician (Saga), 1953

Michael Bolton, singer, 1953

Hagood Hardy, Canadian composer, 1937

Johnny Cash, musician, 1932

Monique Leyrac, Canadian singer, 1928

Fats Domino, musician, 1928

Tony Randall, actor (*The Odd Couple*), 1920

Jackie Gleason, actor (*The Honeymooners*), 1916

Tex Avery, cartoonist, 1908

John Harvey Kellogg, cereal magnate, 1852

Buffalo Bill Cody, showman, 1846

Levi Strauss, inventor of blue jeans, 1829

Victor Hugo, author (*Les Misérables*), 1802

Daily Oddity
Peanuts are one of the ingredients used to make dynamite.

FEBRUARY 27
307 days until next year

In a Days
Polar bears from the Arctic to Australia should celebrate. It's "International Polar Bear Day."

In the News

1594: Henry IV was crowned king of France.

1917: Women in Ontario won the right to vote in provincial elections.

1945: Lebanon became independent.

1964: Italy asked for help in keeping the Leaning Tower of Pisa from falling over.

1974: Canadian singer Joni Mitchell's album *Court and Spark* turned gold.

1974: *People* magazine was first published.

1977: The RCMP arrested Rolling Stones guitarist Keith Richards for possession of heroin and cocaine.

1988: Canada's Elizabeth Manley won silver in women's figure skating at the Calgary Winter Olympics.

1996: Wayne Gretzky moved from the Los Angeles Kings to the St. Louis Blues.

2007: The Shanghai Stock Exchange had its largest drop in 10 years.

Pisces
You are a perceptive person who is governed by your emotions, which means that you allow your heart to control your decisions.
9, 27, 36

#1 Song
1967: "Ruby Tuesday" by The Rolling Stones

Birth Friends Forever

Matt Stairs, Canadian baseball player, 1968

Donal Logue, Canadian actor (*Blade*), 1966

Adam Baldwin, actor (*Firefly*), 1962

Danny Antonucci, Canadian animator (*The Smurfs*), 1957

Michel Forget, Canadian actor, 1942

Van Williams, actor (*The Green Hornet*), 1934

Ralph Nader, consumer activist, 1934

Elizabeth Taylor, actress (*Cleopatra*), 1932

David H. Hubel, Canadian neuroscientist, 1926

John Steinbeck, author (*Of Mice and Men*), 1902

Charles Best, Canadian co-inventor of insulin, 1899

Henry Wadsworth Longfellow, poet, 1807

Daily Oddity
The 27th of every month is "Weird Al Day."

FEBRUARY 28
306 days until next year

In a Days
Pick some skunkweed and thistles. It's "Floral Design Day."
Sorry, am I in your way? Then it must be "Inconvenience Day."
Knock out some teeth in honour of "National Tooth Fairy Day."

In the News
1838: Robert Nelson proclaimed the independence of Lower Canada (Québec).

1935: Nylon was invented.

1939: The erroneous word "dord" was found in *Webster's Dictionary*.

1952: Vincent Massey was sworn in as the first Canadian-born governor general.

1964: The Toronto International Airport terminal building opened.

1983: The final episode of *M*A*S*H* aired.

1991: The first Gulf War ended.

1993: Bureau of Alcohol, Tobacco, Firearms and Explosives (ATF) agents served an arrest warrant to Branch Davidian sect leader David Koresh, commencing the Waco Siege.

1996: Canadian singer Alanis Morissette won 4 Grammy awards.

Pisces
You are a charming and energetic individual, but you lack self-discipline.
2, 6, 10

#1 Song
1974: "Seasons in the Sun" by Terry Jacks

Birth Friends Forever
Fefe Dobson, Canadian singer, 1985
Ali Larter, actress (*Heroes*), 1976
Eric Lindros, Canadian hockey player, 1973
Peter Stebbings, Canadian actor (*Traders*), 1971
Rae Dawn Chong, Canadian actress (*Commando*), 1961
Gilbert Gottfried, comedian, 1955
Bubba Smith, football player, 1945
Brian Jones, musician (The Rolling Stones) 1942
Mario Andretti, racecar driver, 1940
Tommy Tune, dancer, 1939
Frank Gehry, Canadian architect, 1929
Joseph Rouleau, Canadian opera singer, 1929

Daily Oddity
The word "Lent" is derived from the Old English word *lencten*, which means "spring."

FEBRUARY 29
Four years until next leap year

In a Days
Ladies, today is "Sadie Hawkins Day," the only day when a woman can ask a man to marry her.

Gentlemen, today is "Leap Year Day," so if you do end up getting married on this date, you will only have to remember your anniversary once every 4 years.

In the News
1712: To do away with their old calendar, Sweden followed February 29 with February 30.

1812: Premier James Wilson of Tasmania was born.

1880: Premier James Wilson of Tasmania died.

1940: Actress Hattie McDaniel (*Gone with the Wind*) became the first African American to win an Oscar.

1972: Hank Aaron became the first major league baseball player to sign a $200,000 contract.

1980: Gordie Howe scored his 800th goal.

1987: Canada's John Sarish pushed a wheelbarrow containing 3781.36 kg of bricks a distance of 74.07 m.

1989: Canada's Denna Brasseur and Jane Foster became the world's first female jet pilots.

1996: Over 120 people died when a Boeing 737 crashed in the Andes.

2004: The president of Haiti resigned because of a rebel uprising.

Pisces
You are a pragmatic attention-seeker who is always trying to prove your uniqueness.
2, 11, 20

#1 Song
1976: "Love Machine" by The Miracles

Birth Friends Forever
Cam Ward, Canadian hockey player, 1984

Simon Gagné, Canadian hockey player, 1980

Ja Rule, rapper, 1976

Antonio Sabàto Jr., model, 1972

Lyndon Byers, Canadian hockey player, 1964

Tony Robbins, motivational speaker, 1960

Bob Speller, Canadian politician, 1956

Superman, Canadian-created, Krypton-born superhero, 1938

Henri "The Rocket" Richard, Canadian hockey player, 1936

Dinah Shore, talk-show host, 1916

Jimmy Dorsey, bandleader, 1904

Daily Oddity
In the year 2000, 20,000 Canadians were born on this date. This means that in the year 2012, those people will only be 3 years old.

MARCH 1
305 days until next year

In a Days

Get drunk. It's "Beer Day."
Get drunk and read a book. It's "World Book Day."
Get drunk and book a trip. It's "Plan a Solo Vacation Day."
Get a pig drunk. It's "Pig Day."

In the News

1872: Yellowstone became the world's first national park.

1883: The first issue of *The Regina Leader* newspaper was published.

1911: Canada's *Busy Man's Magazine* was renamed *Maclean's*.

1932: The infant son of Charles Lindbergh was kidnapped.

1939: Trans-Canada Air Lines started operations.

1943: Work began in Dawson Creek, BC, on the Alaska Highway.

1944: The Canadian government ended meat rationing during World War II.

1966: A Soviet space probe became the first spacecraft to land on another planet, Venus.

1975: Australia got colour TV.

2002: Spain replaced the peseta with the euro.

2007: Tornadoes tore up the southern U.S., killing 20 people.

Pisces

You are an instinctive and imaginative person; however, you may be prone to bouts of anxiety.
1, 10, 37

#1 Song

1983: "Billie Jean" by Michael Jackson

Birth Friends Forever

Alexander Steen, Canadian hockey player, 1984

Mark-Paul Gosselaar, actor (*Saved by the Bell*), 1974

Ryan Peake, Canadian musician (Nickelback), 1973

Javier Bardem, actor (*No Country for Old Men*), 1969

Susan Auch, Canadian speed skater, 1966

Stewart Elliott, Canadian jockey, 1965

Ron Howard, director (*Apollo 13*), 1954

Alan Thicke, Canadian actor (*Growing Pains*), 1947

Roger Daltrey, musician (The Who), 1944

Monique Bégin, Canadian politician, 1936

Harry Belafonte, singer, 1927

Max Bentley, Canadian hockey player, 1920

David Niven, actor (*The Pink Panther*), 1910

Daily Oddity

March comes in like a lion because the constellation Leo is rising in the east, while it goes out on the Ram (lamb) constellation.

MARCH 2
304 days until next year

In a Days
Release the Hound of the Baskervilles. It's "Sherlock Holmes Day."
God help us all. It's "World Day of Prayer."
Be careful of impromptu pie fights. Today is "National Banana Cream Pie Day."

In the News
1873: The first practical typewriter was constructed.

1877: Belleville, ON, was incorporated as a city.

1899: Mount Rainier National Park was established.

1946: Ho Chi Minh was elected president of North Vietnam.

1947: Ottawa was hit by the biggest snowfall in a single day for March—48.3 cm.

1953: The Academy Awards were first broadcast on TV.

1962: NBA player Wilt Chamberlain scored 100 points in a single game.

1990: Canadian swimmer Mark Tewksbury set a new world record for the 50 m backstroke, 25.06 seconds.

1992: Moldova joined the United Nations.

2008: Riots in Armenia claimed the lives of 8 people.

Pisces
You are a loyal and sensitive individual; however, you have a habit of losing your direction.
2, 11, 22

#1 Song
1986: "Kyrie" by Mr. Mister

Birth Friends Forever
Jay McClement, Canadian hockey player, 1983

Chris Martin, musician (Coldplay), 1977

Daniel Craig, actor (*Casino Royale*), 1968

Jon Bon Jovi, musician (Bon Jovi), 1962

Luc Plamondon, Canadian songwriter, 1942

John Irving, author (*The Cider House Rules*), 1942

Lou Reed, musician, 1942

Al Waxman, Canadian actor (*King of Kensington*), 1935

Mikhail Gorbachev, Russian president, 1931

Desi Arnaz, actor/bandleader (*I Love Lucy*), 1917

Theodor Geisel/Dr. Seuss, author (*The Cat in the Hat*), 1904

Carl Jacobsen, brewer (Carlsberg), 1842

Sam Houston, president of Texas, 1793

Daily Oddity
In Russia, it is customary to answer the telephone with "I'm listening."

MARCH 3
303 days until next year

In a Days
If I weren't so selfish, I'd celebrate "I Want You to Be Happy Day." Get ready to stand at attention for the next 24 hours. It's "National Anthem Day." I'm sure they would do a lot more hitchhiking—today is "What if Cats and Dogs Had Opposable Thumbs Day?"

In the News
1875: The first hockey game to use modern rules was played in Montréal.

1923: *Time* magazine was first published.

1964: Parliament approved the name change of Trans-Canada Air Lines to Air Canada.

1965: The film version of *The Sound of Music*, starring Canadian actor Christopher Plummer, opened.

1982: Statistics Canada confirmed that the country was in a recession.

1991: A video camera caught LAPD officers beating Rodney King.

1994: Former head of the NHL Players Association, Alan Eagleson, was indicted on 32 counts of embezzlement, fraud and racketeering.

2003: Toronto experienced its coldest day since 1873, a chilly –24°C.

2005: Four RCMP officers were killed in the line of duty near Mayerthorpe, AB.

Pisces
You are a compassionate humanitarian who at times dismisses the opinions of those around you.
3, 12, 30

#1 Song
1966: "The Ballad of the Green Berets" by Sgt. Barry Sadler

Birth Friends Forever
Erica Morningstar, Canadian swimmer, 1989

Colton Orr, Canadian hockey player, 1982

Jessica Biel, actress (*The Illusionist*), 1982

Stéphane Robidas, Canadian hockey player, 1977

Jackie Joyner-Kersee, athlete, 1962

Édouard Lock, Canadian choreographer, 1954

Bobby Driscoll, actor (*Treasure Island*), 1937

James Doohan, Canadian actor (*Star Trek*), 1920

Jean Harlow, actress (*Hell's Angels*), 1911

Norman Bethune, Canadian doctor, 1890

Alexander Graham Bell, Scottish-born Canadian inventor, 1847

Madeleine de Verchères, Canadian heroine, 1678

Daily Oddity
Alexander Graham Bell believed that the old sailor greeting, "Ahoy," was the best way to answer the phone.

MARCH 4
302 days until next year

In a Days
Find out why you were named after the milkman. It's "Namesake Day."
Break out the glue stick. It's "International Scrapbooking Industry Day."
Even if it's just marching in a circle, today is "March Forth and Do Something Day."
Swallow a Band-Aid. It's "Healing from the Inside Out Day."

In the News
- 1837: Chicago was incorporated as a city.
- 1861: Abraham Lincoln was inaugurated as U.S. president.
- 1929: Charles Curtis became the first Native American U.S. vice president.
- 1933: Bertha Wilson became the first woman appointed to the Supreme Court of Canada.
- 1969: The RCMP switched from dogsled teams to snowmobiles.
- 1971: Pierre Trudeau, 52, married Margaret Sinclair, 22, in a secret ceremony.
- 1981: Montréal Canadien Guy Lafleur scored his 1000th point.
- 1994: Canadian comic legend John Candy died.
- 1997: The U.S. banned nationally funded human cloning research.
- 2002: Canada permitted stem-cell research using human embryos.
- 2007: The first parliamentary election allowing e-votes took place in Estonia.

Pisces
You are an extremely empathetic individual; however, you are also an introvert, which causes you to retreat from others.
4, 22, 31

#1 Song
1993: "A Whole New World (Theme from *Aladdin*)" by Peabo Bryson and Regina Belle

Birth Friends Forever
Pierre Dagenais, Canadian hockey player, 1978
Rachel Roberts, Canadian model, 1978
Hawksley Workman, Canadian singer, 1975
Iain Baird, Canadian soccer player, 1971
Patrick Roach, Canadian actor (*Trailer Park Boys*), 1969
Catherine O'Hara, Canadian actress (*SCTV*), 1954
Carroll Baker, Canadian country singer, 1949
Sam Langford, Canadian boxer, 1883

Daily Oddity
In Edmonton, a moose was once used to deliver the mail.

MARCH 5
301 days until next year

In a Days
Find out how many people are named Percival and Humperdinck. It's "Fun Facts About Names Day."

If you have a face that can stop a clock, you'll be in high demand. Today is "Stop the Clocks Day."

In the News

1804: Explorer David Thompson began his journey down the Peace River.

1838: Kingston, ON, was incorporated as a town.

1844: *The Toronto Globe* was first published.

1910: Sixty-two rail workers in Roger's Pass, BC, were buried in an avalanche.

1946: Winston Churchill first used the term the "Iron Curtain."

1953: Soviet dictator Josef Stalin died.

1963: Country singer Patsy Cline was killed in a plane crash on her way home from a benefit concert.

1982: Comedian John Belushi (*SNL*) died of a drug overdose.

1985: Canada's Mike Bossy became the first NHL player to score 50 goals in each of 8 consecutive seasons.

1999: Paul Okalik became the first premier of Nunavut.

Pisces
You are a truly perceptive individual; however, you can be a bit irrational at times.
5, 15, 25

#1 Song
1979: "I Will Survive" by Gloria Gaynor

Birth Friends Forever

Jake Lloyd, actor (*The Phantom Menace*), 1989

Niki Taylor, model, 1975

Eva Mendes, actress (*Hitch*), 1974

Kevin Connolly, actor (*Entourage*), 1974

John Frusciante, musician (Red Hot Chili Peppers), 1970

Andy Gibb, singer, 1958

Penn Jillette, magician (Penn and Teller), 1955

Richard Bell, Canadian musician (The Band), 1946

Peter Woodcock, Canadian serial killer, 1939

Dean Stockwell, actor (*Quantum Leap*), 1936

Red Storey, Canadian football player, 1918

Milt Schmidt, Canadian hockey player, 1918

Daily Oddity
In 2006, the most popular baby names in BC were Ethan and Emma.

MARCH 6
300 days until next year

In a Days

If you are the offspring of Angelina Jolie and Brad Pitt, today you should celebrate "Unique Names Day."

Hope you have a gym pass. It's "National Chocolate Cheesecake Day."

In the News

1834: The city of Toronto was incorporated.

1836: Mexican soldiers captured the Alamo after a 13-day siege.

1880: The Royal Canadian Academy of Arts was founded.

1884: The Toronto Public Library opened.

1899: Bayer trademarked aspirin.

1927: Fritz Lang's film *Metropolis* was released.

1964: Cassius Clay renamed himself Muhammad Ali.

1981: News anchor Walter Cronkite retired.

1997: Picasso's painting *Tête de Femme* was stolen from a London art galley.

2008: Many parts of Canada and the U.S. were struck by a blizzard, which lasted until March 10.

Pisces

You are a sensitive person who is always striving for perfection; however, this may cause you to become disillusioned.
6, 16, 26

#1 Song

1959: "Venus" by Frankie Avalon

Birth Friends Forever

Ellen Muth, actress (*Dead Like Me*), 1981

Erik Bedard, Canadian baseball player, 1979

Shaquille O'Neal, basketball player, 1972

Connie Britton, actress (*Friday Night Lights*), 1967

D.L. Hughley, comedian, 1963

Alan Greenspan, economist, 1962

Tom Arnold, actor (*True Lies*), 1959

Rob Reiner, director (*The Princess Bride*), 1947

David Gilmour, musician (Pink Floyd), 1946

Ken Danby, Canadian painter, 1940

Ed McMahon, TV personality, 1923

Will Eisner, comic book artist (*The Spirit*), 1917

Lou Costello, comedian (Abbott & Costello), 1906

Elizabeth Barrett Browning, poet, 1806

Michelangelo, artist, 1475

Daily Oddity

Canada used to have a $3 bill, but got rid of it in 1871.

MARCH 7
299 days until next year

In a Days
As long as it doesn't mean "One who smells," you should celebrate "Learn What Your Name Means Day."

What's that? I can't hear you…"National Behead Day"? Oh, sorry…"National Be Heard Day."

In the News
322: The philosopher Aristotle died.

1867: The British North America Act, which united the provinces of Canada, was first introduced.

1876: Canadian inventor Alexander Graham Bell was granted a patent for the telephone.

1878: The Toronto Stock Exchange was incorporated.

1926: The first transatlantic telephone call took place.

1933: The game Monopoly was invented.

1968: The BBC began broadcasting in colour.

1985: The benefit song "We Are the World" was released.

1996: The first photographs of Pluto's surface were taken.

2005: Thousands of women's voting-rights protesters gathered outside the National Assembly of Kuwait.

Pisces
You are an extremely intuitive individual; however, that ability may cause you to lose focus on the task at hand.
7, 17, 34

#1 Song
2006: "You're Beautiful" by James Blunt

Birth Friends Forever
Éric Godard, Canadian hockey player, 1980

Laura Prepon, actress (*That '70s Show*), 1980

Maxim Roy, Canadian actress (*MVP*), 1972

Rachel Weisz, actress (*The Mummy*), 1971

Denis Boucher, Canadian baseball player, 1968

Bret Easton Ellis, author (*American Psycho*), 1964

Diane Jones-Konihowski, Canadian track coach, 1951

John Heard, actor (*Home Alone*), 1945

Michael Eisner, Disney executive, 1942

Douglas Cardinal, Canadian architect, 1934

Jean-Paul Desbiens, Canadian journalist, 1927

Nicéphore Niépce, inventor of photography, 1765

Daily Oddity
In Cree, Winnipeg and Winnebago both mean "dirty water."

MARCH 8
298 days until next year

In a Days
If it weren't for them, gossip wouldn't exist—and neither would we. Today is "International Women's Day."

They do a better job and get paid less. It's "International Working Women's Day."

In the News
- 1817: The New York Stock Exchange was founded.
- 1855: The Niagara Suspension Bridge—connecting the U.S. with Canada—opened.
- 1911: "International Women's Day" was declared.
- 1918: An outbreak of the Spanish flu became a worldwide pandemic.
- 1936: The first stock car race was held at Daytona Beach, Florida.
- 1945: Canada celebrated "International Women's Day" for the first time.
- 1971: Joe Frazier beat Muhammad Ali.
- 1978: *The Hitchhiker's Guide to the Galaxy* was first broadcast on the radio.
- 1979: A volcano was discovered on one of Jupiter's moons.
- 1980: The Soviet Union held its first rock music festival.
- 1990: Kurt Browning won his second World Men's Figure Skating Championship.
- 1991: U.S. troops arrived home from the Gulf War.

Pisces
You are a rebel, a true original; however, others may sometimes perceive you as being stubborn.
8, 18, 28

#1 Song
1995: "Take a Bow" by Madonna

Birth Friends Forever
Kat Von D, tattoo artist, 1982

James Van Der Beek, actor (*Dawson's Creek*), 1977

Freddie Prinze Jr., actor (*Scooby-Doo*), 1976

Mike Lalor, Canadian hockey player, 1963

John Kapelos, Canadian actor (*Legally Blonde*), 1956

Don Ashby, Canadian hockey player, 1955

Mickey Dolenz, musician (The Monkees), 1945

Buzz Hargrove, Canadian labour leader, 1944

Lynn Redgrave, actress (*Gods & Monsters*), 1943

Susan Clark, Canadian actress (*Webster*), 1940

Charlotte Whitton, Canadian politician, 1896

Daily Oddity
Women blink more than men do.

MARCH 9
297 days until next year

In a Days
Hello. My name is "Nametag Day."
Oh, my gawd! We're all going to die…it's "Panic Day"!!!
Closure that door. It's "Get Over It Day."
I'm not ashamed of Jason Aaron, because today is "Middle Name Pride Day."

In the News
1834: The French Foreign Legion was founded.

1855: The first train crossed the Niagara Falls Suspension Bridge.

1904: Lester Patrick of Brandon, MB, became the first hockey defenceman to score a goal.

1928: The first phone call from Vancouver to England was made.

1959: The Barbie doll made its debut.

1970: The first Arctic Winter Games were held in Yellowknife.

1977: Health and Welfare Canada banned saccharin as a food additive.

1986: The bodies of crewmembers aboard the space shuttle *Challenger* disaster were discovered.

2004: Avian influenza was detected on a farm in BC.

2006: Water was discovered on one of Saturn's moons.

Pisces
You are a daring and original individual who, at times, can be emotionally unsettled.
9, 19, 29

#1 Song
1993: "Informer" by Snow

Birth Friends Forever
Christina Broccolini, Canadian TV host, 1989

Bow Wow, rapper, 1987

Brittany Snow, actress (*Hairspray*), 1986

Chingy, rapper, 1979

Ben Mulroney, Canadian TV host, 1976

Stefie Shock, Canadian singer, 1969

Brian Bosworth, football player, 1965

Juliette Binoche, actress (*Chocolat*), 1964

Phil Housley, hockey player, 1964

Charles Gibson, television journalist, 1943

Bobby Fischer, chess master, 1943

Marlene Streit, Canadian golfer, 1934

Mel Lastman, Canadian politician, 1933

Gerald Bull, Canadian engineer, 1928

Mickey Spillane, author (*Mike Hammer*), 1918

Daily Oddity
Canada's east coast is closer to England than it is to Canada's west coast.

MARCH 10
296 days until next year

In a Days
Hey, Luigi! It's "Mario Day."
It's the best army in the world, so celebrate "Salvation Army Day."
Find out if you're related to a king or killer. It's "Genealogy Day."

In the News
1842: Queen's University was founded in Kingston, ON.

1880: The Salvation Army was founded.

1910: Prince Rupert, BC, was incorporated as a city.

1934: The Toronto Maple Leafs' undefeated streak reached 18 games in a row.

1969: Martin Luther King Jr.'s assassin, James Earl Ray, was sentenced to 99 years in prison.

1982: All 9 planets aligned in a solar display known as "syzygy."

1989: An Air Ontario plane crashed near Dryden, killing 24 people.

1990: Newfoundland and Labrador rescinded their approval to amend Canada's constitution, killing the Meech Lake Accord.

2003: The first hospital in Ontario closed because of the SARS outbreak.

2005: Governor General Adrienne Clarkson announced the creation of a Canadian women's hockey trophy.

Pisces
You are an idealistic and reasonable person; however, you can sometimes be too sensitive.
10, 20, 28

#1 Song
1963: "Walk like a Man" by The Four Seasons

Birth Friends Forever
Carrie Underwood, country singer, 1983

Lyne Bessette, Canadian cyclist, 1975

Timbaland, music producer, 1971

Sharon Stone, actress (*Basic Instinct*), 1958

Shannon Tweed, Canadian model, 1957

Osama bin Laden, Islamic radical, 1957

Paul Haggis, Canadian director (*Crash*), 1953

Kim Campbell, prime minister of Canada, 1947

Chuck Norris, actor (*Walker: Texas Ranger*), 1940

Tommy Hunter, Canadian country singer, 1937

James Earl Ray, assassin, 1928

Emily Pauline Johnson, Canadian poet, 1861

Daily Oddity
The Stanley Cup is the oldest trophy in professional sports.

MARCH 11
295 days until next year

In a Days
If you have a smoke detector or a robot servant, be warned. Today is "Check your Batteries Day."

If this is the second Sunday in March, move your sundial ahead one hour. It's "Daylight Saving Day."

In the News
1845: Self-rising flour was invented.

1892: Canadian inventor of basketball, James Naismith, organized the first-ever public demonstration of the sport.

1897: A meteorite exploded over West Virginia.

1918: Russia's capital moved from Saint Petersburg to Moscow.

1978: Winnipeg Jet Bobby Hull got his 1000th point.

1985: Mikhail Gorbachev became Russia's president.

1987: L.A. King Wayne Gretzky got his 1500th point.

1992: Environment Canada began issuing weekly ozone warnings.

1996: The final hockey game was played at the 72-year-old Montréal Forum. The Canadiens beat the Stars 4–1.

2004: A train bombing in Madrid, Spain, killed over 190 people.

2006: The first female president of Chile was elected.

Pisces
You are an enthusiastic and clear-sighted individual; however, you sometimes manipulate those around you.
2, 11, 22

#1 Song
1958: "Tequila" by The Champs

Birth Friends Forever
Marc-André Gragnani, Canadian hockey player, 1987

Marc-André Grondin, Canadian actor (*C.R.A.Z.Y.*), 1984

Thora Birch, actress (*American Beauty*), 1982

Benji Madden, musician (Good Charlotte), 1979

Joel Madden, musician (Good Charlotte), 1979

Terrence Howard, actor (*Iron Man*), 1969

Jesse Jackson Jr., politician, 1965

Elias Koteas, Canadian actor (*TMNT*), 1961

Leslie Cliff, Canadian swimmer, 1955

Bernie LaBarge, Canadian musician, 1953

Claude Jutra, Canadian director (*Mon oncle Antoine*), 1930

John Weinzweig, Canadian composer, 1913

Lawrence Welk, bandleader, 1903

Daily Oddity
Creston, Fort St. John, Charlie Lake, Taylor and Dawson Creek, BC, do not observe daylight saving time; neither does Saskatchewan.

MARCH 12
294 days until next year

In a Days

I'll take 5 boxes of cookies, please. It's "Girl Scouts Day."

Speak with a bad Australian accent, mate. It's "Canberra Day."

String up a hammock between the photocopier and the water cooler. It's "National Workplace Napping Day."

In the News

1857: A bridge connecting Toronto and Hamilton collapsed, killing 79 people.

1894: Coca-Cola was first sold in a glass bottle.

1912: The first person parachuted from an airplane.

1923: The motion picture soundtrack was patented.

1930: Canadian Victoria Cross recipient Billy Barker—an ace pilot who shot down 53 enemy planes—died.

1955: Saxophonist Charlie Parker died at the age of 34.

1972: After 26 seasons, Gordie Howe retired from hockey.

1987: Brian Orser became the first Canadian male world figure skating champion.

1993: Canada's east coast was battered by a blizzard that killed 110 people.

2003: Fourteen-year-old kidnap victim Elizabeth Smart was recovered.

2004: Canadian peacekeeping forces were deployment to Haiti.

Pisces

You are a naturally curious individual; however, this makes you susceptible to addiction.
2, 11, 22

#1 Song

1985: "Can't Fight This Feeling" by REO Speedwagon

Birth Friends Forever

Pete Doherty, musician (Babyshambles), 1979

Aaron Eckhart, actor (*The Dark Knight*), 1968

Darryl Strawberry, baseball player, 1962

James Taylor, musician, 1948

Peter Whalley, Canadian cartoonist, 1946

Serge Turgeon, Canadian union leader, 1946

Liza Minnelli, singer, 1946

Buckwheat, actor (*The Little Rascals*), 1931

Jack Kerouac, author (*On the Road*), 1922

Irving Layton, Canadian poet, 1912

Simon Newcomb, Canadian astronomer, 1835

John Abbott, Canadian prime minister, 1821

William Lyon Mackenzie, Canadian politician, 1795

Daily Oddity

Coca-Cola was originally green in colour.

MARCH 13
293 days until next year

In a Days
Hold the door open all day long. It's "Good Samaritan Involvement Day."
Set off the fire sprinklers. It's "National Open an Umbrella Indoors Day."

In the News

1781: The planet Uranus was discovered.

1887: Earmuffs were patented.

1906: Women's rights activist Susan B. Anthony died.

1916: Manitoba became the first province to vote for prohibition.

1928: Eileen Vollick became the first Canadian woman to get a pilot's licence.

1971: FLQ member Paul Rose was sentenced to life for the murder of Labour Minister Pierre Laporte.

1986: Microsoft issued shares to the public.

1989: The Northern Lights caused power outages in Québec.

1991: Exxon agreed to pay $1 billion for the Alaskan oil spill clean up.

2003: The footprints of a 350,000-year-old upright-walking human were discovered.

2007: Canada's population reached 31,612,897.

2007: For the first time, a Canadian census included the combined population of all 3 territories.

2008: Gold hit $1000/ounce.

Pisces
You are a courageous individual and an original thinker; however, sometimes you lack confidence.
4, 13, 26

#1 Song
1972: "Heart of Gold" by Neil Young

Birth Friends Forever
Emile Hirsch, actor (*Speed Racer*), 1985

Noel Fisher, Canadian actor (*Medium*), 1984

Danny Masterson, actor (*That '70s Show*), 1976

Common, rapper, 1972

Dana Delany, actress (*China Beach*), 1956

Robin Duke, Canadian comedian (*SCTV*), 1954

William H. Macy, actor (*Fargo*), 1950

Neil Sedaka, singer, 1939

W.O. Mitchell, Canadian author (*Who Has Seen the Wind*), 1914

L. Ron Hubbard, founder of Scientology, 1911

Daily Oddity
Toronto has the largest number of UFO sightings with 34, followed by Vancouver with 31.

MARCH 14
292 days until next year

In a Days
Is it really "International Ask a Question Day"?
Don't eat the paste. It's "National Children's Craft Day."
Get out of your pyjamas and pick up a broom. It's "Organize Your Home Office Day."
Make the radius of my slice 3.14 and don't forget the ice cream. It's "Pi Day."

In the News
1794: The cotton gin was patented.
1889: The Zeppelin was patented.
1916: Saskatchewan women got the provincial vote.
1923: Regina's Pete Parker gave the first play-by-play radio broadcast of a professional hockey game.
1942: The first patient was successfully treated with penicillin.
1964: Jack Ruby was found guilty of the murder of Lee Harvey Oswald, who had assassinated JFK a year earlier.
1978: The total number of people unemployed in Canada hits one million.
1979: Albertan Premier Peter Lougheed won his 3rd term.
1984: Marc Garneau was chosen as the first Canadian to go into space.
1991: Canadian skater Kurt Browning won his 3rd consecutive world figure skating championship.
2005: Over one million Lebanese demonstrated against the Syrian military presence in Lebanon.

Pisces
You are an adventurous and tolerant individual; however, you can be indecisive.
5, 15, 23

#1 Song
1982: "I Love Rock 'n' Roll" by Joan Jett and the Blackhearts

Birth Friends Forever
Mercedes McNab, Canadian actress (*Angel*), 1980
Chris Klein, actor (*American Pie*), 1979
Megan Follows, Canadian actress (*Anne of Green Gables*), 1968
Kirby Puckett, baseball player, 1960
Rick Dees, disc jockey, 1950
Billy Crystal, actor (*City Slickers*), 1948
Quincy Jones, composer and record producer, 1933
Michael Caine, actor (*The Dark Knight*) 1933
Alexander Brott, Canadian composer, 1915
K.C. Irving, Canadian industrialist, 1899
Marc-Aurèle Fortin, Canadian painter, 1888
Albert Einstein, physicist, 1879
Emily Murphy, Canadian women's rights activist (Famous Five), 1868

Daily Oddity
Calgary is Gaelic for "clear running water."

MARCH 15
291 days until next year

In a Days
Watch out for back-stabbers. It's "Brutus Day."
It's a metaphor for impending doom. It's the "Ides of March."
It's "Incredible Kid Day." But aren't kids incredible all the time?
Okay, kids are not incredible all the time. It's "True Confessions Day."

In the News

44 BC: Roman ruler Julius Caesar was stabbed to death by Brutus and several other senators.

1603: Samuel de Champlain embarked on his first voyage to Canada.

1871: The Manitoba legislature opened its first session as a province.

1894: Nova Scotia voted for the prohibition of alcohol.

1964: Elizabeth Taylor and Richard Burton were married in a Montréal hotel.

1973: Alberta Natives received $190,000 in back payment promised to them in an 1877 treaty.

1980: Tracey Wainman, 12, became the youngest Canadian to compete in the World Figure Skating Championships.

1985: The first Internet domain name was registered.

1993: A cyclone in Nova Scotia capsized a boat, killing 33 crewmembers.

2004: The discovery of the most distant natural object in the solar system, 90377 Sedna (a dwarf planet), was announced.

Pisces
You are a born leader and trailblazer; however, you may be perceived as domineering.
6, 16, 24

#1 Song
1953: "The Doggie in the Window" by Patti Page

Birth Friends Forever

Jordan Hastings, Canadian musician (Alexisonfire), 1982

Darcy Tucker, Canadian hockey player, 1975

Eva Longoria, actress (*Desperate Housewives*), 1975

Mark Hoppus, musician (B link-182), 1972

Bret Michaels, musician (Poison), 1963

Dee Snider, singer (Twisted Sister), 1955

David Cronenberg, Canadian director (*The Fly*), 1943

Sybil Adelman, Canadian scriptwriter (*Mary Tyler Moore Show*), 1942

Mike Love, musician (The Beach Boys), 1941

Jack Whyte, Canadian author (*A Dream of Eagles*), 1939

Judd Hirsch, actor (*Taxi*), 1935

Jimmy Swaggart, televangelist, 1935

Punch Imlach, Canadian hockey coach, 1918

Daily Oddity
Originally, the term "ides" (*idus* in Latin) was used to describe the 15th day of March, May, July and October.

MARCH 16
290 days until next year

In a Days
Free all knowledge from captivity. It's "Freedom of Information Day."
Make out with everyone you meet. It's "Lips Appreciation Day."
Celebrate a bird you've never heard of. It's "Curlew Day."

In the News

1843: Construction began on Fort Camosun—the first Hudson's Bay Company post on Vancouver Island.

1955: Montréal Canadien Maurice "Rocket" Richard was suspended from play, triggering a riot at the Montréal Forum.

1958: The Thunderbird became the 50-millionth car produced by Ford.

1968: The Oldsmobile Tornado became the 100-millionth car produced by GM.

1985: Canadian hockey player Eddie "Iceman" Shore died at the age of 83.

1989: Kurt Browning won the men's gold medal at the World Figure Skating Championships.

1998: Pope John Paul II asked God to forgive Roman Catholics for their apathy during the Holocaust.

2003: A worldwide vigil was held in protest of the war in Iraq.

2004: The credit information of 1400 Canadians was breached.

2006: The UN Human Rights Council was established.

Pisces
You are a multitalented visionary; however, you have a habit of marginalizing those around you.
7, 17, 27

#1 Song
1968: "(Sittin' on) the Dock of the Bay" by Otis Redding

Birth Friends Forever

Lauren Graham, actress (*Gilmore Girls*), 1967

Todd McFarlane, Canadian comic book artist (*Spawn*), 1961

Duane Sutter, Canadian hockey player, 1960

Flavor Flav, rapper, 1959

Nancy Wilson, singer (Heart), 1954

Kate Nelligan, Canadian actress (*Premonition*), 1950

Victor Garber, Canadian actor (*Alias*), 1949

Erik Estrada, actor (*CHiPs*), 1949

Richard Desjardins, Canadian singer, 1948

Roger Crozier, Canadian hockey player, 1942

Chuck Woolery, game-show host, 1941

Ray Hnatyshyn, governor general of Canada, 1934

Jerry Lewis, comedian, 1926

Daily Oddity
In Canada, most cars are stolen between 6 AM and noon.

MARCH 17
289 days until next year

In a Days
Start off with a hearty pancake breakfast. It's "Maple Syrup Day."
Then get drunk and start a fight. It's "St. Patrick's Day."
Bring along a needle and thread to the drunk tank. It's "National Quilting Day."
Call your friend in the Arctic to bail you out of jail. It's "International Day of the Seal."

In the News
- 1756: New York first celebrated St. Patrick's Day.
- 1765: The first Canadian St. Patrick's Day was celebrated by Irish troops serving in Québec.
- 1845: The rubber band was patented.
- 1858: One person was killed during a St. Patrick's Day riot in Toronto.
- 1900: The Montréal Shamrocks won the Stanley Cup.
- 1906: Canadian boxer Tommy Burns KO'd his opponent in 80 seconds, retaining his world heavyweight title.
- 1955: Ford workers in Oakville and Windsor ended their 109-day strike.
- 1987: The House of Commons passed a motion supporting free trade with the U.S.
- 1996: The Montréal Canadiens played their first game in the new Montréal Forum.
- 2003: Seventeen suspected cases of SARS were reported in Canada
- 2004: Former Governor General Ray Hnatyshyn was honoured with his own stamp.

Pisces
You are an optimistic and curious individual who is sometimes unreliable.
8, 26, 28

#1 Song
1996: "Because You Loved Me" by Céline Dion

Birth Friends Forever
Andrew Ference, Canadian hockey player, 1979
Andrew "Test" Martin, Canadian pro wrestler, 1975
Melissa Auf der Maur, Canadian musician, 1972
Yanic Truesdale, Canadian actor (*Gilmore Girls*), 1970
Rob Lowe, actor (*West Wing*), 1964
Nick Peros, Canadian composer, 1963
Pat Bolland, Canadian broadcaster, 1958
Gary Sinise, actor (*CSI: NY*), 1955
Craig Ramsay, Canadian hockey player, 1951
Kurt Russell, actor (*The Thing*), 1951
Daniel Lavoie, Canadian singer, 1949
John Wayne Gacy, serial killer, 1942
William John McKeag, Canadian politician, 1928
Nat "King" Cole, singer, 1919

Daily Odditys
Leprechauns are shoemakers to the fairies.

MARCH 18
288 days until next year

In a Days
Don't tell the oil companies. It's "National Biodiesel Day."
Make sure you knock before entering. It's "Awkward Moments Day."
Forgive them for not knocking before entering. It's "Forgive Mom and Dad Day."

In the News
- 37: Caligula was proclaimed emperor of Rome.
- 1850: American Express was founded.
- 1893: Lord Stanley donated a silver cup to be awarded every year to the best hockey team in Canada.
- 1918: Daylight saving time was established in North America.
- 1922: Gandhi was sentenced to 6 years in prison for civil disobedience.
- 1922: The first public bat mitzvah (coming of age for a girl) was held in New York.
- 1944: Mount Vesuvius erupted.
- 1945: Maurice "Rocket" Richard scored his 50th goal of the season.
- 1989: A 4400-year-old mummy was uncovered in Egypt.
- 1997: Canadian singer Joni Mitchell was reunited with the daughter she gave up for adoption years earlier.
- 2003: British Sign Language was recognized as an official language in Britain.

Pisces
You are a sensitive humanitarian who sometimes sacrifices your opinion for the sake of compromise.
9, 19, 29

#1 Song
1992: "Save the Best for Last" by Vanessa L. Williams

Birth Friends Forever
Adam Levine, singer (Maroon 5), 1979
Queen Latifah, actress/rapper (*Hairspray*), 1970
Vanessa L. Williams, actress/singer (*Ugly Betty*), 1963
Mike Rowe, TV personality (*Dirty Jobs*), 1962
Guy Carbonneau, Canadian hockey player, 1960
Ben Cohen, co-founder of Ben & Jerry's ice cream, 1951
Guy Lapointe, Canadian hockey player, 1948
Joy Fielding, Canadian actress (*Gunsmoke*), 1945
Charley Pride, country singer, 1938
John Updike, author (*Rabbit, Run*), 1932
George Plimpton, sports journalist, 1927
Peter Graves, actor (*Airplane*), 1926
Norval Baptie, Canadian speed skater, 1879
Mary Tudor, queen of France, 1496

Daily Oddity
Some hockey players have used the Stanley Cup to baptize their children.

MARCH 19
287 days until next year

In a Days
If you are a depressed actor, rejoice. It's "Act Happy Day."

Hope you like cavities. It's "National Chocolate Caramel Day."

Having healthier old people means having more home-baked goods, so celebrate "Well Elderly Day."

In the News
1885: Louis Riel seized hostages and set up the Provisional Government of Saskatchewan, starting the North West Rebellion.

1915: Pluto was first photographed.

1931: Gambling was legalized in Nevada.

1932: The Sydney Harbour Bridge opened in Australia.

1954: The first prizefight bout was televised in colour.

1964: Québec City had its greatest one-day snowfall—100 cm.

1979: C-SPAN began broadcasting.

1987: Televangelist Jim Bakker resigned as head of the Praise the Lord Club because of a sex scandal.

1990: The first world ice hockey tournament for women was held in Ottawa.

1990: Canadian singer Alannah Myles reached the top of the charts with her song "Black Velvet."

2008: A cosmic burst was observed in space.

Pisces
You are a driven individual with a strong sense of justice; however, you may be blind to the opinions of others.
1, 11, 28

#1 Song
1990: "Black Velvet" by Alannah Myles

Birth Friends Forever
Munro Chambers, Canadian actor (*Godsend*), 1993

Don Sparrow, Canadian illustrator, 1980

Rachel Blanchard, Canadian actress (*Road Trip*), 1976

Bruce Willis, actor (*Die Hard*), 1955

Harvey Weinstein, film producer, 1952

Glenn Close, actress (*Damages*), 1947

Ursula Andress, actress (*Dr. No*), 1936

Burt Metcalfe, Canadian director (*Father of the Bride*), 1935

Patrick McGoohan, actor (*The Prisoner*), 1928

Henry Morgentaler, Canadian gynecologist, 1923

Lomer Gouin, Canadian politician, 1861

Wyatt Earp, gunfighter, 1848

Daily Oddity
Chipmunks emerge from hibernation on this day.

MARCH 20
286 days until next year

In a Days
Kick winter in the groin—it's the first day of spring.
Be mindful of what you swallow when eating with your significant other. It's "Proposal Day."

In the News
1616: After 13 years in prison, poet Sir Walter Raleigh was released from the Tower of London.

1852: *Uncle Tom's Cabin* was first published.

1916: Albert Einstein published his theory of relativity.

1969: John Lennon and Yoko Ono were married.

1974: Hydro Québec workers shut down a project on James Bay after destroying millions of dollars of equipment in a riot.

1995: Sarin gas was released in the Tokyo subway system, killing 12 people.

1999: Legoland opened in California.

2003: The U.S. began military operations in Iraq.

2004: Stephen Harper won the leadership of the newly created Conservative Party of Canada.

2005: Japan had its first major quake, registering a magnitude of 6.6, in over 100 years.

2006: Cyclone Larry destroyed much of Australia's banana crops.

Pisces
You are a compassionate and intuitive person who is sometimes a victim of your own empathy.
2, 22, 29

#1 Song
1977: "Rich Girl" by Daryl Hall & John Oates

Birth Friends Forever
Caroline Brunet, Canadian kayaker, 1969

Stephen Sommers, director (*The Mummy*), 1962

Sting, pro wrestler, 1959

Holly Hunter, actress (*Saving Grace*), 1958

Spike Lee, director (*Malcolm X*), 1957

William Hurt, actor (*The Big Chill*), 1950

Bobby Orr, Canadian hockey player, 1948

Jay Ingram, Canadian TV host (*Daily Planet*), 1945

Pat Riley, basketball coach, 1945

Brian Mulroney, Canadian prime minister, 1939

Fred Rogers, television host (*Mr. Rogers Neighborhood*), 1928

Carl Reiner, actor (*Dick Van Dyke Show*), 1922

Maud Menten, Canadian biochemist, 1879

Daily Oddity
The word "spring" is derived from Indo-European and means "rapid movement."

MARCH 21
285 days until next year

In a Days
Hey, baby, what's your sign? It's "International Astrology Day."
Hold open the door for someone. It's "National Common Courtesy Day."
Spread some manure around. It's "National Agriculture Day."
Hopefully, the necessity for "International Day for the Elimination of Racial Discrimination Day" will soon be eliminated.
Don't forget, it's "Memory Day."

In the News
1413: Henry V became king of England.

1844: Jesus Christ was predicted to return to Earth on this day.

1963: Alcatraz prison closed.

1970: Winnipeg band The Guess Who released their hit song "American Woman."

1970: The first Earth Day was announced.

1973: Canadian hockey player Frank Mahovlich scored his 500th goal.

1980: J.R. Ewing was shot on the season finale of *Dallas*.

1980: The U.S. announced that it would boycott the Moscow Summer Olympics.

1985: Canadian paraplegic Rick Hansen began his wheelchair ride around the world for spinal cord injury research.

1993: Anne Murray was inducted into Canadian Music Hall of Fame.

1994: Wayne Gretzky tied Gordie Howe's 801-goal record.

Aries
You are practical and a quick-thinker; however, you tend to alienate those around you.
3, 9, 30

#1 Song
1955: "The Ballad of Davy Crockett" by Bill Hayes

Birth Friends Forever
Deryck Whibley, Canadian singer (Sum 41), 1980

Kathy Greenwood, Canadian actress (*The Kids in the Hall*), 1962

Matthew Broderick, actor (*The Producers*), 1962

Gary Oldman, actor (*Dracula*), 1958

Timothy Dalton, actor (*James Bond*), 1946

Ed Broadbent, Canadian politician, 1936

Daily Oddity
This day marks the beginning of the astrological year.

MARCH 22
284 days until next year

In a Days
Put on booties and a bonnet to celebrate "As Young as You Feel Day." Directly affect your company's productivity. It's "International Goof-off Day." Drink it up and then pee it out. It's "World Water Day."

In the News
1885: Canadian troops are mobilized because of the Northwest Rebellion.

1894: The first Stanley Cup playoff game was held.

1895: The first demonstration of a motion picture occurred.

1903: Niagara Falls ran dry because of a drought.

1922: Coalminers in BC and Alberta began a 6-month strike.

1923: Canadian Foster Hewitt announced the first radio broadcast of a hockey game.

1960: The first laser was patented.

1978: Karl Wallenda, patriarch of The Flying Wallendas, fell to his death attempting to tightrope walk between 2 hotels.

1993: Intel shipped their first Pentium chips.

1997: The Hale-Bopp Comet came the closest to Earth it has ever been.

2006: Two passengers died when the ferry *Queen of the North* sank in BC's Inside Passage.

Aries
You are an astute and energetic individual who sometimes refuses to compromise.
2, 11, 22

#1 Song
1980: "Another Brick in the Wall" by Pink Floyd

Birth Friends Forever
Reese Witherspoon, actress (*Legally Blonde*), 1976

Elvis Stojko, Canadian figure skater, 1972

John Kordic, Canadian hockey player, 1965

Andrew Lloyd Webber, composer, 1948

Dick Pound, Canadian lawyer, 1942

Dave Keon, Canadian hockey player, 1940

William Shatner, Canadian actor (*Star Trek*), 1931

Marcel Marceau, mime, 1923

Karl Malden, actor (*Patton*), 1912

Gabrielle Roy, Canadian author (*The Tin Flute*), 1909

Chico Marx, comedian (The Marx Brothers), 1887

Ernie Quigley, Canadian sports official, 1880

Daily Oddity
Noon was originally at 3 PM.

MARCH 23
283 days until next year

In a Days
Move over kittens. It's "National Puppy Day."
Avid horseshoe throwers and grenade tossers should celebrate "Near Miss Day."
Everything is "O.K. Day."
There is a 45 percent chance that today is "World Meteorological Day."

In the News

1752: *The Halifax Gazette*—Canada's first regular newspaper—first went on sale.

1889: The temperature in Edmonton reached 22°C—the city's warmest March day ever.

1903: The Wright brothers patented an airplane.

1933: Adolf Hitler was made dictator of Germany.

1956: Pakistan became the first Islamic republic.

1969: Group of Seven artist Arthur Lismer died at the age of 84.

1987: Six American skiers and their Canadian guide died in an avalanche in Kamloops, BC.

1989: The discovery of cold fusion was announced.

2001: The retired *Mir* space station broke up reentering the atmosphere, landing in the Pacific Ocean.

2007: British Royal Navy personnel sailing in Iraqi waters were seized by the Iranian Navy and held for 12 days.

Aries
You are an eager learner and a keen observer who can sometimes be over-analytical.
5, 23, 32

#1 Song
1975: "Lady Marmalade" by LaBelle

Birth Friends Forever
Jan Lisiecki, Canadian pianist, 1995
Luciana Carro, Canadian actress (*Battlestar Galactica*), 1981
Perez Hilton, celebrity blogger, 1978
Michelle Monaghan, actress (*Maid of Honour*), 1976
Yasmeen Ghauri, Canadian model, 1971
David Ford, Canadian kayaker, 1967
Amanda Plummer, actress (*Pulp Fiction*), 1957
Ric Ocasek, musician (The Cars), 1949
Fernand Gignac, Canadian singer, 1934
Akira Kurosawa, director (*Ran*), 1910
Joan Crawford, actress (*The Women*), 1905
William "Captain" Kidd, pirate, 1645

Daily Oddity
The Russian word *mir* has two meanings: "world" and "peace."

MARCH 24
282 days until next year

In a Days
Hope you're looking forward to wearing dentures. It's "National Chocolate-Covered Raisins Day."

There will be plenty of ups and downs today because it's "Yo-Yo Day."

In the News
1837: Lower Canada gave African Canadians the right to vote.

1936: The longest game in NHL history was played between Detroit and Montréal; Detroit scored in the 6th overtime, winning 1–0.

1944: Seventy-six WWII POWs broke out of Stalag Luft III. Their escape inspired the movie *The Great Escape*.

1958: Elvis Presley was inducted into the army.

1964: Prince Edward Island adopted its provincial flag.

1975: Thunder Bay received 102 cm of snow.

1975: The beaver became the official symbol of Canada.

1989: The tanker Exxon Valdez ran aground near Alaska, spilling 240,000 barrels of oil into the water.

2004: Because of an avian flu outbreak, the Canadian Food Inspection Agency ordered the slaughter of 275,000 poultry in BC.

2008: The Kingdom of Bhutan in South Asia held its first-ever general election.

Aries
You are a vigorous person who loves a challenge, but you can be impulsive.
6, 16, 26

#1 Song
1986: "Rock Me Amadeus" by Falco

Birth Friends Forever
Corneille, Canadian singer, 1977
Mike Vanderjagt, Canadian football player, 1970
Angèle Dubeau, Canadian violinist, 1962
Pierre Harvey, Canadian cross-country skier/cyclist, 1957
Doug Jarvis, Canadian hockey player, 1955
Tommy Hilfiger, fashion designer, 1951
Don Jardine, Canadian pro wrestler, 1940
David Suzuki, Canadian scientist, 1936
Steve McQueen, actor (*The Great Escape*), 1930
Onna White, Canadian choreographer, 1922
Joseph Barbera, cartoonist, 1911
Paul Sauvé, Canadian politician, 1907
Harry Houdini, magician, 1874
Honoré Beaugrand, Canadian journalist, 1848

Daily Oddity
Some of the characters in the movie *The Great Escape* were based on Canadian soldiers.

MARCH 25
281 days until next year

In a Days
The Virgin Mary was told she would conceive the Son of God. It's "Lady Day," or the "Feast of Annunciation."

Rock the vote. It's "National Day of Celebration of Democracy."

You're nuts if you don't celebrate "Pecan Day."

In the News
1893: A Toronto cab driver was fined $2 for driving on Sunday.

1903: Canada was left out of the U.S. redefinition of the Alaska-Canada border.

1958: The Avro Arrow took its maiden flight.

1965: RCMP in Montréal seized $25 million worth of heroin.

1969: John Lennon and Yoko Ono held their "Bed-In for Peace" in an Amsterdam hotel.

1982: Colin and Gregory Rankin of Oakville, ON, became North America's first test-tube twins.

1986: The Montréal Canadiens won their 23rd Stanley Cup.

1988: Kurt Browning became the first skater to successfully do a quadruple jump in competition.

2000: Canada's Reform Party became the Canadian Alliance.

2003: Tolkien Reading Day was declared. As well, in Middle Earth—Tolkien's fictional realm—March 25 is also considered "The Fall of Sauron."

Aries
You are fair-minded and self-reliant; however, you tend to neglect your personal needs.

7, 17, 27

#1 Song
1967: "Happy Together" by The Turtles

Birth Friends Forever
Danica Patrick, racecar driver, 1982

Kari Matchett, Canadian actress (*Invasion*), 1970

Jeff Healey, Canadian guitarist, 1966

Sarah Jessica Parker, actress (*Sex and the City*), 1965

Ken Wregget, Canadian hockey player, 1964

Marcia Cross, actress (*Desperate Housewives*), 1962

Elton John, singer, 1947

Aretha Franklin, singer, 1942

Gloria Steinem, feminist, 1934

Howard Cosell, sports reporter, 1918

David Lean, director (*Lawrence of Arabia*), 1908

Walter Little, Canadian politician, 1877

Daily Oddity
Ladybugs, which regularly appear around the Feast of Annunciation, were named after the Virgin Mary.

MARCH 26
280 days until next year

In a Days
Lawyers should forego chasing ambulances and instead celebrate "Legal Assistants Day."

It's "Hallomasgiving Day" or, if you wish, "Make Up Your Own Holiday Day."

In the News

1830: The Book of Mormon was first published.

1908: PEI passed a law banning all automobiles from its roadways.

1921: The Canadian schooner *Bluenose* was launched in Lunenburg, NS.

1926: Montréal Canadiens goaltender Georges Vézina died.

1934: Driving tests were introduced in the UK.

1953: The Salk polio vaccine was announced

1976: Queen Elizabeth II sent the first royal email.

1982: The groundbreaking ceremony for the Vietnam Veterans Memorial in Washington, DC, was held.

1997: The bodies of 39 members of the Heaven's Gate cult were discovered following a mass suicide.

2003: Ontario declared a public health emergency because of the SARS outbreak.

2004: Canada created the One-Tonne Challenge, a government initiative to reduce greenhouse gas emissions.

Aries
You are clear-sighted and practical yet, at times, extremely rigid.
8, 17, 26

#1 Song
1965: "Stop! In the Name of Love" by The Supremes

Birth Friends Forever

Keira Knightley, actress (*Atonement*), 1985

David Bennett, Canadian powerlifter, 1983

Sylvain Grenier, Canadian pro wrestler, 1977

Mike Peca, Canadian hockey player, 1974

Roch Voisine, Canadian singer, 1963

Martin Short, Canadian comedian (*SCTV*), 1950

Diana Ross, singer (The Supremes), 1944

Bob Woodward, journalist, 1943

Yvon Marcoux, Canadian politician, 1941

James Caan, actor (*The Godfather*), 1940

Leonard Nimoy, actor (*Star Trek*), 1931

Tennessee Williams, playwright, 1911

Robert Frost, poet, 1874

Daily Oddity
Twenty-five percent of all cars stolen in Canada are never retrieved.

MARCH 27
279 days until next year

In a Days

Go fly a kite. It's "Kite Flying Day."

Teach someone to share. It's "Education and Sharing Day."

If your dog died and your wife left you, you may have a hit song on your hands. It's "Quirky Country Music Song Titles Day."

In the News

1613: The first English child was born in Canada.

1848: Fredericton, NB, was incorporated as the "Celestial City."

1867: The BNA Act received Royal Assent.

1883: Pile-O'-Bones was made the capital of the NWT, which at the time included Alberta, Saskatchewan and the current NWT; Pile-O'-Bones was later renamed "Regina" in honour of Queen Victoria.

1920: Canadian actress Mary Pickford married Douglas Fairbanks.

1935: John Buchan, author of *The Thirty Nine Steps*, was appointed governor general of Canada.

1970: The supersonic jet Concorde took its maiden flight.

1982: *SCTV* characters Bob and Doug McKenzie (Rick Moranis and Dave Thomas) along with Geddy Lee of Rush, hit number 16 on the pop charts with their song "Take Off."

1998: The FDA approved the sale of Viagra in the U.S.

Aries

You are a charming and logical individual who sometimes isolates yourself from others.
9, 19, 29

#1 Song

1974: "Sunshine on My Shoulders" by John Denver

Birth Friends Forever

Brenda Song, actress (*The Suite Life*), 1988

Chad Denny, Canadian hockey player, 1987

Fergie, singer, 1975

Nathan Fillion, Canadian actor (*Firefly*), 1971

Brent Fitz, Canadian musician (Theory of a Deadman), 1970

Mariah Carey, singer, 1970

Quentin Tarantino, director (*Pulp Fiction*), 1963

Jann Arden, Canadian musician, 1962

Richard Séguin, Canadian singer, 1952

Michael York, actor (*Austin Powers*), 1942

Elsie MacGill, Canadian engineer, 1905

Gloria Swanson, actress (*Sunset Boulevard*), 1899

Daily Oddity

Regina is Latin for "queen."

MARCH 28
278 days until next year

In a Days
Leave your friends a trail of cake crumbs leading into some shadowy woods. It's "National Black Forest Cake Day."
If it's 2010, then today is "Palm Sunday."

In the News

1885: Five-thousand troops from the Dominion of Canada headed west to fight in the North-West Rebellion.

1918: Anti-conscription riots broke out in Québec City; 4 civilians were killed.

1928: The first automatic streetlight system went into operation in Ottawa.

1935: The Canadian Radio Commission banned radio ads on Sundays.

1969: Six thousand students demanding that McGill University become a French-only institution began rioting.

1978: Heritage Canada was incorporated.

1979: The nuclear reactor at Three Mile Island, PA, went into meltdown.

1982: The Edmonton Oilers scored the 2 fastest goals in NHL history—2 goals 24 seconds into the game.

1984: The Brampton, ON, store became the first unionized Eaton's.

1990: Athlete Jesse Owens posthumously won the Congressional Gold Medal.

Aries
You are a positive and helpful person who may become overwhelmed by your insecurities.
1, 10, 11

#1 Song
1972: "A Horse with No Name" by America

Birth Friends Forever

Mira Leung, Canadian figure skater, 1989

Julia Stiles, actress (*Save the Last Dance*), 1981

Richard Kelly, director (*Donnie Darko*), 1975

Shanna Moakler, TV personality, 1975

Nick Frost, actor (*Shaun of the Dead*), 1972

Vince Vaughn, actor (*Wedding Crashers*), 1970

Brett Ratner, director (*Rush Hour*), 1969

Reba McEntire, singer, 1955

Karen Kain, Canadian ballerina, 1951

Dianne Wiest, actress (*Parenthood*), 1948

Joseph Wright Jr., Canadian rower, 1906

Frederick Pabst, brewer, 1836

Daily Oddity
In the pulp novel *Red Trails*, published in 1935, a fictional Mountie named Eric Lewis kept the peace during the North-West Rebellion.

MARCH 29
277 days until next year

In a Days

Mix the sourest fruit in the world with your old prom dress, pour it into a cake pan, bake at 350°F for 15 minutes, and then serve. It's "National Lemon Chiffon Cake Day."

Stop shopping at Wal-Mart for one day and celebrate "National Mom and Pop Business Owners Day."

In the News

1778: James Cook landed on Vancouver Island.

1848: An iceberg in Lake Erie caused Niagara Falls to run dry for 30 hours.

1867: The British Parliament passed the BNA Act, which established the Dominion of Canada.

1886: The first batch of Coca-Cola was brewed in Atlanta, GA.

1966: Cassius Clay (Muhammad Ali) defeated George Chuvalo, the Canadian heavyweight boxing champion, in a 15-round bout in Toronto.

1978: Gordie Howe became the first active 50-year-old hockey player.

1993: PEI's Catherine Callbeck became the first female premier elected in a Canadian general election.

1996: The now defunct Vancouver Grizzlies lost their 21st game in a row.

2004: The Republic of Ireland became the first country to ban smoking in the workplace, bars and restaurants.

Aries

You are a reliable and analytical individual who can sometimes be inflexible.
2, 20, 22

#1 Song

1963: "He's So Fine" by The Chiffons

Birth Friends Forever

Maxim Lapierre, Canadian hockey forward, 1985

Sue Foley, Canadian singer, 1968

Lucy Lawless, actress (*Xena: Warrior Princess*), 1968

Elle Macpherson, model, 1964

Barry Blanchard, Canadian mountaineer, 1959

Brad McCrimmon, Canadian hockey player, 1959

Christopher Lambert, actor (*Highlander*), 1957

Terry Jacks, Canadian musician, 1944

Eric Idle, actor (*Monty Python*), 1943

Jacques Brault, Canadian poet, 1933

Man o' War, racehorse, 1917

Cy Young, baseball player, 1867

Daily Oddity

In 2001, the Vancouver Grizzlies moved down south, where they became the Memphis Grizzlies.

MARCH 30
276 days until next year

In a Days
Watch out for lead poisoning. It's "Pencil Day."
Be sure to write illegibly. Today is "Doctors Day."
Even though they'll probably get stuck in the tunnel slide, today is "Take your Parents to the Playground Day."

In the News
240 BC: The first perihelion passage of Halley's Comet occurred.

1832: The Bank of Nova Scotia was incorporated.

1842: Anesthesia was first used in an operation.

1858: Niagara Falls completely froze over.

1885: Stratford, ON, was incorporated as a city.

1939: Prime Minister Mackenzie King said Canada would not enlist its men for Foreign Service.

1951: The first UNIVAC computer was delivered to the U.S. Census Bureau.

1954: The Yonge Street subway station opened in Toronto.

1972: The last daily ration of rum was issued to Canadian naval personnel.

1981: U.S. President Ronald Reagan was shot in the chest.

1990: Police in Québec arrested 250 of 2000 marchers demonstrating against increased university tuition.

2006: Marcos Pontes became the first Brazilian in space.

Aries
You are an imaginative and headstrong individual; however, this causes you to rush into situations headfirst.
3, 12, 30

#1 Song
1984: "Footloose" by Kenny Loggins

Birth Friends Forever
Scott Moffatt, Canadian singer, 1983
Norah Jones, singer, 1979
Secretariat, racehorse, 1970
Celine Dion, Canadian singer, 1968
Ian Ziering, actor (*Beverly Hills, 90210*), 1964
Doug Wickenheiser, Canadian hockey player, 1961
Laurie Graham, Canadian skier, 1960
Maurice LaMarche, Canadian voice actor, 1958
Liza Frulla, Canadian politician, 1949
Eric Clapton, musician, 1945
Warren Beatty, actor (*Dick Tracy*), 1937
Milton Acorn, Canadian poet, 1923
Vincent van Gogh, painter, 1853

Daily Oddity
Wood Buffalo National Park in Alberta and the Northwest Territories is bigger than Switzerland.

MARCH 31
275 days until next year

In a Days
Feel free to heat, sterilize or combust. It's "Bunsen Burner Day."
Put on your clam diggers to celebrate "National Clams on the Half Shell Day."
Here's citrus in your eye. It's "Oranges and Lemons Day."

In the News
1831: Montréal and Québec City were incorporated as cities.

1889: The Eiffel Tower opened in France.

1914: Seventy-eight seal hunters died during a 2-day winter storm off the coast of Newfoundland.

1949: Newfoundland entered the Dominion of Canada.

1962: Brockville, ON, was incorporated as a city.

1978: Canadian co-discoverer of insulin Charles Best died at the age of 79.

1982: Canada's first fibre optics cable manufacturing plant opened in Saskatoon.

1984: Following in the footsteps of Terry Fox, one-legged runner Steve Fonyo started his journey across Canada to raise money for cancer research by dipping his artificial leg into St. John's Harbour.

2007: In Australia, 2.2 million people took part in the first-ever energy-saving initiative, Earth Hour.

2008: Honolulu's Aloha Airlines filed for bankruptcy.

Aries
You are a steadfast and resourceful person who sometimes suppresses your real emotions.
4, 14, 24

#1 Song
1974: "Hooked on a Feeling" by Blue Swede

Birth Friends Forever
Michael Ryder, Canadian hockey player, 1980

Ewan McGregor, actor (*Trainspotting*), 1971

Angus Young, musician (AC/DC), 1955

Al Gore, Nobel Prize winner, 1948

Rhea Perlman, actress (*Cheers*), 1948

Gabe Kaplan, actor (*Welcome Back, Kotter*), 1945

Christopher Walken, actor (*Pulp Fiction*), 1943

Shirley Jones, actress (*The Partridge Family*), 1934

Richard Chamberlain, actor (*The Bourne Identity*), 1934

Lee Patterson, Canadian actor (*One Life to Live*), 1929

Gordie Howe, Canadian hockey player, 1928

Jean Coutu, Canadian actor, 1925

Johann Sebastian Bach, composer, 1685

Daily Oddity
Steve Fonyo completed his "Journey for Lives" marathon on May 29, 1985. In total, he ran 7294 km and raised $14 million.

APRIL 1
274 days until next year

In a Days
Today is "Free Money at the Bank Day"—just kidding, it's "April Fools' Day."
Celebrate the patron saint of drivers. It's "St. Stupid Day."
If you were recently dumped, celebrate "Sorry Charlie Day."
Lighten up and celebrate "National Fun Day."

In the News
1868: Canada celebrated its first April Fools' Day.

1891: The Wrigley Chewing Gum Company was founded.

1900: Canada made an unsuccessful bid to purchase the Sun.

1918: Alberta declared the prohibition of alcohol.

1924: The Royal Canadian Air Force was formed.

1966: Bigfoot was mistakenly elected prime minister of Canada.

1976: Apple Computers was founded.

1981: The Canadarm was used to open the first beer in space.

1999: The territory of Nunavut joined the Dominion of Canada.

2001: Canadian beavers were given the right to vote.

2003: Newfoundland became the first province to ban cell phones while driving.

2004: Canadians were exempted from being fingerprinted and photographed when entering the U.S.

Aries
You are an organized and pragmatic individual who can, at times, overburden yourself.
1, 9, 18

#1 Song
1867: "I Canadance" by The Funky Fathers of Confederation.

Birth Friends Forever
Jean-Pierre Dumont, Canadian hockey player, 1978

Darren McCarty, Canadian hockey player, 1972

Method Man, rapper, 1971

Scott Stevens, Canadian hockey player, 1964

Debbie Reynolds, actress (*Singin' in the Rain*), 1932

Ken Reardon, Canadian hockey player, 1921

Toshir Mifune, actor (*Seven Samurai*), 1920

Bob Nolan, Canadian country singer, 1908

Lon Chaney Sr., actor (*Phantom of the Opera*), 1883

Daily Oddity
The French used to celebrate New Year's between March 25 and April 1, but when the Gregorian calendar came into effect, New Year's was changed to January 1.

APRIL 2
273 days until next year

In a Days
I'm only saying sorry because it's "Reconciliation Day."
Don't forget to bring your copy of *Everyone Poops* to read on the bus. It's "International Children's Book Day."
Celebrate everyone's favourite sandwich. It's "National Peanut Butter and Jelly Day."

In the News
1840: Torontonians celebrated the marriage of Queen Victoria and Prince Albert with a public ox-roasting in the street.

1917: Jeannette Rankin became the first woman elected to the U.S. Congress.

1968: To pay off the $250 million Expo '67 deficit, the mayor of Montréal created Canada's first lottery.

1972: Charlie Chaplin returned to the U.S. for the first time after being labelled a communist in the '50s.

1975: Construction of the Toronto CN Tower was completed.

1977: Vancouver's newly restored Orpheum Theatre opened.

1990: Rita Johnson became the first female premier of BC.

1992: Gangster John Gotti was sentenced to life in prison for murder and racketeering.

2005: Pope John Paul II died at the age of 84.

2006: Tennessee was hit by over 60 tornadoes, which killed 29 people.

Aries
You are an enthusiastic and vigorous individual; however, sometimes you may find it hard to compromise.
1, 9, 27

#1 Song
1987: "Nothing's Gonna Stop Us Now" by Starship

Birth Friends Forever
Leyla Milani, Canadian actress (*Entourage*), 1982

Rodney King, victim of police brutality, 1965

Emmylou Harris, singer, 1947

Kurt Winter, Canadian musician (The Guess Who), 1946

Donald Jackson, Canadian figure skater, 1940

Marvin Gaye, singer, 1939

Sharon Acker, Canadian actress (*Rin Tin Tin*), 1935

Shirley Douglas, Canadian actress (*Street Legal*), 1934

Jack Webb, actor (*Dragnet*), 1920

Sir Alec Guinness, actor (*Star Wars*), 1914

Paul Triquet, Canadian military officer, 1910

Buddy Ebsen, actor (*The Beverly Hillbillies*), 1908

Hans Christian Andersen, author (*Ugly Duckling*), 1805

Daily Oddity
The CN tower was named after CN Rail, which funded the construction.

APRIL 3
272 days until next year

In a Days
Even though regular mail is still just as slow, it's "Pony Express Day."

Break out your smoking pipe, monocle and suede elbow patches to celebrate "Tweed Day."

If only for the sake of leprechaun gold, it's "National Find-a-Rainbow Day."

In the News
1793: Britain abolished slavery in Canada.

1802: Three-hundred Scottish men and women settled in Sydney, NS.

1863: Canada's first covered skating rink opened in Halifax, NS.

1882: Outlaw Jesse James was shot and killed by Robert Ford.

1895: The libel court case against Oscar Wilde began.

1957: Elvis Presley performed in Ottawa, the only foreign city he ever played in.

1973: The first cell phone call was made.

1975: Chess protégé Bobby Fischer forfeited the title of world champion.

1992: After 45 years, the "Miss Canada Pageant" was cancelled.

1996: "Unabomber" Ted Kaczynski was arrested.

2008: ATA Airlines filed for bankruptcy for the second time in 5 years.

Aries
You are perceptive person with a magnetic personality; however, you are sometimes oversensitive.
1, 9, 19

#1 Song
2001: "Butterfly" by Crazy Town

Birth Friends Forever
Amanda Bynes, actress (*Sydney White*), 1986

Cobie Smulders, Canadian actress (*The L Word*), 1982

Jennie Garth, actress (*Beverly Hills, 90210*), 1972

Lance Storm, Canadian pro wrestler, 1969

Sebastian Bach, Canadian musician (Skid Row), 1968

Eddie Murphy, actor (*SNL*), 1961

Alec Baldwin, actor (*30 Rock*), 1958

Bernard Parent, Canadian hockey player, 1945

Tony Orlando, musician, 1944

Wayne Newton, singer, 1942

Jane Goodall, zoologist, 1934

Marlon Brando, actor (*Godfather*), 1924

Louis Applebaum, Canadian composer, 1918

Allan Dwan, Canadian director (*Sands of Iwo Jima*), 1885

Daily Oddity
Crowned in 1991, Nicole Dunsdon remains the last Miss Canada.

APRIL 4
271 days until next year

In a Days
Watch out pigs and cows. It's "National Cordon Bleu Day."
If you're a man, you will have no use for "National Reading a Roadmap Day."

In the News
1858: The gold rush began along the BC's Fraser River.

1896: The gold rush began in the Yukon.

1917: Women in BC got the provincial vote.

1949: Canada joined NATO.

1957: Fours girls from Ottawa were expelled from school for going to an Elvis Presley concert.

1960: Canadian singer Paul Anka hit number 2 on the charts with "Puppy Love."

1968: Martin Luther King Jr. was assassinated.

1969: The world's first artificial heart was implanted.

1972: The Liberal Party of Canada was registered.

1975: Microsoft was founded.

1988: Toronto Blue Jay George Bell hit 3 home runs in the season opener.

2008: Under suspicion for sexual abuse, the Fundamentalist Church of Jesus Christ of Latter-day Saints in Texas was raided, and 534 women and children were taken into protective custody.

Aries
You are a strong-willed and determined individual; however, you sometimes lack empathy for others.
1, 4, 9

#1 Song
1961: "Blue Moon" by The Marcels

Birth Friends Forever
Jamie Lynn Spears, actress (*Zoey 101*), 1991

Sarah Gadon, Canadian actress (*The Border*), 1987

Roberto Luongo, Canadian hockey player, 1979

Heath Ledger, actor (*The Dark Knight*), 1979

Barry Pepper, Canadian actor (*Saving Private Ryan*), 1970

Robert Downey Jr., actor (*Iron Man*), 1965

Dale Hawerchuk, Canadian hockey player, 1963

Hugo Weaving, actor (*The Matrix*), 1960

Pat Burns, Canadian hockey coach, 1952

Craig T. Nelson, actor (*Coach*), 1944

Anthony Perkins, actor (*Psycho*), 1932

Maya Angelou, poet, 1928

Claude Wagner, Canadian politician, 1925

Jules Léger, governor general of Canada, 1913

Daily Oddity
The average lifespan of a major league baseball is 5 pitches.

APRIL 5
270 days until next year

In a Days

Personally, I don't think that it is a coincidence that "National Fun at Work Day" coincides with "National Alcohol Screening Day."

Add some spice to your life and celebrate "National Raisin and Spice Bar Day."

If you live in Taiwan, break out the broom. It's "Tomb Sweeping Day."

In the News

1790: The first town meeting was held in Grimsby, ON.

1842: The first museum in Canada opened in Saint John, NB.

1908: Edmonton received the first dial telephones in Canada.

1955: British Prime Minister Winston Churchill resigned.

1958: The underwater mountain Ripple Rock, located in Campbell River, BC, was blown up to clear shipping routes. It is still considered one of the world's largest non-nuclear explosions to date.

1971: Canadian climber Frances Phipps became the first woman to reach the North Pole.

1974: Baseball player Hank Aaron tied Babe Ruth's 714th home run record.

1974: Group of Seven member-painter Alexander Young Jackson died at the age of 91.

1998: The world's largest suspension bridge opened in Japan.

Aries

You are a logical visionary, who may, at times, overwork yourself.
1, 5, 9

#1 Song

1989: "The Look" by Roxette

Birth Friends Forever

Pharrell, rapper (The Neptunes), 1973

Thea Gill, Canadian actress (*Queer as Folk*), 1970

Gary Gait, Canadian lacrosse player, 1967

Christopher "Kid" Reid, rapper (Kid 'n Play), 1964

Diamond Dallas Page, pro wrestler, 1956

Mitch Pileggi, actor (*The X-Files*), 1952

Michael Moriarty, Canadian actor (*Law & Order*), 1941

Colin Powell, U.S. Secretary of State, 1937

Roger Corman, film producer (*Death Race*), 1926

Gregory Peck, actor (*To Kill a Mockingbird*), 1916

Bette Davis, actress (*All About Eve*), 1908

Spencer Tracy, actor (*Bad Day at Black Rock*), 1900

W. Atlee Burpee, Canadian horticulturist, 1858

Daily Oddity

At 5959 m, Mount Logan is Canada's highest mountain.

APRIL 6
269 days until next year

In a Days
Wake up! It's "Drowsy Driver Awareness Day."
I just need you to fill out these forms because it's "Hospital Admitting Clerks Day."
Too plaid, it's "Tartan Day."
"Teflon Day" is easier to say than "Polytetrafluoroethylene Day."
Even though most of us have lost them, it's "World Marbles Day."

In the News
1869: Celluloid was patented.

1886: Vancouver was incorporated as a city.

1896: The first modern Olympic Games opened in Greece.

1947: The first Tony Awards were held.

1954: The Montréal Canadiens scored 3 goals in the first 56 seconds of a Stanley Cup playoff game.

1961: Canadian children donated $260,000 to UNICEF.

1972: A bomb exploded at the Cuban Trade Commission in Montréal, killing one person.

1985: Bryan Adams' song "Somebody" hit number 11 on the pop charts.

1994: The Rwandan genocide began.

2004: The Canadian national women's hockey team won the Women's World Ice Hockey Championships.

Aries
You are a multitalented and original thinker; however, at times, you can be single-minded.
1, 9, 24, 33

#1 Song
1956: "Poor People of Paris" by Les Baxter

Birth Friends Forever
Clarke MacArthur, Canadian hockey player, 1985

Candace Cameron, actress (*Full House*), 1976

Zach Braff, actor (*Scrubs*), 1975

Paul Rudd, actor (*Knocked Up*), 1969

Frank Black, musician (The Pixies), 1965

Michel Larocque, Canadian hockey player, 1952

John Ratzenberger, actor (*Cheers*), 1947

André Ouellet, Canadian politician, 1939

Billy Dee Williams, actor (*The Empire Strikes Back*), 1937

Merle Haggard, musician, 1937

Walter Huston, Canadian actor (*The Virginian*), 1884

Joseph Medill, Canadian newspaper editor, 1823

Daily Oddity
Construction on the Canadarm began in April 1974; it would not be completed until 1981.

APRIL 7
268 days until next year

In a Days
Ah-choo, it's "World Health Day."

If you take your coffee in the form of cake, you should celebrate "National Coffee Cake Day."

Since today is "No Housework Day," you have more time to celebrate "National Love Our Children Day."

In the News
1795: France adopted the metre as a measure of length.

1851: Canada Post issued Canada's first stamp.

1868: Thomas D'Arcy McGee became the only Canadian federal politician to be assassinated.

1869: PEI held its last public hanging.

1906: Mount Vesuvius erupted.

1928: While playing the Montréal Maroons, the general manager of the New York Rangers replaced his team's injured goalie on the ice.

1948: The World Health Organization was established.

1969: The Internet was officially born.

1977: The Toronto Blue Jays played their first home game.

1989: A gunman hijacked a bus in Montréal and drove it to Parliament Hill.

2001: The *Mars Odyssey* was launched.

Aries
You are an optimistic person who is filled with zeal; however, you may become aggressive when opposed.
1, 7, 9

#1 Song
1985: "We Are the World" by various singers

Birth Friends Forever
Ève Salvail, Canadian model, 1973

Victor Kraatz, Canadian figure skater, 1971

Steve Graves, Canadian hockey player, 1964

Russell Crowe, actor (*Gladiator*), 1964

Jackie Chan, actor (*Rush Hour*), 1954

Francis Ford Coppola, director (*Godfather*), 1939

David Frost, television host, 1939

Roger Lemelin, Canadian author (*The Quest of Splendour*), 1919

Billie Holiday, singer, 1915

Percy Faith, Canadian composer, 1908

William Wordsworth, poet, 1770

Daily Oddity
Canadian inventor of time zones, Sandford Fleming, designed the Three Penny Beaver stamp, the first stamp to feature an animal.

APRIL 8
267 days until next year

In a Days
Hola! It's "National Empanada Day."

They can put them in the spokes of their wheelchairs—it's "Trading Cards for Grown-ups Day."

In the News

1751: Canada's first inn opened in Nova Scotia.

1820: *The Venus de Milo* was discovered on a Greek island.

1899: Martha Place became the first woman to be executed in an electric chair.

1904: Longacre Square was renamed Times Square in honour of *The New York Times*.

1969: The Montréal Expos played their first game.

1974: Hank Aaron broke Babe Ruth's record with his 715th home run.

1992: Tennis player Arthur Ashe announced that he had AIDS.

2004: Condoleezza Rice testified before the 9/11 Commission.

2006: The bodies of 8 men were found in an Ontario field. The murders were later linked to the Bandidos motorcycle gang.

2008: The world's first building to integrate wind turbines in its construction was completed.

Aries
You are an incisive and resourceful person; however, you tend to suppress your emotions.
1, 8, 9

#1 Song
2008: "Touch My Body" by Mariah Carey

Birth Friends Forever

Taylor Kitsch, Canadian actor (*Friday Night Lights*), 1981

Katee Sackhoff, actress (*Battlestar Galactica*), 1980

Patricia Arquette, actress (*Medium*), 1968

Robin Wright Penn, actress (*The Princess Bride*), 1966

Biz Markie, rapper, 1964

John Schneider, actor (*The Dukes of Hazzard*), 1954

Michael Leshner, Canadian lawyer, 1948

Darlene Gillespie, Canadian actress (*The Mickey Mouse Club*), 1941

Frédéric Back, Canadian short film director, 1924

Raoul Jobin, Canadian tenor, 1906

Mary Pickford, Canadian silent film actress (*Coquette*), 1892

Daily Oddity
Silent screen star Mary Pickford was known as "America's Sweetheart," even though she was born in Toronto.

APRIL 9
266 days until next year

In a Days
In 2003, the Canadian government declared this day "Vimy Ridge Day."
If you hug them too hard, they'll break. It's "National Cherish an Antique Day."

In the News
1413: Henry V was crowned king of England.

1865: Robert E. Lee surrendered to Ulysses S. Grant, ending the American Civil War.

1917: Canadian troops successfully captured the German stronghold at Vimy Ridge. Four thousand Canadians lost their lives, and over 6000 were wounded.

1953: The first 3-D movie premiered.

1957: The Suez Canal opened.

1987: The Supreme Court of Canada ruled that the right to strike was not guaranteed by the constitution.

1987: Wayne Gretzky scored 7 goals in a Stanley Cup game.

2002: The funeral of Elizabeth, the Queen Mother, was held.

2003: Baghdad fell to U.S. forces.

2005: Prince Charles married Camilla Parker Bowles.

Aries
You are a prodigious and resourceful individual who does not necessarily work well with others.
1, 9, 10

#1 Song
1995: "This Is How We Do It" by Montell Jordan

Birth Friends Forever
Kristen Stewart, actress (*Twilight*), 1990

Adam Loewen, Canadian baseball player, 1984

Jay Baruchel, Canadian actor (*Knocked Up*), 1982

Gerard Way, musician (My Chemical Romance), 1977

Jacques Villeneuve, Canadian racecar driver, 1971

Cynthia Nixon, actress (*Sex and the City*), 1966

Paulina Porizkova, model, 1965

Rick Tocchet, Canadian hockey player, 1964

Marc Jacobs, fashion designer, 1963

Dennis Quaid, actor (*Frequency*), 1954

Cheeta, chimpanzee actor, 1932

Richard Hatfield, Canadian politician, 1931

Hugh Hefner, publisher of *Playboy*, 1926

Daily Oddity
In 1922, France donated the land around Vimy Ridge to Canada in gratitude for their sacrifice. Today, the land is home to Canada's largest war monument, the "Canadian National Vimy Memorial."

APRIL 10
265 days until next year

In a Days
You never know when you'll need a kidney, so celebrate "National Sibling Day." Lie about how many strokes you took. It's "Golfers Day."

In the News

1710: The first law regulating copyright was issued.

1841: Halifax, NS, was incorporated as a city.

1866: The American Society for the Prevention of Cruelty to Animals (ASPCA) was founded.

1916: The Professional Golfers' Association of America (PGA) was formed.

1925: *The Great Gatsby* was first published.

1947: National Wildlife Week was founded in Canada to honour conservationist Jack Miner.

1947: The Montréal Royals sold their star player Jackie Robinson to the Brooklyn Dodgers. The next day, Robinson became the first African American to play in major league baseball.

1984: After a 2-month strike, pulp and paper workers in BC went back to work.

1990: Canada's Goods and Services Tax (GST) became law.

1992: The NHL returned to the ice following a 10-day strike.

Aries
You are a risk-taker and a technical expert who has a tendency to become addicted to danger.
10, 19, 20

#1 Song
1989: "She Drives Me Crazy" by Fine Young Cannibals

Birth Friends Forever

Haley Joel Osment, actor (*The Sixth Sense*), 1988

Dion Phaneuf, Canadian hockey player, 1985

Mandy Moore, singer/actress, 1984

Sean Avery, Canadian hockey player, 1980

Sara Renner, Canadian cross-country skier, 1976

Enrico Ciccone, Canadian hockey player, 1970

Steven Seagal, actor (*Hard to Kill*), 1951

Nick Auf der Maur, Canadian politician, 1942

John Madden, football broadcaster, 1936

Omar Sharif, actor (*Dr. Zhivago*), 1932

Max von Sydow, actor (*Strange Brew*), 1929

Harry Morgan, actor (*M*A*S*H*), 1915

Jack Miner, Canadian conservationist, 1865

Joseph Pulitzer, journalist, 1847

Daily Oddity
Good Friday can fall anywhere between March 19 and April 22.

APRIL 11
264 days until next year

In a Days
Hello, hello, hello, hello. It's "Barbershop Quartet Day."
Hope you can stanza "Poetry and Creative Mind Day."
Everything tastes better covered in melted cheese. It's "National Cheese Fondue Day."
In French, it means "lion's tooth." Today is "Dandelion Day."

In the News
1768: A devastating fire destroyed much of Montréal.
1868: The Japanese shogunate was abolished.
1904: Sydney, NS, was incorporated as a city.
1921: The first sports match was broadcast on the radio.
1970: The ill-fated spacecraft *Apollo 13* was launched.
1976: The Apple I computer was created.
1981: U.S. President Ronald Reagan returned to the White House after being shot in the chest.
1989: Philadelphia Flyers goalie Ron Hextall became the first goaltender to score a goal in a playoff game.
2000: Same-sex couples in Canada were granted the same social and tax benefits as heterosexual couples.
2007: Thirty-three people died in the bombing of Algiers.

Aries
You are a persuasive and progressive thinker who may, at times, fight depression.
1, 2, 9

#1 Song
1974: "Bennie & the Jets" by Elton John

Birth Friends Forever
Joss Stone, singer, 1987
Alexandre Burrows, Canadian hockey player, 1981
Tom Thacker, Canadian musician, 1978
Tricia Helfer, Canadian actress (*Battlestar Galactica*), 1974
Trevor Linden, Canadian hockey player, 1970
John Milius, director (*Conan the Barbarian*), 1944
Mark Strand, Canadian poet, 1934
Victor Bouchard, Canadian composer, 1926
Pierre Péladeau, Canadian businessman, 1925
Danny Gallivan, Canadian sportscaster, 1917
Robert Stanfield, premier of Nova Scotia, 1914
Norman McLaren, Canadian animator, 1914

Daily Oddity
The white bunny usually emerges with the Easter moon. In Germany, the white rabbit is a goddess who lays eggs for children.

APRIL 12
263 days until next year

In a Days
If you are half donkey and half horse, then you should celebrate "Mule Day." If you are uptight, then you should celebrate "Walk on Your Wild Side Day." It's "National Liquorice Day," which means we celebrate black liquorice, too.

In the News

1872: Winnipeg was hit with a record 33 cm of snow.

1898: An imported Winton car became Canada's first gas-powered automobile.

1917: Women in Ontario got the provincial vote.

1937: The first jet engine was ground tested.

1945: U.S. President Franklin D. Roosevelt died while still in office.

1955: The first polio vaccine trial was announced.

1960: Maurice Richard scored the last goal of his NHL career.

1961: Astronaut Yuri Gagarin became the first human in space.

1980: Terry Fox began his Marathon of Hope by dipping his prosthetic leg into the Atlantic Ocean.

1982: To protest the invasion of the Falkland Islands, Canada banned all imports from Argentina.

1992: Euro-Disneyland opened.

Aries
You are an ambitious humanitarian who may become obsessed with your vision.
1, 3, 6, 9

#1 Song
1971: "Joy to the World" by Three Dog Night

Birth Friends Forever

Erik Mongrain, Canadian musician, 1980

Claire Danes, actress (*Stardust*), 1979

Ron MacLean, Canadian sportscaster, 1960

Vince Gill, musician, 1957

Richard Martin, Canadian director (*Slap Shot 3*), 1956

Andy Garcia, actor (*The Untouchables*), 1956

Pat Travers, Canadian musician, 1954

David Cassidy, singer (*The Partridge Family*), 1950

Tom Clancy, author (*Patriot Games*), 1947

David Letterman, talk-show host, 1947

Ed O'Neill, actor (*Married with Children*), 1946

Herbie Hancock, composer, 1940

Tiny Tim, musician, 1932

Beverly Cleary, author (*Ramona*), 1916

Daily Oddity
Easter can fall anywhere from late March to late April.

APRIL 13
262 days until next year

In a Days
Treat every day like it's "Blame Someone Else Day."
Hug your cactus. It's "International Plant Appreciation Day."

In the News

1111: Henry V was crowned Holy Roman Emperor.

1742: George Handel performed his *Messiah* for the first time.

1796: The first elephant arrived in the United States.

1877: A U.S. newspaper coined the RCMP slogan "They always get their man."

1898: An avalanche in the Chilkoot Pass killed 60 miners.

1902: The first J.C. Penney department store opened.

1925: Women in Newfoundland got the right to vote in provincial elections.

1953: The CIA launched its mind-control program.

1970: An oxygen tank aboard *Apollo 13* exploded, stranding the crew in space for a time.

1984: Pete Rose got his 4000th hit in his first game as a Montréal Expo.

1992: The Great Chicago Flood occurred.

1997: Tiger Woods became the youngest golfer to win the Masters Tournament.

Aries
You are a profound and incisive person who may become embittered at times.
1, 4, 8, 9

#1 Song
1950: "If I Knew You Were Comin' (I'd've Baked a Cake)" by Eileen Barton

Birth Friends Forever

Rick Schroder, actor (*NYPD Blue*), 1970

Caroline Rhea, Canadian talk-show host, 1964

Ron Perlman, actor (*Hellboy*), 1950

Al Green, singer, 1946

Paul Sorvino, actor (*Goodfellas*), 1939

Cliff Lumsdon, Canadian marathon swimmer, 1931

Don Adams, actor (*Get Smart*), 1926

Samuel Beckett, dramatist and poet, 1906

Alfred Mosher Butts, inventor of Scrabble, 1899

Gordon S. Fahrni, Canadian physician, 1887

Butch Cassidy, outlaw, 1866

Thomas D'Arcy McGee, Canadian politician, 1825

Guy Fawkes, conspirator, 1570

Daily Oddity
Canadian Joseph Coyle invented the egg carton.

APRIL 14
261 days until next year

In a Days
You can feel it coming back at you. It's "Tangible Karma Day."

In the News

1759: George Handel, the composer of *Messiah*, died.

1865: U.S. President Abraham Lincoln was assassinated.

1869: The noon cannon on Parliament Hill was fired for the first time.

1881: The "Four Dead in Five Seconds" gunfight occurred in Texas.

1892: Windsor, ON, was incorporated as a city.

1894: Thomas Edison first demonstrated the kinetoscope.

1912: The *Titanic* struck an iceberg near Newfoundland and sank, killing 1503 passengers.

1927: The first Volvo automobile debuted.

1956: Videotape was demonstrated for the first time.

1968: Katharine Hepburn and Barbra Streisand tied for Best Actress at the Oscars.

1986: Over 90 people died during a hailstorm in Bangladesh, which produced hailstones weighing one kg.

2000: Metallica drummer Lars Ulrich sued Napster.

Aries
You are an intelligent and self-reliant individual; however, you tend to dominate others.
1, 5, 9, 10

#1 Song
1912: "Moonlight Bay" by American Quartet

Birth Friends Forever

Abigail Breslin, actress (*Little Miss Sunshine*), 1996

Win Butler, Canadian musician (Arcade Fire), 1980

Sarah Michelle Gellar, actress (*Buffy: The Vampire Slayer*), 1977

Jason Wiemer, Canadian hockey player, 1976

Adrien Brody, actor (*The Pianist*), 1973

Anthony Michael Hall, actor (*Sixteen Candles*), 1968

André Boisclair, Canadian politician, 1966

Greg Battle, football player, 1964

Brad Garrett, actor (*Everybody Loves Raymond*), 1960

Lothaire Bluteau, Canadian actor (*24*), 1957

Frank Serpico, police officer, 1936

Loretta Lynn, country singer, 1935

Sylvio Mantha, Canadian hockey player, 1902

Daily Oddity
Newfoundland is the iceberg capital of Canada.

APRIL 15
260 days until next year

In a Days
Today is "Equal Pay Day," so ask for the same pay as a doctor.
Why not lift the toilet seat up when you're done? It's "Husband Appreciation Day."
This might be a stab in the dark, but isn't it "Take a Wild Guess Day"?
If you are a vacuum cleaner, you should celebrate "That Sucks Day."

In the News
1892: General Electric was founded.

1920: The Canadian Mint released the Canadian small cent coin.

1923: Insulin was made available to diabetics.

1924: Rand McNally published their first road atlas.

1955: The first McDonald's restaurant opened.

1957: White Rock separated from Surrey, BC, and incorporated as a new city.

1974: Nine women in Québec won $1 million in the first Lottery Canada draw.

1977: Montréal Expos played their first game in Olympic Stadium.

1984: To celebrate the 450th anniversary of Jacques Cartier's discovery of Québec, a fleet of tall ships sailed from St. Malo, France, to Canada.

1992: Canadian actor William Shatner was inducted into the National Association of Broadcasters Hall of Fame.

Aries
You are an imaginative and inspirational person who can sometimes be stubborn.
1, 6, 9, 18

#1 Song
1990: "Nothing Compares 2 U" by Sinead O'Connor

Birth Friends Forever
Emma Watson, actress (*Harry Potter*), 1990

Seth Rogen, Canadian actor (*Superbad*), 1982

Arturo Gatti, Canadian boxer, 1972

Jimmy Waite, Canadian hockey player, 1969

Emma Thompson, actress (*Wit*), 1959

Kevin Lowe, Canadian hockey player, 1959

Dodi Al-Fayed, businessman, 1955

Claudia Cardinale, actress (*Once Upon A Time in the West*), 1939

Elizabeth Montgomery, actress (*Bewitched*), 1933

Roy Clark, country singer, 1933

Alfred S. Bloomingdale, businessman, 1916

Bliss Carman, Canadian poet, 1861

Joseph E. Seagram, Canadian distiller, 1841

Leonardo da Vinci, inventor, 1452

Daily Oddity
Nothing rhymes with the word "silver."

APRIL 16
259 days until next year

In a Days
It's "International Moment of Laughter Day," which is usually achieved when a person wets himself.

Take a hollandaise and enjoy "National Eggs Benedict Day."

In the News
1856: James Douglas, the governor of BC, declared, "all gold found in the province belongs to the Crown."

1907: The medical building at McGill University was destroyed by fire.

1912: Harriet Quimby became the first woman to fly across the English Channel in an airplane.

1943: Dr. Albert Hofmann became the first person to take a trip after discovering the hallucinogenic drug LSD.

1989: Toronto Blue Jay Kelly Gruber hit a single, a double, a triple and a home run in the same game.

1992: After serving 22 years behind bars for a crime he did not commit, David Milgaard was released from prison.

2007: A young gunman killed 32 students at Virginia Tech before turning the gun on himself.

2008: Pope Benedict XVI began his visit of the U.S.

Aries
You are a caring and committed individual who can sometimes become overburdened with tasks.
1, 7, 9, 21

#1 Song
1967: "Somethin' Stupid" by Nancy Sinatra & Frank Sinatra

Birth Friends Forever
Peter Billingsley, actor (*A Christmas Story*), 1971

Martin Lawrence, actor (*Bad Boys*), 1965

Jon Cryer, actor (*Two and a Half Men*), 1965

Ellen Barkin, actress (*Ocean's Thirteen*), 1954

Kareem Abdul-Jabbar, basketball player, 1947

Benoît Bouchard, Canadian politician, 1940

Henri Mancini, composer, 1924

Peter Ustinov, actor (*Spartacus*), 1921

Joseph-Armand Bombardier, founder of Bombardier Inc., 1907

Charlie Chaplin, actor (*Gold Rush*), 1889

Wilbur Wright, aviation pioneer, 1867

Daily Oddity
The Bombardier Company of Canada also designed monorails for Disneyland and subway cars for the New York subway.

APRIL 17
258 days until next year

In a Days
Yada, yada, yada. It's "Blah! Blah! Blah! Day."

If you've ground your teeth down to nubs, you should celebrate "National Stress Awareness Day."

Hope you don't sleep in the nude, because it's "National Wear Your PJs to Work Day."

In the News
1855: Charlottetown, PEI, was incorporated as a city.

1892: Alexander Mackenzie, the 2nd prime minister of Canada, died at the age of 70.

1919: Women in New Brunswick got the provincial vote.

1961: The CIA landed at the Bay of Pigs on a mission to oust Cuban leader Fidel Castro.

1964: The Ford Mustang was unveiled.

1967: Canada announced the creation of the Order of Canada.

1970: National Defence made Yellowknife the permanent headquarters for the Canadian military in the North.

1974: Residents of Saskatchewan were granted free prescription drugs.

1982: Canada became an independent nation from Britain.

2002: Four Canadian soldiers were killed in Afghanistan by "friendly fire" from the U.S. Air Force.

Aries
You are a focused and capable person who sometimes sees the world as simply black and white.
1, 8, 9, 24

#1 Song
1956: "Heartbreak Hotel" by Elvis Presley

Birth Friends Forever
Brad Boyes, Canadian hockey player, 1982

Victoria Beckham, singer (Spice Girls), 1974

Terran Sandwith, Canadian hockey player, 1972

Jennifer Garner, actress (*Daredevil*), 1972

Liz Phair, musician, 1967

Ken Daneyko, Canadian hockey player, 1964

Maynard Keenan, singer (Tool), 1964

Sean Bean, actor (*National Treasure*), 1959

Rowdy Roddy Piper, Canadian pro wrestler, 1954

Gerry McNeil, Canadian hockey player, 1926

William Holden, actor (*The Wild Bunch*), 1918

Nikita Khrushchev, Russian politician, 1894

Daily Oddity
A zillion is a non-specific number.

APRIL 18
257 days until next year

In a Days
Ham it up. It's "World Amateur Radio Day."

As long as you and your pet aren't wearing matching sweatshirts, feel free to celebrate "Pet Owners Independence Day."

In the News

1793: The Upper Canada Gazette became the first newspaper published in Ontario.

1881: Outlaw Billy the Kid escaped from a Lincoln County, NM, jail.

1924: The first crossword puzzle book was published.

1942: The Toronto Maple Leafs won 4 straight to claim the Stanley Cup.

1967: Manitoba imposed a 5% sales tax.

1971: Convicts at the Kingston Penitentiary staged a 4-day riot; 2 inmates were murdered.

1977: Jerome Drayton became the 8th Canadian to win the Boston Marathon.

1990: W.O. Mitchell won the Steven Leacock Humour Award for *According to Jake and the Kid*.

1999: Wayne Gretzky played his last hockey game.

2007: The U.S. Supreme Court voted to uphold the Partial-Birth Abortion Ban Act.

Aries
You are a compassionate and ambitious person who has a tendency to lash out at those trying to help you.
1, 9, 18, 27

#1 Song
1986: "Kiss" by Prince

Birth Friends Forever
Scott Hartnell, Canadian hockey player, 1982

Robyn Regehr, Canadian hockey player, 1980

Melissa Joan Hart, actress (*Sabrina the Teenage Witch*), 1976

Maria Bello, actress (*The Cooler*), 1967

Eric McCormack, Canadian actor (*Will & Grace*), 1963

Conan O'Brien, talk-show host, 1963

Eric Roberts, actor (*Heroes*), 1956

Rick Moranis, Canadian actor (*Spaceballs*), 1953

Pierre Pettigrew, Canadian politician, 1951

Skip Spence, Canadian musician (Jefferson Airplane), 1946

Hayley Mills, actress (*The Parent Trap*), 1946

Ty LaForest, Canadian baseball player, 1917

Daily Oddity
During his heyday, the portion of ice located behind a hockey net was affectionately referred to as "Gretzky's Office."

APRIL 19
256 days until next year

In a Days
If you are a vampire, you may want to stay in your coffin. Today is "Garlic Day."

In the News

1770: Captain Cook discovered Australia.

1862: Canadian explorer Simon Fraser died.

1907: Canadian Native runner Tom Longboat won the Boston Marathon.

1948: Canadian runner Gérard Côté won the Boston Marathon for the 4th time.

1961: The Bay of Pigs invasion concluded unsuccessfully.

1971: Charles Manson was sentenced to death for the murder of Sharon Tate.

1972: Winnipeg announced tougher boxing regulations after Stewart Gray died in a bout with Canadian boxer Al Sparks.

1995: The Alfred P. Murrah Federal Building in Oklahoma City was bombed, killing 168 people.

2000: Wiebo Ludwig was found guilty for the bombing of an oil well in Alberta in 1998.

2008: Bowie Seamount, off the coast of BC, became a Marine Protected Area.

Aries
You are a motivated perfectionist who can sometimes be inflexible.
1, 9, 20

#1 Song
1983: "Come On Eileen" by Dexy's Midnight Runners

Birth Friends Forever

Fiona MacGillivray, Canadian musician (The Cottars), 1989

Hayden Christensen, Canadian actor (*Star Wars*), 1981

Kate Hudson, actress (*Fool's Gold*), 1979

James Franco, actor (*Spider-Man*), 1978

Ashley Judd, actress (*Simon Birch*), 1968

Bob Rock, Canadian music producer, 1954

Tim Curry, actor (*Clue*), 1946

Jayne Mansfield, actress (*Will Success Spoil Rock Hunter?*), 1933

Walter Stewart, Canadian journalist, 1931

Eliot Ness, lawman, 1903

Roland Michener, governor general of Canada, 1900

Daily Oddity
Though it changes every year, on average, Easter Sunday falls on April 19th more often than on any other date.

APRIL 20
255 days until next year

In a Days
If you are a pineapple, you may want to avoid eating for fear of regurgitation. It's "National Pineapple Upside-Down Cake Day."

If you have the munchies, then you are probably celebrating "4:20."

In the News

1534: Jacques Cartier set sail on the voyage that led to the discovery of Canada.

1918: The Canadian government enlisted men aged 20 to 22 for military service.

1918: The Red Baron shot down his 79th and 80th victims.

1963: The FLQ claimed their first victim when they bombed a Montréal army recruiting centre.

1966: Canadian artist Alex Colville won $9000 for his design of the Canadian Centennial coins.

1968: The Canadian-U.S. expedition lead by Ralph Plaistead and Jean-Luc Bombardier reached the North Pole.

1968: Pierre Elliott Trudeau became Canada's 15th prime minister.

1990: The closure of the Kingston Prison for Women in Ontario was announced.

1999: Thirteen students were killed in the Columbine High School shooting.

2008: Danica Patrick became the first female to win an Indy car race.

Aries
You are an energetic visionary who may, at times, live in a fantasy world.
1, 2, 4, 9

#1 Song
1976: "Disco Lady" by Johnnie Taylor

Birth Friends Forever
Joey Lawrence, actor (*Blossom*), 1976

Crispin Glover, actor (*Back to the Future*), 1964

Andy Serkis, actor (*The Lord of the Rings*), 1964

Geraint Wyn Davies, Canadian actor (*Forever Knight*), 1957

Gilles Lupien, Canadian hockey player, 1954

Toller Cranston, Canadian figure skater, 1949

Julien Poulin, Canadian composer, 1946

Ryan O'Neal, actor (*Love Story*), 1941

George Takei, actor (*Star Trek*), 1937

Tito Puente, musician, 1923

Janine Sutto, Canadian actress (*Les Boys III*), 1921

Wop May, Canadian aviator, 1896

Maurice Duplessis, premier of Québec, 1890

Adolf Hitler, German dictator, 1889

Daily Oddity
In Canada, it is more expensive to incarcerate a woman than it is a man.

APRIL 21
254 days until next year

In a Days

Look up! It's "Astronomy Day."

Break out the beef dip. It's "World Cow Chip Day."

If today is the Wednesday in the last full week in April, it's "Administrative Professionals Day."

One dollar, now two, who will give me two dollars? Two dollars, now three, who will give me three dollars? Sold! It's "Auctioneers Day."

In the News

753 BC: Romulus and Remus founded Rome.

1664: The governor of Québec banned littering in the streets.

1918: The infamous Red Baron was shot down and killed over France during a dogfight with Canadian pilot Captain Roy Brown.

1948: Mackenzie King became the longest serving Commonwealth prime minister with 20 years, 10 months and 10 days of service.

1962: The Seattle World's Fair opened.

1985: The Canadian voice of the NHL games, Foster Hewitt, died

1991: The Toronto Argonauts signed Rocket Ismail for $26 million.

1994: The first discovery of planets beyond our solar system (extrasolar planets) was announced.

2008: The Lockheed F-117 Nighthawk stealth aircraft was retired by the U.S. Air Force.

Taurus

You are self-reliant and objective, but those qualities may cause you to be slightly controlling.

3, 4, 5, 6

#1 Song

1961: "Runaway" by Del Shannon

Birth Friends Forever

Vincent Lecavalier, Canadian hockey player, 1980

Jamie Salé, Canadian figure skater, 1977

Ed Belfour, Canadian hockey player, 1965

Alex Baumann, Canadian swimmer, 1964

Michel Goulet, Canadian hockey player, 1960

Michael Timmins, Canadian musician (Cowboy Junkies), 1959

Robert Smith, musician (The Cure), 1959

Tony Danza, actor (*Who's the Boss?*), 1951

Iggy Pop, musician (The Stooges), 1947

Charles Grodin, actor (*Beethoven*), 1935

Queen Elizabeth II of England, 1926

Charlotte Brontë, author (*Jane Eyre*), 1816

Daily Oddity

The tail of the Red Baron's plane is currently on display at Toronto's Royal Military Institute.

APRIL 22
253 days until next year

In a Days
Sorry, Mars, it's "Earth Day."

Although the name of this treat was once a synonym for "pimp," you should still celebrate "National Jelly Bean Day."

If you're a biochemist or simply an alchemist, today is "Chemists Celebrate Earth Day Day."

In the News
1509: Henry VIII acceded to the throne of England.

1932: Lightning struck a flock of wild geese in Elgin, MB. The electricity cooked the geese perfectly, so when they fell to the ground, residents ate them.

1945: The Canadian Army halted its fight against the Germans in the Netherlands in order to feed the starving Dutch people.

1965: The Rolling Stones kicked off their first North American tour in Montréal.

1970: The first Earth Day was celebrated.

1979: As per his probation agreement following a drug possession charge, Keith Richards and the rest of The Rolling Stones gave a benefit concert for the blind in Toronto.

2006: Four Canadian soldiers were killed by a roadside bomb in Afghanistan. It was the worst one-day loss of Canadian soldiers since the Korean War.

Taurus
You are a determined and steadfast individual; however, sometimes you overwork yourself.
4, 6, 8, 12

#1 Song
1958: "Witch Doctor" by David Seville

Birth Friends Forever
Tony Romo, football player, 1980

Dan Cloutier, Canadian hockey player, 1976

Greg Moore, Canadian racecar driver, 1975

Catherine Mary Stewart, Canadian actress (*Weekend at Bernie's*), 1959

Ryan Stiles, Canadian actor (*Whose Line Is It Anyway?*), 1959

Peter Frampton, musician, 1950

Jack Nicholson, actor (*The Bucket List*), 1937

Pierre Hétu, Canadian conductor, 1936

Charlotte Rae, actress (*The Facts of Life*), 1926

Aaron Spelling, television producer (*Charlie's Angels*), 1923

Robert Oppenheimer, father of the atomic bomb, 1904

Daily Oddity
Theta (θ), the 8th letter of the Greek alphabet, is considered the national symbol of Earth Day.

APRIL 23
252 days until next year

In a Days
Today is "Canada Book Day," so be sure to read both the English and French versions of the same book.

In the News

1827: Excavation of the Shubenacadie Canal began, connecting Halifax with the Bay of Fundy.

1830: Catholics in PEI got the right to vote.

1851: Canada's first regular stamp, the Three Penny Beaver, was issued.

1879: Guelph, ON, was incorporated as a city.

1906: Alberta set its provincial speed limit at 10 mph within the city and 20 mph in rural areas.

1968: The first public hearings of the CRTC were held in Ottawa.

1985: The Coca-Cola Company unveiled New Coke.

1988: Pink Floyd's album *Dark Side of the Moon* was bumped from the Billboard 200 after 741 weeks (14 years) there.

2003: The World Health Organization issued a travel advisory to anyone going to Toronto, because of the SARS outbreak.

Taurus
You are a compassionate and inquisitive person who has a strong desire to always be accepted.
4, 6, 8, 12

#1 Song
2008: "Bleeding Love" by Leona Lewis

Birth Friends Forever

Jessica Stam, Canadian model, 1986

Jennifer Heil, Canadian freestyle skier, 1983

Willie Mitchell, Canadian hockey player, 1977

Rheal Cormier, Canadian baseball player, 1967

George Lopez, comedian, 1961

Valerie Bertinelli, actress (*One Day at a Time*), 1960

Michael Moore, filmmaker (*Fahrenheit 9/11*), 1954

Tony Esposito, Canadian hockey player, 1943

Lee Majors, actor (*The Six Million Dollar Man*), 1939

Roy Orbison, musician, 1936

Shirley Temple, actress (*The Littlest Rebel*), 1928

Lester B. Pearson, Canadian prime minister, 1897

Georges Vanier, Canadian diplomat, 1888

Daily Oddity
In 1995, Canada Post issued Canadian superhero stamps, which included Nelvana, Johnny Canuck, Northguard, Fleur de Lys, Captain Canuck and Superman.

APRIL 24
251 days until next year

In a Days
Buy your child a new mattress. It's "National Teach Your Children to Save Day." Expose your butt crack. It's "National Plumber's Day."

In the News
1184 BC: Concealed within the Trojan Horse, Greeks entered the city of Troy.

1866: Telegraph lines connected Victoria to mainland BC.

1942: Lucy Maud Montgomery, author of *Anne of Green Gables*, died at the age of 68.

1952: Canadian actor Raymond Burr (*Perry Mason*) made his television debut.

1952: Alberta's first oil shipment reached Ontario by pipeline.

1953: British Prime Minister Winston Churchill was knighted by Queen Elizabeth II.

1971: Five hundred thousand people in Washington, DC, and 125,000 in San Francisco, CA, marched in protest against the Vietnam War.

1985: The Supreme Court of Canada allowed Sunday shopping.

1993: Canadian rocker Neil Young performed at Farm Aid VI.

2005: Pope Benedict XVI was inaugurated as the 265th pope of the Roman Catholic Church.

Taurus
You are an organized and empathic individual who may overburden yourself.
4, 6, 12, 24

#1 Song
1983: "Beat It" by Michael Jackson

Birth Friends Forever
Kristopher Letang, Canadian hockey player, 1987

Kelly Clarkson, *American Idol* winner, 1982

Nicolas Gill, Canadian Olympic judo champion, 1972

Cedric the Entertainer, comedian, 1964

Dave Ridgway, Canadian football player, 1959

Jean-Paul Gaultier, fashion designer, 1952

Paul Cellucci, U.S. ambassador to Canada, 1948

Claude Dubois, Canadian singer, 1947

Doug Riley, Canadian musician, 1945

Barbra Streisand, singer, 1942

Shirley MacLaine, actress (*The Apartment*), 1934

Alan Eagleson, Canadian hockey promoter, 1933

Daily Oddity
The character of Anne Shirley from Lucy Maud Montgomery's *Anne of Green Gables* is immensely popular in Japan.

APRIL 25
250 days until next year

In a Days

If the bread in your sandwich is green, don't worry, it's "National Zucchini Bread Day."

If you are a woman over the age of 50, not only do you get to order off the seniors' menu, but you also get to celebrate "Red Hat Society Day."

In the News

1792: Nicolas Pelletier, a highwayman (stagecoach robber), became the first person executed by guillotine.

1849: Riots in Montréal ignited when Lord Elgin, the governor general of Canada, signed the Rebellion Losses Bill, which outraged Montréal's English population.

1908: Westmount, Québec, was incorporated as a city.

1940: Women in Québec got the right to vote in provincial elections.

1950: The provinces of BC, Alberta, Saskatchewan, Manitoba, Ontario and PEI signed an agreement to build the Trans-Canada Highway.

1959: The St. Lawrence Seaway was completed.

1972: A 10-month-old cat named Paula fell from the 26th floor of an apartment building and lived.

2007: The funeral for Russia's former head of state Boris Yeltsin was held.

Taurus

You are a dynamic and focused individual who can be inflexible at times.
4, 6, 7, 21

#1 Song

1979: "Heart of Glass" by Blondie

Birth Friends Forever

James Sheppard, Canadian hockey player, 1988

Jason Lee, actor (*My Name is Earl*), 1970

Renée Zellweger, actress (*Bridget Jones*), 1969

Hank Azaria, actor (*The Simpsons*), 1964

Al Pacino, actor (*Scarface*), 1940

Melissa Hayden, Canadian ballerina, 1923

Ella Fitzgerald, singer, 1917

Russ Conway, Canadian actor (*What Ever Happened to Baby Jane?*), 1913

Edward R. Murrow, journalist, 1908

Félix d'Hérelle, Canadian microbiologist, 1873

Daily Oddity

The Cat's Whiskers, Canada's first strip club, opened in Vancouver in 1966.

APRIL 26
249 days until next year

In a Days
Watch your wallet—it's "Hug an Australian Day."

Get underneath a doorway. It's "Richter Scale Day."

Shatter their dreams of adulthood. It's "Take Your Daughters and Sons to Work Day."

In the News

1900: Seven people died when a fire broke out in Hull, ON.

1918: Women in Halifax, NS, got the vote.

1933: Germany's secret police, the Gestapo, was established.

1959: Cuban President Fidel Castro visited Montréal.

1964: Zanzibar and Tanganyika join to form the East African country of Tanzania.

1965: After 15 minutes, a Rolling Stones concert in London, ON, was shut down because of rioting.

1986: The world's worst nuclear disaster occurred at the Chernobyl nuclear power plant in Ukraine.

2005: After 29 years of military occupation, Syria withdrew its troops from Lebanon.

2007: Queen's Pier in Hong Kong was officially closed.

Taurus
You are intelligent and clear-sighted, although you are also set in your ways.
4, 6, 9, 18

#1 Song
1936: "Lost" by Guy Lombardo and the Royal Canadians

Birth Friends Forever
Channing Tatum, actor (*Step Up*), 1980

Ariane Moffatt, Canadian singer, 1979

Tom Welling, actor (*Smallville*), 1977

Jet Li, actor (*The Forbidden Kingdom*), 1963

Kevin James, actor (*The King of Queens*), 1965

Sylvain Simard, Canadian politician, 1945

Michael Kergin, Canadian diplomat, 1942

Jeanne Sauvé, Canadian politician, 1922

A.E. van Vogt, Canadian sci-fi author (*The Beast*), 1912

Paul-Émile Léger, Canadian cardinal, 1904

William Shakespeare, playwright, 1564

Daily Oddity
Canadian sci-fi writer William Gibson coined the word "cyberspace."

APRIL 27
248 days until next year

In a Days
Sorry, vegetarians, it's "National Prime Rib Day."
Collect outstanding debts. It's "Write an Old Friend Day."
Although Canadians don't celebrate "Arbor Day," if we did, we'd spell it with a "u."
If you have a cat, you should let it know that today is "National Hairball Awareness Day."

In the News
1644: Wheat was planted in Canada for the very first time.

1667: John Milton, who at the time was blind and impoverished, sold the rights to his epic poem "Paradise Lost," for the equivalent of $20.

1813: During the War of 1812, U.S. troops captured the capital of Canada, York, which is now Toronto.

1928: Drivers in PEI began driving on the right side of the road.

1967: Expo '67 officially opened in Montréal.

1981: The computer mouse was first introduced.

1990: Women in Québec celebrated the 50th anniversary of getting the provincial vote.

1992: Betty Boothroyd became the first woman elected Speaker of the British House of Commons.

1992: Lina Haddad of Québec gave birth to 3 boys and 2 girls.

2006: Construction commenced on the Freedom Tower located at Ground Zero in New York City.

Taurus
You are a perceptive and discerning individual who at times isolates yourself from others.
4, 6, 9, 18

#1 Song
1992: "Jump" by Kris Kross

Birth Friends Forever
Emma Taylor-Isherwood, Canadian actress (*Mona the Vampire*), 1987

Johnny Devine, Canadian pro wrestler, 1974

Sébastien Lareau, Canadian tennis player, 1973

Michael Mahonen, Canadian actor (*Road to Avonlea*), 1964

Cali Timmins, Canadian actress (*Frasier*), 1963

Ace Frehley, musician (Kiss), 1951

Keith Magnuson, Canadian hockey player, 1947

Casey Kasem, disc jockey, 1932

Jack Klugman, actor (*The Odd Couple*), 1922

Ulysses S. Grant, U.S. president, 1822

Samuel F.B. Morse, inventor of Morse code, 1791

Daily Oddity
With over 50 million visitors, Expo '67 became the most successful Expo of the 20th century, setting a single-day attendance record on its 3rd day, with 569,000 visitors.

APRIL 28
247 days until next year

In a Days
What's that stink? Oh, it's "Sense of Smell Day."
Oh, say, by the way, it's "Great Poetry Reading Day."
Although it's not as much fun as "Demolition Day," today is "Rebuilding Day."

In the News

1789: Captain Bligh and 18 sailors were set adrift following the mutiny on the *Bounty*.

1902: The one-billionth minute since January 1, Year Zero, occurred.

1930: Major league baseball held its first night game.

1932: A yellow fever vaccine for humans was announced.

1968: Halifax resident Walter Sitch, 98, became the first great-great-great-grandfather in Canada.

1969: French President Charles de Gaulle resigned.

1972: Construction of a 1690-km-long highway from Alberta to Tuktoyaktuk began.

1996: The Winnipeg Jets played their last game before moving to Phoenix and becoming the Coyotes.

2001: Dennis Tito became the world's first space tourist, allegedly paying between $12 and $20 million for the opportunity.

Taurus
You are an objective and driven individual who at times suffers from vanity.
4, 6, 10, 20

#1 Song
1974: "The Loco-Motion" by Grand Funk

Birth Friends Forever
George Nozuka, Canadian singer (George), 1986
Jessica Alba, actress (*The Eye*), 1981
Penélope Cruz, actress (*Vanilla Sky*), 1974
John Daly, golfer, 1966
Lloyd Eisler, Canadian figure skater, 1963
Mary McDonnell, actress (*Battlestar Galactica*), 1952
Jay Leno, *Tonight Show* host, 1950
Ginette Reno, Canadian singer, 1946
Harper Lee, author (*To Kill a Mockingbird*), 1926
Ethel Catherwood, Canadian athlete, 1908
Lionel Barrymore, actor (*It's a Wonderful Life*), 1878

Daily Oddity
A "white out," an old tradition of Winnipeg Jets fans that involves wearing all white to home playoff games, still continues in Phoenix.

APRIL 29
246 days until next year

In a Days
Even though they're not kosher, it's still "National Shrimp Scampi Day."
Learn to sign "Where's my allowance?" It's "Mother-Father Deaf Day."
In honour of "National Deaf Day," we should hold a benefit concert called Hearing Aid.

In the News
1628: An ox-drawn plow was used for the first time in Canada.

1880: Alexander Graham Bell's brother, Melville, incorporated the Bell Telephone Company of Canada.

1903: A landslide in Frank, AB, killed 70 miners.

1945: Canadians began air dropping food supplies to the starving Dutch.

1968: The musical *Hair* opened on Broadway.

1973: The Saint John River in New Brunswick flooded, causing $25 million in damages.

1992: After the LAPD officers involved in the beating of Rodney King were acquitted, riots broke out in the streets of Los Angeles and 53 people were killed.

1995: The world's longest sausage strand, 46.3 km long, was unveiled in Kitchener, ON.

2004: After 107 years of production, Oldsmobile built its last car.

Taurus
You are optimistic and possess impeccable attention to detail; however, you may be perceived as being cold-hearted.
4, 6, 11, 22

#1 Song
1943: "I've Heard That Song Before" by Harry James

Birth Friends Forever
Émilie Mondor, Canadian runner, 1981
Jasper Wood, Canadian violinist, 1974
Curtis Joseph, Canadian hockey player, 1967
Robert J. Sawyer, Canadian author (*Wake*), 1960
Michelle Pfeiffer, actress (*Hairspray*), 1958
Daniel Day-Lewis, actor (*There Will Be Blood*), 1957
Gino Quilico, Canadian baritone, 1955
Jerry Seinfeld, comedian (*Seinfeld*), 1954
Serge Bernier, Canadian hockey player, 1947
Al Balding, Canadian golfer, 1924
Duke Ellington, bandleader, 1899
William Randolph Hearst, newspaper publisher, 1863

Daily Oddity
Helen Keller lost her hearing and sight after contracting scarlet fever.

APRIL 30
245 days until next year

In a Days
Sorry, bald dudes, it's "Hairstylist Appreciation Day."
Sorry, joggers, it's "International Walk Day."
Trust me. It really is "National Honesty Day."

In the News
1658: The first French and Native school opened in Canada.

1903: Emily Howard Stowe, the first woman allowed to practice medicine in Canada, died.

1927: Canadian actress Mary Pickford and her husband Douglas Fairbanks became the first celebrities to leave their footprints in cement at Grauman's Chinese Theatre in Hollywood.

1938: In the cartoon short *Porky's Hare Hunt,* the world was introduced to Happy Rabbit, who later became Bugs Bunny.

1945: Adolf Hitler and his wife of one day, Eva Braun, committed suicide.

1950: Construction began on a $95 million interprovincial pipeline, which would carry oil from Alberta to Lakehead, ON.

1987: Brian Mulroney negotiated the Meech Lake Accord.

2008: The skeletal remains of Tsar Nicholas II's son, Alexei Nikolaevich Romanov, and his daughter, Anastasia Nikolaevna Romanov, were indentified by Russian scientists.

Taurus
You are a strong-willed and practical individual who times may overburden yourself.
3, 4, 6, 9

#1 Song
1987: "(I Just) Died in Your Arms" by Cutting Crew

Birth Friends Forever
Andrew Seeley, Canadian singer, 1982

Kirsten Dunst, actress (*Spider-Man*), 1982

Johnny Galecki, actor (*The Big Bang Theory*), 1975

Akon, singer, 1973

Paul Gross, Canadian actor (*Passchendaele*), 1959

Stephen Harper, Canadian prime minister, 1959

Willie Nelson, musician, 1933

Cloris Leachman, actress (*Young Frankenstein*), 1926

Al Lewis, actor (*The Munsters*), 1923

Eve Arden, actress (*Grease*), 1908

Philippe Panneton, Canadian physician, 1895

David Thompson, Canadian explorer, 1770

Daily Oddity
The evening of April 30 is known as "Walpurgis Night" and is sacred among witches' covens. On this night, the boundaries between the living and the dead are said to weaken.

MAY 1
244 days until next year

In a Days

If you're a worker, celebrate "May Day."
If you're a prince disguised as a frog, celebrate "Mother Goose Day."
If you're feeling horny, celebrate "Save the Rhino Day."
Get sent to the office. It's "School Principals Day."
She's not as evil as you think. It's "Stepmother's Day."

In the News

1885: Electric lights were first used to illuminate city streets in Ottawa.

1909: Prohibition went into effect in Ontario.

1912: Canada issued the first $5 bill.

1930: The planet Pluto was officially named by an 11-year-old girl.

1940: The Summer Olympic Games were cancelled because of the war.

1956: The polio vaccine was made available to the public.

1982: Brock Allison completed his cross-Canada unicycle trip in Vancouver.

1989: Disney-MGM Studios opened in Florida.

2004: Cyprus, the Czech Republic, Estonia, Hungary, Latvia, Lithuania, Malta, Poland, Slovakia and Slovenia became members of the European Union.

2008: The Saint John River flooded, causing water levels in Fredericton to reach 8.33 m, the worst flooding in the region in 35 years.

Taurus

You are a compassionate people person who is sometimes so busy helping others that you neglect your own needs.
1, 2, 4, 6

#1 Song

1965: "Mrs. Brown You've Got a Lovely Daughter" by Herman's Hermits

Birth Friends Forever

Wes Anderson, director (*Rushmore*), 1969

D'arcy Wretzky, musician (The Smashing Pumpkins), 1968

Tim McGraw, country singer, 1967

John Woo, director (*Face/Off*), 1946

Joseph Heller, author (*Catch-22*), 1923

Glenn Ford, Canadian actor (*3:10 to Yuma*), 1916

Paul Desruisseaux, Canadian politician, 1905

Calamity Jane, cowgirl, 1852

Prince Arthur, governor general of Canada, 1850

Emily Stowe, Canadian physician and suffragist, 1831

Daily Oddity

The distress call "Mayday" has nothing to do with this day. Mayday actually means "Help me" (*m'aider*) in French.

MAY 2
243 days until next year

In a Days
If you love parliamentary procedure, celebrate "Robert's Rules of Order Day."

Lock your teenager in a room full of crying babies. It's "Prevent Teen Pregnancy Day."

If this is the first Saturday of May, then it's "Free Comic Book Day."

In the News
1670: King Charles II of England approved the opening of the Hudson's Bay Company.

1885: *Good Housekeeping* magazine was first published.

1919: Metalworkers in Winnipeg went on strike for 8-hour workdays.

1964: Northern Dancer became the first Canadian horse to win the Kentucky Derby.

1970: Montréal was awarded the 1976 Summer Olympic Games.

1986: Canada's first artificial heart transplant took place.

1988: In Ottawa, 16,408 tickets for the musical *Cats* were sold, making it the largest ever single-day sale of tickets for a musical in Canada.

2000: The Netherlands unveiled the *Man with Two Hats* memorial, which thanked Canadians for their assistance during World War II.

2008: Cyclone Nargis hit Myanmar, killing 146,000 people.

Taurus
You are intelligent and logical; however, you tend to overburden yourself.
2, 4, 6, 11

#1 Song
1999: "Livin' La Vida Loca" by Ricky Martin

Birth Friends Forever
James Kirk, Canadian actor (*She's the Man*), 1986

Lily Allen, singer, 1985

Pierre-Luc Gagnon, Canadian skateboarder, 1980

Jason Chimera, Canadian hockey player, 1979

Steve Bays, Canadian musician (Hot Hot Heat), 1978

David Beckham, soccer player, 1975

Dwayne "The Rock" Johnson, pro wrestler/actor, 1972

Alan Best, Canadian animation director, 1959

Engelbert Humperdinck, singer, 1936

Elijah McCoy, Canadian inventor, 1843

Abraham Gesner, Canadian inventor of kerosene, 1797

Catherine the Great, empress of Russia, 1729

Daily Oddity
The Hudson's Bay Company is currently owned by an American corporation.

MAY 3
242 days until next year

In a Days
That's strange, it's "Paranormal Day."

If you're a fan of sad, creepy-looking clowns, celebrate "Emmett Kelly Clown Day."

If you're looking for an oceanic version of Groundhog Day, celebrate "Martin Z. Mollusk Day."

Instead of celebrating "Lumpy Rug Day," why not just buy a new rug?

Oh, the irony. It's "National Day of Prayer" and "National Day of Reason."

In the News
1867: The Hudson's Bay Company gave up all claims to Vancouver Island.

1886: M.A. Maclean became the first mayor of Vancouver, BC.

1887: An explosion in a coalmine near Nanaimo, BC, killed 150 people.

1915: Canadian solider John McCrae composed his poem "In Flanders Fields."

1922: Women in PEI won the right to vote.

1963: After being hit by floodwaters, over 1600 residents of Hay River, NWT, had to be airlifted to safety.

1978: The first "spam" (junk mail) was emailed.

1979: Dawson City, Yukon, was submerged under 2 m of water when the Yukon River flooded.

2007: Three-year-old British girl Madeleine McCann was kidnapped while on holiday in Portugal.

Taurus
You are an insightful and optimistic individual, but at times you can be overly analytical.
4, 6, 8

#1 Song
1962: "Soldier Boy" by The Shirelles

Birth Friends Forever
Cheryl Burke, dancer, 1984

Christina Hendricks, actress (*Mad Men*), 1978

Ron Hextall, Canadian hockey player, 1964

Marc Bellemare, Canadian politician, 1956

Doug Henning, Canadian magician, 1947

Sugar Ray Robinson, boxer, 1921

Léopold Simoneau, Canadian tenor, 1916

Stu Hart, Canadian pro wrestler/trainer, 1915

Bing Crosby, singer, 1903

Daily Oddity
It took John McCrae only 20 minutes to write "In Flanders Fields."

MAY 4
241 days until next year

In a Days
Finally, it's "No Pants Day."
Root through other people's trash without getting yelled at. It's "Garage Sale Day."
Put down that bucket of wings and celebrate "Respect for Chickens Day."

In the News
1904: Charles Rolls met Frederick Royce.

1907: Ottawa had its greatest single-day May snowfall, 19.1 cm.

1910: The Royal Canadian Navy was established.

1932: Mobster Al Capone began serving his 11-year prison sentence for tax evasion.

1958: Canadian comedy duo Johnny Wayne and Frank Shuster made their first appearance on *The Ed Sullivan Show*.

1966: Jean Sutherland Boggs became the first female director of the National Art Gallery of Canada.

1972: Vancouver's environmental organization the Don't Make A Wave Committee changed its name to the Greenpeace Foundation.

1979: Margaret Thatcher became the first female prime minister of the UK.

2007: A class 5 tornado nearly destroyed Greensburg, Kansas.

Taurus
You are a rational problem solver, who at times feel unappreciated.
4, 6, 8

#1 Song
1977: "Hotel California" by The Eagles

Birth Friends Forever
Derek Roy, Canadian hockey player, 1983

Lance Bass, singer ('N Sync), 1979

Emily Perkins, Canadian actress (*Ginger Snaps*), 1977

Will Arnett, Canadian actor (*Arrested Development*), 1970

Randy Travis, musician, 1959

Dick Dale, surf rock guitarist, 1937

Mr. Fuji, pro wrestler, 1937

Audrey Hepburn, actress (*Breakfast at Tiffany's*), 1929

Maynard Ferguson, Canadian musician, 1928

Jane Jacobs, Canadian author (*The Death and Life of Great American Cities*), 1916

Charles Boucher de Boucherville, Canadian politician, 1822

Daily Oddity
Frank Shuster's cousin, Joe Shuster, co-created *Superman*.

MAY 5
240 days until next year

In a Days
Break out the hand sanitizer. It's "Join Hands Day."
If you can be run over by an Acme truck and survive, celebrate "Cartoonists Day."
If you regularly inject mascara, celebrate "Makeup Junkie Day."
If you're a middle-aged woman in yoga pants, celebrate "Pilates Day."

In the News
1800: Explorer David Thompson began surveying the North Saskatchewan River.

1862: Mexican forces defeated French occupational forces in the Battle of Puebla.

1941: The fragrance Chanel No. 5 was released.

1970: Winnipeg's The Guess Who topped the charts with "American Woman."

1973: Canadian jockey Ron Turcotte and Secretariat won the Kentucky Derby.

1950: Winds of 80 km/h created waves that broke through the dikes of Winnipeg and flooded the city; one person died.

2008: The Braidwood Inquiry, an investigation into the safety of police Tasers as well the death of Robert Dziekański, who died in a Vancouver airport after being tasered, began in BC.

Taurus
You are an imaginative and down-to-earth individual who may sometimes be perceived as authoritarian.
4, 5, 6, 10

#1 Song
1970: "American Woman/No Sugar Tonight" by The Guess Who

Birth Friends Forever
Skye Sweetnam, Canadian singer, 1988
Wade MacNeil, Canadian musician (Alexisonfire), 1984
Devin Townsend, Canadian musician (Strapping Young Lad), 1972
Naomi Klein, Canadian author (*The Shock Doctrine*), 1970
Shawn Drover, Canadian musician (Megadeth), 1966
James LaBrie, Canadian singer (Dream Theater), 1963
Michael Palin, actor (*Monty Python*), 1943
Lance Henriksen, actor (*Alien*), 1940
Ann B. Davis, actress (*The Brady Bunch*), 1926
Tyrone Power, actor (*Rawhide*), 1914
Karl Marx, political philosopher/author (*The Communist Manifesto*), 1818

Daily Oddity
"American Woman" by The Guess Who was voted the Best Canadian Single of All Time.

MAY 6
239 days until next year

In a Days
Sorry, doctors. It's "Nurses Day."
Sorry, teachers. It's "No Homework Day."
Sorry, billion-dollar diet industry. It's "No Diet Day."

In the News
1889: The Eiffel Tower in Paris officially opened to the public.

1940: John Steinbeck won the Pulitzer Prize for his novel *The Grapes of Wrath*.

1950: A fire in Rimouski, Québec, caused nearly $10 million in damages.

1950 Canadian bandleader Guy Lombardo hit number one on the music charts with his version of the "The Third Man Theme."

1966: The Royal Canadian Mint announced that it would be striking a $20 Centennial gold coin.

1994: The Channel Tunnel between England and France officially opened.

2001: Pope John Paul II became the first pope to enter a mosque.

2002: An animal rights activist assassinated Dutch politician Pim Fortuyn.

2008: The Chaitén volcano in Chile erupted.

Taurus
You are sensitive and intuitive; however, you have a tendency to be a doormat.
4, 6, 12, 16

#1 Song
1950: "The Third Man Theme" by Guy Lombardo and his Royal Canadians

Birth Friends Forever
Martin Brodeur, Canadian hockey player, 1972

Kavan Smith, Canadian actor (*Stargate SG-1*), 1970

Leslie Hope, Canadian actress (*24*), 1965

George Clooney, actor (*ER*), 1961

Roma Downey, actress (*Touched by an Angel*), 1960

Tom Bergeron, game-show host, 1955

Michelle Courchesne, Canadian politician, 1953

Tony Blair, British prime minister, 1953

Bob Seger, singer, 1945

Gilles Grégoire, co-founder of the Parti Québécois, 1926

Orson Welles, director (*Citizen Kane*), 1915

Sigmund Freud, psychiatrist, 1856

Daily Oddity
In the film *Monty Python and the Holy Grail*, French soldiers declare their castle to be owned by Guy de Lombard, a tribute to Guy Lombardo.

MAY 7
238 days until next year

In a Days

If you're a young sheep, protect your hindquarters. It's "National Roasted Leg of Lamb Day."

If you love glue sticks, celebrate "National Scrapbooking Day."

In the News

1849: A fire in Toronto destroyed much of the city.

1920: The first exhibition of the Group of Seven was put on display at the Art Gallery of Ontario.

1950: From May 7 to 21, the Red River flooded Winnipeg, resulting in the evacuation of 10,000 residents. It happened again 47 years later in 1997.

1969: CBC banned all tobacco advertisements from its TV and radio programs.

1975: Canada launched its 3rd communications satellite, *Anik III*, into space.

1983: Canadian-owned horse Sunny's Halo won the Kentucky Derby.

1985: The Edmonton Oilers won their 2nd Stanley Cup.

2002: Openly gay Canadian high school student Marc Hall was permitted to bring his same-sex date to the prom.

2007: The tomb of Herod the Great was discovered near Jerusalem.

Taurus

You are a truth seeker who always makes an impact; however, you take the advice of others for granted.
4, 6, 7, 15

#1 Song

1964: "Hello, Dolly!" by Louis Armstrong

Birth Friends Forever

Jason Tunks, Canadian athlete, 1975

Breckin Meyer, actor (*Rat Race*), 1974

Owen Hart, Canadian pro wrestler, 1965

Amy Heckerling, director (*Clueless*), 1954

Sidney Altman, Canadian molecular biologist, 1939

Claude Raymond, Canadian baseball player, 1937

Isobel Warren, Canadian author, 1935

Darren McGavin, actor (*A Christmas Story*), 1922

Eva Peron, first lady of Argentina (*Evita*), 1919

Gary Cooper, actor (*High Noon*), 1901

Frank J. Selke, Canadian hockey manager, 1893

Daily Oddity

Before becoming a movie star, Errol Flynn used to castrate sheep with his teeth on a sheep ranch in Australia.

MAY 8
237 days until next year

In a Days
Lest we forget, it's "VE (Victory in Europe) Day."
Without them we'd be dumb. It's "National Teachers Day."
Cut your toenails. It's "No Socks Day."

In the News

1886: Coca-Cola was invented.

1907: Canadian boxer Tommy Burns became the new world heavyweight champion.

1908: The University of Alberta was founded.

1914: Paramount Pictures was founded.

1919: An Australian soldier proposed holding a moment of silence to commemorate "The Armistice of World War I," which is now "Remembrance Day."

1945: World War II ended with the unconditional surrender of German troops.

1982: Canadian racecar driver Gilles Villeneuve died in a high-speed accident.

1984: The USSR announced that it would boycott the 1984 Summer Olympics in Los Angeles.

2005: The Canadian War Museum opened.

2008: Steve Nash became the first Canadian to win the NBA MVP Award.

Taurus
You are an ambitious and idealistic individual who at times pushes your beliefs on others.
4, 6, 8

#1 Song
1973: "Tie a Yellow Ribbon Round the Old Oak Tree" by Tony Orlando & Dawn

Birth Friends Forever

Martha Wainwright, Canadian musician, 1976

Enrique Iglesias, singer, 1975

Ray Whitney, Canadian hockey player, 1972

Melissa Gilbert, actress (*Little House on the Prairie*), 1964

David Winning, Canadian director (*Andromeda*), 1961

Stephen Stohn, Canadian producer (*Degrassi: TNG*), 1948

Irwin Cotler, Canadian politician, 1940

Ricky Nelson, singer, 1940

Claude Castonguay, Canadian politician, 1929

Don Rickles, comedian, 1926

Robert Johnson, great-grandfather of rock 'n' roll, 1911

Harry S. Truman, U.S. president, 1884

Daily Oddity
To commemorate the 60th anniversary of VE Day, The Royal Canadian Mint reissued the wartime Victory nickel, which was originally in circulation from 1943 to 1945.

MAY 9
236 days until next year

In a Days
Is it better to celebrate "National Night Shift Workers Day" at night when they're working? Or during the day when they're sleeping?

Eat some paste and come say "Hi." It's "National School Nurse Day."

If you work at a graveyard or a 24-hour convenience store, you should celebrate "National Third Shift Workers Day."

In the News

1671: Disguised as a priest, Thomas Blood unsuccessfully tried to steal the Crown Jewels from the Tower of London.

1886: Halifax experienced its greatest single-day rainfall of over 127 mm.

1887: Frontier showman Buffalo Bill Cody opened his Wild West Show in London, England.

1950: Sci-fi author L. Ron Hubbard released *Dianetics*, which would later evolve into Scientology.

1955: Kermit the Frog made his television debut.

1966: Wanting better pay, 1600 Québec civil servants went on strike for 2 months.

1970: Canadian singer Neil Young with Crosby, Stills, & Nash reached the number 11 position on the pop charts with their song "Woodstock."

1977: A fire in Toronto's downtown destroyed a building scheduled for demolition.

2006: George Preca became the first Maltese saint.

Taurus
You are a brave individual, filled with vigour; however, you direct your frustrations at others.
4, 6, 9, 18

#1 Song
1982: "Ebony and Ivory" by Paul McCartney & Stevie Wonder

Birth Friends Forever

John Ryan Fitzpatrick, Canadian racecar driver, 1988

Pierre Bouvier, Canadian musician (Simple Plan), 1979

Rosario Dawson, actress (*Sin City*), 1979

Steve Yzerman, Canadian hockey player, 1965

John Corbett, actor (*Sex and the City*), 1961

Wendy Crewson, Canadian actress (*Away from Her*), 1956

Billy Joel, musician, 1949

Candice Bergen, actress (*Boston Legal*), 1946

Barbara Ann Scott, Canadian figure skater, 1928

Mike Wallace, journalist (*60 Minutes*), 1918

Don Messer, Canadian musician, 1909

J.M. Barrie, author (*Peter Pan*), 1860

Daily Oddity
Vanilla is used to make chocolate.

MAY 10
235 days until next year

In a Days
Today is "Donate a Day's Wages to Charity Day." But what if you work for a charity?

If the year is 2009, you'd better call your mom. It's "Mother's Day."

In the News
1534: Jacques Cartier landed in Newfoundland.

1857: The Indian Mutiny, India's first war of independence, began.

1872: Victoria Woodhull became the first woman nominated for U.S. president.

1905: King Edward VII approved Manitoba's coat of arms.

1924: J. Edgar Hoover was appointed director of the FBI.

1924: The Alberta Legislature voted to end prohibition in the province.

1954: Bill Haley & The Comets released "Rock Around the Clock."

1970: The most famous photograph in hockey history, *The Goal*, featuring Bobby Orr, was taken.

1994: Nelson Mandela became the first black president of South Africa.

2005: A hand grenade was tossed from the crowd and landed 20 m from George W. Bush while he was speaking publicly in Tbilisi, Georgia; it did not detonate.

Taurus
You are a single-minded and determined individual who at times neglects your own emotions.
2, 4, 6

#1 Song
1951: "How High the Moon" by Les Paul & Mary Ford

Birth Friends Forever
Ryan Getzlaf, Canadian hockey player, 1985

Scott Brison, Canadian politician, 1967

Young MC, rapper, 1967

Linda Evangelista, Canadian model, 1965

Bono, singer (U2), 1960

Gaétan Boucher, Canadian speed skater, 1958

Antonine Maillet, Canadian author (*Pointe-aux-Coques*), 1929

David O. Selznick, film producer, 1902

Fred Astaire, dancer, 1899

John Wilkes Booth, assassin, 1838

Daily Oddity
The woman credited with starting Mother's Day—after she began handing out white carnations in honour of her mother's death—was admitted to a sanatorium after she went crazy trying to stop the holiday from proliferating.

MAY 11
234 days until next year

In a Days
As long as it's not human, enjoy "Eat What You Want Day."
Without them, you'd be breastfeeding in meetings. It's "Child Care Provider Day."
Although they're nothing more than fair-weather friends, celebrate "International Migratory Bird Day."

In the News
1833: The passenger ship *Lady of the Lake* hit an iceberg between Québec and England; 215 people died.

1870: Canada purchased much of the land owned by the Hudson's Bay Company, which included the Prairie Provinces, northern Ontario, northwestern Québec and portions of the NWT, for $11 million.

1927: The Academy of Motion Picture Arts and Sciences was created.

1960: The first birth control pill became available.

1983: In protest of lobster rations, fishermen in Nova Scotia lit 2 fisheries patrol boats on fire, sinking them.

1997: An IBM supercomputer defeated the world's reigning champion chess player.

2002: The second *Man with Two Hats* monument was unveiled in Canada to match the one in the Netherlands. The monuments symbolically link Canada with the Netherlands in a display of appreciation of our service during World War II.

Taurus
You are an imaginative trailblazer who refuses to follow the lead of others.
2, 4, 6, 11

#1 Song
1958: "All I Have to Do Is Dream" by The Everly Brothers

Birth Friends Forever
Erin Lang, Canadian musician (April Wine), 1979

Theresa Burke, Canadian journalist, 1956

Nancy Greene, Canadian alpine skier, 1943

Doug McClure, actor (*The Land That Time Forgot*), 1935

Mort Sahl, Canadian political commentator, 1927

Mitchell Sharp, Canadian politician, 1911

Phil Silvers, comedian, 1911

Salvador Dalí, painter, 1904

Irving Berlin, composer, 1888

Daily Oddity
Sea stars, also known as starfish, have 8 eyes, one on the tip of each arm.

MAY 12
233 days until next year

In a Days
I must say that I feel gay, which means it must be "Limerick Day."
Go swim in her watery bosom. It's "Mother Ocean Day."
Don't answer the phone. It's "National Babysitter's Day."
Spin your arms in continuous circles to celebrate "Windmill Day."
They were here before us. It's "Native American Rights Day."

In the News
1870: *The Manitoba Act* is given Royal Assent, meaning Manitoba is poised to become a province.

1885: After a 4-day battle, the North-West Rebellion came to end, with the Métis rebels defeated by the Canadian government.

1966: The Science Council of Canada was established.

1966: The official flag of Manitoba was unveiled.

1970: Montréal was awarded the 1976 Summer Olympic Games.

1978: It was decided that hurricanes could also be named after men.

1994: Lacrosse was named Canada's national summer sport.

2002: Jimmy Carter became the first U.S. president to visit Cuba since 1959.

2008: Over 69,000 people died in an 8.0-magnitude earthquake in China.

Taurus
You are a deep thinker and a true original; however, at times you sabotage yourself.
3, 4, 6, 12

#1 Song
1953: "The Song from *Moulin Rouge* (Where Is Your Heart)" by Percy Faith

Birth Friends Forever
Emily Van Camp, Canadian actress (*Everwood*), 1986

Mike Weir, Canadian golfer, 1970

Tony Hawk, pro skateboarder, 1968

Bruce McCulloch, Canadian actor (*The Kids in the Hall*), 1961

Bernie Federko, Canadian hockey player, 1956

Gabriel Byrne, actor (*Miller's Crossing*), 1950

Michael Ignatieff, Canadian politician, 1947

George Carlin, comedian, 1937

Johnny Bucyk, Canadian hockey player, 1935

Yogi Berra, baseball player, 1925

Farley Mowat, Canadian author (*Never Cry Wolf*), 1921

Katharine Hepburn, actress (*On Golden Pond*), 1907

Florence Nightingale, nurse, 1820

Daily Oddity
In Canada, First Nations peoples did not gain the right to vote until 1960.

MAY 13
232 days until next year

In a Days
With cheese or with ice cream, it's "National Apple Pie Day."
I told you not to answer the phone. It's "Babysitter Safety Day."

In the News

1873: Canada's first major mining accident occurred in Westville, NS, killing 60 coalminers.

1898: Dawson City was chosen as the capital of the Yukon Territory.

1940: Fleeing invading Nazis forces, Princess Juliana of the Netherlands brought her children to Canada for protection.

1942: Two Canadian ships were sunk by German U-boats in the St. Lawrence River.

1958: Velcro was trademarked.

1983: Nine fishermen in Nova Scotia were charged with piracy stemming from the events of May 11.

1989: Student protestors began a hunger strike in Beijing's Tiananmen Square.

1991: A Sikh RCMP officer in Regina became the first Mountie allowed to wear a turban on duty.

1994: Johnny Carson made his last TV appearance.

2008: The Canadian airline company Jetsgo declared bankruptcy.

Taurus
You are an interesting and empathic individual; however, you are easily distracted.
4, 6, 8, 13

#1 Song
1985: "Don't You (Forget About Me)" by Simple Minds

Birth Friends Forever

Travis Zajac, Canadian hockey player, 1985

Samantha Morton, actress (*In America*), 1977

Darius Rucker, singer (Hootie & the Blowfish), 1966

Stephen Colbert, TV host, 1964

Dennis Rodman, basketball player, 1961

Stevie Wonder, singer, 1950

Ritchie Valens, singer, 1941

Harvey Keitel, actor (*Reservoir Dogs*), 1939

Roch Carrier, Canadian author (*La Guerre, Yes Sir!*), 1937

Bea Arthur, actress (*The Golden Girls*), 1922

Joe Louis, boxer, 1914

Gil Evans, Canadian musician, 1912

Daily Oddity
Every year has at least one Friday the 13th, while no year has more than three of them.

MAY 14
231 days until next year

In a Days
You'd better make a plan to meet and celebrate "National Meeting Planners Appreciation Day."

Proof that they'll give anything its own day, it's "National Buttermilk Biscuit Day."

In the News
1643: Four-year-old Louis XIV became the king of France.

1796: The first smallpox vaccine was administered.

1874: Harvard beat McGill 3–0 in the first-ever football game between Canada and the U.S.

1880: Construction began on the BC portion of the Canadian Pacific Railway.

1946: The Canadian Library Association was founded.

1969: Canada legalized birth control and abortion.

1970: Canadian singer Neil Young parted ways with Crosby, Stills and Nash.

1986: An blizzard with 80 km/h winds hit southern Alberta, knocking over power lines and closing down highways.

1991: Irate truckers lined up in front of Parliament Hill to protest high Canadian taxes.

2005: Pope Benedict XVI observed his first beatification.

Taurus
You are technically and academically inclined, but you become too absorbed in your work.
4, 5, 6, 14

#1 Song
2006: "SOS" by Rihanna

Birth Friends Forever
Amber Tamblyn, actress (*Grudge 2*), 1983

Natalie Appleton, Canadian singer (All-Saints), 1973

Anais Granofsky, Canadian actress (*Degrassi: TNG*), 1973

Sofia Coppola, director (*Lost in Translation*), 1971

Danny Wood, singer (New Kids on the Block), 1969

Cate Blanchett, actress (*Elizabeth*), 1969

Rick Vaive, Canadian hockey player, 1959

Tom Cochrane, Canadian musician, 1953

Robert Zemeckis, director (*Forrest Gump*), 1952

David Byrne, musician (Talking Heads), 1952

Gump Worsley, Canadian hockey player, 1929

Solange Chaput-Rolland, Canadian politician, 1919

Daily Oddity
The emergency signal SOS does not stand for anything.

MAY 15
230 days until next year

In a Days
You love them because you have to, so celebrate "International Day of Families."
Chips Ahoy! It's "National Chocolate Chip Day."
Helping to disguise robbers for 70 years, it's "Nylon Stockings Day."
Lest we forget, it's "Peace Officer Memorial Day."

In the News
1603: Samuel de Champlain embarked on his first voyage to Canada.

1919: The Winnipeg General Strike began, and nearly every worker in the city walked off the job.

1928: Mickey Mouse made his debut.

1935: The Canadian program *Professor Dick and his Question Box* became the first quiz show on television.

1952: Canadian jockey Johnny Longden became the second jockey in history to ride in 4000 races.

1966: Canadian singer Denny Doherty and his group The Mamas & the Papas made it to number one with "Monday, Monday."

1981: The Canadian comedy show *SCTV Network 90* premiered on NBC.

1990: Vincent van Gogh's *Portrait of Doctor Gachet* sold for $82.5 million.

2008: California legalized same-sex marriage.

Taurus
You are a visionary and idea maker who sometimes cuts yourself off from the world.
4, 6, 12, 15

#1 Song
1966: "Monday, Monday" by The Mamas & the Papas

Birth Friends Forever
Justin Morneau, Canadian baseball player, 1981

Jamie-Lynn Sigler, actress (*The Sopranos*), 1981

Caroline Dhavernas, Canadian actress (*Wonderfalls*), 1978

Dwayne DeRosario, Canadian football player, 1978

Emmitt Smith, football player, 1969

Chazz Palminteri, actor (*A Bronx Tale*), 1952

Brian Eno, record producer, 1948

Joseph Wiseman, Canadian actor (*Dr. No*), 1918

L. Frank Baum, author (*Wizard of Oz*), 1856

Daily Oddity
Vincent van Gogh only cut off his earlobe, not his whole ear.

MAY 16
229 days until next year

In a Days
Be nice or they'll write something mean about you. It's "Biographer's Day." It sure beats calling it "Brine Shrimp Day." It's "National Sea-Monkey Day." Instead of "Turning Ugly Outside In Day," today is "Turn Beauty Inside Out Day." Do some butt-crunches at your desk, it's "Employee Health and Fitness Day."

In the News
1811: The phrase "die hard" was coined.

1836: Edgar Allan Poe married his 13-year-old cousin.

1885: The Lake Superior to Fort William portion of the CPR was competed.

1929: The first Academy Awards were held.

1961: John F. Kennedy began his 3-day trip to Canada.

1965: SpaghettiOs were introduced.

1970: Canadian singer Randy Bachman left The Guess Who to found Bachman-Turner Overdrive (BTO).

1975: The first woman reached the top of Mount Everest.

1990: Over 3 million tires in a Québec tire dump caught fire, burning for 4 days.

2006: New Zealand was hit by 7.4-magnitude earthquake.

Taurus
You are a classic extrovert who stands up for your convictions; however, this may cause you to be perceived as egotistical.
4, 6, 7, 16

#1 Song
1974: "The Streak" by Ray Stevens

Birth Friends Forever
Megan Fox, actress (*Transformers*), 1986

Corey Perry, Canadian hockey player, 1985

Jean-Sébastien Giguère, Canadian hockey player, 1977

Tori Spelling, actress (*Beverly Hills, 90210*), 1973

David Boreanaz, actor (*Bones*), 1969

Janet Jackson, singer, 1966

Kevin McDonald, Canadian actor (*The Kids in the Hall*), 1961

Debra Winger, actress (*Betrayed*), 1955

Dafydd Williams, Canadian astronaut, 1954

Liberace, pianist, 1919

Alfred Pellan, Canadian painter, 1906

Henry Fonda, actor (*12 Angry Men*), 1905

Daily Oddity
The man who invented X-Ray Specs also had the bright idea to market brine shrimp as Sea-Monkeys.

MAY 17
228 days until next year

In a Days
Call everyone around the globe and tell them that today is "World Telecommunications Day."

In the News

1775: During the American Revolutionary War, trade with Canada was banned.

1841: A landslide near Québec City killed 32 people.

1878: Inventor Thomas Edison demonstrated his phonograph for the governor general in Ottawa.

1948: The first chapter of the Hell's Angels was started.

1984: Canadian journalist Gordon Sinclair died at the age of 84.

1990: The World Health Organization removed homosexuality from its list of mental illnesses.

1993: Canadian musician Stompin' Tom Connors was awarded an honorary Doctor of Laws degree from St. Thomas University in Fredericton, NB.

1996: Canadian director David Cronenberg premiered his controversial film *Crash* at the Cannes Film Festival.

2007: For the first time since 1953, trains from North and South Korea crossed the Demilitarized Zone.

Taurus
You are sensitive and ambitious yet judgmental at times.
4, 6, 8, 17

#1 Song
1964: "My Guy" by Mary Wells

Birth Friends Forever

Christine Robinson, Canadian water polo player, 1984

Steve Barakatt, Canadian composer, 1973

Josh Homme, singer (Queens of the Stone Age), 1973

Alan Doyle, Canadian musician (Great Big Sea), 1969

Trent Reznor, musician (Nine Inch Nails), 1965

Dave Sim, Canadian comic book artist (*Cerebus the Aardvark*), 1956

Bob Saget, actor (*Full House*), 1956

Sugar Ray Leonard, boxer, 1956

Bill Paxton, actor (*Twister*), 1955

Howard Hampton, Canadian politician, 1952

Dennis Hopper, actor (*Easy Rider*), 1936

Alfred Joseph Casson, Canadian painter, 1898

Daily Oddity
Canadian director Paul Haggis asked David Cronenberg for permission to use the title *Crash* for his 2004 Oscar-winning film.

MAY 18
227 days until next year

In a Days

Don't go to an old folks' home by mistake. It's "International Museum Day."

Get all sweaty before your board meeting. It's "National Bike to Work Day."

Mama Mia, it's-a my favourite day: "National Pizza Party Day."

Lick your computer screen and put on a stamp to celebrate "Send an E-Greeting Card Day."

Today is "Visit Your Relatives Day"—does e-visiting count?

In the News

1765: A large portion of Montréal was destroyed by fire.

1785: Parr Town, NB, changed its name to Saint John.

1897: Bram Stoker's *Dracula* was first published.

1910: Earth passed through the tail of Halley's Comet.

1953: Jackie Cochran became the first woman to break the sound barrier.

1966: Paul-Joseph Chartier was killed in a Parliament Buildings washroom when the bomb he planned to throw into the House of Commons exploded.

1980: Mount St. Helens erupted.

1982: Canadian company Bombardier Inc. won a $1-billion contract to build 825 subway cars for the New York subway system.

2001: Newspaper magnate Conrad Black renounced his Canadian citizenship.

Taurus

You are a steadfast and organized individual; however, you tend to neglect the opinions of others.

4, 6, 9, 18

#1 Song

1997: "MMMBop" by Hanson

Birth Friends Forever

Ryan Cooley, Canadian actor (*Degrassi: TNG*), 1988

Turner Stevenson, Canadian hockey player, 1972

Tina Fey, actress (*30 Rock*), 1970

Chow Yun-Fat, actor (*Crouching Tiger, Hidden Dragon*), 1955

George Strait, country musician, 1952

Bill Wallace, Canadian musician (The Guess Who), 1949

Reggie Jackson, baseball player, 1946

Gordon O'Connor, Canadian politician, 1939

Pope John Paul II, pope, 1920

Perry Como, singer, 1912

Frank Capra, director (*It's a Wonderful Life*), 1897

Daily Oddity

Fingernails grow 4 times faster than toenails.

MAY 19
226 days until next year

In a Days
Celebrate the Dark Lord with "National Devil's Food Cake Day."
Hitch up your horses and get ready to ride shotgun. It's "Stagecoach Day."

In the News

1535: Explorer Jacques Cartier set sail on his 2nd voyage to Canada.

1536: Anne Boleyn was beheaded for adultery.

1780: A combination of forest fire smoke and heavy cloud cover completely shrouded Eastern Canada in darkness.

1962: Marilyn Monroe sang her infamous rendition of "Happy Birthday" to U.S. President John F. Kennedy.

1976: The Soviet Union recognized Canada's proposed 370 km fishing zone.

1984: Workers at *The Vancouver Sun* and *The Province* newspapers returned to work after a 2-month strike.

1984: The Edmonton Oilers won the Stanley Cup.

1996: Canadian astronaut Marc Garneau embarked on his second flight into space aboard the shuttle *Endeavour*.

Taurus
You are a caring and sensible person who may sometimes suffer from mental exhaustion.
1, 4, 6, 10

#1 Song
1961: "Mother-in-Law" by Ernie K-Doe

Birth Friends Forever

David Edgar, Canadian soccer player, 1987

Georges St. Pierre, Canadian UFC fighter, 1981

Jason Gray-Stanford, Canadian actor (*Monk*), 1970

James Gosling, Canadian software developer (Java), 1955

Joey Ramone, musician (The Ramones), 1951

André the Giant, pro wrestler, 1946

Pete Townshend, musician (The Who), 1945

Malcolm X, civil rights activist, 1925

Alex Shibicky, Canadian hockey player, 1914

Percy Williams, Canadian athlete, 1908

Ho Chi Minh, Vietnamese president, 1890

Reginald Aldworth Daly, Canadian geologist, 1871

Daily Oddity
Celsius and Fahrenheit are only equal when they hit −40°.

MAY 20
225 days until next year

In a Days
Hi-diddly-ho, neighbourino! It's "Neighbour Day."
Don't move or use any paper products. It's "Stationery Day."
Is there anything more exciting than "Weights and Measures Day"?
Everything is coming up roses. It's "Flower Day."

In the News
1851: Canada issued its first postage stamps.

1873: Levi Strauss patented his blue jeans design.

1882: Brandon, MB, was incorporated as a city.

1932: Female pilot Amelia Earhart took off on her solo flight across the Atlantic from Newfoundland to Ireland.

1967: A resident of Falcon Lake, MB, claimed that he had encountered a UFO and had been burned by the ship's exhaust.

1980: In a Québec referendum, 60 percent of the population rejected the proposal to separate from Canada.

1986: Sharon Wood and Dwayne Congdon of Canmore, AB, reached the top of Mount Everest.

1995: In a second Québec referendum, the population once again rejected the proposal to separate from Canada.

2003: A BSE-infected cow was found in Alberta, and as a result, many countries banned Canadian beef.

Taurus
You are a curious and practical individual who is prone to erratic behaviour.
2, 4, 6

#1 Song
1984: "Let's Hear It for the Boy" by Deniece Williams

Birth Friends Forever
Busta Rhymes, rapper, 1972

Mindy Cohn, actress (*The Facts of Life*), 1966

Yvon Lambert, Canadian hockey player, 1950

Dave Thomas, Canadian actor (*SCTV*), 1949

Cher, singer, 1946

Joe Cocker, singer, 1944

Stan Mikita, Canadian hockey player, 1940

Otto Jelinek, Canadian figure skater, 1940

Jack Kevorkian, controversial doctor, 1928

Guy Favreau, Canadian lawyer, 1917

James Stewart, actor (*Vertigo*), 1908

Simon Fraser, Canadian explorer, 1776

Daily Oddity
Levi Strauss originally sold tents made of denim, but when prospectors complained about their shoddy cotton trousers, he turned the tents into durable denim pants.

MAY 21
224 days until next year

In a Days
Today is "I Need A Patch For That Day." I hope that includes eyes. Don't forget to leave a tip. It's "National Wait Staff Day."

In the News
1871: "The Maple Leaf Forever" was sung in public for the first time.

1920: XWA radio in Montréal began the first regularly broadcast radio program in North America.

1927: Charles Lindburg landed in Paris, becoming the first person to fly solo across the Atlantic Ocean.

1932: Amelia Earhart landed in Ireland, becoming the first woman to travel solo across the Atlantic Ocean.

1953: Five people were killed when a tornado hit downtown Sarnia, ON.

1965: Ontario unveiled its provincial flag.

1986: Keith Alexander, CEO of Jetco Manufacturing, was sentenced to jail for dumping toxic contaminants into Toronto sewers.

2004: Sherpa Pemba Dorjie climbed Mount Everest in 8 hours and 10 minutes, a new record.

2007: The last surviving clipper ship, *Cutty Sark,* was damaged by fire.

Gemini
You are an intelligent and determined individual who sometimes gets lost in your own beliefs.
3, 4, 6

#1 Song
1955: "Cherry Pink and Apple Blossom White" by Perez Prado

Birth Friends Forever
Adam Gontier, Canadian singer (Three Days Grace), 1978

Jamaal Magloire, Canadian basketball player, 1978

Kardinal Offishall, Canadian rapper, 1976

The Notorious B.I.G., rapper, 1972

Chris Benoit, Canadian pro wrestler, 1967

Jeffrey Dahmer, serial killer, 1960

Judge Reinhold, actor (*Beverly Hills Cop*), 1957

Mr. T, actor (*The A-Team*), 1952

Al Franken, comedian (*SNL*), 1951

Raymond Burr, Canadian actor (*Perry Mason*), 1917

François-Albert Angers, Canadian economist, 1909

Daily Oddity
Terry Fox received more mail than anyone else in Canadian history.

MAY 22
223 days until next year

In a Days
Put a lobster down your pants. It's "National Maritime Day."

In the News

1867: Queen Victoria gave Royal Assent to the BNA Act, creating the Dominion of Canada.

1893: The Montréal Amateur Athletic Association (AAA) won the first Stanley Cup game.

1970: Winnipeg's The Guess Who received 3 gold records for the album and single "American Woman."

1987: Canadian paraplegic Rick Hansen ended his Man in Motion tour to raise money for spinal cord research.

1992: After 30 years on the air, Johnny Carson hosted *The Tonight Show* for the last time.

2003: The first woman in over 58 years played the PGA Tour.

2003: SARS reemerged in Toronto.

2008: Over 200 tornadoes struck the U.S. and parts of Canada.

2008: A 4th severed foot inside a running shoe washed up off the coast of BC.

Gemini
You are an inquisitive and analytical person who has the potential to manipulate others.
4, 5, 8, 9

#1 Song
2005: "Hollaback Girl" by Gwen Stefani

Birth Friends Forever

Marc-Antoine Pouliot, Canadian hockey player, 1985

Maggie Q, actress (*Live Free or Die Hard*), 1979

Katie Price, model, 1978

Alastair Ralphs, Canadian pro wrestler, 1977

Naomi Campbell, model, 1970

Morrissey, singer, 1959

Bernie Taupin, songwriter, 1950

Barbara Parkins, Canadian actress (*Peyton Place*), 1942

Paul Winfield, actor (*City Confidential*), 1941

Michael Sarrazin, Canadian actor (*They Shoot Horses, Don't They?*), 1940

Ron Piché, Canadian baseball player, 1935

Laurence Olivier, actor (*Sleuth*), 1907

James Gladstone, Canadian politician, 1887

Arthur Conan Doyle, author (*Sherlock Holmes*), 1859

Daily Oddity
The name of the Scotsman on the Canadian Tire money is Sandy McTire. He first appeared on the bills in 1958.

MAY 23
222 days until next year

In a Days
Come out of your shell to celebrate "World Turtle Day."
Let's get sticky. It's "National Taffy Day."

In the News

1633: Samuel de Champlain was appointed governor of New France (Québec).

1701: Captain Kidd was hanged for piracy.

1873: The forerunner of the Royal Canadian Mounted Police, the North-West Mounted Police, was established.

1886: The first CPR passenger train to travel across the county arrived at Vancouver.

1929: Canada's first airborne wedding was held on the wings of a biplane over Regina.

1929: After 6 hours and 48 minutes, the first non-stop flight from Winnipeg to Edmonton arrived.

1934: Bank robbers Bonnie and Clyde were shot and killed.

1943: William Aberhart, the founder of Alberta's Social Credit Party, died.

1996: Eight climbers died while trying to reach the summit of Mount Everest.

2007: Jordan Manners became the first Torontonian to be killed in a school shooting.

Gemini
You are an incisive, auspicious and extremely impulsive person.
5, 9, 10, 23

#1 Song
1966: "When a Man Loves a Woman" by Percy Sledge

Birth Friends Forever

Megan Fischer, Canadian Irish dancer, 1985

Brian Campbell, Canadian hockey player, 1979

Matt Hindle, Canadian bobsledder, 1974

Jewel, singer, 1974

Ken Jennings, champion game-show contestant, 1974

Gary Roberts, Canadian hockey player, 1966

Tom Tykwer, director (*Run Lola Run*), 1965

Drew Carey, game-show host (*The Price is Right*), 1958

Reggie Cleveland, Canadian baseball player, 1948

Robert Moog, inventor of the Moog synthesizer, 1934

Joan Collins, actress (*Dynasty*), 1933

Pauline Julien, Canadian singer, 1928

Rosemary Clooney, singer, 1928

Daily Oddity
Otters can get herpes.

MAY 24
221 days until next year

In a Days
Promenade around town in Victorian fashion to celebrate "Victoria Day."
Why do you have to be such a princess on "Tiara Day"?
Punch him in the arm, then give him a wedgie. It's "Brother's Day."

In the News

1830: The song "Mary Had a Little Lamb" was published.

1833: William Logie became the first medical student to graduate in Canada.

1883: The Brooklyn Bridge in New York City opened.

1902: Victoria Day was observed for the first time in Canada.

1918: Canadian women got the right to vote.

1968: FLQ members bombed the U.S. consulate in Québec City.

1995: The Toyota assembly plant in Cambridge, ON, was named the top auto plant in North America.

2000: An *E. coli* outbreak hit Walkerton, ON; 9 people would eventually die.

2001: A 15-year-old Sherpa became the youngest person to climb to the top of Mount Everest.

2004: North Korea banned mobile phones.

Gemini
You are a curious and imaginative individual who sometimes imposes their opinion on others.
5, 6, 9, 12

#1 Song
1961: "Travelin' Man" by Ricky Nelson

Birth Friends Forever

Guillaume Latendresse, Canadian hockey player, 1987

Marc Gagnon, Canadian short-track speed skater, 1975

Will Sasso, Canadian comedian (*Mad TV*), 1974

Kris Draper, Canadian hockey player, 1971

John C. Reilly, actor (*Boogie Nights*), 1965

Pat Verbeek, Canadian hockey player, 1964

Kristin Scott Thomas, actress (*The English Patient*), 1960

Bob Dylan, singer/songwriter, 1941

Tommy Chong, Canadian actor (*Up in Smoke*), 1938

Robert Bateman, Canadian painter, 1930

Lionel Conacher, Canadian athlete, 1900

Queen Victoria, British monarch, 1819

Daily Oddity
Queen Victoria reigned longer than any other monarch in British history.

MAY 25
220 days until next year

In a Days
Annoy your downstairs neighbours by celebrating "National Tap Dance Day." Stop by a saloon on your way home and celebrate "Old Time Player Piano Day."

In the News

1837: Patriots of Lower Canada (Québec) rebelled against the British.

1858: The first boatload of California gold prospectors arrived in BC.

1882: The inaugural meeting of the Royal Society of Canada, which was created to promote science and literature, was held.

1895: Oscar Wilde was sentenced to 2 years in prison for immoral acts.

1905: Peterborough, ON, was incorporated as a city.

1977: *Star Wars* was released.

1987: Canadian jockey Hervé Filion became the first harness-racing driver to win 10,000 races.

2000: The remains of an unidentified Canadian soldier, who was killed in France during WWI, were returned to Canada, where they were laid to rest in the Tomb of the Unknown Soldier in Ottawa.

2001: The first blind person reached the summit of Mount Everest.

2007: Moscow's Ostankino Tower caught fire for the 2nd time.

Gemini
You are an empathic person with strong convictions who can sometimes be a tad judgmental.
5, 7, 9, 14

#1 Song
1943: "That Old Black Magic" by Glenn Miller

Birth Friends Forever

Lauryn Hill, singer (Fugees), 1975

Glen Drover, Canadian musician (Megadeth), 1969

Stacy London, fashion consultant, 1969

Anne Heche, actress (*Men in Trees*), 1969

Mike Myers, Canadian actor (*Austin Powers*), 1963

Rick Nattress, Canadian hockey player, 1962

Rick Wamsley, Canadian hockey player, 1959

Sgt. Slaughter, pro wrestler, 1948

Ian McKellen, actor (*X-Men*), 1939

Robert Ludlum, author (*The Bourne Supremacy*), 1927

Alain Grandbois, Canadian poet, 1900

Max Aitken, Canadian publisher, 1879

Daily Oddity
Erno Rubik, the inventor of the Rubik's Cube, was the first self-made millionaire in a communist country, Hungary.

MAY 26
219 days until next year

In a Days
Warm up your jazz hands. It's "International Jazz Day."
Oh, grape! It's "National Grape Popsicle Day."

In the News
1887: CPR's main line across Canada opened for passenger trains.

1889: The first public elevator opened in the Eiffel Tower.

1894: Nicholas II became tsar of Russia.

1896: A bridge in Victoria, BC, collapsed, killing 55 people.

1906: Saskatoon, SK, was incorporated as a city.

1943: Québec passed a law requiring free and compulsory education within the province.

1969: John Lennon and Yoko Ono held their second Bed-In for Peace in a Montréal hotel.

1977: Mountain climber George Willig climbed the South Tower of the World Trade Center in New York City.

1978: The Montréal Canadiens won their 21st Stanley Cup.

2002: A large ice deposit was discovered on Mars.

2006: Over 5700 people were killed in an earthquake in Java.

Gemini
You are an inspirational person to all around you; however, sometimes your strong belief system may infringe on those around you.
5, 8, 9, 16

#1 Song
2008: "Lollipop" by Lil Wayne

Birth Friends Forever
Helena Bonham Carter, actress (*Fight Club*), 1966

Lenny Kravitz, musician, 1964

Sally Ride, first woman in space, 1951

Hank Williams Jr., singer, 1949

Stevie Nicks, singer (Fleetwood Mac), 1948

Garry Peterson, Canadian musician (The Guess Who), 1945

Teresa Stratas, Canadian soprano, 1938

Phyllis Gotlieb, Canadian author, 1926

Miles Davis, musician, 1926

Peter Cushing, actor (*At the Earth's Core*), 1913

Jay Silverheels, Canadian actor (*The Lone Ranger*), 1912

John Wayne, actor (*The Shootist*), 1907

Daily Oddity
Cherry-flavoured Popsicles are the most popular.

MAY 27
218 days until next year

In a Days
If you don't want to end up looking like a leather-faced lobster, celebrate "Sunscreen Day."

In the News

1703: Peter the Great founded Saint Petersburg.

1846: John Alexander Macdonald made his first-ever speech in Parliament.

1898: The Yukon's first newspaper, *The Klondike Nugget*, was published.

1927: Ford ceased production of its Model T.

1933: Walt Disney released *The Three Little Pigs*, which featured the song "Who's Afraid of the Big Bad Wolf?"

1939: The Dark Knight, Batman, made his first appearance in Detective Comics #27.

1957: CHUM-AM in Toronto became the first radio station in Canada to play rock 'n' roll music.

1963: The Northern Alberta Institute of Technology (NAIT) opened in Edmonton.

1968: The Montréal Expos were awarded a National League baseball franchise.

Gemini
You are an analytical and clear-sighted individual; however, you can be dominating at times.
5, 9, 18, 27

#1 Song
1914: "I Love the Ladies" by Arthur Collins & Byron Harlan

Birth Friends Forever

Jamie Oliver, television chef, 1975

Monika Schnarre, Canadian model, 1971

Northern Dancer, Canadian racehorse, 1961

Ike Hildebrand, Canadian lacrosse player, 1961

Bruce Cockburn, Canadian musician, 1945

Marcel Masse, Canadian politician, 1936

Lee Meriwether, actress (*Batman*), 1935

Ted Rogers, Canadian entrepreneur, 1933

Christopher Lee, actor (*The Lord of the Rings*), 1922

Vincent Price, actor (*The Fly*), 1911

Dashiell Hammett, author (*The Thin Man*), 1894

Wild Bill Hickok, gunfighter, 1837

Daily Oddity
In May 1978, Montréal Expo Willie Stargell hit the longest home run in Olympic Stadium history, 163 metres. To this day, a yellow seat still marks where the ball finally landed.

MAY 28
217 days until next year

In a Days
Sorry, cheeseburger. It's "National Hamburger Day."
Be it sperm, humpback or narwhal, celebrate "Whale Day."

In the News
1845: A fire in Québec City destroyed over 1000 homes.

1930: The Chrysler Building opened in New York City.

1934: Canadian's first set of quintuplets, the Dionnes, were born near North Bay, ON.

1937: Neville Chamberlain was elected prime minister of Britain.

1980: Newfoundland officially adopted its provincial flag.

1988: The Canadian aerosol industry banned CFCs from their spray cans.

1992: Canadian decathlete Dave Steen was appointed to the Canadian Sports Hall of Fame.

1999: After 22 years of restoration, Leonardo da Vinci's *The Last Supper* was put back on display.

2008: Nepal was declared a republic.

Gemini
You are innovative and creative; however, you are constantly on the defensive.
1, 5, 9, 10

#1 Song
1965: "Help Me Rhonda" by The Beach Boys

Birth Friends Forever
David Perron, Canadian hockey player, 1988

Kylie Minogue, singer, 1968

Lynn Johnston, Canadian cartoonist (*For Better or Worse*), 1947

John Fogerty, musician (CCR), 1945

Gladys Knight, singer, 1944

Claude Forget, Canadian politician, 1936

Annette, Cécile, Emilie, Marie and Yvonne Dionne, Canadian identical quintuplets, 1934

Johnny Wayne, Canadian comedian (Wayne and Shuster), 1918

Red Horner, Canadian hockey player, 1909

Ian Fleming, author (*James Bond* novels), 1908

Daily Oddity
The doctor who delivered the Dionne quintuplets made them wards of the Ontario government under his supervision. He then created a theme park called "Quintland," where over 6000 people a day came to ogle the sisters. In their infancy, the Dionne quintuplets endorsed a number of products, including Quaker Oats.

MAY 29
216 days until next year

In a Days
If you call pants "britches" and the washroom "the loo," then you may want to celebrate the English holiday "Oak Apple Day."

In the News
1914: The Canadian Pacific ocean liner *Empress of Ireland* sank in 11 minutes after being hit by a Norwegian ship in the St. Lawrence River; 1012 people died.

1950: The RCMP patrol ship *St. Roch* landed in Nova Scotia, becoming the first ship to circumnavigate North America.

1968: The first female minister was ordained in the Presbyterian Church of Canada.

1970: The Hudson's Bay Company's head office moved from London, England, to Winnipeg, MB.

1979: Canadian silent film star Mary Pickford died at the age of 86.

1985: After 14 months of running across Canada, amputee Steve Fonyo completed his journey, raising $9 million for cancer research.

1999: The space shuttle *Discovery* docked at the International Space Station.

2004: The World War II Memorial opened in Washington, DC.

Gemini
You are a determined and magnetic individual who sometimes finds it hard to stay focused.
1, 5, 9, 11

#1 Song
1994: "I Swear" by All-4-One

Birth Friends Forever
Melanie Brown, musician (Spice Girls), 1975

Eric Lucas, Canadian boxer, 1971

Mike Keane, Canadian hockey player, 1967

Noel Gallagher, musician (Oasis), 1967

Melissa Etheridge, musician, 1961

Nick Mancuso, Canadian actor (*Stingray*), 1948

Jean Coutu, Canadian businessman, 1927

John F. Kennedy, U.S. president, 1917

Hartland Molson, Canadian businessman/senator/brewer, 1907

Bob Hope, comedian, 1903

Beatrice Lillie, Canadian actress (*Around the World in Eighty Days*), 1894

King Charles II of England, 1630

Daily Oddity
The Hudson's Bay Company was incorporated in 1670. It is the oldest commercial corporation in North America and one of the oldest in the world.

MAY 30
215 days until next year

In a Days
To celebrate "Senior Health and Fitness Day," participate in a no-holds-barred, extreme knitting match.

In the News

1832: The 7.8-kilometre-long Rideau Canal opened in eastern Ontario.

1899: Canadian bandit Pearl Hart, a close friend of Calamity Jane, pulled off the last stagecoach holdup in U.S. history.

1922: The Lincoln Memorial was dedicated.

1959: The Auckland Harbour Bridge opened in New Zealand.

1961: Canada's most intense rainstorm occurred in Buffalo Gap, SK; 250 mm of rain fell in less than an hour.

1967: Daredevil Evel Knievel jumped his motorcycle over a row of 16 cars.

1975: Yukon and Northwest Territories both gained seats in the Senate, bumping the number of seats from 102 to 104.

1985: The Edmonton Oilers won their second consecutive Stanley Cup.

1998: Over 5000 people in Afghanistan died in an earthquake.

2008: The office of Winnipeg's former gay mayor Glen Murray was spray painted with anti-gay messages.

Gemini
You are a quick-witted and rebellious individual who is prone to skittishness.
3, 5, 6, 9

#1 Song
1963: "It's My Party" by Lesley Gore

Birth Friends Forever
Mike Bishai, Canadian hockey player, 1979

Cee-Lo, singer (Gnarls Barkley), 1974

Kelley Armstrong, Canadian author (*Bitten*), 1968

Wynonna Judd, country singer, 1964

Tom Morello, musician (Rage Against the Machine), 1964

Jake "The Snake" Roberts, pro wrestler, 1955

Gilles Villemure, Canadian hockey player, 1940

Ruta Lee, Canadian actress (*Seven Brides for Seven Brothers*), 1936

Benny Goodman, bandleader, 1909

Mel Blanc, voice actor (Bugs Bunny), 1908

Pierre-Joseph-Olivier Chauveau, Canadian politician, 1820

Daily Oddity
In the winter, when the Rideau Canal freezes up, some commuters actually ice skate to work on the frozen waterway.

MAY 31
214 days until next year

In a Days
Just because today is "World No-Tobacco Day" doesn't mean you can't smoke other things, like fish.

Suppress your tobacco craving with "National Macaroon Day."

Me think you I should celebrate "Speak in Complete Sentences Day."

In the News
1578: Martin Frobisher sailed from England to Frobisher Bay to mine gold, but mistakenly returned with over 200 tonnes of worthless pyrite.

1877: Brantford, ON, was incorporated as a city.

1927: The last Model T came off the assembly line.

1954: CBWT-TV in Winnipeg became the first television station on the Prairies.

1967: Queen Elizabeth II sent 12 white swans to Ottawa as a Confederation gift.

1985: Barrie, Grand Valley, Orangeville and Tottenham, ON, were hit by a tornado; 12 people were killed.

1997: The Confederation Bridge, which connected PEI and New Brunswick, opened.

2005: Canadian Natalie Glebova was crowned Miss Universe.

2008: Usain Bolt broke the world record in the 100 m sprint, running the distance in 9.72 seconds.

Gemini
You are a practical and individualistic person who, at times, may be perceived as authoritarian.
4, 5, 8, 9

#1 Song
1979: "Hot Stuff" by Donna Summer

Birth Friends Forever
Melissa McIntyre, Canadian actress (*Degrassi: TNG*), 1986

Phil Devey, Canadian baseball player, 1977

Colin Farrell, actor (*Alexander*), 1976

Vampiro, Canadian pro wrestler, 1967

Phil Keoghan, TV personality (*The Amazing Race*), 1967

Brooke Shields, actress (*Lipstick Jungle*), 1965

Leonard Asper, Canadian businessman, 1964

Hugh Dillon, Canadian actor and musician (Headstones), 1963

Corey Hart, Canadian musician, 1962

Clint Eastwood, actor/director (*Dirty Harry*), 1930

Don Ameche, actor (*Cocoon*), 1908

Walt Whitman, poet, 1819

Daily Oddity
Residents wanted to name it the "Fixed Link." The federal government wanted to call it the "Northumberland Strait Crossing." It was called "Confederation Bridge."

JUNE 1
213 days until next year

In a Days
If you're a crazy cat lady, you will love "Hug Your Cat Day."
Fake a family emergency and go celebrate "Leave the Office Early Day."
It's the perfect time to make friends with a prisoner. It's "Pen Pal Day."
If it weren't for their fossils, we'd be riding bicycles. It's "Dinosaur Day."

In the News
- 1831: The Kingston Penitentiary in Ontario officially opened with 6 prisoners.
- 1858: The first Canadian coins were minted.
- 1873: PEI entered Confederation as a province.
- 1882: Winnipeg got gas-powered lighting.
- 1927: In Ontario, drivers were required to have a licence.
- 1938: Superman, a character co-created by Canadian Joe Shuster, made his debut in Action Comics #1.
- 1958: CBC went on the air across Canada.
- 1961: The population of Canada reached 18,238,247.
- 1968: Alberta's provincial flag was approved.
- 1979: The population of Canada reached 23,671,500.
- 2008: A fire on a Universal Studios back lot destroyed the clock tower from *Back to the Future*.

Gemini
You have an insatiable thirst for knowledge; however, you have a problem staying focused on one specific interest.
5, 9, 11

#1 Song
1912: "When I Was 21 and You Were Sweet 16" by Henry Burr & Albert Campbell

Birth Friends Forever
Alanis Morissette, Canadian singer, 1974

Heidi Klum, model, 1973

Oscar the Grouch, muppet, 1969

Paul Coffey, Canadian hockey player, 1961

Michel Plasse, Canadian hockey player, 1948

Ronnie Wood, musician (The Rolling Stones), 1947

Morgan Freeman, actor (*The Shawshank Redemption*), 1937

Marilyn Monroe, actress (*Some Like It Hot*), 1926

Andy Griffith, actor (*Matlock*), 1926

Hap Day, Canadian hockey player, 1901

Daily Oddity
Joe Shuster, the Canadian co-creator of Superman, originally had Clark Kent reporting for *The Daily Star* newspaper, as an homage to *The Toronto Daily Star*, where he worked as a paperboy. The name of the paper was later changed to *The Daily Planet*.

JUNE 2
212 days until next year

In a Days
Only those people who have dentures can honestly celebrate "I Love My Dentist Day."

Sorry, Neapolitan, it's "National Rocky Road Day."

In the News
1692: The witch trials began in Salem, MA.

1800: The first smallpox vaccination in North America was administered in Newfoundland.

1835: P.T. Barnum's circus began touring the U.S.

1896: Marconi submitted an application to patent his radio design.

1917: Canadian pilot and Victoria Cross recipient Billy Bishop shot down 3 German planes behind enemy lines.

1929: A tornado hit Guelph, ON, damaging many of the city's essential services.

1965: The Canadian government set the mandatory retirement age for senators at 75.

1991: The RCMP unveiled their official flag.

2004: *Jeopardy* champion Ken Jennings began his 74-game winning streak.

2007: Prince Henry arrived at Canada's CFB Suffield to begin his military training.

Gemini
You are a very courageous and determined individual; however, you sometimes create situations just so you can solve them.
9, 5, 11

#1 Song
1989: "Rock On" by Michael Damian

Birth Friends Forever
Jewel Staite, Canadian actress (*Firefly*), 1982

Justin Long, actor (Macintosh ads), 1978

Zachary Quinto, actor (*Heroes*), 1977

Dana Carvey, actor (*Wayne's World*), 1955

Larry Robinson, Canadian hockey player, 1951

Joanna Gleason, Canadian actress (*Into the Woods*), 1950

Jerry Mathers, actor (*Leave It to Beaver*), 1948

Charlie Watts, musician (The Rolling Stones), 1941

Stacy Keach, actor (*Mike Hammer*), 1941

Robert Paul, Canadian figure skater, 1937

June Callwood, Canadian journalist, 1924

Florence Bell, Canadian runner, 1910

Daily Oddity
The mandatory retirement age for Air Canada pilots is 60.

JUNE 3
211 days until next year

In a Days
Look on the sunny-side up. It's "Egg Day."
Mmm…"National Doughnut Day."

In the News
1613: Samuel de Champlain reached Ottawa.

1799: The island of St. John was officially proclaimed Prince Edward Island.

1876: Canada introduced lacrosse to Britain.

1888: The poem "Casey at the Bat" was first published.

1961: A 10-day heat wave began in Regina, SK.

1968: The Royal Canadian Mint replaced the silver in coins with nickel alloy.

1972: Thirty-one police officers were injured when a crowd of 2000 fans crashed a Rolling Stones concert in Vancouver.

1983: Canadian record-holder Alian Pumas began dancing for 120 hours and 30 minutes straight.

1989: The SkyDome officially opened in Toronto, ON.

1994: In London's Green Park, Queen Elizabeth unveiled a war memorial honouring Canadian soldiers from both World Wars.

2007: A U.S. naval ship confronted modern-day pirates off the coast of Somalia.

Gemini
You are sharp-witted and extremely charming; however, you are known to have a bit of a temper.
3, 5, 9

#1 Song
1995: "Have You Ever Really Loved a Woman?" by Bryan Adams

Birth Friends Forever
Katie Hoff, swimmer, 1989

Anderson Cooper, news correspondent, 1967

Wally Weir, Canadian hockey player, 1954

Dan Hill, Canadian singer, 1954

Curtis Mayfield, musician, 1942

Larry McMurtry, author (*Lonesome Dove*), 1936

Chuck Barris, game-show host, 1929

Tony Curtis, actor (*The Odd Couple*), 1925

Colleen Dewhurst, Canadian actress (*Anne of Green Gables*), 1924

Daily Oddity
The name SkyDome was chosen in a provincewide contest. Other names submitted included Towerdome, Harbourdome and The Dome. In 2005, the SkyDome was renamed the Rogers Centre.

JUNE 4
210 days until next year

In a Days
Oh, Gouda, it's "Cheese Day."
Sorry, PC, it's "Apple Computer Day."
Well, it's still better than "Frozen Cottage Cheese Day." It's "National Frozen Yogurt Day."

In the News

1768: Ojibway Natives challenged the English soldiers of Fort Michilimackinac to a lacrosse match. Midway through the match, the Natives armed themselves with weapons and seized control of the fort, which they held for a year.

1838: The first recorded baseball game was held in Beachville, ON.

1843: The town of Victoria, BC, was founded.

1973: The ATM was patented.

1976: Canada took jurisdiction over the Continental Shelf.

1980: At the age of 52, Gordie Howe announced his retirement from hockey.

1983: Canadian singer Stan Rogers and 19 other Canadians were killed in an Air Canada flight from Texas to Toronto.

2001: The last king of Nepal ascended to the throne.

Gemini
You are charismatic and influential, but you tend to neglect your personal life.
5, 9, 22

#1 Song
1975: "Thank God I'm a Country Boy" by John Denver

Birth Friends Forever
Shane Kippel, Canadian actor (*Degrassi: TNG*), 1986
Ian White, Canadian hockey player, 1984
François Beauchemin, Canadian hockey player, 1980
Angelina Jolie, actress (*Girl, Interrupted*), 1975
Noah Wyle, actor (*ER*), 1971
Tom Longboat, Canadian marathon runner, 1949
Michelle Phillips, singer (The Mamas & the Papas), 1944
Colette Boky, Canadian soprano, 1935
Dr. Ruth Westheimer, sex therapist, 1928
Dennis Weaver, actor (*McCloud*), 1924
Fernand Leduc, Canadian painter, 1916
Madame Bolduc, Canadian singer, 1894

Daily Oddity
While his official nickname is "Mr. Hockey," some of Gordie Howe's other nicknames include Mr. Everything, Mr. All-Star, The Most, The Great Gordie, The King of Hockey, The Legend, The Man and No. 9.

JUNE 5
209 days until next year

In a Days
Not everyone can afford to be gluttonous. Today is "National Hunger Awareness Day."

Become an eco-maniac. It's "World Environment Day."

Nothing says spring is on its way like "National Gingerbread Day."

In the News
1816: A record-breaking snowstorm hit Québec.

1817: The *Frontenac*, the first Great Lakes steamer, was launched.

1895: Regina MP Nicholas Davin made a motion to give women the right to vote; the House of Commons quickly defeated it.

1915: Women in Denmark got the vote.

1956: Elvis Presley shook his pelvis for the first time on television.

1968: Robert F. Kennedy was shot.

1977: The Apple II personal computer went on sale.

1989: The Toronto Blue Jays lost their first game in the SkyDome.

2002: Dee Dee Ramone, bass player for The Ramones, died.

2003: Temperatures in Pakistan and India exceed 50°C.

Gemini
You are an imaginative and steadfast individual who can be too sensitive on occasion.
5, 9, 23

#1 Song
1966: "Paint It Black" by The Rolling Stones

Birth Friends Forever
Sebastien Lefebvre, Canadian musician (Simple Plan), 1981

Pete Wentz, musician (Fall Out Boy), 1979

Chuck Klosterman, author (*Sex, Drugs, and Cocoa Puffs*), 1972

Mark Wahlberg, actor (*The Italian Job*), 1971

Martin Gelinas, Canadian hockey player, 1970

Kenny G, saxophonist, 1956

Suze Orman, financial advisor, 1951

Spalding Gray, actor (*Swimming to Cambodia*), 1941

Joe Clark, Canadian prime minister, 1939

Roy Herbert Thomson, Canadian publisher, 1894

Pancho Villa, revolutionary, 1878

Pat Garrett, sheriff who killed Billy the Kid, 1850

Daily Oddity
The first song that Elvis Presley sang on television was "Hound Dog."

JUNE 6
208 days until next year

In a Days
Can you bring in the crotch just a bit? It's "National Tailors Day."

In the News

1861: The *Maid of the Mist* became the first boat to successfully navigate the Niagara Falls River.

1891: A tornado destroyed 500 homes in Cornwall, ON.

1891: Canada's first prime minister, John A. Macdonald, died.

1944: Canadian troops stormed the beaches of Normandy, France, in what became known as D-Day.

1957: *Front Page Challenge* was first broadcast on CBC.

1968: Senator Robert F. Kennedy died of the wounds he sustained on June 5, 1968.

1973: The world's tallest totem pole, 52.7 m, was raised in Alert Bay, BC.

1993: The Canadian production of *Kiss of the Spiderwoman* won 7 Tony Awards.

1994: Canadian vets commemorated the 50th anniversary of D-Day.

2002: A meteoroid exploded over the Mediterranean Sea.

Gemini
You are a strategist and an eccentric who sometimes pretends to be something you are not.
5, 9, 24

#1 Song
1944: "I'll Get By (As Long as I Have You)" by Harry James

Birth Friends Forever

François Avard, Canadian scenarist, 1968

Paul Giamatti, actor (*Sideways*), 1967

Max Casella, actor (*Newsies*), 1967

Cam Neely, Canadian hockey player, 1965

Sandra Bernhard, comedian, 1955

Robert Englund, actor (*Nightmare on Elm Street*), 1949

Gary Anderson, musician (Gary U.S. Bonds), 1939

Levi Stubbs, musician (The Four Tops), 1936

V.C. Andrews, author (*Flowers in the Attic*), 1923

Alexandra Romanova, tsarina of Russia, 1872

David Abercrombie, co-founder of Abercrombie & Fitch, 1867

Daily Oddity
The "D" in D-Day stands for Day.

JUNE 7
207 days until next year

In a Days
Sorry, Davy Crocket, it's "Daniel Boone Day."
Sorry, Betamax, it's "VCR Day."
As long as you're not testing out neural disrupters, enjoy "Trial Technology Day."

In the News

1654: King Louis XIV of France was crowned.

1800: Explorer David Thompson reached the mouth of the Saskatchewan River in Manitoba.

1832: Asian cholera, which was brought over by Irish immigrants, killed 6000 residents of Lower Canada.

1893: Mahatma Gandhi performed his first act of civil disobedience.

1909: 16-year-old Canadian actress Mary Pickford made her silent film debut in *The Violin Maker of Cremona*.

1975: Betamax videocassettes officially went on sale.

1982: Graceland—the home of Elvis Presley—officially opened to the public.

1989: Wayne Gretzky won his 9th Hart (MVP) Trophy in 10 years.

2006: The British Houses of Parliament were closed because of an anthrax scare.

Gemini
You are a curious and tenacious individual, but you lack focus.
5, 7, 9

#1 Song
1971: "Want Ads" by The Honey Cone

Birth Friends Forever
Michael Cera, Canadian actor (*Juno*), 1988

Milan Lucic, Canadian hockey player, 1988

Anna Kournikova, tennis player, 1981

Dave Navarro, musician (Jane's Addiction), 1967

Stephane Richu, Canadian hockey player, 1966

Prince, musician, 1958

Liam Neeson, actor (*Rob Roy*), 1952

Tom Jones, singer, 1940

John Turner, Canadian prime minister, 1929

Leo Reise, Canadian hockey player, 1922

Dean Martin, actor (*Rio Bravo*), 1917

Jessica Tandy, actress (*Driving Miss Daisy*), 1909

Daily Oddity
More people lose their virginity in June than any other month.

JUNE 8
206 days until next year

In a Days
Get lost you fruit. It's "Banana Split Day."
Stand erect. It's "Upsy Daisy Day."
Take a dip to celebrate "World Ocean Day."

In the News
1824: Québec City resident Noah Cushing patented the washing machine; it was also the first patent registered in Canada.

1859: The BC Supreme Court was formed.

1887: The punch card calculator was patented.

1949: In an FBI report, Helen Keller, Dorothy Parker, Danny Kaye, Fredric March, John Garfield, Paul Muni and Edward G. Robinson were all named as Communist Party members.

1968: James Earl Ray, the man who assassinated Martin Luther King Jr., was arrested.

1984: New South Wales, Australia, legalized homosexuality.

1992: Out of 5300 applicants, the Canadian Space Agency chose 4 new astronauts: Chris Hadfield, Julie Payette, Robert Stewart and Dafydd Williams.

2008: The Akihabara massacre took place in Tokyo, Japan; 4 people were killed.

Gemini
You are an enthusiastic and talented individual who cannot tolerate boredom.
5, 8, 9

#1 Song
1977: "I'm Your Boogie Man" by K.C. & the Sunshine Band

Birth Friends Forever
Alexandre Despatie, Canadian diver, 1985
Pete Orr, Canadian baseball player, 1979
Kanye West, rapper, 1977
Bryan McCabe, Canadian hockey player, 1975
David Sutcliffe, Canadian actor (*Gilmore Girls*), 1969
Bonnie Tyler, singer, 1951
Marc Ouellet, archbishop of Québec City, 1944
Nancy Sinatra, singer, 1940
Joan Rivers, comedian, 1933
Jerry Stiller, actor (*Seinfeld*), 1927
Alexis Smith, Canadian actress (*Of Human Bondage*), 1921
Frank Lloyd Wright, architect, 1867

Daily Oddity
Canada Post once issued a set of sumo wrestling stamps.

JUNE 9
205 days until next year

In a Days
Call the Queen of Hearts. It's "Croquet Day."

Dress up like a pair of homeless twins to celebrate "Raggedy Ann and Andy Day."

In the News
- **53:** Roman emperor Nero married Claudia Octavia.
- **62:** Roman empress Claudia Octavia committed suicide.
- **68:** Roman emperor Nero committed suicide.
- **1534:** Jacques Cartier became the first European to discover and travel down the St. Lawrence River.
- **1919:** Winnipeg City Council dismissed the police force during the Winnipeg General Strike.
- **1934:** Donald Duck made his debut in the cartoon *The Wise Little Hen*.
- **1947:** The Canadian government ended the wartime rationing of dairy products.
- **1973:** Canadian jockey Ron Turcotte rode racehorse Secretariat to a Triple Crown win.
- **1978:** The Church of Jesus Christ of Latter-day Saints allowed African American men to join the priesthood.
- **2008:** Homes in Lake Delton, WI, were destroyed when a dam holding back a lake burst.

Gemini
You are a versatile, hard worker, though you may be a tad judgmental.

5, 9, 36

#1 Song
2001: "Lady Marmalade" by Christina Aguilera, Lil' Kim, Mya & Pink

Birth Friends Forever
Adamo Ruggiero, Canadian actor (*Degrassi: TNG*), 1986

Andrew Walker, Canadian actor (*Reba*), 1982

Natalie Portman, actress (*The Other Boleyn Girl*), 1981

Gloria Reuben, Canadian actress (*ER*), 1964

Johnny Depp, actor (*Pirates of the Caribbean*), 1963

Michael J. Fox, Canadian actor (*Back to the Future*), 1961

Steve Paikin, Canadian journalist, 1960

Jackie Mason, comedian, 1931

Fernand Seguin, Canadian biochemist, 1922

Les Paul, guitarist, 1915

Bobby Kerr, Canadian sprinter, 1882

Tsar Peter the Great of Russia, 1672

Daily Oddity
Roy G. Biv is a mnemonic used to remember the sequence of colours that are found in a rainbow.

JUNE 10
204 days until next year

In a Days
Check under the hood. It's "National Automotive Service Professionals Day." Do you need some money? Well, then, you'd better start celebrating "Write to Your Father Day."

In the News
1692: The first woman accused of witchcraft was hanged in Salem, MA.

1857: St. Hyacinthe and Trois-Rivières, Québec, were incorporated as cities.

1930: The Winnipeg Rugby Football Club was formed, later becoming the Winnipeg Blue Bombers.

1935: Alcoholics Anonymous was founded.

1937: Canada's 8th prime minister, Robert Laird Borden, died at the age of 83.

1940: Canada declared war on Italy.

1947: The first Saab automobile was produced.

1977: Apple Computers shipped their first personal computer.

1981: Dome Petroleum bought out Hudson's Bay Oil and Gas.

2003: Canada's first legal same-sex marriage took place in Ontario.

Gemini
You are an intelligent and prodigious individual who may become too obsessed with the projects you are working on.
5, 9, 10

#1 Song
1958: "Purple People Eater" by Sheb Wooley

Birth Friends Forever
Sasha Obama, U.S. first daughter, 2001

Leelee Sobieski, actress (*The Glass House*), 1983

Tara Lipinski, figure skater, 1982

Shane West, actor (*ER*), 1978

Elizabeth Hurley, model, 1965

Brent Sutter, Canadian hockey player, 1962

Kim Deal, musician (Pixies), 1961

Preston Manning, Canadian politician, 1942

Judy Garland, actress (*The Wizard of Oz*), 1922

Barry Morse, Canadian actor (*The Fugitive*), 1918

Saul Bellow, Canadian author (*Herzog*), 1915

Hattie McDaniel, actress (*Gone with the Wind*), 1895

Daily Oddity
Labatt's Blue was named after the Winnipeg Blue Bombers.

JUNE 11
203 days until next year

In a Days
Bow your head, pilgrim. It's "Remember the Duke Day."

In the News
1184 BC: The city of Troy was sacked and burned.

1931: Canada proclaimed November 11 (Remembrance Day) a national holiday.

1940: Princess Juliana of the Netherlands and her children arrived in Canada seeking protection from the Nazis during World War II.

1941: Canada's population was 11,506,655.

1966: Dave Bailey became the first Canadian runner to break the 4-minute mile.

1979: Actor John "The Duke" Wayne died.

2001: American terrorist Timothy McVeigh was executed for his involvement in the Oklahoma City bombing.

2008: Canadian Prime Minister Stephen Harper apologized to Canada's First Nations people for the years of abuse that they suffered in residential schools.

2008: Gas in Labrador City, NL, hit $1.505 a litre.

Gemini
You are a focused and skillful individual; however, at times you can be a little single-minded.
2, 5, 9

#1 Song
1984: "Time After Time" by Cyndi Lauper

Birth Friends Forever
Shia LaBeouf, actor (*Transformers*), 1986

Joshua Jackson, Canadian actor (*Dawson's Creek*), 1978

Peter Dinklage, actor (*The Station Agent*), 1969

Sandra Schmirler, Canadian curler, 1963

Hugh Laurie, actor (*House*), 1959

Joe Montana, football player, 1956

Gene Wilder, actor (*Young Frankenstein*), 1933

Johnny Esaw, Canadian broadcaster, 1925

Vince Lombardi, football coach, 1913

Jacques-Yves Cousteau, undersea explorer, 1910

Dai Vernon, Canadian magician, 1894

Richard Strauss, composer, 1864

Daily Oddity
Li'l Abner cartoonist Al Capp designed the oversized Josiah Flintabbatey Flonatin statue in Flin Flon, MB.

JUNE 12
202 days until next year

In a Days
Let me saw you in half. It's "Magic Day."

There are too many eggs in here! Today is "Crowded Nest Awareness Day."

You can either call today "Russia Day" or you can call it by its other moniker: "Day of the Adoption of the Declaration of Sovereignty of the Russian Federation."

In the News
1849: The gas mask was patented.

1901: Montréal made indoor toilets mandatory.

1903: Niagara Falls, ON, was incorporated as a city.

1947: The *Sergeant Preston of the Yukon* radio show—the adventures of a Canadian Mountie—went on the air; it ran until 1955, when it moved to TV.

1979: Bobby Orr was named to the Hockey Hall of Fame.

1985: Wayne Gretzky received his 6th Hart (MVP) Trophy.

1990: The Russia Federation declared its sovereignty.

1994: O.J. Simpson's ex-wife, Nicole Brown Simpson, and her friend, Ronald Goldman, were murdered.

2005: Central Canada was hit by a heat wave that produced temperatures around 31°C with a humidex of 41°C.

Gemini
You are a perceptive and goal-oriented individual; however, sometimes you may be perceived as a bully.

3, 5, 9

#1 Song
2006: "Hips Don't Lie" by Shakira, featuring Wyclef Jean

Birth Friends Forever
William Cuddy, Canadian actor (*Amelia*), 1997

Tasha-Ray Evin, Canadian musician (Lillix), 1985

Christine Sinclair, Canadian soccer player, 1983

Wade Redden, Canadian hockey player, 1977

Gordon Michael Woolvett, Canadian actor (*Andromeda*), 1970

Scott Thompson, Canadian comedian (*The Kids in the Hall*), 1959

Jim Nabors, actor (*The Andy Griffith Show*), 1930

Anne Frank, diarist, 1929

George H. W. Bush, U.S. president, 1924

James Houston, Canadian artist, 1921

Jean Victor Allard, Canadian army general, 1913

Alphonse Ouimet, president of the CBC, 1908

Daily Oddity
Sergeant Preston of the Yukon was the brainchild of the same creators behind *The Lone Ranger* and *The Green Hornet*.

JUNE 13
201 days until next year

In a Days
Sorry, St. Valentine. Today is "Loving Day."
Get out the rusty chainsaws. It's "National Juggling Day."
Put on a bib and boil some water. It's "National Lobster Day."

In the News
1871: A hurricane in Labrador killed 300 people.

1886: A fire destroyed much of Vancouver, BC.

1898: The Yukon Territory joined the Dominion of Canada.

1908: Canadian fighter Tommy Burns knocked out Bill Squires for the world heavyweight boxing championship.

1916: Edmonton's Emily Murphy of "The Famous Five" was appointed the first woman police magistrate in the British Empire.

1935: James "The Cinderella Man" Braddock defeated Max Baer to become heavyweight champion of the world.

1955: The first diamond mine was discovered in Russia.

1977: Martin Luther King Jr. assassin James Earl Ray was recaptured after escaping from prison three days earlier.

2005: Michael Jackson was acquitted of molesting a 13-year-old boy.

Gemini
You are an innovative and stimulating individual who may, at times, shut yourself off from reality.
4, 5, 13

#1 Song
1965: "I Can't Help Myself" by The Four Tops

Birth Friends Forever
Ashley Olsen, actress (*Full House*), 1986

Mary-Kate Olsen, actress (*Full House*), 1986

Danny Syvret, Canadian hockey player, 1985

Jason Spezza, Canadian hockey player, 1983

Natalie MacMaster, Canadian musician, 1972

Rivers Cuomo, musician (Weezer), 1970

Glenn Michibata, Canadian tennis player, 1962

Tim Allen, actor and comedian (*Home Improvement*), 1953

Garnet Bailey, Canadian hockey player, 1948

Malcolm McDowell, actor (*A Clockwork Orange*), 1943

Percy Rodriguez, Canadian actor (*Star Trek*), 1924

Basil Rathbone, actor (*Sherlock Holmes*), 1892

Daily Oddity
The Canadian Women's Rights Group "The Famous Five" was also referred to as "The Valiant Five."

JUNE 14
200 days until next year

In a Days
Chase a monkey around a mulberry bush to celebrate "Pop goes the Weasel Day."

In the News

1789: After his crew mutinied and set him adrift, Captain Bligh finally reached land after floating 7400 km.

1872: Canada legalized trade unions.

1892: A tornado hit the Ottawa Valley, killing 12 people.

1894: Massey Hall opened in Toronto.

1937: CBC Radio's first show, *The Happy Gang*, went on the air; it ran for 22 years.

1942: Anne Frank wrote her first diary entry.

1949: The Yukon recorded its highest temperature, 36.1°C.

1990: Toronto lost the chance to host Expo 2000 to Germany by one vote.

1994: Vancouver fans rioted in the streets after the Canucks lost the Stanley Cup to the Rangers.

2001: China, Russia, Kazakhstan, Kyrgyzstan, Tajikistan and Uzbekistan formed the Shanghai Cooperation Organisation.

Gemini
You are an energetic and opinionated person who is so driven that you sometimes ignore the help of others.
5, 9, 14

#1 Song
1988: "Together Forever" by Rick Astley

Birth Friends Forever

Steve Bégin, Canadian hockey player, 1978

Diablo Cody, screenwriter (*Juno*), 1978

Éric Desjardins, Canadian hockey player, 1969

Steffi Graf, tennis player, 1969

Yasmine Bleeth, actress (*Baywatch*), 1968

Boy George, singer (Culture Club), 1961

Donald Trump, entrepreneur, 1946

Marla Gibbs, actress (*227*), 1931

Ernesto "Che" Guevara, revolutionary, 1928

Joe Morris, Canadian trade unionist, 1913

Burl Ives, actor and singer ("White Christmas"), 1909

Jack Adams, Canadian hockey player, 1895

Daily Oddity
June is the most popular month for getting married.

JUNE 15
199 days until next year

In a Days
You're it! It's "Recess at Work Day."
Shhh! It's "Nature Photography Day."
Why don't you go "Fly a Kite Day"?
Finally, you won't get in trouble for not wearing pants to work. It's "Work@Home Day."

In the News
1752: Using a kite, Benjamin Franklin proved that lightning was, in fact, electricity.

1844: Charles Goodyear patented the process of vulcanization, which is needed to strengthen rubber.

1846: The Oregon Treaty established that the 49th parallel was the border between Canada and the U.S.

1902: The Maritimes switched from Eastern to Atlantic Time.

1944: Tommy Douglas was elected premier of Saskatchewan; he later formed the first socialist government (The Co-operative Commonwealth Federation) in North America.

1995: Richard Weber of Québec skied to Canada's most northernmost point, Ward Hunt Island.

2005: Wayne Gretzky was appointed executive director of Team Canada for the 2006 Winter Olympics.

Gemini
You are an intuitive and sensitive person who can become susceptible to vanity.
5, 6, 9

#1 Song
1972: "Candy Man" by Sammy Davis Jr.

Birth Friends Forever
Neil Patrick Harris, actor (*Doogie Howser, M.D.*), 1973
Bif Naked, Canadian musician, 1971
Jake Busey, actor (*Starship Troopers*), 1971
Leah Remini, actress (*The King of Queens*), 1970
Ice Cube, actor (*Are We There Yet?*), 1969
Courteney Cox, actress (*Friends*), 1964
Mario Gosselin, Canadian hockey player, 1963
Helen Hunt, actress (*As Good As It Gets*), 1963
Jim Belushi, actor (*According to Jim*), 1954
Jim Varney, actor (*Ernest Goes to Camp*), 1949
François-Xavier Garneau, Canadian poet, 1809

Daily Oddity
Canadian politician Tommy Douglas was the grandfather of actor Kiefer Sutherland.

JUNE 16
198 days until next year

In a Days
Eat as much as you can. It's "Fudge Day."
Break down walls by building them. It's "Professional Women in Drywall Day."
Drink as much as you can. It's "Vinegar Day."

In the News

1833: The last duel in Upper Canada took place, resulting in the death of a 19-year-old boy.

1891: John Abbott became the 3rd prime minister of Canada.

1894: An Edmonton-area newspaper first reported the presence of oil in the province.

1898: The Yukon's first newspaper, *The Klondike Nugget*, was published.

1967: Canadian singer Neil Young played at the 3-day long Monterey International Pop Music Festival.

1972: The power was turned on at the largest single-site hydroelectric power project in the western world, located in Churchill Falls, NL.

1981: For his part in freeing 6 American hostages in Iran, Canada's former ambassador to Iran, Ken Taylor, was awarded the U.S. Congressional Gold Medal.

2008: A 5th severed foot inside a running shoe washed up off the coast of BC.

Gemini
You are an imaginative and innovative individual who can, at times, be farsighted.
5, 7, 9

#1 Song
1985: "Heaven" by Bryan Adams

Birth Friends Forever
Keshia Chante, Canadian singer, 1988
Rick Nash, Canadian hockey player, 1984
Missy Peregrym, Canadian actress (*Stick It*), 1982
Brad Gushue, Canadian curler, 1980
Tupac Shakur, rapper, 1971
Steve Larmer, Canadian hockey player, 1961
Gino Vannelli, Canadian singer, 1952
Derek Sanderson, Canadian hockey player, 1946
Lucienne Robillard, Canadian politician, 1945
Raymond Lemieux, Canadian scientist, 1920
Stan Laurel, comedian (Laurel & Hardy), 1890
Arthur Meighen, Canadian prime minister, 1874

Daily Oddity
Only 4% of the world's population is atheist.

JUNE 17
197 days until next year

In a Days
Chill out and celebrate "Iceland Independence Day."
Without them, you'd have to drive yourself crazy. It's "Family Awareness Day."

In the News

1631: After his wife's death, Emperor Shah Jahan I built the Taj Mahal as her tomb.

1753: German immigrants settled in Lunenburg, NS.

1871: Canadian tall woman Anna Swan (7'5") married American tall man Martin Buren (7'2"), becoming the world's tallest married couple.

1885: The Statue of Liberty arrived in New York City.

1944: Iceland declared its independence from Denmark.

1958: A number of Vancouver ironworkers were killed when the Second Narrows Bridge, which connects Vancouver to North Vancouver, collapsed.

1961: Canada's New Democratic Party was founded.

1990: South African leader Nelson Mandela visited Canada.

2006: Close to 400 rioting Edmonton Oilers fans were arrested following a playoff game victory.

Gemini
You are a tenacious person and a progressive thinker; however, when frustrated, you may lash out at others.
5, 7, 8

#1 Song
1971: "It's Too Late/I Feel the Earth Move" by Carole King

Birth Friends Forever
Venus Williams, tennis player, 1980
Jennifer Irwin, Canadian actress (*Superstar*), 1975
Stéphane Fiset, Canadian hockey player, 1970
Will Forte, comedian (*SNL*), 1970
Greg Kinnear, actor (*As Good As It Gets*), 1963
Sam Hamad, Canadian politician, 1958
Joe Piscopo, comedian (*SNL*), 1951
Barry Manilow, musician, 1943
George Hees, Canadian politician, 1910
Ralph E. Winters, Canadian film editor, 1909
Tommy Burns, Canadian boxer, 1881

Daily Oddity
Canadian boxer Tommy Burns was the first fighter to agree to fight an African American boxer, Jack Johnson, in a heavyweight championship bout; he lost.

JUNE 18
196 days until next year

In a Days
Don't tell the wasps and ants that today is "Picnic Day."
Buy everything you want today and return it tomorrow. It's "National Splurge Day."

In the News

1812: America declared war on Britain and its colony, Canada, starting the War of 1812.

1873: Women's rights activist, Susan B. Anthony, was fined $100 for her attempt to vote in the 1872 presidential election.

1923: The first Checker Taxi cab hit the streets.

1980: *The Blues Brothers*, co-starring Canadian comedian Dan Ackroyd, premiered.

1983: Astronaut Sally Ride became the first American woman in space while on a mission to deploy Canada's *Anik C2* communications satellite into orbit.

1985: Bryan Adams enjoyed his 2nd week at number one with his song "Heaven."

1988: A salmon weighing 4.25 kg was caught in Okanagan Lake, BC.

2008: A 6th severed foot inside a running shoe washed up off the coast of BC. It later turned out to be a hoax.

Gemini
You are a positive and adventurous individual who may be overly protective of your emotions.
5, 9, 10

#1 Song
1975: "Love Will Keep Us Together" by The Captain & Tennille

Birth Friends Forever

Martin St. Louis, Canadian hockey player, 1975

Kurt Browning, Canadian figure skater, 1966

Isabella Rossellini, actress (*Blue Velvet*), 1952

Carol Kane, actress (*Scrooged*), 1952

Paul McCartney, musician (The Beatles), 1942

Roger Ebert, film critic, 1942

Jean-Claude Germain, Canadian historian, 1939

Arthur Tremblay, Canadian politician, 1917

Richard Boone, actor (*Have Gun—Will Travel*), 1917

Stanley Knowles, Canadian politician, 1908

Daily Oddity
Twenty-five percent of the U.S. once belonged to Mexico.

JUNE 19
195 days until next year

In a Days
He's as funny as he is obese, so celebrate "Garfield the Cat Day."
It's the mutant offspring of June 19. It's "Juneteenth."
Sorry, strolling. It's "World Sauntering Day."

In the News
1793: Upper Canada prohibited the importation of slaves.

1866: After extinguishing a fire on a passenger train containing 95 barrels of gunpowder, Timothy O'Hea became the first person awarded the Victoria Cross while in Canada.

1903: Regina, SK, was incorporated as a city.

1910: The first Father's Day was celebrated in Spokane, WA.

1914: A dust explosion in Hillcrest, AB, killed 189 miners.

1972: The Canadian Airline Pilots Association went on strike for better airport security.

1973: Gordie Howe joined the Houston Aeros, the same team his sons, Mark and Marty, were on.

1973: Karen Kain and Frank Augustyn of the National Ballet of Canada won first prize for duet ensemble at the Moscow International Ballet Competition.

2006: Construction began on the Svalbard Global Seed Bank—an international seed gene bank.

Gemini
You are strong-willed, with a real sense of purpose; however, you can be stubborn.
5, 9, 10

#1 Song
1931: "(There Ought to Be a) Moonlight Saving Time" by Guy Lombardo

Birth Friends Forever
Paul Dano, actor (*There Will Be Blood*), 1984

Lauren Lee Smith, Canadian actress (*CSI: Crime Scene Investigation*), 1980

Tyson Dux, Canadian wrestler, 1978

Paula Abdul, singer and choreographer, 1962

Kathleen Turner, actress (*Body Heat*), 1954

Salman Rushdie, author (*The Satanic Verses*), 1947

Lou Gehrig, baseball player, 1903

Guy Lombardo, Canadian bandleader, 1902

Cornelius Krieghoff, Canadian painter, 1815

Daily Oddity
In ancient Egypt, when a cat died, its owners would shave their eyebrows as a sign of respect.

JUNE 20
194 days until next year

In a Days
On "Toad Hollow Day of Thank You," you must write a letter to everyone who has helped you in your life; Jack Daniels and Johnny Walker do not count. Whoa, dude, it's "International Surfing Day."

In the News

1837: Queen Victoria succeeded to the British throne.

1840: Samuel Morse patented the telegraph.

1877: A fire in Saint John, NB, wiped out the business district and over 1600 homes.

1877: The University of Manitoba opened.

1908: *Anne of Green Gables* was first published.

1948: *Toast of the Town*, which later became *The Ed Sullivan Show*, made its television debut.

1959: A storm in the Northumberland Strait (New Brunswick) sank 22 boats, drowning 35 fishermen.

1959: A hurricane in Canada's Gulf of St. Lawrence killed 35 people.

1984: Four miners were killed in a cave-in in Sudbury, ON.

2008: *Anne of Green Gables* celebrated its 100th birthday.

Gemini
You are a receptive and intelligent person who tends to lose interest easily.
2, 5, 9

#1 Song
1967: "Groovin'" by The Young Rascals

Birth Friends Forever
Lani Billard, Canadian actress (*Ready or Not*), 1979

Robert Rodriguez, director (*Sin City*), 1968

Nicole Kidman, actress (*Moulin Rouge*), 1967

Lionel Richie, musician (The Commodores), 1949

Anne Murray, Canadian singer, 1945

Brian Wilson, musician (The Beach Boys), 1942

Martin Landau, actor (*Ed Wood*), 1931

Gordon Juckes, Canadian hockey director, 1914

Errol Flynn, actor (*Robin Hood*), 1909

Wilfrid Pelletier, Canadian conductor, 1896

Frank McGill, Canadian athlete, 1894

Daily Oddity
Canadian Tire money is printed on the same material as real money.

JUNE 21
193 days until next year

In a Days
Beat it, spring. It's "Summer Solstice."
Recognize that they've got all the good jobs. It's "Baby Boomer's Recognition Day."
Enjoy some milk to celebrate "Vegan World Day"—wait, no, don't.
Thanks to genetic modification, "Watermelon Seed Spitting Day" is now obsolete.

In the News
- 1813: Canadian heroine Laura Secord left to warn British forces in Canada of an impending attack by the Americans.
- 1887: Queen Victoria celebrated her Golden Jubilee—50 years on the throne.
- 1924: Canadian-born actress Mary Pickford married Douglas Fairbanks Sr.
- 1940: Departing from Vancouver, the *St. Roch* became the first ship to navigate the Northwest Passage west to east; after much hardship, it landed in Halifax 2 years later.
- 1977: A fire in Saint John, NB, claimed the lives of 21 prisoners being held in a city hall jail.
- 1985: *Cocoon*, starring Canadian-born actor Hume Cronyn, opened in theatres.
- 2006: Pluto's 2 moons were named Nix and Hydra.
- 2008: In the quarter-finals of Euro 2008 (soccer), Russia beat the Netherlands 3–1.

Gemini
You are a charming person with a high IQ; however, this may cause you to disregard the opinions of others.
3, 5, 9

#1 Song
1965: "Mr. Tambourine Man" by The Byrds

Birth Friends Forever
Prince William of Wales, British royal, 1982
Yann Danis, Canadian hockey player, 1981
Brandon Flowers, singer (The Killers), 1981
Erica Durance, Canadian actress (*Smallville*), 1978
Anne Carson, Canadian poet, 1950
Joe Flaherty, Canadian actor (*SCTV*), 1941
Michael Ruse, Canadian philosopher, 1940
Jane Russell, actress (*Gentlemen Prefer Blondes*), 1921
Buddy O'Connor, Canadian hockey player, 1916
William Vickrey, Canadian economist, 1914
Jean-Paul Sartre, philosopher, 1905
Norman L. Bowen, Canadian oilman, 1887

Daily Oddity
The image of Laura Secord, found on many chocolate boxes, was used as a marketing tool.

JUNE 22
192 days until next year

In a Days
As long as you don't work with cats, enjoy "Take Your Dog To Work Day." Shave your sporadic patches of body hair. It's "Stupid Guy Thing Day."

In the News

1923: In lieu of prohibition, the Manitoba government decided instead to control of the sale of liquor in the province.

1931: While making her attempt to become the first woman to fly solo across the Atlantic, pilot Ruth Nicholas crashed her plane in Newfoundland.

1968: In Toronto, 3700 blue-collar workers, including garbage collectors, went on strike.

1976: Canada abolished capital punishment.

1983: The Canadian-built Canadarm was first used by NASA to retrieve a satellite in space.

1984: Virgin Airways was launched.

1996: The Canadian Space Agency began its study of sleep in zero gravity.

1991: Governor General Ray Hnatyshyn presented medals to 42 Canadian troops who had served in the Persian Gulf War.

2002: Over 260 people died in a 6.5-magnitude earthquake in Iran.

Cancer
You are a non-materialistic dreamer who is prone to fits of disillusionment.
3, 4, 7

#1 Song
1951: "Too Young" by Nat "King" Cole

Birth Friends Forever
Carson Daly, TV personality, 1973
Kurt Warner, football player, 1971
Mary Lynn Rajskub, actress (*24*), 1971
Steven Page, Canadian musician (Barenaked Ladies), 1970
Amy Brenneman, actress (*Private Practice*), 1964
Dan Brown, author (*The Da Vinci Code*), 1964
John Tenta, Canadian pro wrestler, 1963
Nicholas Lea, Canadian actor (*Once a Thief*), 1962
Cyndi Lauper, singer, 1953
Graham Greene, Canadian actor (*Dances with Wolves*), 1952
Gary Moffet, Canadian musician (April Wine), 1949
Meryl Streep, actress (*Mama Mia*), 1949
Ed Bradley, journalist (*60 Minutes*), 1941
Kris Kristofferson, actor (*Blade*), 1936
John Dillinger, bank robber, 1903
George Vancouver, British explorer, 1757

Daily Oddity
In Ireland, "puck" means to hit someone.

JUNE 23
191 days until next year

In a Days
Close the door. It's "Let It Go Day."
Carve a nude sculpture to celebrate "Marble Day."

In the News
1611: Henry Hudson was set adrift by a mutinous crew in Hudson Bay; he was never seen again.

1713: Acadians were given one year to pledge allegiance to the Commonwealth or leave Canada.

1817: The Bank of Montréal was founded.

1887: Banff National Park in Alberta became Canada's first national park.

1925: Mountaineers first climbed Mount Logan, Canada's highest peak.

1974: Canadian singer Gordon Lightfoot held the number one position on the pop charts for the 2nd week in a row with his song "Sundown."

1975: During a show in Vancouver, singer Alice Cooper fell off the stage, breaking six ribs.

1985: A terrorist bomb aboard an Air India flight departing from Montréal exploded off the coast of Ireland; 329 people died, including the most Canadians ever killed in a commercial flight.

1991: Moldova gained its independence from the Soviet Union.

Cancer
You are an enthusiastic person who is always at the centre of attention, yet you suffer from restlessness.
3, 5, 7

#1 Song
1974: "Sundown" by Gordon Lightfoot

Birth Friends Forever
Duffy, singer, 1984
Brooks Laich, Canadian hockey player, 1983
Emmanuelle Vaugier, Canadian actress (*Smallville*), 1976
Selma Blair, actress (*Hellboy*), 1972
Félix Potvin, Canadian hockey player, 1971
Randy Jackson, *American Idol* judge, 1956
Pierre Corbeil, Canadian politician, 1955
Douglas C. Lord, Canadian businessman, 1950
Myles Goodwyn, Canadian musician (April Wine), 1948
Bob Fosse, choreographer, 1927
Hal Laycoe, Canadian hockey player, 1922
David Lewis, Canadian politician, 1909

Daily Oddity
Cajun people are descendants of Acadians. The word "Cajun" is actually a mispronunciation of the word "Acadian."

JUNE 24
190 days until next year

In a Days

See, touch, taste, smell and hear everything you can. It's "Celebration of the Senses Day."

If you live in Québec, it's "St. Jean Baptiste Day."

If you've reproduced, it's "Descendants Day."

Don't invite any beavers to help you celebrate "Log Cabin Day."

In the News

1497: John Cabot visited Newfoundland.

1509: Henry VIII and Catherine of Aragon were crowned king and queen of England.

1901: The first exhibition to feature Pablo Picasso's work opened.

1916: Canadian-born actress Mary Pickford became the first star to receive a million-dollar film deal.

1918: Canada's first airmail service began.

1949: *Hopalong Cassidy* became the first TV western.

1973: A Canadian teenager set a world record after she limboed under a flaming pole 16.5 cm off the ground.

1990: The day before the season opener, the Montréal Allouettes football club folded.

2004: New York declared capital punishment unconstitutional.

Cancer

You are an objective communicator; however, you have a hard time taking criticism.
3, 6, 7

#1 Song

2002: "Hot in Here" by Nelly

Birth Friends Forever

Michael Del Zotto, Canadian hockey player, 1990

Minka Kelly, actress (*Friday Night Lights*), 1980

Liane Balaban, Canadian actress (*New Waterford Girl*), 1980

Mindy Kaling, actress (*The Office*), 1979

Bernie Nicholls, Canadian hockey player, 1961

Jean Charest, premier of Québec, 1958

Nancy Allen, actress (*RoboCop*), 1950

Mick Fleetwood, musician (Fleetwood Mac), 1947

Peter Weller, actor (*RoboCop*), 1947

Wayne Cashman, Canadian hockey player, 1945

Jeff Beck, musician (The Yardbirds), 1944

Athanase David, Canadian politician, 1882

Daily Oddity

On June 24, 1374, an outbreak of St. John's Dance in Germany caused a number of citizens to dance, gyrate and twitch uncontrollably until they passed out from exhaustion.

JUNE 25
189 days until next year

In a Days
If you're allergic to cats, seafood or just ugly creatures, you'll want to avoid "National Catfish Day."

Forget everything you've learned over the last 10 months, because it's the last week of school.

In the News

1647: The first horses arrived in Canada, a gift from King Louis XIV of France.

1858: BC's first newspaper, *The Victoria Gazette*, was published.

1947: *The Diary of Anne Frank* was first published.

1950: The Korean War began.

1968: Lincoln Alexander became the first African Canadian elected to the House of Commons.

1968: Pierre Elliott Trudeau won the 28th federal general election.

1969: Winnipeg's The Guess Who received a gold record for their hit "These Eyes."

1982: The Greek military abolished the head-shaving requirement for new recruits.

1993: Kim Campbell became Canada's first female prime minister.

2007: While attempting to retrieve his ball from a water hazard, a golfer in Florida was grabbed by an alligator.

Cancer
You are a sensitive and profound thinker who is sometimes on the defensive.
3, 7, 25

#1 Song
1949: "Riders in the Sky" by Vaughn Monroe

Birth Friends Forever
Linda Cardellini, actress (*ER*), 1975

Nisha Ganatra, Canadian director (*Chutney Popcorn*), 1974

Mike Kroeger, Canadian musician (Nickelback), 1972

Yann Martel, Canadian author (*Life of Pi*), 1963

Doug Gilmour, Canadian hockey player, 1963

Roméo Dallaire, Canadian senator, 1946

Carly Simon, singer, 1945

Robert Charlebois, Canadian singer, 1944

Michel Tremblay, Canadian playwright, 1942

Sidney Lumet, director (*Serpico*), 1924

Celia Franca, Canadian ballet dancer, 1921

George Orwell, author (*1984*), 1903

Daily Oddity
The two official animals of Canada are the beaver and the Canadian Horse—a gift from the king of France.

JUNE 26
188 days until next year

In a Days
You're pudding me on—it can't be "National Chocolate Pudding Day."
If you love your own opinion, you should celebrate "National Columnists Day."

In the News
1284: The Pied Piper lured 130 children away from the town of Hamelin, Germany.

1483: Richard III became king of England.

1945: Canada and 50 other nations established the United Nations.

1959: The Saint Lawrence Seaway opened.

1961: The Hockey Hall of Fame opened in Toronto.

1970: Canada's voting age was lowered from 21 to 18.

1974: The first Universal Product Code (UPC) was scanned.

1976: The CN Tower in Toronto opened.

1982: Brock Allison reached Halifax a month and 26 days after embarking on a cross-country unicycle trip.

1989: Canadian coins were minted with a new portrait of Queen Elizabeth.

2002: The G8 world leaders met at Kananaskis in Alberta.

Cancer
You are a nurturing and academic individual who can sometimes become overburdened.
3, 7, 8

#1 Song
1935: "She's a Latin from Manhattan" by Victor Young

Birth Friends Forever
Jason Schwartzman, actor (*Rushmore*), 1980

Ed Jovanovski, Canadian hockey player, 1976

Derek Jeter, baseball player, 1974

Chris O'Donnell, actor (*Batman & Robin*), 1970

Mark McKinney, Canadian actor (*The Kids in the Hall*), 1959

Philippe Couillard, Canadian politician, 1957

Patty Smyth, singer, 1957

Chris Isaak, singer, 1956

Mick Jones, musician (The Clash), 1955

Frank Scott Hogg, Canadian astronomer, 1904

George Hainsworth, Canadian hockey player, 1895

Robert Laird Borden, Canadian prime minister, 1854

Daily Oddity
The first UPC code scanned was on a Wrigley's chewing-gum package.

JUNE 27
187 days until next year

In a Days
Make yourself feel older just for fun. It's "Happy Birthday To You Day." Even though she was a suspected communist, please celebrate "Helen Keller Day." To a woman, every day is "Decide to Be Married Day."

In the News

1759: British General James Wolfe began his siege on Québec.

1854: A Canadian chemist patented a process to distill kerosene from petroleum.

1898: Canadian Joshua Slocum became the first person to solo circumnavigate the globe.

1954: The first nuclear power station opened near Moscow in Russia.

1969: The Stonewall Riots, the start of the gay rights movement, began.

1974: Richard Nixon visited the USSR.

1984: Pierre Trudeau won the Albert Einstein Peace Prize.

1985: Route 66 ceased to be an U.S. highway.

1986: Wayne Gretzky won his 7th Hart (MVP) Trophy.

1995: The RCMP gave Disney exclusive rights to their image; Disney pays them royalties and prevents any copyright infringement.

2008: Bill Gates retired as the chairman of Microsoft.

Cancer
You are a loyal and creative person who can become stagnant at times.
3, 7, 10

#1 Song
1947: "Chi-Baba Chi-Baba (My Bambino Go to Sleep)" by Perry Como

Birth Friends Forever

Aselin Debison, Canadian singer, 1990

Sarah Evanetz, Canadian swimmer, 1975

Tobey Maguire, actor (*Spider-Man*), 1975

J.J. Abrams, producer (*Lost*), 1966

Margo Timmins, Canadian singer (Cowboy Junkies), 1961

Vera Wang, fashion designer, 1949

Frank Mills, Canadian composer, 1942

Charles Bronfman, Canadian industrialist, 1931

Bob "Captain Kangaroo" Keeshan, TV personality, 1927

Helen Keller, deaf and blind activist, 1880

Daily Oddity
Disney animators gave Tinker Bell Marilyn Monroe's measurements.

JUNE 28
186 days until next year

In a Days
Milk a giant blue ox. It's "Paul Bunyan Day."

June 28 is the only date of the year that the month (6) and the day (28) are different perfect numbers.

In the News

1838: Queen Victoria was crowned.

1886: Canada's first transcontinental passenger train departed from Montréal and arrived in BC on July 4.

1914: Franz Ferdinand, archduke of Austria, was assassinated.

1930: A boat in the St. Lawrence River carrying dynamite was struck by lightning; 31 crewmembers died when it exploded.

1975: Rod Serling, creator of *The Twilight Zone*, died.

1981: Canadian hero Terry Fox lost his battle with cancer.

1989: One hundred and thirty Québec nuns got food poisoning from tapioca.

2005: A bill legalizing same-sex marriage in Canada was passed in the House of Commons.

2006: Montenegro was admitted to the UN.

Cancer
You are an artist and a great conversationalist; however, you are easily discouraged.
3, 7, 11

#1 Song
1979: "Ring My Bell" by Anita Ward

Birth Friends Forever

Jasmine Richards, Canadian actress (*Camp Rock*), 1990

Simon Larose, Canadian tennis player, 1978

Gil Bellows, Canadian actor (*Ally McBeal*), 1967

John Cusack, actor (*Say Anything*), 1966

Mary Stuart Masterson, actress (*Benny & Joon*), 1966

John Elway, football player, 1960

Kathy Bates, actress (*Misery*), 1948

Gilda Radner, comedienne (*SNL*), 1946

George Knudson, Canadian golfer, 1937

Pat Morita, actor (*Karate Kid*), 1932

Mel Brooks, director (*Blazing Saddles*), 1926

Daily Oddity
Terry Fox came second in "The Greatest Canadians" vote in 2004.

JUNE 29
185 days until next year

In a Days
Sorry, thighs and breasts. It's "Chicken Wings Day."
Say "gang sign." It's "Camera Day."

In the News

1534: Jacques Cartier discovered Prince Edward Island.

1613: London's Globe Theatre burned to the ground.

1864: Ninety-nine people near St-Hilaire, Québec, were killed in Canada's worst railway disaster.

1871: England gave Canada the right to create new provinces.

1909: Alex Decoteau became the first Aboriginal to join the RCMP.

1922: France transferred ownership of 100 hectares at Vimy Ridge to Canada as thanks for their help during WWI.

1930: Jesuit missionary Jean de Brébeuf and 7 other priests became the first North American saints.

1937: Joseph-Armand Bombardier patented his B7 snowmobile.

1974: While on tour in Canada, Soviet ballet dancer Mikhail Baryshnikov defected.

2007: Apple's iPhone was released.

2008: The world's first pregnant man gave birth to a girl.

Cancer
You are a warm-hearted and sharp individual who tends to not listen to the opinions of others.
3, 7, 11

#1 Song
1989: "Baby Don't Forget My Number" by Milli Vanilli

Birth Friends Forever

Matthew Good, Canadian musician, 1971

Claude Béchard, Canadian politician, 1969

Theoren Fleury, Canadian hockey player, 1968

Murray Foster, Canadian musician, 1967

John Part, Canadian darts player, 1966

Richard Lewis, comedian, 1947

Gary Busey, actor (*The Buddy Holly Story*), 1944

Slim Pickens, actor (*Dr. Strangelove*), 1919

Fulgence Charpentier, Canadian journalist, 1897

Daily Oddity
Sasquatch means "wild man" in Salish.

JUNE 30
184 days until next year

In a Days
As long as it isn't heading directly for Earth, feel free to celebrate "Meteor Day."

In the News

1812: Upper Canada gave U.S. citizens 14 days to leave.

1858: The first Chinese colonists settled in Victoria, BC.

1859: French acrobat Jean Francois Gravelet, better known as the Great Blondin, crossed Niagara Falls on a tightrope.

1912: Canada's deadliest tornado, rated F4 with 416-km winds, swept through Regina, killing 28 people.

1953: The first Chevrolet Corvette was manufactured.

1960: The John George Diefenbaker International Airport opened in Ottawa.

1973: Canada's first National Lesbian Conference was held.

1987: The Canadian Mint introduced the $1 "loonie."

1992: Canadian peacekeepers headed to Sarajevo, bringing food and medicine with them.

2003: Canada's first space telescope was launched.

Cancer
You are charming and witty; however, you are also slightly demanding.
3, 7, 30

#1 Song
2008: "I Kissed a Girl" by Katy Perry

Birth Friends Forever

Michael Phelps, Olympic gold-medal swimmer, 1985

Matt Kirk, Canadian football player, 1981

Monica Potter, actress (*Boston Legal*), 1971

Mike Tyson, boxer, 1966

Steve Duchesne, Canadian hockey player, 1965

Vincent D'Onofrio, actor (*Law & Order: Criminal Intent*), 1959

Murray McLauchlan, Canadian singer, 1948

Ron Harris, Canadian hockey player, 1942

Harry Blackstone Jr., magician, 1934

Orval Tessier, Canadian hockey player, 1933

Lena Horne, singer, 1917

Daily Oddity
Fortune cookies are a North American invention.

JULY 1
183 days until next year

In a Days
If you're a citizen of the best country in the world, celebrate "Canada Day."

If you're reading a book about every day of the year, you're almost finished. It's "Second Half of the Year Day."

If you're a real Canadian, you would celebrate "Postal Code Day" and not "Zip Code Day."

In the News
1858: Canada minted its first one-cent, five-cent, 10-cent and 20-cent coins.

1867: The BNA Act brought the Dominion of Canada into existence.

1873: Prince Edward Island entered the Dominion of Canada

1878: Canada joined the Universal Postal Union.

1908: SOS became the international signal for distress.

1921: The Communist Party of China was created.

1966: Canadian television began broadcasting in colour.

1967: Canada celebrated 100 years as a country.

1980: "O Canada" became Canada's national anthem.

2001: Sixteen people were arrested following a Canada Day riot on Edmonton's Whyte Avenue.

Cancer
You are a determined individual who is full of vigour; however, you are prone to martyrdom.

3, 7, 11

#1 Song
1984: "When Doves Cry" by Prince

Birth Friends Forever
Jarome Iginla, Canadian hockey player, 1977

Liv Tyler, actress (*The Lord of the Rings*), 1977

Missy Elliott, rapper, 1971

Pamela Anderson, Canadian actress (*VIP*), 1967

Michelle Wright, Canadian country singer, 1961

Carl Lewis, athlete, 1961

Diana, Princess of Wales, 1961

Dan Aykroyd, Canadian actor (*SNL*), 1952

Rod Gilbert, Canadian hockey player, 1941

Estée Lauder, cosmetics entrepreneur, 1906

Thomas A. Dorsey, composer, 1899

William Grant Stairs, Canadian explorer, 1863

Daily Oddity
July 1 is the biggest moving day of the year.

JULY 2
182 days until next year

In a Days
I sure wish I could remember what day it is. Oh, yeah—it's "I Forgot Day." If you can understand this book, you should celebrate "National Literacy Day."

In the News
1578: Explorer Martin Frobisher discovered Baffin Island.

1826: The Supreme Court of Newfoundland was founded.

1872: Canada and the U.S. began sharing weather reports via telegraph.

1884: Thirty-one people died in a train accident near Toronto.

1900: The first Zeppelin took flight.

1908: The Royal Mint of Canada was founded.

1937: Pilot Amelia Earhart was last heard from while attempting to fly around the world.

1962: The first Wal-Mart opened.

2002: Adventurer Steve Fossett became the first person to fly in a balloon nonstop around the world.

2004: A Live 8 concert took place in Barrie, ON.

Cancer
You are a sensitive person who is a champion of the little guy; however, you may suffer from feelings of insecurity.
2, 3, 7

#1 Song
1966: "Strangers in the Night" by Frank Sinatra

Birth Friends Forever
Lindsay Lohan, actress (*Mean Girls*), 1986

Ashley Tisdale, actress (*High School Musical 3*), 1985

Joe Thornton, Canadian hockey player, 1979

Evelyn Lau, Canadian author (*Runaway*), 1971

Scotty 2 Hotty, pro wrestler, 1970

Bret "The Hitman" Hart, Canadian pro wrestler, 1957

Jerry Hall, model, 1956

Kevin Michael Grace, Canadian journalist, 1955

Robert Paquette, Canadian singer, 1949

Richard Petty, racecar driver, 1937

Dave Thomas, founder of Wendy's, 1932

Charles Tupper, 6th prime minister of Canada, 1821

Daily Oddity
July 2 is the midway point of every year, including leap years.

JULY 3
181 days until next year

In a Days
If you're a vampire, you should celebrate "Stay Out of the Sun Day" every day. Thank Bloody Mary for not killing you. It's "Compliment Your Mirror Day."

In the News

1608: Samuel de Champlain founded Québec City.

1838: The Toronto Examiner newspaper was founded.

1844: The last great auk (a penguin relative) was killed.

1886: The linotype machine replaced typesetting.

1893: Kamloops, BC, was incorporated as a city.

1901: The first automobile was driven in Calgary.

1944: Temperatures in Goose Bay, NL, hit 37.8°C, the hottest on record.

1990: Fifty thousand fans attended the Toronto Blue Jays 44th home game.

1991: A teenager was sentence to 16 months detention for setting a $30 million tire fire in Hagersville, ON, in 1990.

1992: Thirty-four Mohawks were acquitted by a jury for their part in the Oka standoff in 1990.

2006: An asteroid flew a mere 432,308 km from Earth.

Cancer
You are an analytical and intelligent person who tends to isolate yourself from others at times.
3, 7, 21

#1 Song
1992: "Baby Got Back" by Sir Mix-a-Lot

Birth Friends Forever

Wade Belak, Canadian hockey player, 1976

Kevin Hearn, Canadian musician (Barenaked Ladies), 1969

Yeardley Smith, voice actress (Lisa, *The Simpsons*), 1964

Tom Cruise, actor (*Mission Impossible*), 1962

Montel Williams, talk-show host, 1959

Matthew Fraser, Canadian journalist, 1958

Dave Barry, humorist, 1947

Ace Bailey, Canadian hockey player, 1903

Franz Kafka, author (*The Metamorphosis*), 1883

Richard Bedford Bennett, Canadian prime minister, 1870

King Louis XI, French monarch, 1423

Daily Oddity
Lemons have more sugar than strawberries.

JULY 4
180 days until next year

In a Days

If you think that all Canadians live in igloos, you should celebrate "Independence Day."

Nothing says "21st century" like "Boom Box Day."

Put down the mutton and celebrate "Independence from Meat Day."

In the News

1634: The territory of Trois-Rivières, which later became the province of Québec, was founded.

1865: Lewis Carroll's *Alice's Adventures in Wonderland* was first published.

1886: The first Canadian transcontinental train arrived in Port Moody, BC.

1893: A tug-of-war team from Ontario won the world championship at the Chicago World's Fair.

1939: The lowest July temperature in Canada, −12°C, was reached at Fort Ross, NWT.

1974: Two hundred and fifty icebergs were spotted off the eastern shore of Newfoundland.

1997: NASA's *Pathfinder* space probe landed on Mars.

2008: Canadian serial killer Karla Homolka was released from prison.

2008: The Fallen Four Memorial Site, honouring the RCMP officers who lost their lives in 2005, opened in Mayerthorpe, AB.

Cancer

You are an outgoing and loyal individual; however, you have a hard time listening to the opinions of others.
3, 4, 7

#1 Song

1955: "Rock Around the Clock" by Bill Haley & His Comets

Birth Friends Forever

Andy Creeggan, Canadian musician (Barenaked Ladies), 1971

Koko, the sign-language-using gorilla, 1971

Andy Walker, Canadian television personality, 1967

David Jensen, Canadian disc jockey, 1950

Neil Simon, playwright (*The Odd Couple*), 1927

Leona Helmsley, the "Queen of Mean," 1920

Ann Landers, advice columnist, 1918

Meyer Lansky, gangster, 1902

Louis B. Mayer, Canadian film producer, 1882

Ulysses S. Grant III, Civil War soldier, 1881

Nathaniel Hawthorne, author (*The Scarlet Letter*), 1804

Daily Oddity

Between 1900 and 1920, tug-of-war was an Olympic sport.

JULY 5
179 days until next year

In a Days
Today may be "Cherry Pit Spitting Day," but someone needs to tell those cherry pits that spitting is rude.

In the News

1610: Thirty-nine colonists set sail from Bristol, England, for Newfoundland.

1865: The Salvation Army was founded.

1930: George Stathakis died when he plunged over Niagara Falls in a barrel.

1937: Spam, the luncheon meat, was introduced.

1937: It was 45°C in Midale, SK.

1946: The bikini was unveiled.

1970: An Air Canada plane crashed while landing in Los Angeles; 109 passengers were killed.

1975: Canadian rock group Bachman-Turner Overdrive peaked at number 2 with their single "Hey You."

1975: Arthur Ashe became the first African American to win the singles title at Wimbledon.

1996: Dolly the sheep was cloned.

1997: Canadian singer Sarah McLachlan held the first Lilith Fair—an all-female music festival.

2003: The World Health Organization declared the SARS outbreak contained.

Cancer
You are a charming visionary who tends to gravitate towards unstable relationships.
3, 5, 7

#1 Song
1995: "Waterfalls" by TLC

Birth Friends Forever

Jesse Crain, Canadian baseball player, 1981

Eva Green, French actress (*Casino Royale*), 1980

RZA, rapper, 1969

Nardwuar the Human Serviette, Canadian marvel, 1968

Edie Falco, actress (*The Sopranos*), 1963

Brad Loree, Canadian stuntman, 1960

Bill Watterson, cartoonist (*Calvin and Hobbes*), 1958

Doug Wilson, Canadian hockey player, 1957

Huey Lewis, musician, 1950

Robbie Robertson, Canadian musician, 1944

Niels Jannasch, Canadian curator, 1924

P.T. Barnum, circus ringmaster, 1810

Daily Oddity
Five people have died going over Niagara Falls in a barrel.

JULY 6
178 days until next year

In a Days
Hope you like Big Gulps and nachos from 7-Eleven. It's "Take your Webmaster to Lunch Day."

In the News

1892: A fire, which burned for 3 days, destroyed much of St. John's, Newfoundland.

1906: The Lord's Day Observance Act was passed, banning all work, sports and entertainment on Sundays.

1921: It was 40°C in Québec—the province's warmest day ever.

1924: Winnipeg-born spy William Stephenson, the inspiration for James Bond, sent the first photo via radio.

1933: The first MLB All-Star Game was held.

1935: The Canadian-designed Fairchild 82A bush plane made its first flight.

1957: John Lennon met Paul McCartney.

1975: A hailstone weighing 249 g fell near Wetaskiwin, AB.

1994: CFL expansion team the Shreveport Pirates played their first CFL game.

2002: Smoke from a forest fire just south of Québec blocked out the sky.

Cancer
You are a driven and optimistic individual who may become too obsessed with attaining your goals.
3, 6, 25

#1 Song
1976: "Afternoon Delight" by The Starland Vocal Band

Birth Friends Forever

Gregory Smith, Canadian actor (*Small Soldiers*), 1983

50 Cent, rapper, 1975

Ron Duguay, Canadian hockey player, 1957

Geoffrey Rush, actor (*Shine*), 1951

John Byrne, Canadian comic book artist (*X-Men*), 1950

Brad Park, Canadian hockey player, 1948

Jean-Pierre Blackburn, Canadian politician, 1948

George W. Bush, U.S. president, 1946

Sylvester Stallone, actor (*Rambo*), 1946

Bill Haley, musician, 1925

Nancy Reagan, U.S. first lady, 1921

George Stanley, designer of the Canadian flag, 1907

Daily Oddity
The Baltimore Stallions were the first CFL expansion team to win the Grey Cup.

JULY 7
177 days until next year

In a Days

Oh, fudge, it's "Chocolate Day."

Even if you only have a son, throw a dress on him and enjoy "Father-Daughter Take a Walk Day."

In the News

1534: Jacques Cartier traded furs with the Mi'kmaq tribe in the first known exchange between Europeans and Natives of the Gulf of St. Lawrence.

1928: Sliced bread was sold for the first time.

1930: Construction began on Hoover Dam.

1938: July 5 to 17 was the worst heat wave in Canadian history; 780 people died.

1946: Howard Hughes' spy plane prototype crash-landed in Beverly Hills.

1947: The supposed UFO crash at Roswell, NM, occurred.

1954: Rainbow Stage, Canada's longest-running outdoor theatre, opened in Winnipeg.

1969: The Official Languages Act was passed, declaring French and English as Canada's official languages.

2007: The worldwide eco-concert Live Earth took place.

Cancer

You are an ambitious and goal-orientated individual who at times may find yourself disillusioned.

3, 7, 25

#1 Song

1959: "Lonely Boy" by Paul Anka

Birth Friends Forever

Michelle Kwan, figure skater, 1980

Patrick Lalime, Canadian hockey player, 1974

Nathalie Simard, Canadian singer, 1969

Joe Sakic, Canadian hockey player, 1969

Cree Summer, Canadian voice actress (*Tiny Toons*), 1969

Jorja Fox, actress (*CSI: Crime Scene Investigation*), 1968

Paula Devicq, Canadian actress (*Party of Five*), 1965

Jean Leclerc, Canadian actor (*All My Children*), 1948

Joel Siegel, film critic, 1943

Ringo Starr, drummer (The Beatles), 1940

Satchel Paige, baseball player, 1906

Daily Oddity

The Canadian government directs all UFO sightings to Ufology Research in Manitoba.

JULY 8
176 days until next year

In a Days
If you are a con artist, flim-flam man, shady Pete, bunko man or just a cheat, you should celebrate the "Annual Soapy Smith Wake," named for Alaska's most prominent con man.

In the News
1874: The Mounties began their march west.

1892: The Great Fire of 1892 broke out in St. John's, NL.

1906: Despite opposition from the Church, streetcars in Winnipeg began running on Sundays.

1934: The Vancouver Symphony gave its first performance.

1943: Harry Oakes, a Canadian millionaire, was discovered burned and beaten in his own home; his murder remains a mystery.

1981: The first Ontario Games for the Physically Disabled opened in Burlington.

1987: Statistics Canada showed that more than half of Canada's population was over the age of 30.

2000: Stockwell Day was elected the first leader of the Canadian Alliance Party.

2003: British Columbia permitted same-sex marriage.

Cancer
You are a strong-willed and motivated individual who sometimes neglects people for personal projects.
3, 7, 8

#1 Song
1969: "In the Year 2525" by Zager & Evans

Birth Friends Forever
Sophia Bush, actress (*One Tree Hill*), 1982

Kathleen Robertson, Canadian actress (*Beverly Hills, 90210*), 1973

Beck, musician, 1970

Billy Crudup, actor (*The Watchmen*), 1968

Toby Keith, country singer, 1961

Kevin Bacon, actor (*Footloose*), 1958

Terry Puhl, Canadian baseball player, 1956

Anjelica Huston, actress (*The Witches*), 1951

Wolfgang Puck, celebrity chef, 1949

Raffi, Canadian children's entertainer, 1948

Antonio Lamer, Canadian chief justice, 1933

John D. Rockefeller, philanthropist, 1839

Daily Oddity
Honey will never go bad.

JULY 9
175 days until next year

In a Days
If you are diabetic, you'd better bring along some extra insulin because today is "Sugar Cookie Day."

In the News

1793: Upper Canada passed the Act Against Slavery, which prohibited the importation of slaves into Lower Canada.

1843: The first iron steamship built in Canada, the *Prince Albert*, was launched.

1923: The first Chuckwagon Race was held at the Calgary Stampede.

1944: Canadian forces captured Caen, France, during the Battle of Normandy.

1958: The largest wave in history, 524 m high, struck the Alaskan fjord Lituya Bay.

1960: Seven-year-old Roger Woodward survived the 49 m plunge over Horseshoe Falls at Niagara Falls.

1991: Over 400 residents of St. Lazare, MB, were forced to flee their homes when a train carrying corrosive acetic anhydride (an acid that releases toxic fumes) derailed.

2003: The Canadian government made the decision to allow the use of marijuana for medicinal purposes.

Cancer
You are an organized and sensitive individual who can become frustrated when things don't go as planned.
3, 7, 9

#1 Song
2006: "Promiscuous" by Nelly Furtado, featuring Timbaland

Birth Friends Forever

Jacob Hoggard, Canadian singer (Hedley), 1984

Maggie Ma, Canadian actress (*Final Destination 3*), 1982

Jack White, musician (The White Stripes), 1975

Courtney Love, musician (Hole), 1964

Tom Hanks, actor (*Forrest Gump*), 1956

Jimmy Smits, actor (*NYPD Blue*), 1955

Margie Gillis, Canadian choreographer, 1953

Chris Cooper, actor (*Adaptation*), 1951

O.J. Simpson, football player, 1947

Red Kelly, Canadian hockey player, 1927

Clarence Campbell, Canadian hockey executive, 1905

Daily Oddity
Roger Woodward was the first person to go over Horseshoe Falls by accident and live.

JULY 10
174 days until next year

In a Days
If today is "Don't Step on a Bee Day," then what are you allowed to step on?

In the News

- **988:** The city of Dublin, Ireland, was founded.
- **1789:** Canadian explorer Alexander Mackenzie reached the Mackenzie Delta.
- **1913:** The temperature in Death Valley, CA, reached 56.7°C.
- **1920:** New Brunswick voted for the prohibition of alcohol.
- **1938:** Howard Hughes flew around the world in 91 hours, setting a new world record.
- **1946:** The first Canadian drive-in opened in Stony Creek, ON.
- **1987:** Winnipeg bandleader Jimmy King (Jimmy King Orchestra and the Golden Boy Brass) died at the age of 67.
- **1991:** Grace MacInnis, BC's first female MP, died at the age of 85.
- **2002:** Canadian Kenneth Thomson purchased Rubens' painting *The Massacre of the Innocents* for $76.2 million USD.

Cancer
You are an analytical visionary who sometimes spends too much time being a bystander instead of a participant.
3, 7, 10

#1 Song
1990: "Step by Step" by New Kids on the Block

Birth Friends Forever

Jessica Simpson, singer, 1980

Adam Foote, Canadian hockey player, 1971

Rik Emmett, Canadian musician (Triumph), 1953

Kim Mitchell, Canadian singer, 1952

Arlo Guthrie, musician, 1947

Alice Munro, Canadian author (*The Bear Came over the Mountain*), 1931

Suzanne Cloutier, Canadian actress (*Othello*), 1927

Fred Gwynne, actor (*The Munsters*), 1926

Harvey Ball, creator of the smiley face, 1921

Saul Bellow, Canadian author (*Mr. Samler's Planet*), 1915

Joe Shuster, Canadian cartoonist (*Superman*), 1914

Nikola Tesla, inventor, 1856

Daily Oddity
In a 1972 *Time* magazine article, when asked how many ballistic missiles were pointed at Toronto, Leonid Brezhnev, the leader of the USSR, responded, "None—I have nothing against the Indians."

JULY 11
173 days until next year

In a Days
Sorry, cow, it's "Chicken Appreciation Day."
Sorry, beach, it's "Swimming Pool Day."
Sorry, chicken, it's "Cow Appreciation Day."
Stand up and be counted. It's "World Population Day."

In the News
1750: A fire destroyed much of Halifax, NS.
1859: Charles Dickens' *A Tale of Two Cities* was published.
1889: Tijuana, Mexico, was founded.
1896: Wilfrid Laurier became Canada's first French-speaking prime minister.
1911: The Canadian Professional Golfers Association was founded.
1914: Babe Ruth made his MLB debut.
1955: The U.S. added "In God We Trust" to their currency.
1971: The Canadian Forces Air Demonstration Team became the Snowbirds.
1990: The Oka Crisis, a violent land dispute between the Mohawk Nation and the town of Oka, Québec, began.
2004: West Edmonton Mall suffered millions of dollars in damage from hail and flooding rain.

Cancer
You are an empathic and resourceful individual; however, you sometimes fall victim to your own vanity.
2, 3, 7

#1 Song
1965: "Satisfaction" by The Rolling Stones

Birth Friends Forever
Tanith Belbin, Canadian ice dancer, 1984
Lil' Kim, rapper, 1975
Michael Rosenbaum, actor (*Smallville*), 1972
Michael Geist, Canadian columnist, 1968
Greg Grunberg, actor (*Heroes*), 1966
Al MacInnis, Canadian hockey player, 1963
Lisa Rinna, actress (*Days of Our Lives*), 1963
Richie Sambora, musician (Bon Jovi), 1959
Bill Barber, Canadian hockey player, 1952
Liona Boyd, Canadian classical guitarist, 1949
Jean-Guy Talbot, Canadian hockey player, 1932
Yul Brynner, actor (*Westworld*), 1920

Daily Oddity
Canadian classical guitarist Liona Boyd dated Pierre Trudeau for eight years.

JULY 12
172 days until next year

In a Days
Grab a wiener and celebrate "Hot Dog Day."

In the News

1543: Henry VIII married his 6th and final wife, Catherine Parr.

1812: The U.S. invaded Canada through Windsor, ON, starting the War of 1812.

1874: The Ontario Agricultural College, later renamed the University of Guelph, was founded.

1876: Signorina Maria Spelterini walked backwards on a tightrope across Niagara Falls.

1912: Montréal transport workers went on strike.

1962: The Rolling Stones played their first concert.

1963: Terrorists in Montréal blew up a statue of Queen Victoria.

1981: Forty-eight thousand woodworkers went on strike in BC.

1998: Canadian painter Serge Lemoyne died.

2006: The terrorist group Hezbollah initiated its Operation True Promise, which began the 2006 Lebanon War.

Cancer
You are a born caregiver and a practical person; however, at times you can become controlling.
3, 4, 7

#1 Song
1961: "Tossin' and Turnin'" by Bobby Lewis

Birth Friends Forever

Melissa O'Neil, Canadian singer, 1988

Topher Grace, actor (*That '70s Show*), 1978

Bruny Surin, Canadian athlete, 1967

Tonya Lee Williams, Canadian actress (*The Young and the Restless*), 1958

Richard Simmons, fitness guru, 1948

Bill Cosby, comedian, 1937

Gordon Pinsent, Canadian actor (*Away From Her*), 1930

Bob Fillion, Canadian hockey player, 1921

Pierre Berton, Canadian journalist, 1920

Ned Hanlan, Canadian rower, 1855

William Osler, Canadian physician, 1849

Julius Caesar, Roman emperor, 100 BC

Daily Oddity
The necktie, originally worn by Roman soldiers, was designed to keep them warm in the winter and allow them to wipe away sweat in the summer.

JULY 13
171 days until next year

In a Days
Don't make out with a woman for 24 hours. It's "Embrace Your Geekness Day." If you love monotony, then you should celebrate "International Puzzle Day." Hide the ammo. It's "Disgruntled Workers Day."

In the News

1923: The original "Hollywoodland" sign was unveiled; "land" was later dropped from the sign in 1949.

1931: Walter Zeller opened Canada's first Zellers store.

1953: Sir Alec Guinness, of *Star Wars* fame, starred in Shakespeare's *Richard III*, which opened the first season of the Stratford Festival in Ontario.

1981: The first issue of Canada's music industry magazine *The Record* premiered.

1982: Canada hosted the first All-Star Game to be played outside the U.S.

1995: Canadian singer Geddy Lee (Rush) sang "O Canada" at the All-Star Game.

2004: For the first time ever, the CRTC refused to renew the licence of a Québec radio station because it broadcast crude material.

2007: Canadian newspaper magnate Conrad Black was found guilty of fraud and obstruction of justice.

Cancer
You are an imaginative and intuitive individual who may suffer from periods of depression.
3, 7, 13

#1 Song
1970: "Mama Told Me (Not to Come)" by Three Dog Night

Birth Friends Forever
Sheldon Souray, Canadian hockey player, 1976

Deborah Cox, Canadian singer, 1974

Cameron Crowe, director (*Almost Famous*), 1957

Claude Giroux, Canadian midget wrestler (Dink the Clown), 1956

Mila Mulroney, wife of former Canadian PM Brian Mulroney, 1953

Cheech Marin, actor (*Up in Smoke*), 1946

Harrison Ford, actor (*Star Wars*), 1942

Patrick Stewart, actor (*Star Trek: TNG*), 1940

Hubert Reeves, Canadian astrophysicist, 1932

Bob Crane, actor (*Hogan's Heroes*), 1928

Ken Mosdell, Canadian hockey player, 1922

Julius Caesar, Roman emperor, 100 BC

Daily Oddity
Julius Caesar was born on either July 12 or 13 by caesarean section. The operation was later named after him.

JULY 14
170 days until next year

In a Days
Hear ye! Hear ye! Today is "International Town Criers Day."
If you are French and like to eat cake, you should celebrate "Bastille Day."

In the News

1775: Spanish explorer Bruno Hecata claimed Vancouver Island for Spain.

1789: During the French Revolution, Parisians stormed the Bastille and freed 7 prisoners.

1881: Billy the Kid was shot and killed by Sheriff Pat Garrett.

1933: All political parties in Germany were outlawed save for the Nazi Party.

1976: Canada abolished capital punishment.

1990: PEI resident Edward "Fast Eddy" McDonald performed 8437 loops with his yo-yo in one hour, setting a new world record.

1990: The world's largest cherry pie was baked in Oliver, BC. It weighed 17,119 kg and was made of 16,692 kg of cherry filling.

2000: Eleven people died in a tornado near Pine Lake, AB.

2002: French President Jacques Chirac was saved from an assassination attempt by a Canadian tourist during Bastille Day celebrations.

Cancer
You are a driven and clear-sighted individual who tends to neglect yourself for others.
3, 5, 7

#1 Song
1950: "Mona Lisa" by Nat "King" Cole

Birth Friends Forever
Chris Steele, Canadian musician (Alexisonfire), 1984

Ellen Reid, Canadian musician (Crash Test Dummies), 1966

Matthew Fox, actor (*Lost*), 1966

Jackie Earle Haley, actor (*Watchmen*), 1961

Robert Bourassa, Canadian politician, 1933

Harry Dean Stanton, actor (*Big Love*), 1926

Ingmar Bergman, director (*The Seventh Seal*), 1918

Gerald Ford, U.S. president, 1913

Northrop Frye, Canadian literary critic, 1912

Woody Guthrie, musician, 1912

Daily Oddity
Canada's first birthday was on a Monday.

JULY 15
169 days until next year

In a Days
Time to fake a communicable disease—it's the start of "Hug Week."

Nobody likes you. Everybody hates you. Why don't you go enjoy "Gummi Worm Day"?

Just to be clear, today is "Baby Food Day," and not "Baby as Food Day."

In the News
1691: Henry Kelsey became the first European to record sightings of buffalo and grizzly bears as he travelled through the Canadian Prairies.

1701: Québec resident Pierre Joubert was born on this day and lived for a record 113 years.

1799: The Rosetta Stone, a tablet used to decipher hieroglyphics, was uncovered in Rosetta, Egypt.

1846: The first issue of *The Hamilton Spectator* was published.

1870: The Manitoba and the Northwest Territories entered the Dominion of Canada.

1997: Fashion designer Gianni Versace was gunned down outside his Miami home.

2000: Canadian baritone Louis Quilico died.

2004: Peterborough, ON, was hit with 235 mm of rain, which blocked up the city's sewer system and flooded the streets.

Cancer
You are an imaginative person and a true humanitarian; however, you are unable to cooperate with others.
3, 7, 15

#1 Song
1973: "Bad, Bad Leroy Brown" by Jim Croce

Birth Friends Forever
Brian Austin Green, actor (*Beverly Hills, 90210*), 1973

Steve Thomas, Canadian hockey player, 1963

Lolita Davidovich, Canadian actress (*Cobb*), 1961

Forest Whitaker, actor (*The Last King of Scotland*), 1961

Barry Melrose, Canadian hockey player, 1956

Marky Ramone, musician (Ramones), 1956

Linda Ronstadt, singer, 1946

Ed Litzenberger, Canadian hockey player, 1932

Clive Cussler, author (*Sahara*), 1931

Richard Garneau, Canadian journalist, 1930

Bertram N. Brockhouse, Canadian physicist, 1918

Rembrandt, artist, 1606

Daily Oddity
In the province of Manitoba, it used to be illegal to sing while in the bathroom.

JULY 16
168 days until next year

In a Days
On "National Personal Chef's Day," does Chef Boyardee count as a personal chef?

In the News

1783: The British Crown gave land grants to American loyalists in Québec.

1860: New Westminster, BC, was incorporated as a city.

1880: Emily Howard Stowe became the first woman given a licence to practice medicine in Canada.

1945: Using uranium mined in Port Hope, ON, U.S. scientists detonated the first atomic bomb in New Mexico.

1970: Manitoba allowed French to be taught in public schools.

1975: A fire in Guelph, ON, destroyed the Bell Organ factory, which was established in 1864.

1979: Saddam Hussein became president of Iraq.

1988: Wayne Gretzky married actress Janet Jones.

1999: John F. Kennedy Jr. and his wife Carolyn Bessette Kennedy died in a plane crash off Martha's Vineyard.

2007: Eight people died in a 6.6-magnitude earthquake in Japan.

Cancer
You are a creative and emotional individual who at times may become embittered with your station in life.
3, 7, 16

#1 Song
1983: "Every Breath You Take" by The Police

Birth Friends Forever

Corey Feldman, actor (*The Lost Boys*), 1971

Will Ferrell, comedian (*SNL*), 1967

Claude Lemieux, Canadian hockey player, 1965

Pierre Roland Renoir, Canadian artist, 1958

Michael Flatley, founder of Lord of the Dance, 1958

Stewart Copeland, drummer (The Police), 1952

Pierre Paradis, Canadian politician, 1950

Ginger Rogers, dancer, 1911

Orville Redenbacher, popcorn magnate, 1907

Carmen Lombardo, Canadian saxophonist and brother of composer Guy Lombardo, 1903

"Shoeless" Joe Jackson, baseball player, 1888

Daily Oddity
Although she became the first woman to openly practice medicine in Canada in 1867, Emily Howard Stowe did not receive her licence until 1880.

JULY 17
167 days until next year

In a Days
Just because today is "Get to Know your Customers Day," doesn't mean that it's also "Get to Like your Customers Day."

In the News

1673: The population of New France (Québec) was 6705.

1762: Catherine II became tsarina of Russia.

1820: John A. Macdonald first arrived in Canada from Scotland.

1886: Saskatchewan's first stagecoach robbery took place.

1897: The Klondike Gold Rush began.

1955: Disneyland opened in Anaheim, CA.

1976: The Olympic Games opened in Montréal.

1978: Canada and the U.S. agreed to allow Canadian prisoners in American jails, and vice-versa, to serve out their sentences in their home country.

1995: Calgary Police Chief Christine Silverberg became the first woman appointed chief of police in any Canadian city.

2007: The worst airplane crash in Brazil's history occurred, killing 199 people.

Cancer
You are an intuitive and tenacious individual who can be manipulative at times.
3, 7, 8

#1 Song
1960: "I'm Sorry" by Brenda Lee

Birth Friends Forever

Marc Savard, Canadian hockey player, 1977

M.I.A., rapper, 1977

Cory Doctorow, Canadian activist, 1971

Jonathan Potts, Canadian voice actor, 1961

Bryan Trottier, Canadian hockey player, 1956

Christopher Chappell, Canadian cricket player, 1955

David Hasselhoff, actor (*Baywatch*), 1952

Gale Garnett, Canadian singer, 1942

Donald Sutherland, Canadian actor (*Dirty Sexy Money*), 1934

Phyllis Diller, comedian, 1917

Art Linkletter, Canadian TV-show host, 1912

James Cagney, actor (*The Public Enemy*), 1899

Daily Oddity
Cricket used to be an Olympic event.

JULY 18
166 days until next year

In a Days
Ladies and gentlemen, start your licking. It's "National Ice Cream Day."

In the News

1739: The population of New France (Québec) reached 42,701.

1818: A plague of grasshoppers in Winnipeg's Red River Valley destroyed crops in a matter of minutes.

1925: Adolf Hitler published *Mein Kampf*.

1945: A naval ammunition barge caught fire in Halifax, NS; half the city's population was evacuated and no one was killed.

1968: Intel Corporation was founded.

1968: Twenty-four thousand postal workers nationwide began a 3-week strike.

1976: During the Montréal Olympic Games, 14-year-old Romanian gymnast Nadia Comaneci scored a perfect 10 on the uneven parallel bars.

1990: Canadian comedian Johnny Wayne of Wayne & Schuster fame died at the age of 72.

1996: Québec's Saguenay River began to flood.

Cancer
You are an enthusiastic individual with great mental clarity; however, you have a tendency to be a follower and not a leader.
3, 7, 9

#1 Song
1999: "Wild Wild West" by Will Smith

Birth Friends Forever

Kristen Bell, actress (*Veronica Mars*), 1980

Vin Diesel, actor (*xXx*), 1967

Ricky Skaggs, country musician, 1954

Jack Layton, Canadian politician, 1950

Steven W. Mahoney, Canadian politician, 1947

Martha Reeves, singer (Martha and the Vandellas), 1941

Hunter S. Thompson, gonzo journalist, 1937

Ted Harris, Canadian hockey player, 1936

Margaret Laurence, Canadian author (*The Stone Angel*), 1926

John Glenn, astronaut, 1921

Nelson Mandela, president of South Africa, 1918

Hume Cronyn, Canadian actor (*Cocoon*), 1911

Margaret Brown, the Unsinkable Molly Brown, 1867

Daily Oddity
The name of the Manitoba town Gimli means "home of the gods."

JULY 19
165 days until next year

In a Days
Surf's up, Moondoggie. It's "Woodie Wagon Day."
If participating in "Toss Away Could-haves and Should-haves Day," please recycle.

In the News

1577: Explorer Martin Frobisher entered Frobisher Bay, NWT.

1654: Québec resident Marguerite Sedilot became the country's youngest bride when she married at the age of 11.

1848: Women's bloomers were first introduced at a Women's Rights Convention in New York.

1908: The 300th anniversary of Champlain's founding of Québec City was celebrated.

1918: Spanish flu outbreak began; 30,000 Canadians died.

1937: The Bank of Canada issued the country's first bilingual currency.

1980: Canada boycotted the Summer Olympics in Moscow.

1981: Hailstones the size of tennis balls fell on Toronto, causing millions of dollars in damage.

1996: Canadian singer Céline Dion performed during the opening ceremonies of the Summer Olympic Games in Atlanta.

Cancer
You are an energetic humanitarian who can be a little farsighted at times.
3, 7, 19

#1 Song
1963: "Surf City" by Jan & Dean

Birth Friends Forever
Jared Padalecki, actor (*Supernatural*), 1982

Jean-Sébastien Aubin, Canadian hockey player, 1977

Scott Walker, Canadian hockey player, 1973

Anthony Edwards, actor (*ER*), 1962

Atom Egoyan, Canadian director (*The Sweet Hereafter*), 1960

Brian May, musician (Queen), 1947

Dick Irvin, Canadian hockey player, 1892

Max Fleischer, animator (*Superman*), 1883

Lizzie Borden, accused axe-murderer, 1860

Samuel Colt, gunsmith, 1814

Daily Oddity
The St. John's Newfoundland Regatta is the longest running sporting event in Canadian history. It is believed to have started in 1816.

JULY 20
164 days until next year

In a Days
Suck it! It's "National Lollipop Day."

In the News
1871: The trial of Louis Riel for treason began in Regina.

1905: Regina and Edmonton were announced as the capitals of Saskatchewan and Alberta.

1928: Hungary ordered the nomadic Romany people to settle permanently or face taxation.

1933: In Germany, 200 Jewish merchants were arrested and paraded through the streets.

1945: The first Family Allowance payments were issued to Canadian families.

1976: Hank Aaron broke Babe Ruth's 44-year-old record with his 755th home run.

1985: James Keegstra, a teacher in Alberta, was fined $5000 by the courts for telling his students that the Holocaust never happened.

1996: Torrential rains caused a dam near Québec's Lac Ha! Ha! to rupture, destroying 150 homes.

2005: Royal Assent was officially granted to same-sex marriage in Canada.

Cancer
You are a pioneer and a vibrant spirit who can get too focused on one specific task.
3, 7, 10

#1 Song
1982: "Eye of the Tiger" by Survivor

Birth Friends Forever
Sandra Oh, Canadian actress (*Grey's Anatomy*), 1971

Josh Holloway, actor (*Lost*), 1969

Vitamin C, singer, 1969

Chris Cornell, musician (Soundgarden), 1964

Jim Prentice, Canadian politician, 1956

Tantoo Cardinal, Canadian actress (*North of 60*), 1950

Diana Rigg, actress (*The Avengers*), 1938

Natalie Wood, actress (*West Side Story*), 1938

Mort Garson, Canadian composer, 1924

Alexander the Great, military leader, 356 BC

Daily Oddity
Killing a ladybug is bad luck.

JULY 21
163 days until next year

In a Days
I don't know how you get into it in the first place, but today is "National Get Out of the Doghouse Day."

In the News

1576: Explorer Martin Frobisher named Frobisher Bay after himself.

1730: The population of New France (Québec) reached 33,682.

1873: Jesse James successfully robbed his first train.

1896: *The Kiss* became the first film shown in Canada.

1963: Eighteen people died when a freighter from Britain and a freighter from Bermuda collided in the St. Lawrence Seaway.

1969: Neil Armstrong walked on the Moon.

1975: The Canadian Human Rights Commission was established.

1983: It was −89°C at Vostok Base, Antarctica—the coldest temperature ever recorded.

1996: Canadian cyclist Clara Hughes won Canada's first medal (bronze) at the Olympics Games in Atlanta.

2007: The 7th and final book in the series—*Harry Potter and the Deathly Hallows*—was released.

Cancer
You are a motivated and independent thinker who can sometimes be too confrontational.
3, 7, 21

#1 Song
1975: "The Hustle" by Van McCoy

Birth Friends Forever

Josh Hartnett, actor (*Pearl Harbor*), 1978

Jon Lovitz, comedian (*SNL*), 1957

Robin Williams, actor (*Jumanji*), 1951

Art Hindle, Canadian actor (*Dallas*), 1948

Cat Stevens/Yusuf Islam, singer, 1948

Anton Kuerti, Canadian pianist and composer, 1938

Marcel Gauthier, Canadian wrestler, 1928

Norman Jewison, Canadian director (*Fiddler on the Roof*), 1926

Don Knotts, actor (*Three's Company*), 1924

Rudolph A. Marcus, Canadian chemist, 1923

Marshall McLuhan, Canadian literary critic, 1911

Ernest Hemingway, author (*The Old Man and the Sea*), 1899

Daily Oddity
Mosquitoes prefer blondes.

JULY 22
162 days until next year

In a Days
Listen to the sound of my voice. Today is "Health and Happiness with Hypnosis Day."

If you catch 'em, you cook 'em. It's "Rat-Catchers Day."

Quit playing with your words. It's "Spoonerism Day."

In the News
1629: Olivier le Noir became the first African American in Québec.

1847: Canada was given the power to raise its own taxes.

1892: Fire destroyed much of St. John's, NL.

1915: The Canadian inventor of time zones, Sandford Fleming, died at the age of 88.

1934: Bank robber John Dillinger was killed.

1948: Newfoundland voted to join Canada.

1968: A fire destroyed much of the Basilica of St. Boniface in Winnipeg.

1981: Women in Québec were allowed to enter bars.

1997: The Blue Water Bridge opened between Michigan and Ontario.

2005: Police in London, England, killed an innocent man whom they believed was a suicide bomber.

Cancer
You are a caring and sensitive individual; however, you get confused between your head and your heart.
3, 4, 7

#1 Song
1931: "I Found a Million-Dollar Baby (in a Five-and-Ten-Cent Store)" by The Pennsylvanians

Birth Friends Forever
A.J. Cook, Canadian actress (*Final Destination 2*), 1978

Rufus Wainwright, Canadian singer, 1973

Colin Ferguson, Canadian actor (*Eureka*), 1972

John Leguizamo, actor (*Spawn*), 1964

Willem Dafoe, actor (*Spider-Man*), 1955

Gilles Duceppe, Canadian politician, 1947

Danny Glover, actor (*Lethal Weapon*), 1946

Ron Turcotte, Canadian jockey, 1941

Alex Trebek, Canadian game-show host, 1940

Terence Stamp, actor (*Superman*), 1938

Oscar de la Renta, fashion designer, 1932

William Spooner, father of spoonerisms (play on words), 1844

Daily Oddity
Alberta has been rat-free for over 50 years.

JULY 23
161 days until next year

In a Days
You look so sexy in that babushka. It's "Gorgeous Grandma Day."
Get ready to punch people in the face. It's "Hot Enough for You Day."

In the News
1840: The Act of Union created the Province of Canada.

1903: Ford Motors sold its first car.

1908: Canadian runner Bobby Kerr won Olympic gold in London for the 220 yd sprint.

1956: John Jearmey became the first male swimmer to cross Lake Ontario.

1967: Winnipeg hosted the Pan-American Games.

1975: Saskatchewan Roughrider George Reed scored his 127th career touchdown.

1983: An Air Canada plane ran out of fuel and glided to a landing at Gimli, MB.

1986: Prince Andrew married Sarah Ferguson.

1987: The Head-Smashed-In Buffalo Jump Interpretive Centre officially opened in Alberta.

2002: Pope John Paul II arrived in Toronto for World Youth Day.

Leo
You are a sociable person who is filled with conviction; however, you may be perceived as being slightly authoritarian.
5, 14, 23

#1 Song
1967: "Light My Fire" by The Doors

Birth Friends Forever
Steve Jocz, Canadian musician (Sum 41), 1981

Jonathan Gallant, Canadian musician (Billy Talent), 1976

Omar Epps, actor (*House*), 1973

Philip Seymour Hoffman, actor (*Capote*), 1967

Slash, guitarist (Guns N' Roses), 1965

Woody Harrelson, actor (*Cheers*), 1961

Blair Thornton, Canadian musician (BTO), 1950

Charles Harrelson, hitman and father of Woody Harrelson, 1938

Red Dutton, Canadian hockey player, 1898

Raymond Chandler, author (*The Big Sleep*), 1888

Alexandre-Antonin Taché, Canadian archbishop, 1832

Daily Oddity
When the CFL and the Rugby Association merged, neither the Ottawa Rough Riders nor the Saskatchewan Roughriders would change their name.

JULY 24
160 days until next year

In a Days
Forget the parking lot—it's "National Drive-thru Day."
Why did the chicken cross the road? Because it was "Tell an Old Joke Day."

In the News
1956: Comedy duo Dean Martin and Jerry Lewis performed together for the last time.

1966: The first BASE (Building Antenna Span Earth) jump took place.

1967: While visiting Montréal, French President Charles de Gaulle declared, "Vive le Québec libre!" ("Long live free Québec!").

1969: *Apollo 11*, containing Neil Armstrong and Buzz Aldrin, landed in the Pacific Ocean.

1988: Nine-year-old Canadian Emma Houlston landed her single-engine plane in Halifax after flying from Vancouver.

1988: Edmontonians made the world's largest milkshake with 20,271 kg of ice cream.

1995: Regina resident Dick Assman appeared on the *Late Show with David Letterman*.

1996: Canadian swimmer Marianne Limpert won Olympic silver in the 200 m individual medley.

2005: Lance Armstrong won his 7th consecutive Tour de France.

Leo
You are an energetic and inspiring individual who, at times, can be very uncompromising.
8, 15, 42

#1 Song
1951: "Come On-a My House" by Rosemary Clooney

Birth Friends Forever
Bindi Irwin, daughter of Steve Irwin, 1998

Megan Park, Canadian actress (*Charlie Bartlett*), 1986

Patrice Bergeron, Canadian hockey player, 1985

Anna Paquin, Canadian actress (*X-Men*), 1982

Jennifer Lopez, singer, 1969

Barry Bonds, baseball player, 1964

Pam Tillis, country singer, 1957

Lynda Carter, actress (*Wonder Woman*), 1952

Robert Farnon, Canadian composer, 1917

"Honest" Ed Mirvish, Canadian businessman, 1914

Amelia Earhart, aviatrix, 1897

Alexandre Dumas, author (*The Three Musketeers*), 1802

Daily Oddity
RSVP is French for "Répondez s'il vous plaît," which means "Please reply."

JULY 25
159 days until next year

In a Days
Sorry, there's just no time to celebrate "Out of Time Day."

If you don't celebrate "System Administrator Appreciation Day," you may find all your computer files "accidentally" deleted.

In the News

1755: Thousands of Acadians were sent to the British colonies in America, including Louisiana, where they became Cajuns.

1814: One of the bloodiest battles during the War of 1812 took place near Niagara Falls; 878 British and Canadians soldiers were killed.

1917: Income taxes were first introduced in Canada as a "temporary" measure.

1944: Operation Spring—5021 Canadians were killed at Normandy in one of the bloodiest battles in Canadian history.

1946: Dean Martin and Jerry Lewis performed together for the first time.

1978: The world's first test-tube baby was born.

1984: Svetlana Savitskaya became the first female to do a space walk.

1990: Lucien Bouchard formed the Bloc Québécois.

2007: Pratibha Patil became India's first female president.

Leo
You are an innovative and practical person who sometimes loses sight of reality.
7, 14, 34

#1 Song
1985: "Everytime You Go Away" by Paul Young

Birth Friends Forever
Noel Callahan, Canadian actor (*Stargate SG-1*), 1989

Heather Marks, Canadian model, 1988

Louise Brown, first test-tube baby, 1978

Matt LeBlanc, actor (*Friends*), 1967

Denis Coderre, Canadian politician, 1963

Alain Robidoux, Canadian snooker player, 1960

Thurston Moore, musician (Sonic Youth), 1958

Iman Abdulmajid, model, 1955

Maureen Forrester, Canadian contralto, 1930

Eddie Mazur, Canadian hockey player, 1929

Whipper Billy Watson, Canadian pro wrestler, 1917

Daily Oddity
July 25 is St. Christopher's Day—the patron saint of travellers.

JULY 26
158 days until next year

In a Days
Put on your chaps. It's "National Cowboy Day."
Rev up your engine-less car to celebrate "Soap Box Derby Day."

In the News

1842: G. Riley patented an improved method for brewing beer.

1881: CPR lines were completed up to Winnipeg.

1889: One hundred people made a pilgrimage to a church in Lac Ste. Anne, AB; the annual pilgrimage continues to this day.

1982: London, ON resident, Karen Baldwin, 18, became Canada's first Miss Universe winner.

1982: NASA launched Canada's *Anik D1 Comsat* into orbit.

1983: Former Toronto Argonaut Cookie Gilchrist became the first player to refuse induction into the CFL Hall of Fame.

1991: The CFL took ownership of the near-broke Ottawa Rough Riders.

1995: John Labatt Ltd. was sold to a Belgian brewery for $2.7 billion.

2005: Mumbai, India, received 995 mm of rain within a 24-hr period.

Leo
You are an influential and logical person; however, you have a tendency to become addicted to danger.
8, 17, 26

#1 Song
1999: "Genie in a Bottle" by Christina Aguilera

Birth Friends Forever

Miriam McDonald, Canadian actress (*Degrassi: TNG*), 1987

Dave Baksh, Canadian musician (Sum 41), 1980

Sandra Bullock, actress (*Speed*), 1964

Kevin Spacey, actor (*American Beauty*), 1959

Angela Hewitt, Canadian pianist, 1958

Rick Martin, Canadian hockey player, 1951

Mick Jagger, singer (The Rolling Stones), 1943

Bobby Rousseau, Canadian hockey player, 1940

Stanley Kubrick, director (*The Shining*), 1928

Peter Lougheed, Canadian politician, 1928

Aldous Huxley, author (*A Brave New World*), 1894

Carl Jung, psychiatrist, 1875

Daily Oddity
Beer magnate John Molson almost died in a shipwreck on his way to Canada from England.

JULY 27
157 days until next year

In a Days
Without them, you wouldn't exist or get your allowance, so celebrate "Parents' Day."

As long as your houseplant isn't part of a "grow-op," celebrate "Take Your Houseplant for a Walk Day."

If you're looking to break both your legs, celebrate "Walk on Stilts Day."

In the News

1866: The first successful underwater telegraph cable, connecting Newfoundland to Wales, was completed.

1891: The final spike of the Calgary–Edmonton Railway was driven, nearly a year after construction began.

1897: Toronto experienced its greatest one-day rainfall, 98.6 mm.

1921: Canadian scientist Frederick Banting isolated insulin from the pancreatic duct of a dog.

1965: A musical based on *Anne of Green Gables* premiered in Charlottetown, PEI.

1996: A pipe bomb exploded at the Summer Olympic Games in Atlanta, killing one person and injuring 111.

1996: Canadian sprinter Donovan Bailey became the fastest man alive, running the 100 m sprint in 9.84 seconds at the Summer Olympics in Atlanta.

2002: The worst air show disaster in history occurred in the Ukraine; 85 people died.

Leo
You are a positive and motivated individual who is sometimes overly controlling.
7, 17, 27

#1 Song
1991: "(Everything I Do) I Do It for You" by Bryan Adams

Birth Friends Forever

Charlotte Arnold, Canadian actress (*Degrassi: TNG*), 1989

Jonathan Rhys-Meyers, actor (*The Tudors*), 1977

Alex Rodriguez, baseball player, 1975

Craig Wolanin, Canadian hockey player, 1967

Juliana Hatfield, musician, 1967

André Dupont, Canadian hockey player, 1949

Peggy Fleming, figure skater, 1948

Édith Butler, Canadian songwriter, 1942

Norman Lear, TV producer (*All in the Family*), 1922

Gérard Côté, Canadian runner, 1913

Herbert Jasper, Canadian physiologist, 1906

Jack Laviolette, Canadian hockey player, 1879

Daily Oddity
A first edition of *Anne of Green Gables* was once auctioned off for $24,000 USD.

JULY 28
156 days until next year

In a Days
If it's brown, drink it down. It's "National Chocolate Milk Day."
It's the best way to receive bad news, so celebrate "Singing Telegram Day."

In the News

1586: The first potato arrived in England.

1615: Samuel de Champlain discovered Lake Huron.

1847: London and Brantford, ON, were incorporated as cities.

1890: The first electric street lighting was installed in Trois-Rivières, Québec.

1914: Canada joined the war effort.

1933: The first singing telegram was sent.

1945: A U.S. bomber crashed into the Empire State Building.

1979: An egg was safely dropped from the CN Tower observation deck; shaving cream and cotton cushioned its fall.

1994: A crowd of 35,000 people attended the first Lollapalooza music festival at Molson Park in Barrie, ON.

2008: For the second time in 80 years, the Grand Pier in England burned down.

Leo
You are a strategic and vigorous individual who steps on those who get in your way.
2, 8, 10

#1 Song
1981: "Jessie's Girl" by Rick Springfield

Birth Friends Forever

Hannah Lochner, Canadian actress (*Dawn of the Dead*), 1993

Dustin Milligan, Canadian actor (*90210*), 1985

Marc Dupré, Canadian humorist, 1973

Steve Staios, Canadian hockey player, 1973

Elizabeth Berkley, actress (*Saved by the Bell*), 1972

Annie Perreault, Canadian short-track speed skater, 1971

Lori Loughlin, actress (*90210*), 1964

Terry Fox, Canadian hero, 1958

Sally Struthers, actress (*All in the Family*), 1948

Jim Davis, cartoonist (*Garfield*), 1945

Russ Jackson, Canadian football player, 1936

Beatrix Potter, author (*Peter Rabbit*), 1866

Daily Oddity
The song "Happy Birthday" was originally called "Good Morning to All."

JULY 29
155 days until next year

In a Days
Blast off, it's "Rocket Day."
Leave a good tip. Today is "St. Martha's Day"—the patron saint of housekeepers.

In the News

1848: Construction of the first suspension bridge over the Niagara Gorge was completed.

1900: The last spike was driven on the White Pass and Yukon Railway from Skagway to Whitehorse.

1907: With financial assistance from Canadian Lord Strathcona, Robert Baden-Powell formed the Boy Scouts.

1921: Adolf Hitler became the leader of the National Socialist German Workers' Party.

1948: After a 12-year hiatus, the first Summer Olympics since the start of World War II were held.

1981: Canadian swimmer Alex Baumann set a world record in the 200 m individual medley.

1981: Prince Charles married Lady Diana Spencer.

2005: Astronomers discovered the dwarf planet known as Eris.

2008: A 5.4-magnitude earthquake hit Chino Hills in Southern California.

Leo
You are a sociable and prophetic leader; however, you tend to suppress individuality.
2, 11, 22

#1 Song
2003: "Crazy in Love" by Beyoncé, featuring Jay-Z

Birth Friends Forever

Ryan Braun, Canadian baseball player, 1980

Wil Wheaton, actor (*Stand by Me*), 1972

Martina McBride, country singer, 1966

Dean Haglund, Canadian actor (*The X-Files*), 1965

Tim Gunn, fashion personality, 1953

Ken Burns, documentary filmmaker (*Jazz*), 1953

Geddy Lee, Canadian musician (Rush), 1953

Peter Jennings, Canadian journalist, 1938

Ted Lindsay, Canadian hockey player, 1925

Lloyd Bochner, Canadian actor (*Dynasty*), 1924

Benito Mussolini, Italian dictator, 1883

Daily Oddity
Married men tip better than single men do.

JULY 30
154 days until next year

In a Days
If you can find it on a map, celebrate Vanuatu's "Independence Day."

In the News
1844: Four sailors in Nova Scotia were hanged for piracy.

1945: 4500 Canadian soldiers returned from fighting in Europe.

1954: Elvis Presley performed for the first time.

1962: The Trans-Canada Highway opened.

1975: Labour Leader Jimmy Hoffa disappeared.

1975: Canadian Cindy Nicholas, 17, swam the English Channel in 9 hr and 46 min—a women's world record.

1982: The RCMP seized $22-million worth of hashish.

1990: The first Saturn automobile was introduced.

1992: Canadian swimmer Mark Tewksbury won Olympic gold for the men's 100 m backstroke in Barcelona.

1992: Canadian co-creator of *Superman*, Joe Schuster, died at the age of 78.

2003: The last "classic" Volkswagen Beetle was released.

2008: A 22-year-old man was stabbed and beheaded while riding from Edmonton to Winnipeg on a Greyhound bus.

Leo
You are an energetic person who has great potential; however, you tend to be narrow-minded at times.
3, 12, 21

#1 Song
1989: "Batdance" by Prince

Birth Friends Forever
Hilary Swank, actress (*Million-Dollar Baby*), 1974

Tom Green, Canadian comedian, 1971

Christopher Nolan, director (*The Dark Knight*), 1970

Lisa Kudrow, actress (*Friends*), 1963

Laurence Fishburne, actor (*The Matrix*), 1961

Kate Bush, singer, 1958

Réal Cloutier, Canadian hockey player, 1956

Delta Burke, fashion designer, 1956

Jean Reno, actor (*The Professional*), 1948

Arnold Schwarzenegger, actor (*Terminator*), 1947

Paul Anka, Canadian singer, 1941

Buddy Guy, blues guitarist, 1936

Sid Krofft, Canadian TV producer (*H.R. Pufnstuf*), 1929

Henry Ford, industrialist, 1863

Emily Brontë, author (*Wuthering Heights*), 1818

Daily Oddity
Ontario's licence plates were once made of patent leather.

JULY 31
153 days until next year

In a Days
I know it is "Jump for Jelly Beans Day," but couldn't we change it to "Run for Rum," instead?

In the News

1874: The first Russian Mennonites arrived in Manitoba.

1913: Alys Bryant became the first woman in Canada to fly solo.

1917: Allied Forces, including Canada, mounted the Passchendaele offensive; thousands of Canadian soldiers lost their lives during the assault.

1957: The Distant Early Warning (DEW) Line radar stations became operational.

1976: Canadian Greg Joy jumped 2.23 m for the silver medal in high jump at the Montréal Olympic Games.

1987: Black Friday—A class F-4 tornado ripped through Edmonton, killing 27 people.

1989: CBC Newsworld débuted.

1996: Alanis Morissette kick-started her first Canadian tour in Vancouver.

2006: Dictator Fidel Castro handed over temporary power to his brother Raúl.

Leo
You are a determined and nurturing individual who sometimes spreads yourself too thin.
4, 13, 24

#1 Song
1996: "Macarena" by Los Del Rio

Birth Friends Forever
B.J. Novak, actor (*The Office*), 1979
Dean Cain, actor (*Lois & Clark*), 1966
J.K. Rowling, author (*Harry Potter* series), 1965
Brian Skrudland, Canadian hockey player, 1963
Fatboy Slim, musician, 1963
Wesley Snipes, actor (*Blade*), 1962
Dale Hunter, Canadian hockey player, 1960
Derek Smith, Canadian hockey player, 1954
Yvon Deschamps, Canadian humorist, 1935
Bryan Hextall, Canadian hockey player, 1913

Daily Oddity
Summer is the most hazardous season.

AUGUST 1
152 days until next year

In a Days
My spider-sense is tingling. It must be "Spiderman Day."
If you ever want to get lucky again, celebrate "Girlfriends Day."
You weren't a treat to raise, so celebrate "Respect for Parents Day."
Cover yourself in fleas and lick yourself. It's "Work like a Dog Day."
Settling inane bets for over 20 years, it's "World Wide Web Day."

In the News
1908: Fernie, BC, was destroyed by fire.

1941: The first Jeep was introduced.

1944: Anne Frank made the last entry into her diary.

1957: Canada and the U.S. formed NORAD (North American Air Defense Command).

1968: The Canadian Mint began replacing silver with nickel in Canadian currency save for commemorative coins.

1971: The Canadian government ended its censoring of letters to and from prisoners.

1976: The closing ceremonies for the Montréal Olympic Games were held.

1981: MTV went on the air.

1985: The world's tallest unsupported flagpole, 133 m, was erected in Vancouver.

2008: The official 6th severed foot was discovered, the only foot found in the U.S.

Leo
You are an imaginative and prodigious individual who sometimes isolates yourself from others.
1, 2, 17

#1 Song
1954: "Sh-Boom" by The Crew-Cuts

Birth Friends Forever
Beckie Scott, Canadian cross-country skier, 1974

Tanya Reid, Canadian actress (*Stargate SG-1*), 1972

Sam Mendes, director (*American Beauty*), 1965

Adam Duritz, musician (Counting Crows), 1964

Coolio, rapper, 1963

Richard Roeper, film critic, 1960

André Gagnon, Canadian pianist, 1942

Jerry Garcia, musician (The Grateful Dead), 1942

Dom DeLuise, comedian, 1933

Herman Melville, author (*Moby Dick*), 1819

Daily Oddity
The first video played on MTV was "Video Killed the Radio Star" by the Buggles.

AUGUST 2
151 days until next year

In a Days
Sorry, ketchup, but it's "National Mustard Day."

In the News
- 1610: Henry Hudson first sailed into Hudson Bay.
- 1786: Explorer James Strange claimed Vancouver Island for Britain.
- 1862: Victoria, BC, was incorporated as a city.
- 1870: The world's first underground tube railway opened in London, England.
- 1922: Alexander Graham Bell, Canadian inventor of the telephone, died.
- 1932: The positron—the antiparticle of the electron—was discovered.
- 1932: Icelanders in Gimli, MB, held their first annual Icelandic Festival (*Islendingadagurinn*).
- 1963: China bought $300 million worth of wheat from Canada.
- 1990: Iraq invaded Kuwait.
- 2003: A massive forest fire ravaged the Okanagan.
- 2005: An Air France Flight crashed at Toronto Pearson International Airport; all the passengers survived.

Leo
You are a determined and intellectual person who can be impatient at times.
2, 8, 28

#1 Song
1960: "Itsy Bitsy Teenie Weenie Yellow Polkadot Bikini" by Brian Hyland

Birth Friends Forever
Harry Smith, Canadian pro wrestler, 1985
Edward Furlong, actor (*Terminator 2*), 1977
Mary-Louise Parker, actress (*Weeds*), 1964
Isabel Allende, author, 1942
Wes Craven, director (*Scream*), 1939
Dave Balon, Canadian hockey player, 1938
Garth Hudson, Canadian musician (The Band), 1937
Peter O'Toole, actor (*Lawrence of Arabia*), 1932
John McCormack, Canadian hockey player, 1925
Myrna Loy, actress (*The Thin Man*), 1905
Jack Warner, Canadian film producer, 1892
John Alexander Douglas McCurdy, Canadian pilot, 1886

Daily Oddity
The sea serpent Ogopogo is said to live in Okanagan Lake, BC.

AUGUST 3
150 days until next year

In a Days
If it weren't for them, who would older brothers torment? It's "Sisters Day."

If you're looking to solidify a good character witness for your upcoming trial, celebrate "Friendship Day."

In the News

1527: The first known letter in North America was sent by John Rut while he was in St. John's, NL.

1751: Canada's first printing press was founded in Nova Scotia.

1876: Canadian inventor Alexander Graham Bell made the world's very first phone call.

1900: The Firestone Tire Company was founded.

1918: Canadian ace pilot Billy Bishop was awarded the Distinguished Flying Cross for shooting down 25 German planes in 12 days.

1949: The National Basketball Association (NBA) was founded.

1958: The *Billboard* Hot 100 was created.

1978: The Commonwealth Games opened in Edmonton.

1989: Canada's first infant heart transplant operation took place in Ottawa.

2004: The Statue of Liberty reopened for the first time since 9/11.

Leo
You are a courageous and pioneering individual who at times suffers from restlessness.
5, 23, 32

#1 Song
1975: "Jive Talkin'" by The Bee Gees

Birth Friends Forever
Dominic Moore, Canadian hockey player, 1980

Evangeline Lilly, Canadian actress (*Lost*), 1979

Tom Brady, football player, 1977

Patrick Wilson, actor (*Watchmen*), 1973

Brent Butt, Canadian actor (*Corner Gas*), 1966

James Hetfield, musician (Metallica), 1963

Marcel Dionne, Canadian hockey player, 1951

Martha Stewart, TV personality, 1941

Vic Vogel, Canadian bandleader, 1935

Tony Bennett, singer, 1926

Elmar Tampõld, Canadian architect, 1920

Frank Arthur Calder, Canadian politician, 1915

Daily Oddity
In 2005, Edmontonian Finola Hackett won the first-ever Canwest Spelling Bee by correctly spelling the word "otiosity," which means idleness.

AUGUST 4
149 days until next year

In a Days
Whip out your dinghy and celebrate "Coast Guard Day."
It's a lot tastier than "Paint Chip Day," it's "National Chocolate Chip Day."

In the News
1637: A Huron council in Ontario blamed the smallpox epidemic on the Jesuits (Black Robes).

1693: Dom Perignon invented Champagne.

1769: Prince Edward Island came into existence when the British Crown separated the island of St. Jean from Nova Scotia.

1821: *The Saturday Evening Post* was first published as a weekly newspaper.

1875: Children's storyteller Hans Christian Andersen died.

1944: Anne Frank and her family were discovered by the Gestapo.

1978: The Molson Brewery Company purchased the Montréal Canadiens hockey team for $20 million.

1996: The Summer Olympic Games in Atlanta closed with Canada winning 3 gold medals, 11 silver and 8 bronze.

2005: Michaëlle Jean was announced as Canada's first black governor general.

Leo
You are a curious and radical thinker who sometimes alienates those around you.
4, 8, 44

#1 Song
2000: "It's Gonna Be Me" by 'N Sync

Birth Friends Forever
Dylan and Cole Sprouse, child actors (*The Suite Life*), 1992

Stefan Brogren, Canadian actor (*Degrassi: TNG*), 1972

Jeff Gordon, racecar driver, 1971

Daniel Dae Kim, actor (*Lost*), 1968

Roger Clemens, baseball player, 1962

Barack Obama, first African American U.S. president, 1961

Maurice Richard, Canadian hockey player, 1921

Louis Armstrong, jazz musician, 1901

Tom Thomson, Canadian painter, 1877

Louis Vuitton, fashion designer, 1821

Percy Shelley, poet, 1792

Daily Oddity
Croquet, polo and rope climbing were once Olympic events.

AUGUST 5
148 days until next year

In a Days
Lock the kids in the basement. It's "National Night Out."

In the News

1305: William Wallace, the inspiration behind *Braveheart*, was captured by the English and transported to London for his trial and subsequent execution.

1583: The first English colony in North America was established at St John's, NL.

1689: Over 1000 Iroquois warriors attacked the settlement of Lachine, New France (Québec), killing 24 colonists and kidnapping 90.

1858: The first transatlantic telegraph cable connecting Newfoundland to Ireland was established.

1913: Canada's first airplane fatality occurred near Victoria, BC.

1914: Canada joined Britain in the war against Germany.

1957: *American Bandstand* made its debut.

1962: Nelson Mandela was put in prison, where he stayed for the next 32 years.

1960: Canada's 9th prime minister, Arthur Meighen, died at the age of 86.

2004: Hundreds lined up in Toronto for a book signing by former U.S. president Bill Clinton.

Leo
You are a logical person with an impeccable fashion sense; however, you are prone to fits of rage.
8, 9, 23

#1 Song
1978: "Miss You" by The Rolling Stones

Birth Friends Forever

Erik Guay, Canadian alpine skier, 1981

Terri Clark, Canadian country singer, 1968

Adam "MCA" Yauch, musician (Beastie Boys), 1964

Jerry Ciccoritti, Canadian director (*Due South*), 1956

Greg Leskin, musician (The Guess Who), 1947

Loni Anderson, actress (*WKRP in Cincinnati*), 1946

Neil Armstrong, astronaut, 1930

Selma Diamond, Canadian actress (*Night Court*), 1920

Betty Oliphant, Canadian ballerina, 1918

John Huston, director (*The Maltese Falcon*), 1906

Tom Thomson, Canadian painter, 1877

Joseph Merrick, the "Elephant Man," 1862

Daily Oddity
The Rolling Stones took their name from a 1950 Muddy Waters' song entitled "Rollin' Stone."

AUGUST 6
147 days until next year

In a Days
Gargle, gargle. It's "National Fresh Breath Day."

In the News

1866: Vancouver Island became part of the province of British Columbia.

1926: Escape artist Harry Houdini spent 91 minutes underwater in a sealed tank before escaping—his greatest escape ever.

1930: William Lyon Mackenzie King resigned as Canada's prime minister.

1945: The U.S. dropped an atomic bomb on Hiroshima, killing 70,000 people instantly; thousands died later as a result of radiation poisoning.

1964: Prometheus, the world's oldest tree, was cut down by a graduate student while he was conducting research.

1991: Aulavik National Park on Banks Island opened; the name *Aulavik* means "where people travel" in Inuit.

2002: Joe Clark announced his decision to resign as the leader of Canada's Progressive Conservative Party.

2004: Svend Robinson, former NDP MP, plead guilty to stealing a $5000 ring; he received 100 hours of community service as punishment.

Leo
You are a driven and perceptive individual who sometimes pushes yourself too far.
8, 9, 42

#1 Song
1984: "Ghostbusters" by Ray Parker Jr.

Birth Friends Forever
Jon Benet Ramsey, child beauty pageant contestant, 1990

Soleil Moon Frye, actress (*Punky Brewster*), 1976

Geri Halliwell, singer (Spice Girls), 1972

M. Night Shyamalan, director (*The Sixth Sense*), 1970

Michelle Yeoh, actress (*Crouching Tiger, Hidden Dragon*), 1962

Dino Bravo, Canadian pro wrestler, 1949

Roch La Salle, Canadian politician, 1929

Andy Warhol, artist, 1928

Paul Hellyer, Canadian politician, 1923

Robert Mitchum, actor (*Night of the Hunter*), 1917

Lucille Ball, actress (*I Love Lucy*), 1911

John Campbell, governor general of Canada, 1845

Daily Oddity
Harry Houdini first encountered a straitjacket when he was visiting an insane asylum in St. John, NB.

AUGUST 7
146 days until next year

In a Days
Get a suntan while you still can—summer is officially half over.
Imagine everyone nude. It's "Professional Speakers Day."
Be a beacon. It's "Lighthouse Day."
Don't get too wrapped up in "Preposterous Packaging Day."

In the News
1606: The "Scottish play," *Macbeth*, was performed for the first time.

1679: The first ship to sail the upper Great Lakes, *Le Griffon*, was launched.

1858: Ottawa was officially named the capital of Canada.

1867: Following Confederation, John A. Macdonald began campaigning in Canada's first general election.

1930: Richard Bennett became Canada's 9th prime minister following Mackenzie King's resignation.

1955: Tokyo Telecommunications Engineering, the forerunner of Sony, sold its first transistor radio.

1974: Philippe Petit walked across a high wire connecting the twin towers of the World Trade Center.

2007: Barry Bonds broke Hank Aaron's record by hitting his 756th home run.

2008: Russia invaded the neighbouring country of Georgia.

Leo
You are a practical person with a strong sense of conviction; however, this makes you somewhat confrontational.
8, 9, 34

#1 Song
1980: "Magic" by Olivia Newton-John

Birth Friends Forever
Sidney Crosby, Canadian hockey player, 1987

Samantha Ronson, disc jockey, 1977

Charlize Theron, actress (*Monster*), 1975

David Duchovny, actor (*The X-Files*), 1960

Bruce Dickinson, singer (Iron Maiden), 1958

Kerry Chater, Canadian musician (Gary Puckett & the Union Gap), 1945

Garrison Keillor, radio host, 1942

James "The Amazing" Randi, Canadian magician, 1928

Carl "Alfalfa" Switzer, actor (*The Little Rascals*), 1927

Dorothy Walton, Canadian tennis player, 1909

Mata Hari, spy, 1876

Anna Swan, Canadian tall woman (7'6"), 1846

Daily Oddity
Canadian magician "The Amazing Randi" has an ongoing challenge in which he will award $1 million to anyone who can demonstrate supernatural ability; no one has ever claimed the prize.

AUGUST 8
145 days until next year

In a Days
Oh yeahhh! It's "Kool-Aid Day."

Don't get accidentally shot in the process. It's "Sneak Some Zucchini onto Your Neighbour's Porch Night."

Turn off the lights, take off your pants and celebrate "The Date to Create."

After that rendezvous, you'll definitely agree that today is "Happiness Happens Day."

In the News
1907: Canadian bandit Bill "The Grey Fox" Miner broke out of prison and fled to the U.S., where he continued his pilfering ways.

1918: John Croke became the first Newfoundlander to win the Victoria Cross.

1918: Canadian forces mounted a 4-day assault on German troops in Amiens, France. This date also marked the beginning of "Canada's Hundred Days," a string of continuous victories for the brave Canucks.

1934: The first nonstop transatlantic flight from Canada to England occurred.

1963: The Great Train Robbery—15 train robbers in England stole £2.6 million.

1991: Tim Horton's was sold to Wendy's International Inc. for $300 million.

2000: After 136 years at the bottom of the ocean, the sunken Confederate submarine *H.L. Hunley* was raised.

2007: Brooklyn was hit by a tornado for the first time since 1889.

Leo
You are socially aware and have strong values; however, you may be confrontational at times.
8, 17, 26

#1 Song
1987: "I Still Haven't Found What I'm Looking For" by U2

Birth Friends Forever
JC Chasez, singer ('N Sync), 1976

Scott D'Amore, Canadian pro wrestler, 1974

Scott Stapp, singer (Creed), 1973

Mike Zanier, Canadian hockey player, 1962

The Edge, musician (U2), 1961

Don Most, actor (*Happy Days*), 1953

Ken Dryden, Canadian hockey player/senator, 1947

Jacques Hétu, Canadian composer, 1938

Connie Stevens, singer, 1938

Dustin Hoffman, actor (*Tootsie*), 1937

Dino De Laurentiis, producer (*Hannibal*), 1919

Daily Oddity
The first Tim Horton's opened in Hamilton, ON, in 1964.

AUGUST 9
144 days until next year

In a Days
Though it's a bit abstract, today is "International Art Appreciation Day."
They were here a long time before us, so celebrate "International Day of the World's Indigenous People."

In the News
1173: Construction began on the Tower of Pisa; it wasn't completed until 200 years later.

1483: The Sistine Chapel opened.

1842: The U.S.-Canadian border east of the Rocky Mountains was established.

1930: Canadian runner Percy Williams set a world record, sprinting 100 m in 10:03 seconds.

1945: The U.S. dropped an atomic bomb on Nagasaki, killing 70,000 people.

1974: Richard Nixon became the first U.S. president to resign.

1988: Edmonton Oiler Wayne Gretzky was traded to the Los Angeles Kings.

1992: The Summer Olympic Games in Barcelona closed, with Canadians bringing home 6 gold medals, 5 silver and 7 bronze.

2004: Dar Heatherington, a city councillor in Lethbridge, AB, resigned after faking her own kidnapping.

Leo
You are a positive and an inspirational person; however, at times you tend to dominate over others.
8, 9, 45

#1 Song
1966: "Summer in the City" by The Lovin' Spoonful

Birth Friends Forever
Shane O'Brien, Canadian hockey player, 1983

Eric Bana, actor (*Hulk*), 1968

Gillian Anderson, actress (*The X-Files*), 1968

Deion Sanders, football and baseball player, 1967

Brett Hull, Canadian hockey player, 1964

Whitney Houston, singer, 1963

Stuart Hughes, Canadian stage actor, 1959

Melanie Griffith, actress (*Working Girl*), 1957

Sam Elliott, actor (*Roadhouse*), 1944

John Gomery, Canadian jurist, 1932

Jacques Parizeau, Canadian politician, 1930

André Bessette, Canadian faith healer, 1845

Daily Oddity
Over 976,000 Canadians identify themselves as being Aboriginal (indigenous).

AUGUST 10
143 days until next year

In a Days

If you're hungry like the wolf, you should celebrate "National Duran Duran Appreciation Day."

If you're hungry like a camper, you should celebrate "S'mores Day."

In the News

1840: *The Star of the East* became the first balloon to fly in Canada.

1907: John Underwood became the first Canadian to be lifted into the air by a kite, floating 3 m above the ground for 15 minutes.

1948: *Candid Camera* made its television debut.

1949: The *Avro Canada* took its maiden flight.

1966: Winnipegger Brian Parks won the world bridge trophy.

1977: Serial killer David Berkowitz ("Son of Sam") was arrested.

1981: 23,000 Canadian Union of Postal Workers went back to work after a 42-day strike.

1995: Concerned with fish stocks, the Canadian government shut down BC's Fraser River salmon fishery.

1995: NASA donated a moon rock to the Cosmodome in Québec.

2008: A series of explosions at a propane facility shook Toronto, causing a number of evacuations.

Leo

You are a persuasive strategist who sometimes can be dismissive.
8, 9, 37

#1 Song

1974: "Feel Like Makin' Love" by Roberta Flack

Birth Friends Forever

Sam Gagner, Canadian hockey player, 1989

Devon Aoki, actress (*Sin City*), 1982

Angie Harmon, actress (*Law & Order*), 1972

Antonio Banderas, actor (*The Mask of Zorro*), 1960

Rosanna Arquette, actress (*Pulp Fiction*), 1959

Florent Vollant, Canadian musician (Kashtin), 1959

Ronnie Spector, singer (The Ronettes), 1943

Eddie Fisher, singer, 1928

Norma Shearer, Canadian actress (*The Divorcee*), 1902

Charles Darrow, inventor of Monopoly, 1889

James Wilson Morrice, Canadian painter, 1865

Daily Oddity

At least one in every 3 Taiwanese funeral processions includes a stripper.

AUGUST 11
142 days until next year

In a Days
Time to cut your foot on broken glass. It's "Play in the Sand Day."

In the News
1883: The first CPR construction train pulled into the tent settlement known as Calgary.

1914: The temperature in St. John's, NL, hit 41°C.

1929: Babe Ruth hit his 500th home run.

1934: The first prisoners arrived at the island prison of Alcatraz.

1941: The use of silk was banned in Canada in order to conserve wartime supplies for parachutes.

1988: The terrorist organization Al-Qaeda was formed.

1988: Montréal Expo Gary Carter hit his 300th home run.

1990: Canadian soldiers arrived at the land dispute in Oka, Québec, to support police in their standoff against Mohawk warriors.

1996: Canadian Formula One driver Jacques Villeneuve won the Grand Prix of Hungary.

2003: Temperatures in Paris, France, reached 44°C; 144 people died.

Leo
You are a tenacious and logical person who can be somewhat critical at times.
8, 9, 22

#1 Song
1910: "Casey Jones" by Billy Murray & American Quartet

Birth Friends Forever
Ben Gibbard, musician (The Postal Service), 1976

Marie-France Dubreuil, Canadian figure skater, 1974

Veda Hille, Canadian singer, 1968

Marc Bergevin, Canadian hockey player, 1965

Jim Lee, comic book artist (*X-Men*), 1964

Hulk Hogan, pro wrestler, 1953

Steve Wozniak, Apple co-founder, 1950

Jim Kale, Canadian musician (The Guess Who) 1943

Israel "Izzy" Asper, Canadian media magnate, 1932

Alex Haley, author (*Roots*), 1921

Chuck Rayner, Canadian hockey player, 1920

Walter Bowman, Canadian soccer player, 1870

Daily Oddity
Twelve out of Canada's 15 largest oil deposits are located in Alberta.

AUGUST 12
141 days until next year

In a Days
Break your hip while attempting to skateboard? It's "International Youth Day."
Today is tailor-made for "Sewing Machine Day."
When you find out what a vinyl record is, celebrate "Vinyl Record Day."

In the News

1851: Isaac Singer patented the sewing machine.

1892: The first electric streetcars began operating in Toronto.

1908: The Ford Motor Company built the first Model T.

1964: South Africa was banned from the Olympic Games because of apartheid.

1981: IBM's first Personal Computer was released.

1990: The most complete skeleton of a *Tyrannosaurus rex* was discovered in South Dakota.

1992: Canada, Mexico and the U.S. completed their negotiations for the North American Free Trade Agreement (NAFTA).

1994: MLB players went on strike, cancelling that year's World Series.

2004: Andre Ouellet resigned as the head of Canada Post because of his involvement in the Sponsorship Scandal.

Leo
You are a responsible and determined individual; however, you can be too confident in yourself.
3, 12, 21

#1 Song
1978: "Three Times a Lady" by The Commodores

Birth Friends Forever

Dominique Swain, actress (*Face/Off*), 1980

Cindy Klassen, Canadian speed skater, 1979

Hayley Wickenheiser, Canadian hockey player, 1978

Brad Lukowich, Canadian hockey player, 1976

Casey Affleck, actor (*Ocean's 11*), 1975

Pete Sampras, tennis player, 1971

Mark Knopfler, musician (Dire Straits), 1949

Roy Romanow, Canadian politician, 1939

George Hamilton, actor (*Zorro, the Gay Blade*), 1939

Norris & Ross McWhirter, co-founders of the *Guinness Book of Records*, 1925

Zerna Sharp, author (*Dick and Jane*), 1889

Cecil B. DeMille, director (*Cleopatra*), 1881

Daily Oddity
An image of a *T. rex* is hidden somewhere on the Canadian $2 coin.

AUGUST 13
140 days until next year

In a Days

Today may be "National Underwear Day," but it doesn't say anything about it being "Clean Underwear Day."

Even though they are freaks of nature, we should still celebrate "International Left-Handers Day"

In the News

3114 BC: The start of the Mayan calendar, which ends in 2012.

1918: Women were allowed to enlist in the U.S. Marine Corps.

1941: The Canadian Women's Army Corps was formed.

1955: The Canso Causeway linking Cape Breton Island to Nova Scotia's mainland was opened.

1977: Winnipeg rock group Bachman-Turner Overdrive (BTO) broke up.

1988: Ronald J. Dossenbach set a new record when he rode his bike from Vancouver to Halifax in 13 days.

1992: Manitoba courts ruled that mandatory Christian prayer in schools was unconstitutional.

1997: The controversial cartoon *South Park* first aired.

2008: Michael Phelps won the most gold medals by an athlete in Olympic history with his victory in the men's 200 m butterfly; he went on to win 8 gold medals in total.

Leo

You are a proficient and ambitious individual who abandons your dreams if they become too hard to obtain.
4, 13, 21

#1 Song

2007: "Beautiful Girls" by Sean Kingston

Birth Friends Forever

Marty Turco, Canadian hockey player, 1975

Patrick Carpentier, Canadian racecar driver, 1971

Danny Bonaduce, actor (*The Partridge Family*), 1959

Herb Ritts, photographer, 1952

Bobby Clarke, Canadian hockey player, 1949

John Stocker, Canadian voice actor (*Sailor Moon*), 1947

Erin Fleming, Canadian actress (*Adam-12*), 1941

Don Ho, musician, 1930

Fidel Castro, Cuban leader, 1926

Alfred Hitchcock, director (*The Birds*), 1899

Annie Oakley, sharpshooter, 1860

Daily Oddity

On average, men spend 11 minutes in the shower while women spend 13.

AUGUST 14
139 days until next year

In a Days
Sit. Roll over. Shake a paw. It's "Assistance Dog Day."

In the News

1885: Japan's first patent was issued to the inventor of a rustproof paint.

1908: The world's first beauty contest was held in Folkestone, England.

1919: The first flight between Montréal and Québec City took place; it took 5 hours.

1934: Canadian brewer John Labatt was kidnapped and held for $150,000 ransom; he was later released unharmed; it was the first ransom kidnapping in Canadian history.

1936: The last public execution was held in the U.S.

1958: The Winnipeg Blue Bombers defeated the Edmonton Eskimos 29–21 in the first CFL game.

1968: Montréal was awarded a National League baseball franchise.

1994: The elusive terrorist "Carlos the Jackal" was apprehended.

2003: The United Church of Canada approved same-sex marriages.

Leo
You are an outgoing and charismatic individual who sometimes becomes emotionally isolated.
5, 15, 32

#1 Song
1944: "Swinging on a Star" by Bing Crosby

Birth Friends Forever
Kyle Turris, Canadian hockey player, 1989

Josh Gorges, Canadian hockey player, 1984

Mila Kunis, actress (*That '70s Show*), 1983

Steve Braun, Canadian actor (*The Immortal*), 1976

Jay Manuel, Canadian TV host (*Canada's Next Top Model*), 1972

Bill Mavreas, Canadian cartoonist, 1968

Halle Berry, actress (*Monster's Ball*), 1966

Sarah Brightman, soprano, 1960

Magic Johnson, basketball player, 1959

Gary Larson, cartoonist (*The Far Side*), 1950

Danielle Steel, author, 1947

Steve Martin, actor (*The Jerk*), 1945

David Crosby, musician (Crosby, Stills and Nash), 1941

Doc Holliday, gambler/dentist, 1851

Daily Oddity
Citronella irritates mosquitos' feet.

AUGUST 15
138 days until next year

In a Days
Sorry, loners, it's "Best Friends Day."
Calm down! It's "National Relaxation Day."
Trim those mutton chops, mister. It's "National Men's Grooming Day."

In the News
1057: The real Scottish king Macbeth was killed in battle.

1822: The population of Upper Canada was 120,000, while Lower Canada had 500,000 inhabitants.

1947: The Canadian Catholic Church abolished meatless Tuesdays and Fridays.

1950: The RCMP took over policing in BC.

1965: The Beatles played Shea Stadium in New York City.

1969: The Woodstock Music and Art Festival opened.

1971: The first Banff Festival of the Arts opened.

1971: Hurricane Beth dropped 296 mm of rain on Halifax, NS, washing out bridges and highways.

1974: The Metropolitan Toronto Zoo opened.

2007: Over 500 people died when an 8.0-magnitude earthquake hit Peru.

Leo
You are a goal-oriented and motivated individual, which makes you appear cold-hearted at times.
6, 9, 32

#1 Song
1953: "Vaya con Dios (May God Be with You)" by Les Paul & Mary Ford

Birth Friends Forever
Joe Jonas, singer (Jonas Brothers), 1989

Martin Biron, Canadian hockey player, 1977

Brendan Morrison, Canadian hockey player, 1975

Natasha Henstridge, Canadian actress (*Species*), 1974

Ben Affleck, actor (*Daredevil*), 1972

Debra Messing, actress (*Will & Grace*), 1968

Craig MacTavish, Canadian hockey player, 1958

Princess Anne, British royalty, 1950

Patsy Gallant, Canadian singer, 1948

Oscar Peterson, Canadian jazz pianist, 1925

Julia Child, cook, 1912

Napoleon Bonaparte, emperor of France, 1769

Daily Oddity
Watermelons are 93% water.

AUGUST 16
137 days until next year

In a Days
Have I every told you the one about "Joke Day"?
Warm up your kicking leg. It's "Sandcastle Day."
Six billion impersonators can't be wrong. It's "Elvis Presley Remembrance Day."

In the News
1665: The first Canadian horses—12 mares and 2 stallions, a gift from Louis XIV—arrived in Canada.

1858: The Bank of Canada was chartered.

1896: Gold was discovered in Canada's Klondike River.

1930: The first coloured cartoon with sound was created.

1962: Ringo Star replaced Pete Best in The Beatles.

1966: Canadian George Chuvalo became Canadian heavyweight boxing champion.

1974: Canadian Cindy Nicholas swam across Lake Ontario in 15 hours, a new record.

1979: Former Canadian Prime Minister John Diefenbaker died.

1989: Trading on the TSX came to a halt when a geomagnetic storm disrupted microchips.

2008: Usain Bolt ran the 100 m dash in 9.69 seconds at the Beijing Olympics.

Leo
You are a calculating attention-seeker who can easily become emotionally disconnected.
8, 9, 61

#1 Song
1987: "Who's That Girl" by Madonna

Birth Friends Forever
Sarah-Jeanne Labrosse, Canadian actress (*Bon Cop, Bad Cop*), 1991

Steve Carell, actor (*The Office*), 1962

Angela Bassett, actress (*ER*), 1958

Madonna, a "material girl," 1958

James Cameron, Canadian director (*Titanic*), 1954

Kathie Lee Gifford, TV personality, 1953

Stockwell Day, Canadian politician, 1950

Julie Newmar, actress (*Batman*), 1933

Frank Gifford, football player, 1930

Fess Parker, actor (*Davy Crockett*), 1924

Charles Bukowski, poet, 1920

Peter Fiddler, Canadian surveyor, 1769

Daily Oddity
60% of weddings are held in the summer, 75% of them on a Saturday.

AUGUST 17
136 days until next year

In a Days
Please don't ask me what the meaning of "Meaning of –Is- Day" is. Kill yourself a b'ar. It's "Davy Crockett's Birthday."

In the News
1706: A new law required taverns in Québec to close at 9 PM.

1959: Oil was discovered in the Yukon.

1965: The Beatles played Maple Leaf Gardens.

1965: Four treasure hunters drowned in Oak Island, NS, while searching for Captain Kidd's treasure.

1970: Canadian architect Arthur Erickson won top architectural honours for his Expo '70 design.

1982: Montréal Expo Gary Carter made his 1000th hit.

1982: The first compact discs (CDs) were released.

1985: Canadian singer Corey Hart played his first show as a headliner.

1988: Two Canadians sailed a catamaran through the Northwest Passage—the first to do so via wind power.

2008: Swimmer Michael Phelps won his 8th consecutive gold medal in a single Olympics.

Leo
You are an innovative and self-confident individual who sometimes ignores good advice.
8, 17, 22

#1 Song
1902: "Bill Bailey, Won't You Please Come Home" by Arthur Collins

Birth Friends Forever
Donnie Wahlberg, singer (New Kids on the Block), 1969

Don Sweeney, Canadian hockey player, 1966

Colin James, Canadian musician, 1964

Sean Penn, actor (*Milk*), 1960

Kirk Stevens, Canadian snooker player, 1958

Belinda Carlisle, singer (The Go-Go's), 1958

Robert Joy, Canadian actor (*CSI: NY*), 1951

Robert De Niro, actor (*Goodfellas*), 1943

Maureen O'Hara, actress (*The Parent Trap*), 1920

Mae West, actress (*Sex*), 1893

Samuel Goldwyn, film producer, 1882

Davy Crockett, frontiersman, 1786

Daily Oddity
Seeing 3 butterflies together is bad luck.

AUGUST 18
135 days until next year

In a Days
Oh say, by the way, it is "Bad Poetry Day."

In the News
1868: Helium was discovered.

1958: Vladimir Nabokov's controversial novel *Lolita* was first published in North America.

1969: Jimi Hendrix played Woodstock.

1972: Canadian doctor Norman Bethune's birthplace in Gravenhurst, ON, was declared a national historic site.

1978: Canadian Maurice "King of the Banjo" Bolyer died.

1979: The Dempster Highway from Dawson, Yukon, to Inuvik, NWT, was opened.

1986: Canadian folksingers Ian Tyson and Sylvia Fricker reunited for a concert at Kingswood Music Theatre.

1988: Former Montréal Canadien Guy Lafleur signed with the New York Rangers.

2005: American Dennis Rader, the BTK (bind, torture and kill) serial killer, was sentenced to 175 years in prison.

Leo
You are a determined individual who has many humanitarian pursuits; however, you may become too obsessed with your goals.
8, 9, 99

#1 Song
1985: "The Power of Love" by Huey Lewis & the News

Birth Friends Forever
Frances Bean Cobain, daughter of Kurt Cobain, 1992

Andy Samberg, comedian (*SNL*), 1978

Régine Chassagne, Canadian musician (Arcade Fire), 1977

Edward Norton, actor (*Fight Club*), 1969

Patrick Swayze, actor (*Dirty Dancing*), 1952

Robert Redford, actor (*Out of Africa*), 1936

William R. Bennett, premier of BC, 1932

Bramwell Tillsley, Canadian Salvation Army general, 1931

Pierre Grondin, Canadian surgeon, 1925

Shelley Winters, actress (*Lolita*), 1920

Max Factor, cosmetics industrialist, 1904

Simon Fraser, Canadian explorer, 1776

Daily Oddity
A Canadian invented the Wonderbra.

AUGUST 19
134 days until next year

In a Days

Safely store your carry-on in the overhead compartment. It's "Aviation Day."

If you're Irish, you'll want to celebrate "National Potato Day."

If you're a pigeon, you'll want to poop on "Sculpture Day."

In the News

1809: The first Canadian steamship was launched on the St. Lawrence River.

1902: Nude protest parades were held in BC.

1935: The temperature in Nova Scotia and PEI reached 38°C.

1942: Canadian troops began raid on German-occupied Dieppe, France.

1957: Robert Bédard won the Canadian Tennis Championship.

1972: Hamilton Tiger Cat Tommy Joe Coffey made his 632nd catch.

1981: A riot broke out in Toronto following the cancellation of an Alice Cooper concert.

1983: Toronto Argonaut Terry Greer made 16 pass receptions in one game.

1992: A ceremony to honour those who died 50 years earlier at Dieppe was held.

2005: Toronto was hit by a series of storms that caused major flooding in the city.

Leo

You are an inspiring and intellectual individual who sometimes believes your own hype.

8, 9, 99

#1 Song

1937: "Satan Takes a Holiday" by Tommy Dorsey

Birth Friends Forever

Matthew Perry, Canadian actor (*Friends*), 1969

Kyra Sedgwick, actress (*The Closer*), 1965

Kevin Dillon, actor (*Entourage*), 1965

John Stamos, actor (*ER*), 1963

Jonathan Frakes, actor (*Star Trek: TNG*), 1952

Susan Jacks, Canadian singer, 1948

Bill Clinton, U.S. president, 1946

Qaqaq Ashoona, Canadian sculptor, 1928

Norman Brooks, Canadian singer, 1928

Gene Roddenberry, creator of *Star Trek*, 1921

Coco Chanel, designer, 1883

Orville Wright, aviation pioneer, 1871

Daily Oddity

In Montréal, 1816 was considered the year with no summer, thanks to snow and frost from June to September.

AUGUST 20
133 days until next year

In a Days
If you're an obnoxious talk-show host or an insipid DJ, you should celebrate "National Radio Day."

In the News

1858: Charles Darwin first published his theory of evolution.

1882: The first CPR train reached Regina.

1907: The University of Saskatchewan was founded.

1969: Frank Zappa disbanded The Mothers of Invention after their Canadian tour.

1976: Gordon Lightfoot released the single "The Wreck of the Edmund Fitzgerald," a song about an ore carrier that sank on Lake Superior.

1987: Canada banned smoking in public service offices, to take effect on January 1, 1988.

1991: The August Coup began, leading to the collapse of the Soviet Union.

1998: The Supreme Court of Canada ruled that Québec couldn't split from Canada without federal approval.

2007: A severed foot in a running shoe washed up on the coast of BC.

Leo
You are an analytical and empathetic individual who tends to put others before yourself.
2, 8, 9

#1 Song
1979: "My Sharona" by The Knack

Birth Friends Forever
Amy Adams, actress (*Enchanted*), 1974
Fred Durst, singer (Limp Bizkit), 1970
James Marsters, actor (*Buffy the Vampire Slayer*), 1962
Patricia Rozema, Canadian director (*Kitt Kittredge*), 1958
Cynthia "Cindy" Nicholas, Canadian swimmer, 1957
Gary Lalonde, Canadian musician (Honeymoon Suite) 1955
Robert Plant, singer (Led Zeppelin), 1948
Connie Chung, TV journalist, 1946
Isaac Hayes, singer, 1942
Don King, boxing promoter, 1931
Mario Bernardi, Canadian conductor, 1930
Amor de Cosmos, BC premier, 1825

Daily Oddity
Lake Superior is the second largest lake in the world.

AUGUST 21
132 days until next year

In a Days
They can't get work, but they can get their own day. It's "Poet's Day."
Pull your pants up to your armpits. It's "Senior Citizen's Day."

In the News

1583: The first Canadian shipwreck occurred off Sable Island, NS; 85 people died.

1847: The Canada Life Insurance Company was founded.

1862: Billy Barker discovered gold in Barkerville, BC.

1879: The Virgin Mary appeared to a number of people in Ireland.

1911: An employee of the Louvre stole the *Mona Lisa*.

1964: Canadian diver Bette Singer set a new record of 93.5 m.

1987: Geraldine Kenney-Wallace was named the first woman chairman of the Science Council of Canada.

2002: Jean Chrétien announced that he would be stepping down as Canada's prime minister effective February 2004.

2006: A UFO was spotted near the Pickering Nuclear Generating Station in Ajax, ON.

Leo
You are an imaginative and pragmatic person who tends to isolate yourself from others.
8, 9, 12

#1 Song
1969: "Honky Tonk Women" by The Rolling Stones

Birth Friends Forever

Hayden Panettiere, actress (*Heroes*), 1989

Usain Bolt, Jamaican sprinter, 1986

Josée Chouinard, Canadian figure skater, 1969

Carrie-Anne Moss, Canadian actress (*The Matrix*), 1967

Kim Cattrall, Canadian actress (*Sex and the City*), 1956

Joe Strummer, singer (The Clash), 1952

Keith Hart, Canadian pro wrestler, 1952

Wilt Chamberlain, basketball player, 1939

Kenny Rogers, "The Gambler," 1938

Christopher Robin Milne, *Winnie-the-Pooh* inspiration, 1920

Toe Blake, Canadian hockey player, 1912

Count Basie, bandleader, 1904

Daily Oddity
The next total solar eclipse visible from Canada will be in 2017.

AUGUST 22
131 days until next year

In a Days
Knock out all of your teeth. It's "National Tooth Fairy Day."

In the News
565: A monk reported seeing a monster in Loch Ness.

1884: The Calgary and District Agricultural Society Fair, the precursor to the Calgary Stampede, was first held.

1886: A man swam through Niagara Rapids wearing a lifejacket.

1901: Cadillac was founded.

1914: Canada's War Measures Act received Royal Assent.

1935: The world's first Social Credit government was elected in Edmonton.

1964: The Beatles held their first Canadian concert in Vancouver, BC.

1979: Former prime minister John Diefenbaker was buried on the University of Saskatchewan campus.

1992: The Charlottetown Accord was signed.

1992: Canadian singer Tom Cochrane's "Life Is a Highway" peaked at number 6 on the charts.

2004: The painting *The Scream* was stolen from a museum in Norway.

2007: The Texas Rangers scored 30 runs against the Baltimore Orioles.

Leo
You are farsighted and courageous; however, you can sometimes only see things in black and white.
8, 9, 32

#1 Song
1995: "Kiss from a Rose" by Seal

Birth Friends Forever
Nicolas Macrozonaris, Canadian athlete, 1980

Jeff Stinco, Canadian musician (Simple Plan), 1978

Howie D, singer (Backstreet Boys), 1973

Kristen Wiig, comedian (*SNL*), 1973

GZA, rapper, 1966

Tori Amos, singer, 1963

Frank Marino, Canadian musician (Mahogany Rush), 1954

Rita Johnston, Canadian politician, 1935

Ray Bradbury, author (*The Martian Chronicles*), 1920

Paul Comtois, Canadian politician, 1895

Ezra Butler Eddy, Canadian businessman, 1827

Daily Oddity
Dracontology is the study of sea monsters.

AUGUST 23
130 days until next year

In a Days
Eat it or bathe with it, it's your choice. It's "National Sponge Cake Day."

In the News

1305: William Wallace, the inspiration for *Braveheart*, was executed for high treason.

1820: A lost pig wandered into a Bank of Montréal.

1882: Pile-O'-Bones was renamed Regina.

1890: Moncton, NB, was incorporated as a city.

1904: Tire chains for automobiles were patented.

1943: Trans-Canada Airlines (now Air Canada) began its transatlantic service.

1954: The first Hercules transport aircraft took flight.

1957: Saskatchewan opened its 740 km stretch of Trans-Canada Highway, the first province to complete its portion.

1978: Calgarian Helen Vanderburg won the gold medal for synchronized swimming at the World Aquatic Championships.

2006: After 8 years in captivity, an Austrian woman escaped her captor, who had abducted her at the age of 10.

Virgo
You are a rigorous individual and a real problem solver; however, sometimes you isolate yourself from others.
8, 9, 32

#1 Song
1949: "Some Enchanted Evening" by Perry Como

Birth Friends Forever

Kobe Bryant, basketball player, 1978

Scott Caan, actor (*Ocean's 11*), 1976

River Phoenix, actor (*Stand By Me*), 1970

Roger Avary, Canadian producer (*Pulp Fiction*), 1965

Chris Potter, Canadian actor (*The Pacifier*), 1960

Shelley Long, actress (*Cheers*), 1949

Keith Moon, musician (The Who), 1946

Barbara Eden, actress (*I Dream of Jeannie*), 1934

Pierre Gauvreau, Canadian painter, 1922

Gene Kelly, dancer, 1912

William Southam, Canadian newspaper publisher, 1843

Daily Oddity
Birthday candles symbolize Artemis, the goddess of the moon.

AUGUST 24
129 days until next year

In a Days
Well, butter me up and cover me in maple syrup, it's "National Waffle Day."

In the News

1456: The Gutenberg Bible was completed.

1814: After American troops burned and looted York (Toronto), the British (Canadians) set fire to the White House in Washington.

1831: Charles Darwin was invited to travel on the HMS *Beagle*.

1891: Thomas Edison patented the film camera.

1908: Canadian boxer Tommy Burns KO'd Bill Squires to win the world heavyweight championship.

1909: Construction on the Panama Canal began.

1912: Alaska became a U.S. territory.

1944: The Battle of Normandy in France ended; 5021 Canadians died.

1972: Canadians Gordie Howe and Jean Beliveau were inducted into the International Hockey Hall of Fame.

2006: The term "planet" was redefined, and Pluto was downgraded to a dwarf planet.

Virgo
You are a seeker of knowledge and a very progressive-minded person; however, sometimes you spend too much time as a bystander.
3, 5, 42

#1 Song
1958: "Little Star" by The Elegants

Birth Friends Forever

Kyle Schmid, Canadian actor (*The Covenant*), 1984

Chad Michael Murray, actor (*One Tree Hill*), 1981

Derek Morris, Canadian hockey player, 1978

Andrew Brunette, Canadian hockey player, 1973

Jean-Luc Brassard, Canadian skier, 1972

Cal Ripken Jr., baseball player, 1960

Mike DeRosier, Canadian musician (Heart), 1951

Rocky Johnson, Canadian pro wrestler (father of The Rock), 1944

Kenny Baker, actor (R2-D2 in *Star Wars*), 1934

Yasser Arafat, Palestinian leader, 1929

René Lévesque, premier of Québec, 1922

Alex Colville, Canadian painter, 1920

Daily Oddity
The ℞ on prescriptions is a form of the astrological symbol for the god Jupiter.

AUGUST 25
128 days until next year

In a Days
Just say you were wrong, so we can enjoy "Kiss and Make Up Day."
Enjoy someone else's pit stains. It's "National Second-Hand Wardrobe Day."

In the News
1785: The first issue of *The Montréal Gazette* was published.

1814: British (Canadian) troops burned down the American Library of Congress.

1878: The first issue of *The Saskatchewan Herald* was published.

1906: King Edward VII approved Saskatchewan's coat of arms.

1910: The Yellow Cab company was founded.

1937: A polio outbreak hit southern Ontario.

1943: Franklin Delano Roosevelt became the first U.S. president to officially visit Canada.

1981: *Voyager 2* passed Saturn.

1989: *Voyager 2* passed Neptune.

1994: St. Marys, ON, was chosen as the home of the Canadian Baseball Hall of Fame and Museum.

2003: The Canadian government conceded ownership of 39,000 sq km between Great Bear Lake and Great Slave Lake to the Tli Cho (Dogrib First Nation).

Virgo
You are a perceptive and resourceful individual who can be impulsive at times.
3, 5, 26

#1 Song
1981: "My Sharona" by The Knack

Birth Friends Forever
Stacey Farber, Canadian actress (*Degrassi: TNG*), 1987

Blake Lively, actress (*Gossip Girl*), 1987

Claudia Schiffer, model, 1970

Rachael Ray, chef, 1968

Tim Burton, director (*Beetlejuice*), 1958

Elvis Costello, musician, 1954

Rob Halford, singer (Judas Priest), 1951

Fariborz Lachini, Canadian composer, 1949

Gene Simmons, musician (Kiss), 1949

Conrad Black, Canadian publisher, 1944

Jacques Demers, Canadian hockey coach, 1944

Carol Bolt, Canadian playwright, 1941

Sean Connery, actor (*James Bond* films), 1930

Monty Hall, Canadian game-show host (*Let's Make a Deal*), 1923

Leonard Bernstein, conductor, 1918

Daily Oddity
The longest recorded kiss lasted 130 hours and 2 minutes.

AUGUST 26
127 days until next year

In a Days
Lick yourself. It's "National Dog Day."

They work as hard as men and they smell twice as nice. It's "Women's Equality Day"

In the News

1834: John A. Macdonald began practising law in Kingston, ON.

1858: The first news was dispatched via the telegraph.

1891: Manitobans received their first-ever published weather forecasts.

1957: Joseph Burr Tyrrell, discoverer of dinosaur fossils in Alberta, died.

1961: The International Hockey Hall of Fame opened in Toronto.

1972: Swimmer Mark Spitz won his 7th Olympic gold medal in Munich, Germany.

1987: September 11 was proclaimed "9-1-1 Emergency Number Day."

1987: A fire destroyed the Canadian National Exhibition's Music Building.

2004: Vancouver Canuck Todd Bertuzzi pleaded not guilty for assaulting Colorado Avalanche player Steve Moore.

2006: Elizabeth May was elected leader of the Canadian Green Party.

2007: A 2nd severed foot inside a running shoe washed up off the coast of BC.

Virgo
You are a logical thinker and a team player; however, at times you may be considered too self-effacing.

3, 5, 62

#1 Song
2008: "Disturbia" by Rihanna

Birth Friends Forever
Petey Williams, Canadian pro wrestler, 1981

Macaulay Culkin, actor (*Home Alone*), 1980

Shirley Manson, singer (Garbage), 1966

Nancy Martinez, Canadian singer, 1960

Rick Hansen, wheelchair athlete, 1957

Bryon Baltimore, Canadian hockey player, 1952

Peter Appleyard, Canadian musician, 1928

Naïm Kattan, Canadian essayist, 1928

Jessie Gray, Canada's first woman surgeon, 1910

Mother Teresa, missionary, 1910

John Buchan, governor general of Canada, 1875

Daily Oddity
The average age of Air Canada pilots is 42.

AUGUST 27
126 days until next year

In a Days
I forgive you, world. It's "Global Forgiveness Day."

In the News

1793: In honour of the Duke of York, the capital of Upper Canada was named York.

1883: Krakatoa, a volcanic island in Indonesia, erupted.

1912: Thomas Wilby and Jack Haney set out on the first cross-Canada motor trip.

1978: Bob Macoritti of the Saskatchewan Roughriders kicked 7 field goals against the Toronto Argonauts, a new CFL record.

1980: Both *The Ottawa Journal* and *The Winnipeg Tribune* went under.

1990: The Canadian Army was ordered to use whatever force necessary to end the Oka standoff.

1998: The Canadian dollar reached 64.02 cents US.

2003: Mars made its closest approach to Earth—55,758,005 km.

2008: Barack Obama became the first African American to be nominated for president by a major U.S. political party.

Virgo
You are articulate and a lateral thinker; however, you may be too smart for your own good.
3, 5, 28

#1 Song
1997: "Mo Money Mo Problems" by The Notorious B.I.G., Puff Daddy & Mase

Birth Friends Forever

Alexa Vega, actress (*Spy Kids*), 1988

Sarah Neufeld, Canadian musician (Arcade Fire), 1979

Mase, rapper, 1977

Cory Bowles, Canadian actor (*Trailer Park Boys*), 1973

Mike Smith, Canadian actor (*Trailer Park Boys*), 1972

Adam Oates, Canadian hockey player, 1962

Normand Brathwaite, Canadian radio host, 1958

Alex Lifeson, Canadian musician (Rush), 1953

Paul Reubens, actor (Pee-Wee Herman), 1952

Sgt. Slaughter, pro wrestler, 1948

Ed Gein, serial killer, 1906

Samuel Goldwyn, film producer, 1882

Daily Oddity
The Canadian Minister of Finance always wears a brand-new pair of shoes to present the annual budget in the House of Commons.

AUGUST 28
125 days until next year

In a Days
Go to school with no clothes on. It's "Dream Day."

In the News
1845: *Scientific American* was first published.

1859: A geomagnetic storm allowed the aurora borealis to be seen around the world.

1861: Toronto's first mayor, William Lyon Mackenzie, died at the age of 66.

1872: "Wild Bill" Hickok staged the first Wild West show in Canada near Niagara Falls.

1898: Caleb Bradham named his soft-drink invention Pepsi-Cola.

1920: The Pantages Theatre opened in Toronto.

1941: Dominion Observatory Time became Canada's official time.

1963: Martin Luther King Jr. gave his "I Have a Dream" speech.

1996: Prince Charles and Princess Diana were divorced.

2008: The governor general of Canada announced the creation of the Sacrifice Medal.

Virgo
You are a communicator and an excellent advisor; however, sometimes that may lead to an air of superiority.
6, 16, 24

#1 Song
1983: "Sweet Dreams" by Eurythmics

Birth Friends Forever
LeAnn Rimes, country singer, 1982

Pierre Turgeon, Canadian hockey player, 1969

Jason Priestley, Canadian actor (*Beverly Hills, 90210*), 1969

Jack Black, actor (*School of Rock*), 1969

Shania Twain, Canadian country singer, 1965

Amanda Tapping, Canadian actress (*The X-Files*), 1965

Paul Martin, Canadian prime minister, 1938

Andy Bathgate, Canadian hockey player, 1932

John Perkins, Canadian blues musician, 1931

Jack Kirby, comic book legend (*Captain America*), 1917

Robertson Davies, Canadian journalist, 1913

Daily Oddity
If you dream of a blackbird, your life will be dull for the next few months.

AUGUST 29
124 days until next year

In a Days
If you are a pothead, you'll be glad to know that today is "More Herbs, Less Salt Day."

In the News

1844: The Mohawks won the first Europeans vs. Natives lacrosse game.

1898: Goodyear Tire was founded.

1907: The Québec Bridge collapsed during construction, killing 75 workers.

1919: Prince Edward Island removed its ban on automobiles.

1987: Canadian swimmer Jocelyn Muir completed her 60-day marathon swim around Lake Ontario, setting a record for the longest international marathon.

1994: Canadian swimmer Carlos Costa swam across the Straits of Messina in Italy in 23.5 hours.

1996: Former BC premier W.R. Bennett was found guilty of insider trading.

2004: Canada left the 2004 Summer Olympics with only 12 medals, its lowest count since Seoul in 1988.

2005: Hurricane Katrina killed more than 1800 people and caused billions of dollars in damage across the U.S. Gulf Coast.

Virgo
You are an independent person who is full of wisdom; however, you are too rebellious at times.
3, 5, 11

#1 Song
1995: "You Are Not Alone" by Michael Jackson

Birth Friends Forever

Lauren Collins, Canadian actress (*Degrassi: TNG*), 1986

Geneviève Jeanson, Canadian cyclist, 1981

David Desrosiers, Canadian musician (Simple Plan), 1980

Chieu Luu, Canadian journalist, 1979

Carla Gugino, actress (*Sin City*), 1971

Chris A. Hadfield, Canadian astronaut, 1959

Michael Jackson, singer, 1958

Robin Leach, TV host, 1941

Elliott Gould, actor (*Ocean's 11*), 1938

Peter Jennings, Canadian news anchor, 1936

Mr. Blackwell, fashion critic, 1922

Charlie Parker, musician, 1920

Ingrid Bergman, actress (*Notorious*), 1915

Aurel Joliat, Canadian hockey player, 1901

Daily Oddity
Prince Rupert, BC, is the cloudiest city in Canada.

AUGUST 30
123 days until next year

In a Days
Realign your hamster's chakras. It's "National Holistic Pet Day."

Put some marshmallows in your toaster and celebrate "National Toasted Marshmallow Day."

In the News
1835: Melbourne, Australia, was founded.

1836: Houston, TX, was founded.

1957: Canadian singer Paul Anka's hit "Diana" peaked at number one on the UK charts.

1967: Thurgood Marshall became the first African American on the U.S. Supreme Court.

1988: Canada's Vicki Keith ended her marathon swim of all 5 Great Lakes.

1990: Canadian singer Paul Anka became an American citizen.

2003: Canada began supplying medicine to developing countries to help fight AIDS/HIV.

2004: The Canadian Passport Office asked for the government's permission to use facial recognition technology to help detect terrorists.

Virgo
You are an ambitious and inspirational person who may be perceived as authoritarian.

1, 17, 19

#1 Song
1974: "(You're) Having My Baby" by Paul Anka

Birth Friends Forever
Andy Roddick, tennis player, 1982

Cameron Diaz, actress, 1972

Paul Oakenfold, disc jockey, 1963

Michael Chiklis, actor (*The Shield*), 1963

Lewis Black, comedian (*Root of Evil*), 1948

John Phillips, singer (The Mamas and the Papas), 1935

Don Getty, premier of Alberta, 1933

Ted Williams, baseball player, 1918

Fred MacMurray, actor (*My Three Sons*), 1908

Raymond Massey, Canadian actor (*The Fountainhead*), 1896

Andrew Onderdonk, Canadian railway contractor, 1848

Mary Shelley, author (*Frankenstein*), 1797

Daily Oddity
American inventor Thomas Edison bought the light bulb patent from two Toronto inventors, Henry Woodward and Matthew Evans.

AUGUST 31
122 days until next year

In a Days
If you're a minion of Satan, you should celebrate "Love Litigating Lawyers Day."

In the News

1527: The first letter was written and sent from Canada; it was sent to Henry VIII.

1888: Jack the Ripper claimed his first victim.

1976: Canada's Carallyn Bowes became the first woman to run across the country, from Halifax to Burnaby, in 133 days.

1981: The RCMP charged Clifford Olson with first-degree murder in the deaths of 9 children; he was sentenced to life in prison with no chance of parole.

1985: Canadian singer Bryan Adams' song "Summer of '69" peaked at number 5 on the pop charts.

1988: The Canada-U.S. Free Trade Agreement went into effect.

1997: Princess Diana died in a car accident.

2006: *The Scream*, which was stolen on August 22, 2004, was recovered.

2008: A listeriosis outbreak, linked to Maple Leaf Foods products, hit Canada; 6 people died.

Virgo
You are an empathic and energetic individual who is so busy helping others that you neglect your own needs.
3, 4, 5

#1 Song
1998: "I Don't Want to Miss a Thing" by Aerosmith

Birth Friends Forever

Mark Johnston, Canadian swimmer, 1979

Scott Niedermayer, Canadian hockey player, 1971

Zack Ward, Canadian actor (*Crossing Jordan*), 1970

Deborah Gibson, singer, 1970

Ralph Krueger, Canadian hockey coach, 1959

Richard Gere, actor (*Pretty Woman*), 1949

Van Morrison, musician, 1945

Jos LeDuc, Canadian pro wrestler, 1944

Jean Béliveau, Canadian hockey player, 1931

James Coburn, actor (*In Like Flint*), 1928

Félix-Antoine Savard, Canadian priest, 1896

Caligula, Roman emperor, 12

Daily Oddity
Grapes explode in the microwave.

SEPTEMBER 1
121 days until next year

In a Days
If you have a job or are pregnant, you should celebrate "Labour Day."

If you are a human-poultry hybrid, you should celebrate "Chicken Boy's Day."

In the News

1860: The cornerstone of the Canadian Parliament Buildings was laid.

1905: Alberta and Saskatchewan entered the Dominion of Canada.

1914: The world's last passenger pigeon died.

1951: Canadian women's rights advocate Nellie McClung died.

1978: Edmonton Eskimo Jackie Parker was named the CFL's outstanding player of the quarter century.

1980: Because of his spreading cancer, Terry Fox cancelled his Marathon of Hope at Thunder Bay, ON.

1982: Canada adopted the Canadian Charter of Rights and Freedoms.

1985: The wreck of the *Titanic* was located off the coast of Newfoundland.

1995: Paul Bernardo was found guilty of the first-degree murders of 2 Ontario schoolgirls.

2006: Luxembourg began broadcasting all television programs in digital.

Virgo
You are a persuasive visionary who at times overextends yourself.
1, 3, 5

#1 Song
1926: "Bye Bye, Blackbird" by Gene Austin

Birth Friends Forever

Jeffrey Buttle, Canadian figure skater, 1982

Polly Shannon, Canadian actress (*Trudeau*), 1976

Scott Speedman, Canadian actor (*Underworld*), 1975

J.D. Fortune, Canadian singer (INXS), 1973

Brian Bellows, Canadian hockey player, 1964

Gloria Estefan, singer, 1957

Dr. Phil McGraw, talk-show host, 1950

Conway Twitty, country singer, 1933

Kenneth Thomson, Canadian businessman, 1923

Yvonne De Carlo, Canadian actress (*The Munsters*), 1922

Edgar Rice Burroughs, author (*Tarzan* series), 1875

Henri Bourassa, Canadian politician, 1868

Daily Oddity
In 1703, passenger pigeons were such a threat to farmers that a Québec bishop excommunicated the species.

SEPTEMBER 2
120 days until next year

In a Days
Wave a white flag to celebrate "V-J Day" (Japan surrendered on this date in 1945).

In the News

1578: Canada's first Christian church service was held.

1651: Martin Boutet was named Québec's first town crier.

1912: The first official Calgary Stampede Rodeo was held.

1961: Shirley Giles and G. Marcellus were appointed Canada's first women bank managers.

1969: The first ATM was installed in the U.S.

1972: Forty-two people were killed when a firebomb was thrown into a Montréal café.

1995: During the Canadian National Exhibition in Toronto, the Nimrod plane crashed into Lake Ontario; 7 people were killed.

1998: A Swissair flight crashed near Peggy's Cove, PEI, killing 229 people.

2005: The Canadian government deployed an Airbus to transport Canadians stranded in New Orleans, post Hurricane Katrina, to an air force base in Texas.

Virgo
You are a direct and perceptive individual who can be single-minded at times.
3, 5, 11

#1 Song
1990: "Blaze of Glory" by Jon Bon Jovi

Birth Friends Forever

Dany Sabourin, Canadian hockey player, 1980

Stéphane Matteau, Canadian hockey player, 1969

Salma Hayek, actress (*Frida*), 1966

Lennox Lewis, boxer, 1965

Keanu Reeves, Canadian actor (*The Matrix*), 1964

Guy Laliberté, Canadian founder of Cirque du Soleil, 1959

Tony Alva, skateboarder, 1957

Mario Tremblay, Canadian hockey player, 1956

Mark Harmon, actor (*NCIS*), 1951

Terry Bradshaw, football commentator, 1948

Glen Sather, Canadian hockey player, 1943

C. Wilson Markle Jr., Canadian inventor of the film colourization process, 1938

Daily Oddity
The Calgary Stampede was originally called The Last and Best Great West Frontier Days Celebration.

SEPTEMBER 3
119 days until next year

In a Days
If you have a pouch or enjoy wrestling crocodiles or drinking Foster's Lager, you should celebrate "Australian National Flag Day."

In the News
1189: Richard the Lionheart was crowned king of England.

1894: Canada celebrated Labour Day for the first time.

1929: The Dow Jones Industrial Average reached an all-time high of 381.17, soon followed by the Great Wall Street Crash of 1929.

1970: Football coach Vince Lombardi died.

1979: Canada's CFMT-TV, the world's first private multilingual television station, went on the air.

1987: Canada's Cirque du Soleil performed in Los Angeles.

1989: During the Canadian National Exhibition airshow, 2 Snowbird jets collided; one pilot died.

1992: Canadian Prime Minister Brian Mulroney announced that a referendum (the Charlottetown Accord) would be held on October 26.

1995: The Internet site eBay was founded.

Virgo
You are an inquisitive individual; however, sometimes you can be perceived as a "Yes" person.
4, 26, 36

#1 Song
2006: "SexyBack" by Justin Timberlake

Birth Friends Forever
Cone McCaslin, Canadian musician (Sum 41), 1980

Marianna Komlos, Canadian bodybuilder, 1969

Charlie Sheen, actor (*Platoon*), 1965

Steve Jones, musician (Sex Pistols), 1955

Albert DeSalvo, serial killer (Boston Strangler), 1931

Armand Vaillancourt, Canadian sculptor, 1929

Mort Walker, creator of *Beetle Bailey*, 1923

Alan Ladd, actor (*Shane*), 1913

Paul Kane, Canadian painter, 1810

Guy Carleton, governor of Québec, 1724

Jean-Baptiste Gaultier La Vérendrye, Canadian fur trader, 1713

Daily Oddity
Birthdays were celebrated as far back as 3000 BC by the Egyptians; however, only those of the queen and male members of the royal family were celebrated.

SEPTEMBER 4
118 days until next year

In a Days
Extra! Extra! It's "Newspaper Carriers Day."

In the News
1880: John A. Macdonald signed an agreement to begin construction of the CPR.

1886: Geronimo surrendered.

1888: George Eastman registered the name Kodak.

1950: A 452 kg tuna was caught in St. Ann Bay, NS.

1950: The comic *Beetle Bailey* made its debut.

1957: The Ford Edsel was introduced.

1972: Swimmer Mark Spitz won his 7th Olympic gold medal in Munich, Germany.

1972: In Game 2 of the Super Series, Canada beat the USSR 4–1.

1984: Brian Mulroney became Canada's prime minister after winning the federal election.

1985: Mila Mulroney, the prime minister's wife, gave birth to the couple's son, Nicolas Mulroney.

1997: Canada's Gordie Howe, 69, became the only hockey player to play in 6 consecutive decades, after he played in the IHL's Detroit Vipers home opener.

1998: Google was founded.

Virgo
You are a quick-witted truth seeker who sometimes comes off as being too intense.
3, 5, 22

#1 Song
2008: "Whatever You Like" by T.I.

Birth Friends Forever
Beyoncé Knowles, singer, 1981

Wes Bentley, actor (*American Beauty*), 1978

Françoise Yip, Canadian actress (*Rumble in the Bronx*), 1972

Mike Piazza, baseball player, 1968

Sergio Momesso, Canadian hockey player, 1965

Damon Wayans, comedian (*In Living Color*), 1960

Bryan Mauricette, Canadian cricket player, 1946

Ron Ward, Canadian hockey player, 1944

Dick York, actor (*Bewitched*), 1928

Bert Olmstead, Canadian hockey player, 1926

Paul Harvey, radio broadcaster, 1918

Edward Dmytryk, Canadian director (*The Cain Mutiny*), 1908

Donald McKay, Canadian naval architect, 1810

Daily Oddity
The odds of winning the 6/49 are 1 in 13,983,816.

SEPTEMBER 5
117 days until next year

In a Days
If you're hoping to be unemployed soon, you should celebrate "Be Late for Something Day."

In the News

1698: Tsar Peter I of Russia enforced a new tax on beards.

1755: Acadians unwilling to take an oath of allegiance were expelled from Canada.

1944: An earthquake hit Cornwall, ON.

1945: Soviet spy Igor Gouzenko defected to Canada, bringing Russian secrets with him.

1945: Canada's first nuclear power reactor, ZEEP—the Zero Energy Experimental Pile—went online in Chalk River, ON.

1972: Palestinian terrorist group "Black September" attacked 11 Israeli athletes during the Munich Olympic Games.

1990: After a 55-day standoff (Oka), the Mercier Bridge through the Kahnawake reserve reopened.

1997: Mother Teresa of Calcutta died.

2007: Canadian television personality David Onley replaced James Bartleman as lieutenant-governor of Ontario.

Virgo
You are an astute and energetic person who has a tendency to put others before yourself.
3, 5, 23

#1 Song
1992: "End of the Road" by Boyz II Men

Birth Friends Forever

Stacey Dales, Canadian basketball player, 1979

Laura Bertram, Canadian actress (*Ready or Not*), 1978

Rose McGowan, actress (*Grindhouse: Planet Terror*), 1973

Shane Sewell, Canadian pro wrestler, 1972

Michael Keaton, actor (*Batman*), 1951

Paul William Roberts, Canadian author (*The Palace of Fears*), 1950

Freddie Mercury, singer (Queen), 1946

Werner Herzog, director (*Grizzly Man*), 1942

Raquel Welch, actress (*One Million Years B.C.*), 1940

Bob Newhart, comedian, 1929

Frank Shuster, Canadian comedian (Wayne and Shuster), 1916

Jack Daniel, whiskey magnate, 1850

Jesse James, outlaw, 1847

Louis XIV, king of France, 1638

Louis VIII, king of France, 1187

Daily Oddity
Most people die of natural causes between 4 and 5 PM.

SEPTEMBER 6
116 days until next year

In a Days
Turn off the TV and pick up the *TV Guide*. It's "Read a Book Day."

In the News
1897: The Saskatchewan Roughriders football club was formed.

1952: The first Canadian TV station, CBFT in Montréal, went on the air.

1972: Team Canada and the USSR tied 4–4 in Game 3 of the Summit Series.

1977: Canadian author Leslie MacFarlane, who wrote the first 20 books of *The Hardy Boys* series, died at the age of 74.

1977: Canada changed all its highway signs to metric (except in Nova Scotia and Québec).

1987: Saskatchewan Roughrider Dave Ridgway kicked a 60-yard field goal, a CFL record.

1989: Canadian musician Neil Young won MTV's Best Video Award for his video "This Note's For You," which lampooned advertising.

1995: Baseball player Cal Ripken Jr. set a record by playing in his 2131st consecutive game.

1997: 2.5 billion people tuned into to their television sets to watch Princess Diana laid to rest.

Virgo
You are a curious and tenacious individual who sometimes neglects your personal life.
3, 5, 42

#1 Song
1995: "Gangsta's Paradise" by Coolio

Birth Friends Forever
Foxy Brown, rapper, 1979

Sarah Strange, Canadian actress (*Men in Trees*), 1974

Nina Persson, singer (The Cardigans), 1974

Greg Rusedski, Canadian tennis player, 1973

Dolores O'Riordan, singer (The Cranberries), 1971

Angela Chalmers, Canadian sprinter, 1963

Jeff Foxworthy, comedian, 1958

Michaëlle Jean, governor general of Canada, 1957

Swoosie Kurtz, actress (*Pushing up Daisies*), 1944

Roger Waters, musician (Pink Floyd), 1943

W.A.C. Bennett, BC premier, 1900

George Herrick Duggan, Canadian engineer, 1862

Daily Oddity
You burn more calories sleeping than you do watching TV.

SEPTEMBER 7
115 days until next year

In a Days
Who wants some hugs? It's "National Grandparent's Day."
Who wants some meat? It's "Salami Day."
It's "Neither Snow Nor Rain Day," so be prepared for sleet.

In the News
1572: Canada's first business transaction took place when a fisherman in Labrador bought 4 scallops.

1921: The first Miss America Pageant was held.

1975: Winnipeg's The Guess Who played their final concert at the Montréal Forum.

1977: Canada's Cindy Nicholas became the first woman to swim the English Channel there and back, nonstop.

1980: A Terry Fox telethon raised $10 million for cancer research.

1988: Guy Lafleur, Tony Esposito and Brad Park were inducted into the Hockey Hall of Fame.

1991: A hailstorm hit Calgary, resulting in 116,000 insurance claims and $340 million in damages.

2008: The U.S. government took control of Fannie Mae and Freddie Mac, its largest mortgage-financing companies, during the subprime mortgage crisis.

Virgo
You are an incisive and innovative individual; however, your actions may sometimes be perceived as obstructive.
3, 5, 44

#1 Song
1989: "Hangin' Tough" by New Kids on the Block

Birth Friends Forever
Evan Rachel Wood, actress (*The Wrestler*), 1987

Aleksandra Wozniak, Canadian tennis player, 1987

Eazy-E, rapper (N.W.A.), 1963

Corbin Bernsen, actor (*Major League*), 1954

Chrissie Hynde, singer (The Pretenders), 1951

Julie Kavner, actress (Marge Simpson), 1950

Jacques Lemaire, Canadian hockey player, 1945

Beverley McLachlin, Chief Justice of Canada, 1943

Buddy Holly, singer, 1936

Allan Blakeney, Saskatchewan premier, 1925

Clarence Campbell, Canadian NHL president, 1905

Elizabeth I, queen of England, 1533

Daily Oddity
Canada at one time used playing cards as money.

SEPTEMBER 8
114 days until next year

In a Days
If you're reading this, you are inadvertently celebrating "International Literacy Day." As long as you're not self-employed, celebrate "National Boss/Employee Exchange Day."

In the News
1504: Michelangelo's *David* was unveiled.

1911: Mount Royal College opened in Calgary.

1921: Margaret Gorman, 16, became the first Miss America.

1930: Scotch Tape hit the market.

1952: Canada got television.

1954: Marilyn Bell, 16, swam across Lake Ontario in 20 hours.

1964: The Beatles played the Montréal Forum.

1966: *Star Trek* premiered.

1968: An FLQ bomb exploded in Québec City.

1971: Canada's Gordie Howe retired for the first time; he didn't officially retire until 1980.

1972: The USSR beat Canada 5–3 in Game 4 of the Summit Series.

1974: U.S. President Gerald Ford pardoned Richard Nixon.

2004: Canada gave $20 million to the UN for peacekeeping in Sudan.

Virgo
You are a determined individual with strong beliefs who may force your values on others.
3, 5, 36

#1 Song
1997: "Honey" by Mariah Carey

Birth Friends Forever
Pink, singer, 1979

Jay McKee, Canadian hockey player, 1977

Brooke Burke, model, 1971

David Arquette, actor (*Scream*), 1971

Neko Case, musician, 1970

Rogatien "Rogie" Vachon, Canadian hockey player, 1945

Barbara Frum, Canadian broadcaster, 1937

Patsy Cline, singer, 1932

Peter Sellers, actor (*Pink Panther*), 1925

Mimi Parent, Canadian painter, 1924

Sid Caesar, comedian, 1922

Frank "Pep" Leadley, Canadian football player, 1898

Robert McLaughlin, Canadian car manufacturer, 1871

Richard I, king of England, 1157

Daily Oddity
Salt is the only rock that humans can eat.

SEPTEMBER 9
113 days until next year

In a Days
Go hug a grizzly. It's "Teddy Bear Day."

If you wear army fatigues in an urban setting, you should celebrate "Wonderful Weirdoes Day."

In the News
1898: The Ottawa Football Club became the Ottawa Rough Riders.

1919: Alexander Graham Bell's hydrofoil set a world speed record of 122 km/h.

1956: Elvis Presley debuted on *The Ed Sullivan Show*.

1964: For the first time ever, a Canadian province (Québec) borrowed money ($100 million) from another province (BC).

1965: Simon Fraser University opened in Burnaby, BC.

1970: Canada banned DDT, effective January 1, 1971.

1979: Canadian cartoonist Lynn Johnson's *For Better or For Worse* premiered.

1984: Pope John Paul II began his 12-day tour of Canada.

1988: David Lam became the first Chinese Canadian lieutenant-governor of British Columbia.

2005: The Halifax Airport Terminal was named after Nova Scotia premier Robert Stanfield.

Virgo
You are an ingenious and benevolent individual who suppresses your need to have fun.

3, 5, 28

#1 Song
1956: "Hound Dog/Don't Be Cruel" by Elvis Presley

Birth Friends Forever
Michelle Williams, actress (*Dawson's Creek*), 1980

Michael Bublé, Canadian singer, 1975

Félix Rodríguez, baseball player, 1972

Rachel Hunter, model, 1969

Adam Sandler, comedian (*SNL*), 1966

Hugh Grant, actor (*Notting Hill*), 1960

John Kricfalusi, Canadian animator (*Ren & Stimpy*), 1955

Tom Wopat, actor (*The Dukes of Hazzard*), 1951

Bruce Palmer, Canadian musician (Buffalo Springfield), 1946

Otis Redding, singer, 1941

H.R. MacMillan, Canadian businessman, 1885

Leo Tolstoy, author (*War and Peace*), 1828

Daily Oddity
Elvis Presley loved bumper cars.

SEPTEMBER 10
112 days until next year

In a Days
Oops. It's "Swap Ideas Day," not "Swap Wives Days."

In the News

1937: Over 1500 cases of infantile paralysis (poliomyelitis) were reported in Canada; 56 children died.

1939: Canada declared war on Germany.

1941: The Alberta government closed schools because of a polio outbreak.

1945: "Mike the Headless Chicken" was decapitated; he lived headless for 18 months.

1960: The Halifax International Airport opened.

1978: Toronto Argonaut coach Leo Cahill became the first CFL coach to be fired twice by the same football club.

1986: Montréal Canadien Serge Savard was inducted into the Hockey Hall of Fame.

1995: Canada's Jacques Villeneuve won the Indy Car racing title.

2000: After 22 years, *Cats* closed on Broadway.

2004: Canada announced $500 million to help cattle farmers, following restricted trade in 2003 because of mad cow disease.

Virgo
You are a far-seeing strategist who may become emotionally debilitated at times.
3, 5, 81

#1 Song
1988: "Sweet Child O' Mine" by Guns N' Roses

Birth Friends Forever

Coco Rocha, Canadian model, 1988

Jordan Staal, Canadian hockey player, 1988

Ryan Phillippe, actor (*Cruel Intentions*), 1974

Guy Richie, director (*Snatch*), 1968

Joe Nieuwendyk, Canadian hockey player, 1966

Colin Firth, actor (*Pride & Prejudice*), 1960

Vic Toews, Canadian politician, 1952

Margaret Trudeau, former wife of Pierre Trudeau, 1948

Karl Lagerfeld, fashion designer, 1933

Arnold Palmer, golfer, 1929

Jean Vanier, Canadian disabilities advocate, 1928

Yma Súmac, singer, 1922

Rin Tin Tin, canine hero, 1918

Daily Oddity
During the Alberta poliomyelitis epidemic, school lessons were published in newspapers.

SEPTEMBER 11
111 days until next year

In a Days
Be wary of people trying to check out your glutes. It's "National Hot Cross Buns Day."

In the News

1754: Anthony Henday became the first European in Alberta.

1888: The world's oldest sound recording, a message by Canadian Governor General Lord Stanley, was made.

1941: Construction commenced on the Pentagon.

1956: Canadian pilot Billy Bishop died at the age of 62.

1961: The World Wildlife Fund was founded.

1973: Helen Hunley became Alberta's first woman Solicitor General.

1987: Canadian actor Lorne Greene (*Bonanza*) died at the age of 72.

2001: 9/11: 2974 people died when two terrorist-hijacked airplanes were flown into the World Trade Center in NYC; another plane hit the Pentagon in Virginia; a 4th crashed in Pennsylvania.

2007: Stephen Harper became the first Canadian prime minister to address the Australian Parliament.

Virgo
You are a perceptive and clear-sighted individual who can sometimes be quite stubborn.
2, 3, 5

#1 Song
1991: "The Promise of a New Day" by Paula Abdul

Birth Friends Forever
Zack Stortini, Canadian hockey player, 1985

Mike Comrie, Canadian hockey player, 1980

Ludacris, rapper, 1977

Harry Connick Jr., singer and actor, 1967

Moby, musician, 1965

Brad Bird, animation director (*The Incredibles*), 1957

Brian de Palma, director (*Scarface*), 1940

Oliver Jones, Canadian jazz pianist, 1934

Harry Somers, Canadian composer, 1925

Dalton Camp, Canadian journalist, 1920

Pinto Colvig, voice actor (Goofy), 1892

O. Henry, author (*The Gift of the Magi*), 1862

Daily Oddity
Twenty-four Canadians died in the 9/11 attacks.

SEPTEMBER 12
110 days until next year

In a Days
If you still live in your parents' basement, you should celebrate "Video Game Day." You have so much to live for! It's "World Suicide Prevention Day."

In the News

1609: Henry Hudson discovered the Hudson River.

1646: Huron fur traders arrived in New France (Québec) with 14,515 kg of beaver pelts.

1759: British soldiers captured Québec City.

1858: Gold was found in Tangier, NS.

1874: Maple Ridge, BC, was founded.

1940: Cave paintings were discovered in France.

1959: *Bonanza* premiered.

1974: The Canadian Egg Marketing Agency ordered 28 million eggs destroyed because of improper storage.

1993: Canadian actor Raymond Burr (*Perry Mason*) died at the age of 76.

1996: Rocky Mountain Railtours ran the longest passenger train in Canadian history, with 34 cars.

2007: The Burj Dubai in Dubai surpassed the CN Tower as the world's tallest freestanding building (321 m).

Virgo
You are a rational person with a dualistic personality who is sometimes too focused on work.
3, 5, 66

#1 Song
1999: "Unpretty" by TLC

Birth Friends Forever

Jennifer Hudson, actress (*Dreamgirls*), 1981

Ruben Studdard, *American Idol* contestant, 1978

Martin Lapointe, Canadian hockey player, 1973

Neil Peart, Canadian musician (Rush), 1952

Barry White, singer, 1944

Michael Ondaatje, Canadian author (*The English Patient*), 1943

George Chuvalo, Canadian boxer, 1937

Ian Holm, actor (*The Lord of the Rings*), 1931

George Jones, country singer, 1931

Desmond Llewelyn, actor (Q, *James Bond* films), 1914

Jesse Owens, athlete, 1913

Donald MacDonald, Canadian politician, 1909

Daily Oddity
On September 12, 2003, Canada's PC Party released a statement describing Liberal leader Dalton McGuinty as an "Evil reptilian kitten-eater from another planet."

SEPTEMBER 13
109 days until next year

In a Days
Listen up chrome-domes, it's "Bald is Beautiful Day."

In the News

1503: Michelangelo began work on *David*.

1759: British troops defeated the French near Québec City in the Battle of the Plains of Abraham.

1922: The world's hottest temperature, 57°C, was recorded in Al Aziziyah, Libya.

1981: The first annual Terry Fox 10-K run was held.

1986: The Canadian Country Music Awards were first broadcast.

1988: Hurricane Gilbert became the strongest recorded hurricane in the Western Hemisphere.

1989: Desmond Tutu led the largest anti-apartheid march in South African history.

2001: Civilian air traffic resumed in the U.S. following the 9/11 attacks.

2004: Canada's first same-sex divorce took place.

2006: Kimveer Gill went on a killing spree at Montréal's Dawson College, killing 2 students and injuring 19 others before turning the gun on himself.

Virgo
You are a driven individual and a true pioneer; however, those qualities may cause you to overwork yourself.
3, 5, 67

#1 Song
2001: "Fallin'" by Alicia Keys

Birth Friends Forever

Angel Williams, Canadian pro wrestler, 1981

Fiona Apple, singer, 1977

José Théodore, Canadian hockey player, 1976

Craig Rivet, Canadian hockey player, 1974

Stella McCartney, fashion designer, 1971

Dave Mustaine, musician (Megadeth), 1961

Nell Carter, actress (*Gimme a Break*), 1948

Peter Cetera, singer (Chicago), 1944

David Clayton-Thomas, Canadian singer (Blood, Sweat & Tears), 1941

Richard Kiel, actor (*Moonraker*), 1939

Mel Tormé, singer, 1925

Roald Dahl, author (*The Witches*), 1916

Laura Secord, Canadian heroine (War of 1812), 1775

Daily Oddity
The Battle of the Plains of Abraham only lasted 15 minutes, but 1300 men were killed or injured.

SEPTEMBER 14
108 days until next year

In a Days
Stand aside crullers. It's "National Cream-Filled Doughnut Day."

In the News

1752: The British Empire adopted the Gregorian calendar and skipped ahead 11 days (today would have originally been September 3).

1917: Russia was officially proclaimed a republic.

1936: Canadian nurse Dorothea Palmer was arrested for distributing birth-control information.

1948: A groundbreaking ceremony was held in New York City for the headquarters of the United Nations.

1960: The Organization of the Petroleum Exporting Countries (OPEC) was founded.

1987: The Toronto Blue Jays hit 10 home runs in a 9-inning game, a new MLB record.

1994: The MLB season was cancelled because of a strike.

1995: Body Worlds, an exhibition featuring deceased human bodies, first opened in Japan.

2001: Canada held its largest vigil on Parliament Hill for the victims of 9/11.

Virgo
You are an energetic and disciplined individual who can also be very critical at times.
3, 5, 14

#1 Song
1976: "Play That Funky Music" by Wild Cherry

Birth Friends Forever
Amy Winehouse, singer, 1983
Mike Ward, Canadian comedian, 1973
Nas, rapper, 1973
Faith Ford, actress (*Murphy Brown*), 1964
Callum Keith Rennie, Canadian actor (*Battlestar Galactica*), 1960
Sam Neill, actor (*Jurassic Park*), 1947
Walter Koenig, actor (*Star Trek*), 1936
Maurice Vachon, Canadian pro wrestler, 1929
Clayton Moore, actor (*The Lone Ranger*), 1914
Frank Amyot, Canadian canoeist, 1904
Ivan Pavlov, father of classical conditioning, 1849

Daily Oddity
The Battle of the Plains of Abraham was named after the farmer who owned the field where the conflict took place.

SEPTEMBER 15
107 days until next year

In a Days
If you're tone deaf, please don't celebrate "International Sing-Out Day." Sideswipe a P.T. Cruiser. It's "National Woman Road Warrior Day."

In the News
1835: Charles Darwin reached the Galápagos Islands.

1935: Germany adopted the swastika flag.

1960: Maurice "Rocket" Richard retired from the NHL with 544 goals.

1970: Manitoba lowered its voting age to 18.

1976: Team Canada beat Czechoslovakia in the inaugural Canada Cup tournament.

1978: Ontario's Jean-Luc Lafrenière, 11, became the first school patroller to be killed by a car while on duty.

1979: ABBA kicked off their first North American tour in Vancouver.

1987: Team Canada beat the USSR in the Canada Cup.

1988: Mother Teresa gave a speech in Montréal.

1992: Canadian planes delivered relief supplies to famine-stricken Somalia.

2004: NHL commissioner Gary Bettman announced a lockout, and the 2004–05 hockey season was cancelled.

Virgo
You are an inquisitive and affectionate individual who sometimes damages your personal relationships by overstretching yourself.
3, 5, 6

#1 Song
1978: "Boogie Oogie Oogie" by A Taste of Honey

Birth Friends Forever
Henry, Prince of Wales, 1984

Patrick Marleau, Canadian hockey player, 1979

Heidi Montag, reality-show star, 1968

Dan Marino, football player, 1961

Joel Quenneville, Canadian hockey player, 1958

Harry Sinden, Canadian hockey player, 1958

Tommy Lee Jones, actor (*JFK*), 1946

Oliver Stone, director (*JFK*), 1946

Norma MacMillan, Canadian actress (*Little House on the Prairie*), 1921

Fay Wray, Canadian actress (*King Kong*), 1907

Agatha Christie, author (*Murder on the Orient Express*), 1890

Marco Polo, explorer, 1254

Daily Oddity
All three games of the '87 Canada Cup ended in a 6–5 score.

SEPTEMBER 16
106 days until next year

In a Days
Thanks to all the hairspray used in the '80s, we now have to celebrate "Preservation of the Ozone Day."

In the News
1887: The first softball game was played.

1893: Calgary was incorporated as Alberta's first city.

1908: General Motors was founded.

1914: Sam Hughes formed the Canadian Aviation Corps.

1916: Prohibition went into effect in Ontario.

1957: Asian flu hit Canada.

1974: Gary Carter played his first game as a Montréal Expo.

1974: Canada's first female RCMP constable was sworn in.

1987: The Montréal Protocol to protect the ozone layer from depletion was signed.

1991: Canadian-born Jenny Jones premiered her talk show.

1996: CBC announcer Bob Cole was inducted into the Hockey Hall of Fame.

2004: Manitoba lifted its ban on same-sex marriage.

Virgo
You are generally an optimistic and generous individual who has a hard time focusing on a specific task.
3, 5, 7

#1 Song
1960: "The Twist" by Chubby Checker

Birth Friends Forever
Nick Jonas, musician (Jonas Brothers), 1992

Alexis Bledel, actress (Gilmore Girls), 1981

Amy Poehler, comedian (SNL), 1971

Marc Anthony, singer, 1968

Molly Shannon, actress (SNL), 1964

Jennifer Tilly, Canadian actress (Liar Liar) 1959

David Copperfield, magician, 1956

Mickey Rourke, actor (The Wrestler), 1956

Eric Vail, Canadian hockey player, 1953

Ed Begley Jr., actor (Arrested Development), 1949

Peter Falk, actor (Columbo), 1927

B.B. King, musician, 1925

Lauren Bacall, actress (The Big Sleep), 1924

Allan Funt, TV personality, 1914

H.A. Rey, author (Curious George), 1898

James Jerome Hill, Canadian railway financier, 1838

Daily Oddity
Winnipeg's Harry Wasylyk invented the green garbage bag.

SEPTEMBER 17
105 days until next year

In a Days
If you are an American woman, you should celebrate "Guess Who Day."
If you want to qualify for health care, you'd better celebrate "Citizenship Day."

In the News
1908: Thomas Selfridge became the first airplane fatality while flying with Orville Wright.

1916: The Red Baron shot down his first victim.

1920: The NFL was formed.

1949: Over 100 died when the SS *Noronic* caught fire in the Toronto Harbour.

1956: Australia got television.

1971: Guy Lafleur played his first NHL game as a Montréal Canadien.

1976: *The Enterprise*, NASA's first space shuttle, was unveiled.

1978: *Battlestar Galactica*, starring Canadian actor Lorne Greene, debuted.

1983: Vanessa L. Williams became the first black Miss America.

1984: Brian Mulroney was sworn in as Canada's 18th prime minister.

1987: The last episode of *T.J. Hooker*, starring Canadian William Shatner, aired.

1996: *Spin City*, starring Canadian Michael J. Fox, debuted.

Virgo
You are a decisive and motivated individual who tends to bottle up your emotions.
3, 5, 8

#1 Song
1982: "Hard to Say I'm Sorry" by Chicago

Birth Friends Forever
Garth Murray, Canadian hockey player, 1982

Chuck Comeau, Canadian musician (Simple Plan), 1979

Shawn Horcoff, Canadian hockey player, 1978

Peter Lhotka, Canadian director (*Jake and the Kid*), 1962

Baz Luhrmann, director (*Australia*), 1962

Hank Ilesic, Canadian football player, 1959

John Ritter, actor (*Three's Company*), 1948

David Emerson, Canadian politician, 1945

Anne Bancroft, actress (*The Graduate*), 1931

Roddy McDowall, actor (*Planet of the Apes*), 1928

Hank Williams, musician, 1923

James Alexander Calder, Canadian politician, 1868

Daily Oddity
Lester B. Pearson won the Noble Peace Prize for his peacekeeping work.

SEPTEMBER 18
104 days until next year

In a Days
If you have the need for speed, you should celebrate "Air Force Day." You can play with it and eat it. It's "National Play-Doh Day."

In the News

1837: Tiffany and Co. opened.

1851: *The New York Times* was first published.

1885: Riots broke out in Montréal in protest of compulsary smallpox vaccination.

1919: Women in the Netherlands got the vote.

1932: Actress Peg Entwistle committed suicide by jumping from the "H" in the Hollywood sign.

1942: The CBC was authorized.

1970: Jimi Hendrix was found dead in a London hotel.

1975: Heiress/outlaw Patty Hearst was arrested.

1992: Nine miners died in an explosion near a NWT gold mine.

1992: Canada's *The Kids in the Hall* sketch show debuted on CBS.

1997: Media mogul Ted Turner donated $1 billion to the UN.

2001: The first letter containing anthrax was mailed in the U.S.

Virgo
You are an artistic and sensitive individual who tends to isolate yourself from others.
3, 5, 81

#1 Song
1986: "Stuck with You" by Huey Lewis & the News

Birth Friends Forever

Xzibit, rapper, 1974

Lance Armstrong, cyclist, 1971

Jada Pinkett Smith, actress (*The Matrix Reloaded*), 1971

James Gandolfini, actor (*The Sopranos*), 1961

Dee Dee Ramone, musician (The Ramones), 1952

Darryl Sittler, Canadian hockey player, 1950

Frankie Avalon, singer, 1939

Fred Willard, actor (*Best in Show*), 1939

Ralph Backstrom, Canadian hockey player, 1937

Greta Garbo, actress (*Romance*), 1905

John Diefenbaker, Canadian prime minister, 1895

Grey Owl, Canadian naturalist, 1888

Daily Oddity
Pogonip is a type of ice fog. Folklore says that it can cause severe injury to the lungs if inhaled.

SEPTEMBER 19
103 days until next year

In a Days
Arrgh! Who wants to buy bootlegged DVDs? It's "Talk Like a Pirate Day."

In the News
1889: Forty-five people died in a rockslide in Québec City.

1900: Butch Cassidy and the Sundance Kid committed their first robbery together.

1934: Bruno Hauptmann was arrested for the murder of the Lindbergh baby.

1952: Charlie Chaplin was banned from the U.S.

1959: Nikita Khrushchev was banned from Disneyland.

1960: The University of Alberta opened a new campus in Calgary, AB.

1961: Betty and Barney Hill claimed that a UFO tried to abduct them.

1970: The first Glastonbury Festival was held in England.

2003: Hurricane Isabel killed one person and caused power outages in Ontario.

2005: Canada and Denmark settled their dispute over Hans Island ownership, with sovereignty going to Canada.

Virgo
You are a jovial individual with a thirst for knowledge; however, you sometimes spread yourself too thin.
3, 5, 19

#1 Song
1990: "Release Me" by Wilson Phillips

Birth Friends Forever
Tegan and Sara Quin, Canadian singers (Tegan and Sara), 1980

Trisha Yearwood, country singer, 1964

Daniel Lanois, Canadian record producer, 1951

Twiggy, model, 1949

Jeremy Irons, actor (*Kafka*), 1948

Sylvia Tyson, Canadian singer, 1940

Ed Westfall, Canadian hockey player, 1940

Adam West, actor (*Batman*), 1928

James Lipton, TV host (*Inside the Actors Studio*), 1926

William Golding, author (*Lord of the Flies*), 1911

Ferry Porsche, automobile designer, 1909

Daily Oddity
At 507,451 km^2, Baffin Island is Canada's largest island.

SEPTEMBER 20
102 days until next year

In a Days
Today is definitely not "Big Whopper Liar Day."
Sorry, oranges, it's "International Eat an Apple Day."
Remove all the salt from the ocean. It's "International Coastal Clean Up Day."
Don't forget to bring along your poop bags. It's "Responsible Dog Ownership Day."
Every day should be "Wife Appreciation Day."

In the News
1503: The name "Newfoundland" was first used.

1816: The first stagecoach line from York to Niagara opened.

1946: The first Cannes Film Festival was held.

1973: Singer Jim Croce ("Bad, Bad Leroy Brown") died in a plane crash.

1973: Billie Jean King beat Bobby Riggs in the Battle of the Sexes tennis match.

1979: Lee Iacocca was elected president of Chrysler.

1982: NFL players began a 57-day strike.

1984: Pope John Paul II held an outdoor mass in Ottawa.

1998: Cal Ripken Jr. sat out a game, ending his record 2632 consecutive MLB games streak.

2001: U.S. President George W. Bush declared a "war on terror."

Virgo
You are an independent thinker and a natural-born leader who alienates those who don't conform to your ideas.
3, 5, 20

#1 Song
1988: "Don't Worry, Be Happy" by Bobby McFerrin

Birth Friends Forever
John Tavares, Canadian hockey player, 1990

Jason Bay, Canadian baseball player, 1978

Enuka Okuma, Canadian actress (*Sue Thomas: F.B. Eye*), 1976

Leah Pinsent, Canadian actress (*Made in Canada*), 1968

Guy Lafleur, Canadian hockey player, 1951

Sophia Loren, actress (*El Cid*), 1934

Dr. Joyce Brothers, advice columnist, 1928

Jay Ward, animator (*Rocky & Bullwinkle*), 1920

Jelly Roll Morton, jazz pianist, 1885

Upton Sinclair, author (*Oil!*), 1878

Sidney Olcott, Canadian director, 1873

Daily Oddity
For a good harvest, Newfoundland folklore recommends burying your dead dog under a fruit tree.

SEPTEMBER 21
101 days until next year

In a Days
Shut up! It's "International Day of Peace."
If you like borrowing clothes, you should celebrate "Women's Friendship Day."
Hit the ball into the clown's mouth—it's "Miniature Golf Day."
Thank goodness it's "World Gratitude Day."

In the News
- 1897: "Yes, Virginia, there is a Santa Claus" was published in *The New York Sun*.
- 1928: Canada Post introduced airmail stamps.
- 1929: Calgary Stampeder Gerry Seiberling threw the first legal forward pass in CFL history during a game against the Edmonton Eskimos.
- 1937: *The Hobbit*, by J.R.R. Tolkien, was first published.
- 1992: The Ottawa Senators rejoined the NHL.
- 1995: In New Delhi, a statue of the Hindu god Ganesh began drinking spoonfuls of milk.
- 1995: The Canadian Mint issued the first toonie.
- 2004: Construction of the Burj Dubai began in Dubai.
- 2008: The last-ever baseball game was played at Yankee Stadium.

Virgo
You are a true original with your finger on the pulse of what's hip; however, you easily become frustrated with those around you.
3, 5, 12

#1 Song
1981: "Endless Love" by Diana Ross & Lionel Richie

Birth Friends Forever
Nicole Richie, celebrity, 1981
Liam Gallagher, singer (Oasis), 1972
Luke Wilson, actor (*Rushmore*), 1971
Tyler Stewart, Canadian musician (Barenaked Ladies), 1967
Faith Hill, country singer, 1967
David James Elliott, Canadian actor (*J.A.G.*), 1960
Bill Murray, actor (*SNL*), 1950
Stephen King, author (*The Shining*), 1947
Leonard Cohen, Canadian singer, 1934
Chuck Jones, animator (*Looney Tunes*), 1912
Howie Morenz, Canadian hockey player, 1902
H.G. Wells, author (*War of the Worlds*), 1866

Daily Oddity
The Ottawa Senators were absent from the NHL from 1934 until the team was reformed in 1992.

SEPTEMBER 22
100 days until next year

In a Days
Dear Diary, I can't believe it's "Dear Diary Day."
If you have hairy toes, enjoy "Hobbit Day."
Sorry, dark chocolate. It' "National White Chocolate Day."
Play the piano. It's "Elephant Appreciation Day."
Get out the rake. It's the "Autumnal Equinox."

In the News
1888: *National Geographic* magazine was first published

1972: USSR beat Team Canada 5–4 in Game 5 of the Summit Series.

1976: The new Glenbow Centre opened in Calgary.

1987: The first quintuplets since the Dionnes were born in Ontario.

1988: Prime Minister Brian Mulroney apologized on behalf of Canada for the internment of Japanese Canadians during WWII.

1992: The WWF stated that Canada was losing one sq km of wilderness every hour because of city sprawl.

1994: *Friends*, starring Canadian actor Matthew Perry, premiered.

1996: Canada's Jacques Villeneuve won the Formula One Grand Prix of Portugal.

2004: Canada forgave the debts of Senegal, Ghana and Ethiopia.

Virgo
You are an active person and a trailblazer who often finds yourself on the defensive.
3, 5, 22

#1 Song
1970: "Ain't No Mountain High Enough" by Diana Ross

Birth Friends Forever
Frodo Baggins, hobbit, 2968
Bilbo Baggins, hobbit, 2890
Laura Vandervoort, Canadian actress (*Smallville*), 1984
Ethan Moreau, Canadian hockey player, 1975
Bonnie Hunt, actress (*Beethoven*), 1961
Scott Baio, actor (*Happy Days*), 1961
Joan Jett, musician, 1958
Nick Cave, musician, 1957
Debby Boone, singer, 1956
Serge Garant, Canadian conductor, 1929
Charles B. Huggins, Canadian surgeon, 1901
Louise McKinney, Canadian women's rights activist, 1868

Daily Oddity
On "Hobbit Day," many fans of *The Lord of the Rings* series go barefoot all day.

SEPTEMBER 23
99 days until next year

In a Days
Check the Powwow Calendar! It's "Native American Day."

In the News
1846: The planet Neptune was discovered.

1889: The Nintendo Koppai company was founded; it originally produced playing card games.

1908: The University of Alberta began to offer instruction.

1985: Guy Lafleur was dismissed from his public-relations job with the Montréal Canadiens.

1991: Canadians Mike Bossy and Denis Potvin were inducted into the Hockey Hall of Fame.

1992: Canada's Manon Rhéaume became the first woman to play an NHL game when she tended goal for the Tampa Bay Lightning for one period.

1992: Bill Comrie purchased the BC Lions from the CFL.

2002: The web browser Mozilla Firefox was first released.

2004: Hurricane Jeanne hit Haiti, killing 1070 people.

Libra
You are a resourceful and multitalented individual who sometimes gives in too easily.
3, 5, 32

#1 Song
1984: "Let's Go Crazy" by Prince

Birth Friends Forever
Donald Audette, Canadian hockey player, 1969

Jason Alexander, actor (*Seinfeld*), 1959

Bruce Springsteen, musician, 1949

Anne Wheeler, Canadian director (*Bye Bye Blues*), 1946

Julio Iglesias, singer, 1943

Simon Nolet, Canadian hockey player, 1941

Gerald Stairs Merrithew, Canadian educator, 1931

Ray Charles, musician, 1930

John Coltrane, jazz saxophonist, 1926

Mickey Rooney, actor (*Andy Hardy* films), 1920

"Typhoid Mary" Mallon, first carrier of typhoid, 1869

Kublai Khan, Mongolian ruler, 1215

Augustus Caesar, Roman emperor, 63 BC

Daily Oddity
Only 45 students attended the first day of classes at the University of Alberta.

SEPTEMBER 24
98 days until next year

In a Days
!Yippy; Today is. "Punctuation Day"?
Eat some fibre and run a lap. It's "National Women's Health and Fitness Day."

In the News

1685: Playing cards were first used as money in New France (Québec).

1890: The Church of Jesus Christ of Latter-day Saints renounced polygamy.

1927: Conn Smythe changed the name of the Toronto St. Patricks hockey team to the Toronto Maple Leafs.

1948: Honda was founded.

1950: Dense smoke from forest fires blocked out the sun over parts of Canada.

1957: The Molson family purchased the Montréal Canadiens.

1969: Ontario banned DDT, effective January 1, 1970.

1988: Canada's Ben Johnson won a gold medal after he ran the 100 m dash in 9.79 seconds at the Summer Olympic Games in Seoul, Korea.

1991: Beloved children's author Theodor "Dr. Seuss" Geisel died.

2004: Same-sex marriage was legalized in Nova Scotia.

Libra
You are an intellectual who strives for harmony in both work and pleasure; however, your intellect may cause you to isolate yourself from the rest of the world.
6, 15, 24

#1 Song
2008: "So What" by Pink

Birth Friends Forever

Karl Alzner, Canadian hockey player, 1988

Mike Gallay, Canadian comedian, 1975

Nia Vardalos, Canadian actress (*My Big Fat Greek Wedding*), 1962

Kevin Sorbo, actor (*Hercules*), 1958

Phil Hartman, Canadian actor (*SNL*), 1948

Joe "Mean" Greene, football player, 1946

Linda McCartney, photographer, 1941

Jim Henson, creator of the Muppets, 1936

Sean McCann, Canadian actor (*Night Heat*), 1935

F. Scott Fitzgerald, author (*The Great Gatsby*), 1896

Arthur Guinness, brewer, 1725

Daily Oddity
Taser is an acronym for Thomas A. Swift's Electric Rifle. Tom Swift was a fictional adventurer/inventor, prominently featured in a series of books for young adults.

SEPTEMBER 25
97 days until next year

In a Days
If you were in Dexy's Midnight Runners, The Archies or Chumbawamba, you should celebrate "One Hit Wonder Day."

Something smells fishy. Oh, it's "Maritime Day."

In the News
1844: Canada defeated the U.S. in the first international cricket match.

1926: William Lyon Mackenzie King was sworn in as prime minister.

1926: The NHL granted franchises to the Chicago Blackhawks and Detroit Red Wings.

1976: The Montréal Expos played their last game at Jarry Park.

1979: The *Montréal Star* newspaper stopped publication after 110 years.

1981: Sandra Day O'Connor became the first female Associate Justice of the U.S. Supreme Court.

1983: British Prime Minister Margaret Thatcher arrived in Canada for a 3-day visit.

1996: Canadian singer Céline Dion reached number one on the *Billboard* Top 200 for record sales.

2008: China launched its 3rd manned spacecraft.

Libra
You are an acerbic and progressive-thinking individual who is sometimes considered too frank when dealing with others.
6, 16, 36

#1 Song
1969: "Sugar, Sugar" by The Archies

Birth Friends Forever
T.I., rapper, 1980

Catherine Zeta-Jones, actress (*Chicago*), 1969

Will Smith, actor (*I Am Legend*), 1968

Joey Saputo, Canadian businessman, 1964

Sonia Benezra, Canadian TV host, 1960

Carol Vadnais, Canadian hockey player, 1945

Michael Douglas, actor (*Wall Street*), 1944

Ron Stewart, Canadian football player, 1934

Ian Tyson, Canadian singer, 1933

Glenn Gould, Canadian pianist, 1932

Barbara Walters, journalist, 1929

Fletcher Christian, *Bounty* mutineer, 1764

Daily Oddity
In 2006, the song "Sugar, Sugar," co-composed by Canadian Andy Kim, was inducted into the Canadian Songwriters Hall of Fame.

SEPTEMBER 26
96 days until next year

In a Days
Dear lover, I hope you enjoy "Love Note Day."
Eat 4000 kg of krill. It's "Shamu the Whale Day."
Set up a date with Mrs. Butterworth. It's "National Pancake Day."

In the News

1907: Newfoundland became a dominion within the British Empire.

1908: Ed Reulbach became the only pitcher to throw 2 no-hitters in the same day.

1934: The *Queen Mary* was launched.

1960: The first televised presidential candidate debate took place between Nixon and JFK.

1973: The Concorde made its first nonstop flight across the Atlantic.

1984: Canadian actor Walter Pidgeon (*Forbidden Planet*) died at the age of 78.

1988: Canada's Ben Johnson was stripped of his Olympic gold medal after he tested positive for steroids.

1993: Canadian Dave Munday took his 2nd plunge over Niagara Falls in a barrel.

2008: A Swiss inventor became the first person to fly across the English Channel using a jet pack.

Libra
You are a tenacious and resourceful individual who can be slightly compulsive.
8, 17, 26

#1 Song
1983: "Total Eclipse of the Heart" by Bonnie Tyler

Birth Friends Forever

Ashley Leggat, Canadian actress (*Discovery Kids*), 1986

Serena Williams, tennis player, 1981

Shannon Hoon, singer (Blind Melon), 1967

Olivia Newton-John, actress (*Grease*), 1948

John Gray, Canadian playwright (*Billy Bishop Goes to War*), 1946

Robert Cade, inventor of Gatorade, 1927

Réal Caouette, Canadian politician, 1917

Jack LaLanne, fitness guru, 1914

George Gershwin, composer, 1898

T.S. Eliot, author (*The Hollow Men*), 1888

Johnny Appleseed, environmentalist, 1774

Francis of Assisi, founder of the Franciscan Order, 1181

Daily Oddity
In 1950, forest fires burning in BC and Alberta blocked out the sun over parts of the UK.

SEPTEMBER 27
95 days until next year

In a Days
Quick, take my picture. It's "World Tourism Day."
Give thanks for your double chin. It's "Ancestor Appreciation Day."

In the News

1839: Fifty-eight Québec rebels were exiled to Australia.

1905: Einstein's $E=mc^2$ equation was first published.

1937: The Balinese tiger was declared extinct.

1954: The Muscular Dystrophy Association of Canada was founded.

1954: *The Tonight Show* premiered.

1972: Canada banned the sale of firecrackers.

1989: Jeff Petkovich and Peter DeBernardi became the first 2-man team to go over Horseshoe Falls and survive.

2004: Calgary Health Region investigated an *E. coli* outbreak, which affected more than 600 people.

2005: Michaëlle Jean was sworn in as Canada's new governor general.

2008: The first Chinese astronaut performed a space walk.

Libra
You are an objective humanitarian who may be perceived as a perfectionist.
9, 18, 27

#1 Song
1977: "*Star Wars* Theme" by Meco

Birth Friends Forever

Daeg Faerch, Canadian actor (*Halloween*), 1996

Avril Lavigne, Canadian singer, 1984

Travis MacRae, Canadian singer, 1983

Lil Wayne, rapper, 1982

Gwyneth Paltrow, actress (*Iron Man*), 1972

Clara Hughes, Canadian cyclist, 1972

Peter MacKay, Canadian politician, 1965

Irvine Welsh, author (*Trainspotting*), 1961

André Viger, Canadian marathoner, 1952

Tom Braidwood, Canadian actor (*The X-Files*), 1948

Meat Loaf, singer, 1947

Jack Goldstein, Canadian artist, 1945

Randy Bachman, Canadian musician (BTO), 1943

Wilford Brimley, actor (*Cocoon*), 1934

Harry Blackstone Sr., magician, 1885

Daily Oddity
The name of every continent ends with the same letter it starts with.

SEPTEMBER 28
94 days until next year

In a Days
Turn off your floodlights. It's "National Good Neighbour Day."
It's "Hug a Vegetarian Day," but not too hard, they're fragile.

In the News
1867: Toronto was named the capital of Ontario.

1928: The United Kingdom banned cannabis.

1928: Alexander Fleming first noticed a bacteria-killing mould, which subsequently led to his discovery of penicillin.

1929: Joe Hess made the first interception return for a touchdown in Canadian football history.

1945: The Calgary Bronks changed their name to the Calgary Stampeders.

1971: The UK banned the medicinal use of cannabis.

1972: Team Canada defeated the USSR in the 8th and final game of the Summit Series.

1991: Jazz trumpeter Miles Davis died.

2000: Pierre Trudeau, former Canadian prime minister, died at the age of 80.

2008: The first privately funded spacecraft, the *Falcon 1*, was launched into orbit.

Libra
You are a lover of all things beautiful; however, your passion for perfection may push away those close to you.
1, 10, 19

#1 Song
1980: "Another One Bites the Dust" by Queen

Birth Friends Forever
Hilary Duff, singer, 1987
Dustin Penner, Canadian hockey player, 1982
Éric Lapointe, Canadian singer, 1969
Naomi Watts, actress (*The Ring*), 1968
Janeane Garofalo, comedian, 1964
Grant Fuhr, Canadian hockey player, 1962
Ron Fellows, Canadian racecar driver, 1959
Stéphane Dion, Canadian politician, 1955
Wei Chen, Canadian journalist, 1951
Nick St. Nicholas, Canadian musician (Steppenwolf), 1943
Ed Sullivan, TV show host, 1901
Thomas Crapper, inventor of the ballcock, 1836

Daily Oddity
Thomas Crapper did not invent the toilet; however, he did invent the ballcock that helps toilets flush.

SEPTEMBER 29
93 days until next year

In a Days
If the year is 2009 and you are of the Jewish faith, you should celebrate "Rosh Hashanah."

In the News
1898: Canada held a referendum in which 278,380 people voted for the prohibition of alcohol, while 264,693 voted against it.

1902: Banks in Dawson City, Yukon, announced that they would no longer accept gold dust as legal tender.

1916: John D. Rockefeller became the world's first billionaire.

1930: The Hamilton Tigers played the University of BC in the first Canadian football game to be played under lights.

1962: Canada launched its first orbiting satellite, *Alouette 1*.

1966: The Chevrolet Camaro was introduced.

2003: Hurricane Juan hit Halifax, NS, killing 4 people.

2004: The Montréal Expos played their final game in Montréal before moving to Washington, DC.

2008: The Dow Jones suffered a 777.68-point drop, the biggest drop in a single trading session.

Libra
You are a practical leader who is sometimes dissatisfied with yourself.
2, 11, 20

#1 Song
2005: "Gold Digger" by Kanye West, featuring Jamie Foxx

Birth Friends Forever
Mark Fraser, Canadian hockey player, 1986

Dallas Green, Canadian musician (City and Colour), 1980

Wade Brookbank, Canadian hockey player, 1977

Dave Andreychuk, Canadian hockey player, 1963

Les Claypool, musician (Primus), 1963

Andrew Dice Clay, comedian, 1957

Bryant Gumbel, TV personality, 1948

Ian McShane, actor (*Deadwood*), 1942

Jerry Lee Lewis, musician, 1935

Stan Berenstain, children's author (*Berenstain Bears* series), 1923

Gene Autry, singing cowboy, 1907

Daily Oddity
Queen Elizabeth II appears on the Canadian $1000 bill.

SEPTEMBER 30
92 days until next year

In a Days
Make sure you're not sitting on chewing gum. It's "National Seat Check Day."

In the News

1888: Jack the Ripper killed his 3rd and 4th victims.

1901: The vacuum cleaner was patented.

1927: Babe Ruth hit his 60th home run of the season.

1955: James Dean died in a car accident at the age of 24.

1968: The Boeing 747 was unveiled.

1981: Calgary was awarded the 1988 Winter Olympic Games.

1990: The Dalai Lama unveiled the Canadian Tribute to Human Rights in Ottawa.

2002: The CBC caused a fan uproar when it announced that Hockey Night in Canada host Ron MacLean would not be returning; he eventually did.

2005: Cartoon renderings of the Islamic prophet Muhammad sparked outraged when they appeared in a Danish newspaper.

2006: A highway overpass on Autoroute 19 in Laval, Québec, collapsed, killing 5 people.

Libra
You are a sensitive and uncompromising individual who can be perceived as being too judgmental.
3, 12, 21

#1 Song
1991: "Good Vibrations" by Marky Mark & the Funky Bunch

Birth Friends Forever

Lacey Chabert, actress (*Party of Five*), 1982

Camilla D'Errico, Canadian artist, 1980

Eric Stoltz, actor (*Pulp Fiction*), 1961

S.M. Stirling, Canadian author (*Snow Brother*), 1953

Harry Jerome, Canadian sprinter, 1940

Len Cariou, Canadian stage-actor (*Sweeny Todd*), 1939

Johnny Mathis, singer, 1935

Angie Dickinson, actress (*The Killers*), 1931

Truman Capote, author (*In Cold Blood*), 1924

Eddie James, Canadian football player, 1907

Henry Larsen, explorer and RCMP officer, 1899

Dr. John Rae, Canadian explorer, 1813

Daily Oddity
The electric chair was invented by a dentist.

OCTOBER 1
91 days until next year

In a Days
Talk about a hot dog, it's "Fire Pup Day."
Talk about a veggie dog, it's "World Vegetarian Day."
Talk about puréed hot dogs, it's "International Day of Older Persons."

In the News
1869: The world's first postcards were issued.

1890: Yosemite and Yellowstone in the U.S. became National Parks.

1903: The first modern World Series was held.

1908: Ford began selling its Model T for $825 USD.

1962: The first *Tonight Show Starring Johnny Carson* aired.

1966: CBC began broadcasting in colour.

1971: Walt Disney World opened in Florida.

1982: The first CD player hit the market.

1988: Canada's Lennox Lewis defeated Riddick Bowe at the Seoul Olympics, winning Canada's first boxing gold medal in 56 years.

2008: The French-language debate for the 2008 federal election was televised.

Libra
You are a steadfast and positive individual who may at times become obsessive.
1, 10, 19

#1 Song
1997: "4 Seasons of Loneliness" by Boyz II Men

Birth Friends Forever
Denis Gauthier, Canadian hockey player, 1976

Cliff Ronning, Canadian hockey player, 1965

Julie Andrews, actress (*Mary Poppins*), 1935

Richard Harris, actor (*Harry Potter* films), 1930

Jimmy Pattison, Canadian businessman, 1928

George Peppard, actor (*The A-Team*), 1928

Tom Bosley, actor (*Happy Days*), 1927

Jimmy Carter, U.S. president, 1924

Walter Matthau, actor (*The Odd Couple*), 1920

Bonnie Parker, outlaw (Bonnie & Clyde), 1910

William Boeing, aircraft engineer, 1881

Daily Oddity
Leaves turn colours because the chlorophyll used to make them green is shut off for the winter.

OCTOBER 2
90 days until next year

In a Days
Sorry, Guardian Devils. It's "Guardian Angels Day."

Play with some string. It's "National Frugal Fun Day."

If you want that vomit cleaned up, you'd better celebrate "National Custodial Workers Day."

In the News
1535: Jacques Cartier landed at Stadacona (Québec City).

1758: Canada's first elected Parliament met.

1887: A 3.6 m sturgeon was caught in BC.

1950: The first *Peanuts* comic strip was published

1991: The Toronto Blue Jays became the first team in sports history to draw 4 million fans in one season.

1991: Hazen Argue—Canada's longest serving parliamentarian—died at 70; he was first elected at age 24.

1994: The biggest Canadian pumpkin, which weighed 408 kg, was crowned.

1995: Alanis Morissette's album *Jagged Little Pill* reached number one on the *Billboard* chart.

2006: Five Amish schoolgirls were shot and killed by Charles Carl Roberts in Pennsylvania, before he turned the gun on himself.

Libra
You are a bright and gifted individual who may at times become too confrontational.
2, 11, 20

#1 Song
1959: "Mack the Knife" by Bobby Darin

Birth Friends Forever
George Pettit, Canadian singer (Alexisonfire), 1982

Sam Roberts, Canadian singer, 1974

Kelly Ripa, television personality, 1970

Al Connelly, Canadian musician, 1960

Glenn Anderson, Canadian hockey player, 1960

Sting, musician, 1951

Annie Leibovitz, photographer, 1949

Donna Karan, fashion designer, 1948

Eric Peterson, Canadian actor (*Corner Gas*), 1946

Don McLean, songwriter, 1945

Bud Abbott, actor (Abbott & Costello), 1895

Groucho Marx, actor (The Marx Brothers), 1890

Daily Oddity
The Canadian prime minister's licence plate number is CAN 001.

OCTOBER 3
89 days until next year

In a Days
Put in your dentures and celebrate "World Smile Day."
Put on your jeans cut-offs. It's "National Denim Day."

In the News

1535: Jacques Cartier landed at Hochelaga (Montréal).

1863: The U.S. declared the last Thursday in November "Thanksgiving Day."

1927: Canadian PM Mackenzie King made the first transatlantic phone call to the UK.

1951: NY Giants' Bobby Thomson hit a home run in the bottom of the 9th to win the National League pennant after being down 14 games (The "Shot Heard 'Round the World").

1955: Captain Kangaroo and *The Mickey Mouse Club* debuted.

1986: The SkyDome groundbreaking ceremony was held.

2003: During a stage performance, a tiger attacked Roy Horn of Siegfried & Roy.

2008: U.S. President George W. Bush signed the $700 billion bailout bill for the U.S. financial systems.

Libra
You are a strong-willed and ambitious individual who sometimes wears yourself too thin.
3, 12, 21

#1 Song
1988: "Love Bites" by Def Leppard

Birth Friends Forever

Amanda Walsh, Canadian TV personality, 1981

Sheldon Brookbank, Canadian hockey player, 1980

Neve Campbell, Canadian actress (*Scream*), 1973

Gwen Stefani, singer, 1969

Clive Owen, actor (*Sin City*), 1964

Tommy Lee, musician (Mötley Crüe), 1962

Hart Bochner, Canadian actor (*Die Hard*), 1956

Stevie Ray Vaughan, musician, 1954

Al Sharpton, social rights activist, 1954

Lindsey Buckingham, musician (Fleetwood Mac), 1949

Chubby Checker, musician, 1941

Jean Ratelle, Canadian hockey player, 1940

Glenn Hall, Canadian hockey player, 1931

A.Y. Jackson, Canadian painter, 1882

Daily Oddity
All polar bears are left-handed.

OCTOBER 4
88 days until next year

In a Days
Sorry, Hallmark. It's "World Card Making Day."
Breaker, breaker, over and out, it's "Ten-Four Day."

In the News

1537: The first English-language Bible was printed.

1873: Gimli, MB, was founded.

1883: The Orient Express began operation.

1895: The first U.S. open Golf Championship was held.

1909: The cornerstone of the Saskatchewan Legislature was laid.

1927: Sculpting commenced on Mt. Rushmore.

1957: The *Sputnik I* satellite was launched.

1957: The Avro Arrow was unveiled at a ceremony in Malton, ON.

1982: Laurie Skreslet became the first Canadian to reach the top of Mount Everest.

1982: Canadian pianist Glenn Gould died.

1996: Céline Dion's album *Falling Into You* was certified multi-platinum.

2002: The Queen arrived in Canada to mark her Golden Jubilee as Queen of Canada.

Libra
You are a level-headed and gregarious individual who is easily distracted.
4, 13, 22

#1 Song
1966: "Cherish" by The Association

Birth Friends Forever

Lil Mama, rapper, 1989

Kristina Lenko, Canadian ice skater, 1980

Justin Williams, Canadian hockey player, 1981

Alicia Silverstone, actress (*Clueless*), 1976

Liev Schreiber, actor (*Defiance*), 1967

Susan Sarandon, actress (*Dead Man Walking*), 1946

Anne Rice, author (*Interview with a Vampire*), 1941

Milan Chvostek, Canadian director (*The Nature of Things*), 1932

Charlton Heston, actor (*Planet of the Apes*), 1923

Buster Keaton, comedian (*The General*), 1895

Louis-Hippolyte Lafontaine, Canadian prime minister, 1807

Daily Oddity
The Bible is the most shoplifted book.

OCTOBER 5
87 days until next year

In a Days
Sleep, shower and eat in a stranger's house. It's "Bed and Breakfast Day."
Find a short pier and enjoy "Long Walk Day."

In the News

1864: The city of Calcutta, India, was almost totally destroyed by a cyclone; 60,000 died.

1869: The Bay of Fundy was ravaged by a hurricane.

1921: The World Series was broadcast over the radio for the first time.

1944: The Canadian Air Force shot down its first German fighter jet over France.

1947: The first televised White House address was given by U.S. President Harry S. Truman.

1969: *Monty Python*'s Flying Circus premiered.

1970: Members of the FLQ terrorist group kidnapped the British Trade Commissioner to Canada.

1984: Marc Garneau became the first Canadian in space.

2003: Canadian citizen Maher Arar was freed from a Syrian jail.

Libra
You are a sensitive and determined individual who may lose your perspective at times.
8, 15, 33

#1 Song
1997: "Candle in the Wind 1997" by Elton John

Birth Friends Forever

Jesse Palmer, Canadian football player, 1978

Kate Winslet, actress (*Titanic*), 1975

Grant Hill, basketball player, 1972

Mario Lemieux, Canadian hockey player, 1965

Patrick Roy, Canadian hockey player, 1965

Michael Andretti, racecar driver, 1962

Bernie Mac, comedian (*Ocean's 11*), 1957

Bob Geldof, singer (The Boomtown Rats), 1951

Ralph Goodale, Canadian politician, 1949

Steve Miller, singer (Steve Miller Band), 1943

Ray Kroc, founder of McDonald's, 1902

Alexander Keith, Canadian brewer, 1795

Daily Oddity
Lighters were invented before matches.

OCTOBER 6
86 days until next year

In a Days
Line your hat with mercury. It's "Mad Hatter Day."

In the News
1582: Because of the implementation of the Gregorian calendar, Italy, Poland, Portugal and Spain skipped October 6.

1882: A fire in Miramichi, NB, killed more than 500 people.

1889: Thomas Edison showed his first motion picture.

1927: *The Jazz Singer*, the first talking movie, opened.

1945: A billy goat was ejected from Wrigley Field during the World Series ("Curse of the Billy Goat").

1966: LSD was declared illegal in the U.S.

1967: Canada's largest rainfall in a 24 hr period, 192.6mm, occurred in Ucluelet, BC.

1973: Two people spotted UFOs near St-Mathias, Québec.

1989: Ray Hnatyshyn was appointed Canada's new governor general,

2004: The Supreme Court of Canada began a 3-day hearing to determine the legality of same-sex marriage under the Canadian Constitution.

Libra
You are a versatile and inspirational individual who is unable to focus on only one task at a time.
6, 15, 24

#1 Song
1958: "It's All in the Game" by Tommy Edwards

Birth Friends Forever
Daniel Brière, Canadian hockey player, 1977

Jeremy Sisto, actor (*Law & Order*), 1974

Ioan Gruffudd, actor (*Fantastic Four*), 1973

Amy Jo Johnson, actress (*Flashpoint*), 1970

Elisabeth Shue, actress (*Adventures in Babysitting*), 1963

Gerry Wilmot, Canadian hockey announcer, 1914

Carole Lombard, actress (*The Gay Bride*), 1908

Ernest Lapointe, Canadian politician, 1876

Reginald Fessenden, Canadian inventor, 1866

Isaac Brock, Canadian military officer, 1769

James McGill, Canadian philanthropist, 1744

Daily Oddity
Canadian Gerry Wilmot is recognized in the *Guinness Book of Records* as the world's fastest-speaking broadcaster.

OCTOBER 7
85 days until next year

In a Days
Whether you're bathing or just brewing some gin in it, enjoy "Bathtub Day."

In the News

1737: Iron ore was smelted in Canada for the first time.

1763: Cape Breton was annexed to Nova Scotia.

1952: *American Bandstand* debuted.

1955: Allen Ginsberg's poem "Howl" was read publicly for the first time.

1959: The first photos of the far side of the moon were transmitted back to Earth.

1982: *Cats* opened on Broadway.

1983: Cabbage Patch dolls debuted.

1995: Montréal Canadiens retired the number one sweater of goaltender Jacques Plante.

2001: Canada became involved in the war in Afghanistan.

2002: Canadian citizen Maher Arar was deported to Syria by American officials on suspicion of being associated with Al-Qaeda.

2003: Arnold Schwarzenegger was elected governor of California.

Libra
You have a magnetic personality and are very sociable; however, you can be too self-righteous.
6, 17, 22

#1 Song
1982: "Jack and Diane" by John Cougar

Birth Friends Forever

Shawn and Aaron Ashmore, Canadian actors, 1979

Taylor Hicks, *American Idol* winner, 1976

Daniel Boucher, Canadian musician, 1971

Thom Yorke, singer (Radiohead), 1968

Dave Bronconnier, Canadian politician, 1962

Simon Cowell, *American Idol* judge, 1959

Yo-Yo Ma, cellist, 1955

John Mellencamp, singer, 1951

Graeme Ferguson, Canadian co-inventor of IMAX, 1929

Jean-Paul Riopelle, Canadian artist, 1923

Francis X. Boucher, Canadian hockey player, 1901

Louis-Joseph Papineau, Canadian politician, 1786

Daily Oddity
Goaltender Jacques Plante originated retrieving the puck from behind the net and passing it to a team member.

OCTOBER 8
84 days until next year

In a Days
If you wish to lose the respect of your peers, celebrate "Bring your Teddy Bear to Work and School Day."

In the News
1904: Edmonton, AB, and Prince Albert, SK, were incorporated as cities.

1967: Guerilla leader Che Guevara was captured in Bolivia.

1975: Montréal Canadien Guy Lafleur scored his first NHL goal.

1978: Gilles Villeneuve won his first Formula 1 race at the Montréal Grand Prix.

1984: Canada's Anne Murray won the Country Music Association's Album of the Year Award for *A Little Good News*.

1992: *Reconciliation*, a monument honouring 90,000 Canadian peacekeepers, was unveiled in Ottawa.

2001: U.S. President George W. Bush announced the establishment of the Office of Homeland Security.

2005: Television personality Martha Stewart began serving her prison sentence after being convicted of insider trading.

Libra
You are an optimistic and determined individual who has a habit of isolating yourself.
8, 17, 26

#1 Song
2002: "A Moment Like This" by Kelly Clarkson

Birth Friends Forever
Raffi Torres, Canadian hockey player, 1981

Matt Damon, actor (*The Bourne Ultimatum*), 1970

Sigourney Weaver, actress (*Alien*), 1949

Johnny Ramone, musician (The Ramones), 1948

Chevy Chase, comedian (*SNL*), 1943

R.L. Stine, author (*Goosebumps* series), 1943

Jesse Jackson, civil rights activist, 1941

Paul Hogan, actor (*Crocodile Dundee*), 1939

Walter Gretzky, Canadian hockey dad, 1938

Frank Herbert, author (*Dune*), 1920

Ray Lewis, Canadian track-and-field athlete, 1910

Ozias Leduc, Canadian painter, 1864

Daily Oddity
Because of the implementation of the Gregorian calendar, the date October 8, 1582, does not exist in the history books of Italy, Poland, Portugal or Spain.

OCTOBER 9
83 days until next year

In a Days
Email your friends and tell them that it's "World Post Day."
What are you looking at? It's "World Sight Day."
By Odin's beard, it's "Leif Erickson Day."

In the News
1003: Leif Erickson became the first European to reach North America, landing at Newfoundland.

1874: The General Postal Union, which coordinates the worldwide postal system, was created.

1967: Guerrilla leader Che Guevara was executed for attempting to incite a revolution in Bolivia.

1974: Hervé Filion became the first North American/Canadian to win 5000 harness races.

1980: The *Winnipeg Sun* was first published.

1982: Wayne Gretzky scored his 200th goal.

1986: *The Phantom of the Opera* debuted in London, England.

1989: A UFO landing was reported in Russia.

2006: North Korea allegedly tested a nuclear device.

Libra
You are a problem solver and an observer who may be perceived as too critical.
9, 18, 27

#1 Song
1995: "Fantasy" by Mariah Carey

Birth Friends Forever
Jodelle Ferland, Canadian actress (*Cold Squad*), 1994

Sean Lennon, son of John Lennon, 1975

P.J. Harvey, musician, 1969

Carling Bassett-Seguso, Candian tennis player, 1967

Guillermo del Toro, director (*Hellboy*), 1964

Linwood Boomer, Canadian actor (*Little House on the Prairie*), 1955

Tony Shalhoub, actor (*Monk*), 1953

Sharon Osbourne, TV personality, 1952

John Lennon, musician (The Beatles), 1940

Alastair Sim, actor (*A Christmas Carol*), 1900

Aimee Semple McPherson, Canadian evangelist, 1890

Daily Oddity
Thursday is a tribute to the Norse god Thor.

OCTOBER 10
82 days until next year

In a Days
Decorate your cake and eat it, too. It's "Cake Decorating Day."
Take a mental health day. It's "World Mental Health Day."
Dress classier than you are. It's "Tuxedo Day."

In the News
1851: The worst natural disaster in PEI history occurred when a gale destroyed 80 fishing boats, killing 130 people.

1903: Henry Ford began production at his plant in Walkerville, ON; the plant produced 117 cars in its first year.

1970: Québec Vice-Premier Pierre Laporte was the 2nd person kidnapped by the FLQ.

1978: Female pages were hired for the House of Commons for the first time.

1992: Canadian k.d. lang's "Constant Craving" peaked at number 38 on the *Billboard* chart.

2005: An education strike began in BC, closing down 40,000 schools.

2008: In protest to the expansion of gas wells near Dawson Creek, BC, anonymous letters were sent to the media warning oil and gas companies to leave the area alone.

Libra
You are a perceptive and rational individual who suppresses your inner emotions.
1, 10, 19

#1 Song
1987: "Here I Go Again" by Whitesnake

Birth Friends Forever
Chris Pronger, Canadian hockey player, 1974
Dale Earnhardt Jr., racecar driver, 1974
Karen Percy, Canadian skier, 1966
Ron Flockhart, Canadian hockey player, 1960
David Lee Roth, singer (Van Halen), 1954
Nora Roberts, author (*One Summer*), 1950
Peter Mahovlich, Canadian hockey player, 1946
Great Antonio, Canadian strongman, 1925
Ed Wood, director (*Plan 9 from Outer Space*), 1924
Thelonious Monk, jazz pianist, 1917
Louis Cyr, Canadian strongman, 1863

Daily Oddity
Canadian strongman Louis Cyr is said to have been able to lift 1869 kg on his back.

OCTOBER 11
81 days until next year

In a Days
If you think you are gay, celebrate "National Coming Out Day."
If you know you are gay, celebrate "Nation Sausage Pizza Day."

In the News
1754: British explorer Anthony Henday made the first European contact with the Blackfoot tribe in Alberta.

1869: The Red River Rebellion began when Louis Riel prevented a surveyor from taking Métis land in St. Vital, MB.

1927: The Toronto Symphony Orchestra performed its first concert.

1952: The first hockey game was televised in Canada (Montréal vs. Detroit).

1975: *Saturday Night Live*, hosted by George Carlin, premiered.

1984: Canadian-born Mario Lemieux scored on his first NHL shift.

1984: Kathryn Sullivan became the first American woman to perform a space walk.

2000: The 100th space shuttle mission took off.

2008: The new "Hockey Night in Canada" anthem premiered.

2009: World-renowned detectives Vicki and Donny von Tricket wed.

Libra
You are resourceful, with a magnetic personality; however, you sometimes overindulge.
2, 11, 20

#1 Song
1976: "Disco Duck" by Rick Dees

Birth Friends Forever
Michelle Trachtenberg, actress (*Gossip Girl*), 1985
Martha MacIsaac, Canadian actress (*Emily of New Moon*), 1984
Jason Arnott, Canadian hockey player, 1974
Luke Perry, actor (*90210*), 1966
Joan Cusack, actress (*SNL*), 1962
Gregory Dudek, Canadian roboticist, 1958
Daryl Hall, musician (Hall & Oates), 1946
Raymond Moriyama, Canadian architect, 1929
Jean Vander Pyl, voice actress (Wilma Flintstone, *The Flintstones*), 1919
George Hodgson, Canadian swimmer, 1893
Eleanor Roosevelt, U.S. first lady, 1884
Mary Macleod, Canadian pioneer, 1852
Henry Heinz, ketchup magnate, 1844

Daily Oddity
Dr. Seuss coined the word "nerd."

OCTOBER 12
80 days until next year

In a Days
Hide the glassware. It's "International Moment of Frustration Scream Day." God bless you if you celebrate "Clergy Appreciation Day."

In the News

- **1535:** Jacques Cartier was introduced to tobacco.
- **1773:** The first insane asylum opened in the U.S.
- **1810:** The first Oktoberfest was held.
- **1823:** The first raincoat was sold.
- **1901:** The Executive Mansion was renamed the White House.
- **1917:** The First Battle of Passchendaele took place.
- **1957:** Lester B. Pearson won the Nobel Prize for peacekeeping.
- **1960:** A new airport terminal opened in Regina.
- **1962:** Typhoon Freda hit Vancouver, killing 7 people.
- **1986:** Vancouver's Expo '86 closed.
- **1999:** The 6 billionth human was born.
- **2008:** A sour gas pipeline near Dawson Creek, BC, was bombed by eco-terrorists.

Libra
You are a strong-willed person and a true pioneer; however, you may be perceived as being too reactionary.
3, 12, 21

#1 Song
1998: "One Week" by Barenaked Ladies

Birth Friends Forever

Mike Green, Canadian hockey player, 1985

Marie Wilson, Canadian actress (*As the World Turns*), 1974

Kirk Cameron, actor (*Growing Pains*), 1970

Dwayne Roloson, Canadian hockey player, 1969

Martie Maguire, musician (Dixie Chicks), 1969

Hugh Jackman, actor (*X-Men*), 1968

Jane Siberry, Canadian musician, 1955

Danielle Proulx, Canadian actress (*C.R.A.Z.Y.*), 1952

Luciano Pavarotti, tenor, 1935

Guido Molinari, Canadian painter, 1933

Louis Hémon, Canadian author (*Maria Chapdelaine*), 1880

Aleister Crowley, occultist, 1875

Daily Oddity
Oktoberfest runs for 16 days between September and October and originated as a celebration of the marriage between Prince Ludwig of Bavaria to Princess Therese von Sachsen-Hildburghausen.

OCTOBER 13
79 days until next year

In a Days
Put extra padding in your britches! It's "National Kick Butt Day."
If an Italian explorer discovered your country, celebrate "Columbus Day."
If you pronounce it "turk-eh," celebrate "Canadian Thanksgiving."

In the News
- 54: Nero ascended to the Roman throne.
- 1812: British commander Isaac Brock died in battle near Queenston, ON.
- 1884: Greenwich Mean Time was established.
- 1917: The Miracle of the Sun, in which the sun zig-zagged across the sky, occurred in Portugal.
- 1971: The first night game in World Series history was played.
- 1972: A Uruguayan rugby team crashed in the Andes; the incident inspired the film *Alive*.
- 1984: Marc Garneau, the first Canadian in space, returned to Earth.
- 1992: Canadian author Michael Ondaatje won the Booker Prize for his novel *The English Patient*.
- 2008: The Dow Jones Industrial Average gained 936.42 points, the largest single-day increase in its history.

Libra
You are an analytical and focused individual who may be too driven.
4, 13, 22

#1 Song
1988: "Red Red Wine" by UB40

Birth Friends Forever
Sacha Baron Cohen, comedian (Ali G), 1971
Jerry Rice, football player, 1962
Marie Osmond, TV entertainer, 1959
Sammy Hagar, singer (Van Halen), 1947
Paul Simon, musician (Simon and Garfunkel), 1941
Nana Mouskouri, singer, 1934
Walter "Killer" Kowalski, Canadian pro wrestler, 1925
Margaret Thatcher, UK prime minister, 1925
Edward Blake, Canadian politician, 1833
John William Dawson, Canadian geologist, 1820

Daily Oddity
Canadian Thanksgiving began as a celebration of the safe return of Martin Frobisher from his journey through the Northwest Passage.

OCTOBER 14
78 days until next year

In a Days
Well, it sure beats having hair and being in jail. It's "Be Bald and Be Free Day."

In the News

1586: Mary, Queen of Scots, was put on trial for conspiracy.

1789: George Washington proclaimed the first U.S. Thanksgiving.

1926: A.A. Milne's *Winnie-the-Pooh,* inspired by a Winnipeg bear, was first published.

1958: The U.S. conducted nuclear weapon tests in Nevada.

1964: Martin Luther King Jr. became the youngest recipient of the Nobel Prize.

1966: The Montréal Metro opened.

1979: Wayne Gretzky scored his first NHL goal.

1979: The first Gay Rights March was held in the U.S.

1982: The U.S. declared a "War on Drugs."

2004: A Boeing 747 crashed just after taking off from Halifax International Airport.

2008: Conservative leader Stephen Harper was re-elected prime minister of Canada.

Libra
You are a receptive team player; however, you may be too self-indulgent.
8, 6, 23

#1 Song
1962: "Monster Mash" by Bobby Pickett

Birth Friends Forever

Usher, singer, 1978

Kelly Schumacher, Canadian basketball player, 1977

Natalie Maines, musician (Dixie Chicks), 1974

Steve Coogan, actor (*Hamlet 2*), 1965

David Kaye, Canadian voice actor (*Beast Wars*), 1964

Isaac Mizrahi, fashion designer, 1961

Dave "The Hammer" Schultz, Canadian hockey player, 1949

Ralph Lauren, fashion designer, 1939

Ron Lancaster, American-born CFL player, 1938

Yvon Durelle, Canadian boxer, 1929

Roger Moore, actor (James Bond), 1927

C. Everett Koop, U.S. Surgeon General, 1916

e.e. cummings, poet, 1894

Dwight D. Eisenhower, U.S. president, 1890

Daily Oddity
In October, Romans celebrated the goddess of fruit, Pomona. Her symbol was the apple.

OCTOBER 15
77 days until next year

In a Days
Leave me alone. It's "National Grouch Day."

In the News
1878: The Edison Electric Light Company began operating.

1912: Thomas Wilby and Jack Haney reached Port Alberni, BC, to complete the first cross-Canada motor trip.

1917: Notorious spy Mata Hari was executed.

1954: Hurricane Hazel hit south-central Ontario; 83 people died.

1981: RCMP seized $200 million of methaqualone at the Collingwood, ON, airport; it is still the largest drug seizure in Canadian history.

1986: U of T professor John Polanyi won the Nobel Prize for Chemistry.

1989: Wayne Gretzky became the all-time NHL leading points scorer with 1851 points.

1990: Soviet leader Mikhail Gorbachev won the Nobel Peace Prize.

1997: The first supersonic land-speed record was set.

2007: In New Zealand, 17 activists were arrested in anti-terrorism raids.

Libra
You are adventurous and a born educator; however, you are prone to fits of jealousy.
6, 15, 24

#1 Song
1977: "You Light Up My Life" by Debby Boone

Birth Friends Forever
Jesse Levine, Canadian tennis player, 1982

Charline Labonté, Canadian hockey player, 1982

Sarah Ferguson, Duchess of York, 1959

Betsy Clifford, Canadian alpine skier, 1953

Penny Marshall, actress (*Laverne & Shirley*), 1942

Willie O'Ree, Canadian hockey player, 1935

Warren Miller, ski and snowboarding filmmaker, 1924

Lee Iacocca, Chrysler CEO, 1924

Mario Puzo, author (*The Godfather*), 1920

John Kenneth Galbraith, Canadian economist, 1908

Friedrich Nietzsche, philosopher, 1844

Marie-Marguerite d'Youville, first Canadian Native canonized, 1701

Daily Oddity
Thomas Edison was afraid of the dark.

OCTOBER 16
76 days until next year

In a Days
Let's eat. It's "World Food Day."
Sorry, Hardware Store. It's "Department Store Day."
How would one define "Dictionary Day"?
If you want to remain employed, celebrate "Bosses Day."

In the News
1793: Marie Antoinette was beheaded.

1841: Queen's University in Kingston, ON, was founded.

1911: Winnipeg received electricity.

1923: The Walt Disney Company was founded.

1970: In response to the October Crisis, Trudeau invoked Canada's War Measures Act.

1976: Canadian hockey legend Lanny McDonald scored a hat trick in 2 minutes, 54 seconds.

1987: A 3-hour-old infant from Surrey, BC, became the world's youngest heart transplant recipient.

1989: Roberta Jamieson became Ontario's first Aboriginal ombudsman.

2008: A second natural gas pipeline was bombed by eco-terrorists in Dawson Creek, BC.

Libra
You are a person of observation and wit; however, you can be too overconfident at times.
6, 12, 26

#1 Song
2008: "Live Your Life" by T.I., featuring Rihanna

Birth Friends Forever
Trevor Blumas, Canadian actor (*Ice Princess*), 1984

John Mayer, musician, 1977

Paul Kariya, Canadian hockey player, 1974

Flea, musician (Red Hot Chili Peppers), 1962

Tim Robbins, actor (*The Shawshank Redemption*), 1958

Fred Turner, Canadian musician (BTO), 1943

Tom Monaghan, founder of Domino's Pizza, 1937

Angela Lansbury, actress (*Murder, She Wrote*), 1925

Wallace Turnbull, Canadian aeronautical engineer, 1870

Oscar Wilde, author (*The Picture of Dorian Grey*), 1854

Noah Webster, author (*Webster's Dictionary*), 1758

Daily Oddity
The Cardiff Giant was a hoax created after an argument over a Bible passage stating that giants once lived on Earth.

OCTOBER 17
75 days until next year

In a Days
Take a second golf swing and celebrate "Mulligan Day."
Grab your quill pen. It's "Black Poetry Day."

In the News

1671: The first Hudson's Bay Company furs were auctioned off in England.

1814: A wave of beer (1,222,688 L) drowned 9 people in England.

1931: Al Capone was convicted of tax evasion.

1967: The musical *Hair*, composed by Canadian Galt MacDermot, opened on Broadway.

1970: Pierre Laporte, Québec vice-premier, was murdered by the FLQ.

1974: Mark Kent, 17, arrived in St. John's, becoming the first person to run across Canada.

1986: CKND-TV became the first station in Manitoba to broadcast in stereo.

2004: Frederick Banting, Alexander Graham Bell, Tommy Douglas, Terry Fox, Wayne Gretzky, John A. Macdonald, Lester B. Pearson, David Suzuki, Pierre Trudeau and Don Cherry were announced as the 10 finalists in "The Greatest Canadian" challenge.

Libra
You are an objective and adventurous person, but when confused, you strike out at those around you.
8, 17, 26

#1 Song
1972: "My Ding-a-Ling" by Chuck Berry

Birth Friends Forever
Wyclef Jean, singer, 1972
Eminem, rapper, 1972
Rick Mercer, Canadian comedian (*Rick Mercer Report*), 1969
Norm MacDonald, Canadian comedian (*SNL*), 1963
Alan Jackson, country singer, 1958
Margot Kidder, Canadian actress (*Superman*), 1948
George Wendt, actor (*Cheers*), 1948
Dave Cutler, Canadian football player, 1945
Evel Knievel, daredevil, 1938
Rita Hayworth, actress (*Cover Girl*), 1918
Arthur Miller, playwright (*Death of a Salesman*), 1915
Irene Ryan, actress (*The Beverly Hillbillies*), 1902

Daily Oddity
October is the cheapest month to buy a bike.

OCTOBER 18
74 days until next year

In a Days
Oh, sweet! It's the "Sweetest Day."
Fellas, since it's "World Menopause Day," why not celebrate "Long Distance Day"?
Take a faux photo. It's "World Toy Camera Day."

In the News

1851: Herman Melville's *Moby Dick* was first published.

1877: The world's first telephone service was installed in Hamilton, ON.

1929: The Supreme Court of Canada ruled that women are "persons" under Canadian law.

1954: Texas Instruments unveiled the Regency Tr-1, the world's first practical transistor radio.

1968: Bob Beamon set a long-jump record of 8.90 m at the Olympics.

1980: The first African elephant was born in Canada at the Toronto Zoo.

1994: Canadian musician Neil Young of Crazy Horse received a gold record for the album *Sleeps With Angels*.

2007: Benazir Bhutto returned to Pakistan after 8 years in exile; she would later become its prime minister.

Libra
You are a complex and inspirational person; however, you neglect your own needs.
9, 18, 27

#1 Song
2000: "Come On Over Baby" by Christina Aguilera

Birth Friends Forever
Zac Efron, actor (*Scrubs*), 1987

Alex Tagliani, Canadian racecar driver, 1972

Jean-Claude Van Damme, actor (*Blood Sport*), 1960

Patrick Morrow, Canadian mountaineer, 1952

Lee Harvey Oswald, JFK assassin, 1939

Mike Ditka, football coach, 1939

Iona Campagnolo, Canadian politician, 1932

George C. Scott, actor (*Patton*), 1927

Chuck Berry, musician, 1926

Klaus Kinski, actor (*Fitzcarraldo*), 1926

Hugh "Buddy" MacMaster, Canadian musician, 1924

Pierre Elliott Trudeau, Canadian prime minister, 1919

Daily Oddity
PEI didn't have public transit until October 2005.

OCTOBER 19
73 days until next year

In a Days
Go to the bar. It's "Evaluate Your Life Day."
Wear rubber pants. It's "Electricity Day."

In the News

1216: King Henry III ascended to the throne of England at the age of 9.

1957: Maurice "Rocket" Richard scored his 500th goal.

1966: Canadian cosmetics magnate Elizabeth Arden died at the age of 81.

1976: Chimpanzees were placed on the Endangered Species list.

1987: Black Monday: The TSX dropped 407 points; Dow Jones dropped 508 points.

2004: A Toronto lawyer successfully challenged a traffic ticket on the grounds that the traffic sign was not bilingual.

2005: The trial of Saddam Hussein, president of Iraq, for crimes against humanity began in Baghdad.

2006: Environment Minister Rona Ambrose introduced the Clean Air Act, which was criticized by environmentalists and the Opposition.

Libra
You are an independent free spirit who can be quite combative.
1, 10, 19

#1 Song
2008: "Womanizer" by Britney Spears

Birth Friends Forever

Jason Reitman, Canadian director (*Juno*), 1977

Dan Smith, Canadian hockey player, 1976

Trey Parker, co-creator of *South Park*, 1969

Jon Favreau, director (*Iron Man*), 1966

Evander Holyfield, boxer, 1962

Divine, actor (*Hairspray*), 1945

John Lithgow, actor (*3rd Rock from the Sun*), 1945

Peter Tosh, musician, 1944

Tommy Ambrose, Canadian composer, 1939

Marilyn Bell, Canadian swimmer, 1937

John McLoughlin, Canadian fur trader, 1784

Daily Oddity
Elizabeth Arden's real name was Florence Nightingale Graham. She dropped out of nursing school to enter the field of skincare and cosmetics.

OCTOBER 20
72 days until next year

In a Days
Orange you happy that today is "National Fruit Day"?
Sorry, conditioner. It's "Shampoo Day."

In the News
1671: New France (Québec) colonists were ordered to marry newly landed French females or lose their fur-trading rights.

1955: J.R.R. Tolkien's *The Return of the King* was first published.

1956: Canada launched its first weather rockets.

1967: The most famous footage of Bigfoot was released.

1968: Former First Lady Jacqueline Kennedy married Aristotle Onassis.

1973: The Sydney Opera House opened.

1977: Several members of the rock band Lynyrd Skynyrd died in a plane crash.

1992: The Toronto Blue Jays won the first World Series outside the U.S.

2004: The Canadian dollar closed at $0.8029, the highest since 1993.

2008: Canadian Liberal Party leader Stéphane Dion announced his resignation.

Libra
You are progressive and artistic, which can drive you to exhaustion.
2, 11, 20

#1 Song
1949: "That Lucky Old Sun" by Frankie Laine

Birth Friends Forever
John Krasinski, actor (*The Office*), 1979

Leila Josefowicz, Canadian violinist, 1977

Julie Payette, Canadian astronaut, 1963

Johnny Dee, Canadian musician (Honeymoon Suite), 1961

Viggo Mortensen, actor (*The Lord of the Rings*), 1958

Tom Petty, musician, 1950

Jerry Orbach, actor (*Law & Order*), 1935

Mickey Mantle, baseball player, 1931

Tommy Douglas, Canadian politician, 1904

Jelly Roll Morton, composer, 1890

Bela Lugosi, actor (*Dracula*), 1882

Nellie McClung, Canadian women's rights advocate, 1873

Daily Oddity
It is bad luck to sleep in the light of a full moon.

OCTOBER 21
71 days until next year

In a Days
Don't bother putting on any skin moisturizer today. It's "Reptile Awareness Day."

In the News

1854: Florence Nightingale was assigned to the Crimean War.

1878: Canadian brewer John Labatt's India Pale Ale won the gold medal at the International Exposition in Paris.

1879: Thomas Edison tested the first electric light bulb.

1945: Women in France got the vote.

1945: Argentine politician Juan Perón married actress Evita (Ana Perón).

1959: The Guggenheim Museum opened in New York City.

1976: Canadian-born writer Saul Bellow won the Nobel Prize for Literature.

1988: Canadian musician Robbie Robertson's self-titled album was certified gold.

2003: The first photos of the dwarf planet Eris were taken.

Libra
You are an idealistic perfectionist who, when not motivated, may become destructive.
3, 12, 21

#1 Song
1990: "Black Cat" by Janet Jackson

Birth Friends Forever

Anouk Leblanc-Boucher, Canadian short-track speed skater, 1984

Charlotte Sullivan, Canadian actress (*Smallville*), 1983

Mélanie Turgeon, Canadian alpine skier, 1976

Carrie Fisher, actress (*Star Wars*), 1956

Brian Tobin, premier of Newfoundland, 1954

Michel Brière, Canadian hockey player, 1949

Judge Judy, television judge, 1942

Manfred Mann, musician, 1940

Carl Brewer, Canadian hockey player, 1938

Whitey Ford, baseball player, 1928

Dizzy Gillespie, jazz trumpeter, 1917

Oswald Avery, Canadian bacteriologist, 1877

Daily Oddity
If you spend too much time in a graveyard reading the names on the tombstones, it is believed that you will lose your memory.

OCTOBER 22
70 days until next year

In a Days
What do I have to do to get you behind the wheel of "Used Car Day"?

In the News

- 1797: The first recorded parachute jump occurred.
- 1883: The Metropolitan Opera House opened.
- 1924: Toastmasters International was founded.
- 1934: Bank robber Pretty Boy Floyd was shot and killed.
- 1964: Jean-Paul Sartre turned down the Nobel Prize for Literature, stating: "A writer must refuse to allow himself to be transformed into an institution."
- 1964: The new design was selected for the Canadian flag.
- 1966: The Supremes became the first all-female group to have a number-one album.
- 2002: Canadian Yann Martel won the Booker Prize for his novel *Life of Pi*.
- 2008: For the first time since 2005, the loonie dropped below $0.80 USD as the 2008 economic crisis hit Canada.
- 2008: India launched its first unmanned lunar mission, *Chandryaan-1*.

Libra
You are an imaginative and empathetic individual who is sometimes perceived as being demanding.
4, 13, 22

#1 Song
1999: "Smooth" by Santana, featuring Rob Thomas

Birth Friends Forever

Kara Lang, Canadian soccer player, 1986
Spike Jonze, director (*Adaptation*), 1969
Shaggy, musician, 1968
Ron Tugnutt, Canadian hockey player, 1967
Brian Boitano, figure skater, 1963
Jeff Goldblum, actor (*The Fly*), 1952
Yvan Ponton, Canadian actor (*Slap Shot*), 1945
Catherine Deneuve, actress (*The Hunger*), 1943
Annette Funicello, actress (*Beach Party*), 1942
Christopher Lloyd, actor (*Back to the Future*), 1938
Curly Howard, comedian (The Three Stooges), 1903
Louis Riel, Canadian folk hero/Métis leader, 1844
Franz Liszt, composer, 1811
Daniel Boone, frontiersman, 1734

Daily Oddity
Though he refused the Nobel Prize, Jean-Paul Sartre did ask for the monetary prize; his request was refused.

OCTOBER 23
69 days until next year

In a Days
Preserve this moment by celebrating "Canning Day."
You should get that spot checked out. It's "National Mole Day."

In the News

1867: The first 72 members of the Canadian Senate were appointed.

1911: The first aircraft was used in war.

1930: The first mini-golf tournament was held.

1958: An earthquake trapped 174 miners in Springhill, NS; 74 miners died.

1958: The Smurfs made their first appearance.

1967: Brenda Robertson became the first woman elected to the New Brunswick legislature.

1971: "Sweet City Woman" by Calgary's The Stampeders peaked at number 8 on the pop charts.

1993: The Toronto Blue Jays won their 2nd World Series.

2001: Apple released the iPod.

2004: Thirty-five people died when an earthquake hit northern Japan.

Scorpio
You are a rational, helpful individual who takes on too much responsibility.
4, 9, 21

#1 Song
1987: "Bad" by Michael Jackson

Birth Friends Forever

Ryan Reynolds, Canadian actor (*Wolverine*), 1976

Lucie Laroche, Canadian freestyle skier, 1968

Doug Flutie, American-born CFL player, 1962

Sam Raimi, director (*Spider-Man*), 1959

"Weird Al" Yankovic, musical parodist, 1959

Dwight Yoakam, country singer, 1956

Ang Lee, director (*Brokeback Mountain*), 1954

Michael Crichton, author (*Jurassic Park*), 1942

Anita Roddick, founder of The Body Shop, 1942

Pelé, soccer player, 1940

Johnny Carson, TV host, 1925

Lawren Harris, Canadian painter, 1885

Daily Oddity
On this date in 1874, the winner of an oyster-opening contest in Montréal shucked 300 oysters in 30 minutes.

OCTOBER 24
68 days until next year

In a Days
Inhale a Band-Aid. It's "Lung Health Day."
If you're a member of a clichéd street gang, celebrate "Bandanna Day."
If you're full of it, celebrate "National Bologna Day."

In the News
1901: Annie Edson Taylor, 63, became the first person to go over Niagara Falls in a barrel and survive.

1903: To confuse the other team, a football coach in Saskatchewan sewed football-shaped patches to his players' jerseys.

1917: Russia's October Revolution began.

1921: Nova Scotia's *Bluenose* won the International Schooner Championships.

1926: Houdini gave his last performance.

1929: Black Thursday: The stock market crashed.

1945: The United Nations was formed.

1990: The RCMP allowed Native officers to wear hair braids on duty.

1991: Céline Dion released her duet "Beauty and the Beast."

2008: Bloody Friday: Stock exchanges experienced record declines.

Scorpio
You're a hardworking leader, but you expect too much from others.
4, 8, 16

#1 Song
2006: "Money Maker" by Ludacris, featuring Pharrell

Birth Friends Forever
Shenae Grimes, Canadian actress (*90210*), 1989

Aubrey Graham, Canadian actor (*Degrassi: TNG*), 1986

Keyshia Cole, singer, 1983

Kevin Kline, actor (*Dave*), 1947

Jerry Edmonton, Canadian musician (Steppenwolf), 1946

F. Murray Abraham, actor (*Scarface*), 1939

Robert Mundell, Canadian economist, 1932

The Big Bopper, singer, 1930

Normie Kwong, CFL player/lieutenant-governor of Alberta, 1929

Hubert Aquin, Canadian novelist, 1915

Bob Kane, creator of Batman, 1915

Paul Grégoire, archbishop of Montréal, 1911

Daily Oddity
Anna Edson Taylor went over Niagara Falls to make money; she died destitute.

OCTOBER 25
67 days until next year

In a Days
Warm up the defibrillator. It's "National Greasy Foods Day."
Put down that greasy food and celebrate "Make a Difference Day."

In the News

1768: Port La Joie, PEI, was renamed Charlottetown.

1852: The Toronto Stock Exchange opened.

1923: Canadian Frederick Banting jointly won the Nobel Prize for discovering insulin.

1951: Montréal became the first Canadian city to reach a population of one million people.

1969: Winnipeg's The Guess Who were awarded a gold record for "Laughing."

1982: The Canadian Senate named July 1 Canada Day.

1993: Jean Chrétien became prime minister of Canada.

1995: Alanis Morissette's album *Jagged Little Pill* was certified multiplatinum.

2004: Fidel Castro banned all transactions using American money, effective November 8, 2004.

Scorpio
You are a perceptive, goal-oriented individual who sets standards that are too high.
6, 15, 24

#1 Song
1982: "Who Can It Be Now?" by Men at Work

Birth Friends Forever
Conchita Campbell, Canadian actress (*The 4400*), 1995

Katy Perry, singer, 1984

Milena Roucka, Canadian model, 1979

Jonathan Torrens, Canadian actor (*Jonovision*), 1972

Ed Robertson, Canadian musician (Barenaked Ladies), 1970

Wendel Clark, Canadian hockey player, 1966

Nancy Cartwright, voice actress (Bart Simpson, *The Simpsons*), 1957

Billy Barty, legendary little person, 1924

Ivan M. Niven, Canadian mathematician, 1915

Pablo Picasso, painter, 1881

Johann Strauss II, composer, 1825

Joseph Montferrand, Canadian strongman, 1802

Daily Oddity
Toronto, Vancouver and Montréal contain one-third of Canada's population.

OCTOBER 26
66 days until next year

In a Days
Oh, God, it's "World Priest Day."
Oh, God, it's "Mother-in-Law Day."

In the News
1861: The Pony Express was discontinued.

1881: The "Gunfight at the O.K. Corral" occurred.

1951: Joe Louis came out of retirement to box Rocky Mariano; Marciano won.

1965: The Beatles were appointed Members of the Order of the British Empire.

1984: "Baby Fae" received a baboon heart transplant.

1990: Wayne Gretzky scored his 2000th NHL point.

1992: The Charlottetown Accord was defeated in a Canada-wide referendum.

1997: Jacques Villeneuve became the first Canadian to win the World Championship of Drivers.

2000: Canadian pro wrestler Bret "the Hitman" Hart retired.

2001: The U.S. Patriot Act became law.

2005: Hundreds of Ontario residents were forced to evacuate their homes after *E. coli* was found in the water supply.

Scorpio
You are a born leader and a true humanitarian who can sometimes be too controlling.
5, 15, 23

#1 Song
1968: "Hey Jude" by The Beatles

Birth Friends Forever
Steve Kelly, Canadian hockey player, 1976

Keith Urban, country singer, 1967

Kelly Rowan, Canadian actress (*The O.C.*), 1965

Thomas Cavanagh, Canadian actor (*Ed*), 1964

Natalie Merchant, singer, 1963

Cary Elwes, actor (*The Princess Bride*), 1962

Dylan McDermott, actor (*The Practice*), 1961

Hillary Clinton, U.S senator, 1947

Jaclyn Smith, actress (*Charlie's Angels*), 1947

Pat Sajak, game-show host, 1946

Arthur Sifton, Canadian politician, 1858

Daily Oddity
Brushing your teeth uses 10 litres of water if you leave the tap running.

OCTOBER 27
65 days until next year

In a Days
Pee in your colleagues' Corn Flakes. It's "Cranky Co-worker Day."

In the News
- 1275: Amsterdam was founded.
- 1682: Philadelphia was founded.
- 1871: Canadian strongman David MacDonald lifted 725 kg; unfortunately, the exertion killed him.
- 1904: The first New York City subway line opened.
- 1951: Radiation treatment for cancer was first used in Canada.
- 1957: Maurice Richard scored his 500th NHL goal.
- 1985: George Kapeynes of Hamilton climbed the CN Tower's 1760 stairs in 8 minutes.
- 1994: The U.S. prison population reached one million.
- 1998: The *National Post* was launched.
- 2000: The RCMP arrested 2 suspects in connection with the 1985 bombing of Air India Flight 182.

Scorpio
You are an active and practical person who can sometimes be too aggressive.
9, 18, 27

#1 Song
1986: "True Colors" by Cyndi Lauper

Birth Friends Forever
Kristi Richards, Canadian freestyle skier, 1981
Scott Weiland, singer (Stone Temple Pilots), 1967
Simon Le Bon, singer (Duran Duran), 1958
Fran Lebowitz, author (*Metropolitan Life*), 1950
John Gotti, gangster, 1940
John Cleese, actor (*Fawlty Towers*), 1939
Sylvia Plath, author and poet (*The Bell Jar*), 1932
Gilles Vigneault, Canadian singer, 1928
Dylan Thomas, poet, 1914
Theodore Roosevelt, U.S. president, 1858
Isaac Singer, founder of Singer sewing machines, 1811
James Cook, explorer, 1728

Daily Oddity
Back in the olden days, many structures were painted red because red paint was the cheapest to purchase.

OCTOBER 28
64 days until next year

In a Days
Break out the acne cream. It's "National Chocolates Day."

In the News
1824: Canada's first medical school opened in Montréal.

1886: The Statue of Liberty was dedicated.

1889: Vancouver's Stanley Park was dedicated.

1942: The Alaska Highway, from Dawson Creek, BC, to Fairbanks, AK, was completed.

1968: Jim Day, Jim Elder and Tom Gayford of the Canadian Equestrian Team won Canada's only gold medal at the Mexico City Olympics.

1970: Gary Gabelich set a land-speed record in a rocket car (*The Blue Flame*) powered by natural gas.

1973: Racehorse Secretariat won his last race at the Canadian International Stakes.

1987: Montréal Expo Tim Wallach was named the National League Player of the Year.

2004: The Supreme Court of Canada ruled that Newfoundland and Labrador were justified in postponing pay equality to women during a financial crisis.

Scorpio
You are a committed and ingenious person who can sometimes be too timid.
4, 14, 24

#1 Song
1969: "Suspicious Minds" by Elvis Presley

Birth Friends Forever
Joaquin Phoenix, actor (*Walk the Line*), 1974

Julia Roberts, actress (*Pretty Woman*), 1967

Benoît Hogue, Canadian hockey player, 1966

Kevin Dineen, Canadian hockey player, 1963

Bill Gates, software magnate, 1955

Bruce Jenner, athlete, 1949

Pierre Desjardins, Canadian football player, 1941

Gary Cowan, Canadian golfer, 1938

Joan Plowright, actress (*Jane Eyre*), 1929

Paraskeva Clark, Canadian golfer, 1919

Francis Bacon, painter, 1909

Edith Head, Hollywood costume designer, 1897

Eliphalet Remington, gun manufacturer, 1793

Daily Oddity
The 2575 km Alaska Highway was built so that Canada could quickly move supplies and munitions north in case Japanese forces attacked.

OCTOBER 29
63 days until next year

In a Days
Put down that porridge. It's "Oatmeal Day."
Look at pornography and download free music. It's "Internet Day."

In the News
1618: Adventurer Walter Raleigh was beheaded.

1863: The International Red Cross was formed.

1886: New York held its first ticker-tape parade.

1929: Black Tuesday—The NYSX crashed, marking the start of the Great Depression.

1960: Cassius Clay (Muhammad Ali) won his first fight.

1969: ARPANET, the precursor to the Internet, was created.

1975: Vancouver experienced its greatest October rainfall, 60.7 mm.

1987: Montréal Canadiens goaltender Patrick Roy was handed an 8-game suspension for slashing.

1998: Astronaut John Glenn, 77, became the oldest person to go into space.

2004: In a video, Osama bin Laden took responsibility for the 9/11 attacks.

Scorpio
You are a direct and intelligent person who sometimes withdraws into a world of your own.
2, 11, 20

#1 Song
1963: "Sugar Shack" by Jimmy Gilmer & the Fireballs

Birth Friends Forever
Eric Staal, Canadian hockey player, 1984

Chelan Simmons, Canadian actress (*Kyle XY*), 1982

Brendan Fehr, Canadian actor (*Roswell*), 1977

Winona Ryder, actress (*Heathers*), 1971

Mike Gartner, Canadian hockey player, 1959

Dan Castellaneta, voice actor (Homer Simpson, *The Simpsons*), 1957

Denis Potvin, Canadian hockey player, 1953

Richard Dreyfuss, actor (*Jaws*), 1947

Ralph Bakshi, cartoonist (*Fritz the Cat*), 1938

Jon Vickers, Canadian tenor, 1926

Dominick Dunne, author (*The Winners*), 1925

Daily Oddity
The word "candy" is derived from the Arabic word *quandi*, which means "crystallized sugar."

OCTOBER 30
62 days until next year

In a Days
Hide the body. It's "Create a Great Funeral Day."
Get a priest to egg-sorcise your fridge. It's "Haunted Refrigerator Night."
It's the only vegetable kids will eat. Celebrate "National Candy Corn Day."
Hide the eggs and toilet paper. It's "Devil's Night."

In the News
1869: The first photograph was put in print, a picture of Prince Arthur.

1918: A ceasefire was declared in WWI; armistice soon followed.

1922: Benito Mussolini became prime minister of Italy.

1938: Orson Welles created mass hysteria when his radio adaptation of *The War of the Worlds* was broadcast.

1957: Albertans voted for a greater diversity of liquor outlets.

1968: Frank Sinatra recorded "My Way," with lyrics provided by Canada's Paul Anka.

1988: The Philip Morris Company bought Kraft Foods for $13.1 billion USD.

1995: Québec sovereigntists lost the referendum for independence from Canada, 50% to 49%.

Scorpio
You are an organized and objective person who has a hard time finding proper balance in your life.
5, 15, 32

#1 Song
2002: "Dilemma" by Nelly, featuring Kelly Rowland

Birth Friends Forever
Iain Hume, Canadian soccer player, 1983

Sarah Carter, Canadian actress (*DOA*), 1980

Ian D'Sa, Canadian singer (Billy Talent), 1975

Adam "Edge" Copeland, Canadian pro wrestler, 1973

Gavin Rossdale, musician (Bush), 1967

Harry Hamlin, actor (*L.A. Law*), 1951

Henry Winkler, actor (*Happy Days*), 1945

Joanna Shimkus, Canadian actress (*The Virgin & the Gypsy*), 1943

Charles Atlas, bodybuilder, 1893

Ezra Pound, poet, 1885

Fyodor Dostoevsky, author (*Crime and Punishmen*t), 1821

Daily Oddity
Bats hang upside down because their legs are too tiny and light to hold their bodies up.

OCTOBER 31
61 days until next year

In a Days
Dig up a corpse. It's "Halloween."
It's the only fruit kids will eat. It's "National Carmel Apple Day."
Let me saw you in half to celebrate "Magic Day."
If you use the Celtic calendar, you'll want to celebrate summer's end: "Samhain."

In the News
1918: Because of an influenza outbreak, the Alberta government prohibited all public meetings involving 7 people or more.

1926: Magician Harry Houdini died from a ruptured appendix.

1936: The Boy Scouts of the Philippines was founded.

1959: Lee Harvey Oswald tried to renounce his U.S. citizenship while he was in Moscow.

1961: Joseph Stalin's body was removed from Lenin's tomb.

1987: The Reform Party of Canada was founded.

2002: The Supreme Court of Canada ruled that all prisoners have the right to vote.

2007: Rogers Communications took possession of CityTV.

2008: A 3rd pipe bomb was detonated at a gas well near Dawson Creek, BC.

Scorpio
You are a determined and perceptive individual who may at times emotionally isolate yourself.
5, 15, 32

#1 Song
2004: "My Boo" by Usher and Alicia Keys

Birth Friends Forever
Justin Chatwin, Canadian actor (*Dragon Ball*), 1982

Fiona Smith, Canadian hockey player, 1973

Vanilla Ice, rapper, 1967

Adam Horovitz, rapper (Beastie Boys), 1966

Rob Schneider, actor (*SNL*), 1963

Peter Jackson, director (*The Lord of the Rings*), 1961

John Candy, Canadian comedian (*SCTV*), 1950

Michael Landon, actor (*Little House on the Prairie*), 1936

Dan Rather, television journalist, 1931

Dale Evans, singing cowgirl, 1912

Newsy Lalonde, Canadian hockey player, 1887

John Keats, poet, 1795

Daily Oddity
Halloween is the second biggest holiday in Canada after Christmas.

NOVEMBER 1
60 days until next year

In a Days
If you've been canonized or play football for New Orleans, celebrate "All Saints' Day."
If you're a drunken loner, celebrate "National Authors' Day."
Fall back. It's the end of Daylight Saving Time.

In the News
1512: The ceiling of the Sistine Chapel was unveiled.
1604: Shakespeare's *Othello* premiered.
1611: Shakespeare's *The Tempest* premiered.
1896: The first bare-breasted photo of a woman appeared in *National Geographic* magazine.
1924: NHL granted Boston the first U.S. hockey franchise.
1939: Trans-Canada Air Lines began daily flights across the country.
1939: The first rabbit born from artificial insemination was unveiled.
1952: Foster Hewitt gave the play-by-play in Canada's first English-language hockey telecast.
1992: *Maclean's* magazine named McGill Canada's best university.
2008: Two Québec radio DJs tricked U.S. vice-presidential candidate Sarah Palin into thinking she was speaking with the French president.

Scorpio
You are an intelligent and energetic individual who may perceive yourself as being superior.
4, 7, 17

#1 Song
1991: "Romantic" by Karyn White

Birth Friends Forever
Aishwarya Rai, actress (*Bride & Prejudice*), 1973
Toni Collette, actress (*The Sixth Sense*), 1972
Jenny McCarthy, model, 1972
Tie Domi, Canadian hockey player, 1969
Lyle Lovett, country singer, 1957
Phil Myre, Canadian hockey player, 1948
Ralph Klein, premier of Alberta, 1942
Marcia Wallace, voice actress (Edna Krabappel, *The Simpsons*), 1942
Al Arbour, Canadian hockey player, 1932
Gordon R. Dickson, Canadian sci-fi author (*The Dragon Knight*), 1923
Paul-Émile Borduas, Canadian painter, 1905
Emma Albani, Canadian soprano, 1847

Daily Oddity
The word "vagina" was derived from the sheath that Roman soldiers used to hold their swords.

NOVEMBER 2
59 days until next year

In a Days
Chip away at your tombstone. It's "Plan Your Epitaph Day."
Don't even bother to breathe. It's "Zero Tasking Day."
Stock up on crackers. It's "Cookie Monster Day."

In the News
1898: Johnny Campbell became the first cheerleader.

1936: The CBC was established.

1947: *The Spruce Goose*, the aircraft with the largest wingspan, made its first and last flight.

1957: The Levelland UFO case, history's most notorious UFO sighting, occurred.

1959: Canadian goaltender Jacques Plante wore the first goalie mask.

1984: Velma Barfield became the first woman executed in the U.S. in nearly 20 years.

1992: A goat in Québec made it into the *Guinness Book of Records* after giving birth to 6 kids.

1998: The Friendly Giant (Bob Homme) was awarded the Order of Canada.

2000: The first crew of astronauts arrived at the International Space Station.

Scorpio
You are a logical and good-natured individual who is sometimes viewed as a meddler.
2, 11, 20

#1 Song
1990: "Ice Ice Baby" by Vanilla Ice

Birth Friends Forever
Luke Schenn, Canadian hockey player, 1989

Tamara Hope, Canadian actress (*Whistler*), 1984

Nelly, rapper, 1974

David Schwimmer, actor (*Friends*), 1966

k.d. lang, Canadian musician, 1961

Pat Buchanan, politician, 1938

Steve Ditko, comic book artist (*Dr. Strange*), 1927

Father David Bauer, Canadian hockey player/priest, 1924

Bill Mosienko, Canadian hockey player, 1921

Burt Lancaster, actor (*Airport*), 1913

Jean-Marie-Rodrigue Villeneuve, archbishop of Québec, 1883

Marie Antoinette, queen of France, 1755

Daily Oddity
The Friendly Giant (Bob Homme) was only 5'6" tall.

NOVEMBER 3
58 days until next year

In a Days
Stop! It's "National Traffic Directors Day."
Turn up the stereotypes and celebrate "Cliché Day."
Hold the mayo. It's "Sandwich Day."

In the News
1644: The first religious marriage between a French Canadian and a Native woman took place.

1817: The Bank of Montréal opened.

1869: The Hamilton Football Club (Tiger Cats) was founded.

1911: Chevrolet was founded.

1913: Income tax was first introduced in the U.S.

1930: Canada and the U.S. were connected by the world's first vehicular tunnel from Windsor, ON, to Detroit, MI.

1957: A dog named Laika became the first animal to enter Earth's orbit, aboard *Sputnik 2*.

1998: Artist Bob Kane, the creator of *Batman*, died.

2007: With doubt hanging over his re-election, Pakistan president Pervez Musharraf suspended the constitution and declared a state of emergency in Pakistan; his re-election was later confirmed.

Scorpio
You are a driven and resourceful individual who sometimes forgets your own needs.
5, 9, 14

#1 Song
1998: "The First Night" by Monica

Birth Friends Forever
Tim McIlrath, singer (Rise Against), 1979

Jim McKenzie, Canadian hockey player, 1969

Debbie Rochon, Canadian actress (*Santa Claws*), 1968

Dolph Lundgren, actor (*Rocky IV*), 1957

Dennis Miller, comedian, 1953

Kate Capshaw, actress (*Indiana Jones and the Temple of Doom*), 1953

Roseanne Barr, comedian, 1952

William Kurelek, Canadian artist, 1927

Bronislau Nagurski, Canadian football player, 1908

Billy Barker, Canadian fighter pilot, 1894

Vilhjalmur Stefansson, Canadian explorer, 1879

Daily Oddity
In olden times, after a wedding ceremony, the couple would drink mead (fermented honey) for a good moon cycle; thus, the honeymoon was created.

NOVEMBER 4
57 days until next year

In a Days
Rock the vote. It's "U.S. Election Day"
Giving new meaning to chicken breasts, it's "National Chicken Lady Day."
Don't shower with your television. It's "Use your Common Sense Day."

In the News

1920: Canada broadcast the world's first commercial radio show.

1922: Archaeologists uncovered the entrance to the tomb of King Tutankhamun.

1924: Nellie Tayloe Ross was elected the first female U.S. governor.

1970: A 13-year-old "feral child" named Genie, who had lived most of her life in a locked basement, was discovered in Los Angeles.

1992: Canadian goaltender Manon Rhéaume became the first woman to sign a professional hockey contract.

1993: Jean Chrétien was sworn in as Canada's 20th prime minister.

1995: Israeli Prime Minister Yitzhak Rabin was assassinated.

2008: Barack Obama was elected the first African American U.S. president.

Scorpio
You are rational and clear-sighted individual; however, you tend to be too opinionated.
4, 13, 22

#1 Song
2007: "Kiss Kiss" by Chris Brown

Birth Friends Forever
Alexz Johnson, Canadian actress (*Instant Star*), 1986

Éric Fichaud, Canadian hockey player, 1975

Matthew McConaughey, actor (*Sahara*), 1969

Sean Combs, rapper, 1969

Ralph Macchio, actor (*The Karate Kid*), 1961

Kathy Griffin, comedian, 1960

Jacques Villeneuve Sr., Canadian racecar driver, 1953

Laura Bush, U.S. first lady, 1946

Howie Meeker, Canadian hockey player, 1924

Art Carney, actor (*The Honeymooners*), 1918

Walter Cronkite, news broadcaster, 1916

Will Rogers, cowboy, 1879

Daily Oddity
A beaver's front teeth never stop growing.

NOVEMBER 5
56 days until next year

In a Days
Blow up Parliament (just kidding). It's "Guy Fawkes Day."

In the News
1605: Political agitator Guy Fawkes and others attempted to blow up the British Houses of Parliament, in what is known as the "Gunpowder Plot."

1872: Susan B. Anthony attempted to vote for the first time; she was fined $100.

1895: George B. Selden patented the automobile.

1955: Montréal Canadien Jean Béliveau scored a hat trick in 44 seconds, the second fastest hat trick on record.

1977: Canadian bandleader Guy Lombardo died at the age of 75.

1980: The World's Biggest Bookstore opened in Toronto, with 1.5 million books on 27.3 km of shelves.

1995: André Dallaire broke into 24 Sussex Drive in an attempt to assassinate Canadian Prime Minister Jean Chrétien.

2006: Former Iraq President Saddam Hussein was found guilty for crimes against humanity and was sentenced to death.

Scorpio
You are an analytical and socially aware individual who may wear yourself thin.
2, 8, 23

#1 Song
1971: "Gypsies, Tramps & Thieves" by Cher

Birth Friends Forever
Ryan Adams, musician, 1974
Famke Janssen, actress (*GoldenEye*), 1965
Tilda Swinton, actress (*Adaptation*), 1960
Bryan Adams, Canadian musician, 1959
Robert Patrick, actor (*Terminator 2*), 1958
Sam Shepard, actor (*The Notebook*), 1943
Art Garfunkel, musician (Simon & Garfunkel), 1941
Ike Turner, musician, 1931
Vivien Leigh, actress (*Gone with the Wind*), 1913
Roy Rogers, cowboy, 1911
Cooney Weiland, Canadian hockey player, 1904
Alphonse Desjardins, Canadian journalist, 1854

Daily Oddity
Every November 5, British residents burn effigies of the "Old Guy" (Fawkes). The dishevelled look of the effigies later led to the term "bum."

NOVEMBER 6
55 days until next year

In a Days
Today blows. It's "Saxophone Day."
Hope you like takeout. It's "National Men Make Dinner Day."
Put on a beard of bees to celebrate "Guinness World Record Day."

In the News

1879: Canada observed Thanksgiving for the first time.

1917: Canada's "Fighting Tenth" took Passchendaele; nearly 240,000 soldiers died during the 4-month battle.

1968: Canadian surgeons performed the first plastic cornea implant on a human eye.

1984: Former Saskatchewan cabinet minister Colin Thatcher was found guilty of murdering his ex-wife.

1991: Canadians extinguished the last of the 751 oil well fires started by Saddam Hussein's troops at the end of the Gulf War.

1995: Canada's Mark Messier scored his 500th NHL goal.

1997: An escaped flamingo was spotted among the geese on the Ottawa River.

1999: Australia voted to remain a part of the British monarchy.

2000: The Marijuana Party of Canada was registered.

Scorpio
You are a direct and ingenious individual who can also be single-minded at times.
6, 12, 26

#1 Song
1979: "Heartache Tonight" by The Eagles

Birth Friends Forever
Andrew Murray, Canadian hockey player, 1981

Mike Maurer, Canadian football player, 1975

Rebecca Romijn, actress (*X-Men*), 1972

Ethan Hawke, actor (*Reality Bites*), 1970

Jean-Marc Chouinard, Canadian fencer, 1963

Maria Shriver, TV journalist, 1955

Ken Read, Canadian downhill skier, 1955

Fred Penner, Canadian children's entertainer, 1946

Sally Field, actress (*Brothers & Sisters*), 1946

James A. Naismith, Canadian inventor of basketball, 1861

Adolphe Sax, inventor of the saxophone, 1814

Daily Oddity
The biggest trend of 1936 was swallowing goldfish.

NOVEMBER 7
54 days until next year

In a Days
Can I get a witness? It's "Notary Public Day."
Wake one up from hibernation and celebrate "Bear Hug Day."
Sorry, books, it's "Magazine Day."

In the News
1492: The first recorded meteorite hit Earth.

1873: Alexander Mackenzie became Canada's 2nd prime minister.

1885: The Canadian Pacific Railway was completed

1908: Butch Cassidy and the Sundance Kid were allegedly killed in Bolivia.

1917: Trotsky and Lenin led the Bolsheviks in a coup d'état.

1961: Woodrow Lloyd succeeded Tommy Douglas as premier of Saskatchewan.

1982: Edmonton's Warren Moon became the first quarterback to complete 5000 passing yards.

1990: Mary Robinson became the first female president of the Republic of Ireland.

1991: Magic Johnson announced that he had HIV.

1994: The first Internet radio show was broadcast.

2002: Iran banned all U.S. advertisements from its country.

Scorpio
You are an inquisitive and inspiring individual who at times neglects your loved ones.
3, 9, 32

#1 Song
1983: "Islands in the Stream" by Kenny Rogers, with Dolly Parton

Birth Friends Forever
Melyssa Ford, Canadian model, 1976

Jason and Jeremy London, actors, 1972

Jamie Drummond, Canadian wine steward, 1971

Tanya Dubnicoff, Canadian cyclist, 1969

Michael Heidt, Canadian hockey player, 1963

Christopher Knight, actor (*The Brady Bunch*), 1957

Joni Mitchell, Canadian musician, 1943

Mary Travers, singer (Peter, Paul & Mary), 1937

Audrey McLaughlin, Canadian politician, 1936

Billy Graham, evangelist, 1918

Leon Trotsky, Russian revolutionary, 1879

Daily Oddity
Lotteries have the worst gambling odds, craps the best.

NOVEMBER 8
53 days until next year

In a Days
Skip going home. It's "National Parents as Teachers Day."

Skip dinner and go straight to dessert. It's "Cook Something Bold and Pungent Day."

Sassy skunks and saucy spectators should succumb to celebrating "International Tongue Twister Day."

In the News
1793: The Louvre opened to the public.

1873: Winnipeg was incorporated as a city.

1895: X-rays were discovered.

1917: The Canadian Press (CP) news service was established.

1942: Montréal Canadien Maurice Richard scored his first NHL goal.

1944: The First Canadian Army was victorious in the battle of the Scheldt, in the southwestern Netherlands and northern Belgium.

1962: The Royal Canadian Mint was ordered to revert the nickel back to its original round shape.

1971: The NHL granted franchises to Long Island and Atlanta,

1993: Canada's Céline Dion announced her engagement to her manager, René Angélil.

1995: Country Dick Montana, singer for the Beat Farmers, collapsed and died on stage during a concert in Whistler, BC.

Scorpio
You are an eager and determined student who may at times go on the defensive.

4, 16, 28

#1 Song
1988: "Wild, Wild West" by The Escape Club

Birth Friends Forever
Jully Black, Canadian singer, 1977

Parker Posey, actress (*Josie & the Pussy Cats*), 1968

Gordon Ramsay, chef, 1966

Alan Graham Frew, Canadian singer (Glass Tiger), 1959

Mary Hart, TV personality, 1950

Bonnie Raitt, singer, 1949

Morley Safer, Canadian TV journalist, 1931

Gordon Churchill, Canadian politician, 1898

Clarence Gagnon, Canadian painter, 1881

Bram Stoker, author (*Dracula*), 1847

Milton Bradley, board game magnate, 1836

Vlad the Impaler, prince/inspiration for Dracula, 1431

Daily Oddity
Manitoba has won curling's Brier Cup 26 times, more than any other province.

NOVEMBER 9
52 days until next year

In a Days
Everyone save for prisoners should celebrate "World Freedom Day."

In the News

1620: *Mayflower* pilgrims spotted Cape Cod, MA.

1861: The first recorded football game in Canada was played.

1872: The *Manitoba Free Press*, later the *Winnipeg Free Press*, was founded.

1888: Jack the Ripper claimed his last victim.

1905: Alexander Rutherford was elected Alberta's first premier.

1921: Albert Einstein was awarded the Nobel Prize in Physics.

1965: The Northeast Blackout left several U.S. and Canadian cities in darkness for about 13 hrs.

1967: *Rolling Stone* magazine was first published.

1972: Canada's *Anik 1* communications satellite was launched from Cape Canaveral, FL.

1985: Garry Kasparov, 22, became the youngest World Chess Champion.

1989: The Berlin Wall fell.

2001: Canadian discount airline Canada 3000 filed for bankruptcy.

Scorpio
You are a socially conscious, energetic person who easily becomes dissatisfied.
9, 18, 27

#1 Song
1974: "You Ain't Seen Nothing Yet" by Bachman-Turner Overdrive

Birth Friends Forever

Vanessa Minnillo, TV personality, 1980

Sisqó, singer, 1978

Nick Lachey, singer, 1973

Gabrielle Miller, Canadian actress (*Corner Gas*), 1973

Chris Jericho, Canadian pro wrestler, 1970

Teryl Rothery, Canadian actress (*The X-Files*), 1965

Sandra "Pepa" Denton, musician (Salt-N-Pepa), 1965

Bob Nault, Canadian politician, 1955

Gaétan Hart, Canadian boxer, 1953

Lou Ferrigno, actor (*The Incredible Hulk*), 1951

Clyde Wells, Canadian politician, 1937

Carl Sagan, astronomer, 1934

Dorothy Dandridge, actress (*Carmen Jones*), 1923

Pierrette Alarie, Canadian soprano, 1921

Spiro Agnew, U.S. vice president, 1918

Daily Oddity
The word *anik* is Inuit for brother.

NOVEMBER 10
51 days until next year

In a Days
780-403-204-604, it's "Area Code Day."
If your area code consists of gumdrops, celebrate "Gingerbread House Day."

In the News

1871: Henry Stanley uttered the phrase, "Dr. Livingstone, I presume?"

1918: Ottawa received a coded message from Europe stating that all fighting would end on November 11, 1918.

1926: Vincent Massey became Canada's first ambassador to the U.S.

1931: Famous Five member Henrietta Edwards died.

1958: The Hope Diamond was donated to the Smithsonian.

1969: *Sesame Street* premiered.

1975: Twenty-nine crewmembers died when the *Edmund Fitzgerald* sank on Lake Superior.

1986: Canadian hockey coach Francis "King" Clancy died.

2007: During the Ibero-American Summit in Chile, the king of Spain asked the president of Venezuela, "Why don't you just shut up?"—which later became a popular catchphrase.

Scorpio
You are a meticulous knowledge-seeker who can easily become obsessive.
7, 8, 13

#1 Song
1939: "Address Unknown" by the Ink Spots

Birth Friends Forever

Brittany Murphy, actress (*8 Mile*), 1977

Ellen Pompeo, actress (*Grey's Anatomy*), 1969

Tracy Morgan, comedian (*SNL*), 1968

Neil Gaiman, author (*The Sandman*), 1960

Sinbad, comedian, 1956

Kevin Spraggett, Canadian chessmaster, 1954

Tim Rice, lyricist (*The Lion King*), 1944

Roy Scheider, actor (*Jaws*), 1932

Ennio Morricone, composer (*A Fistful of Dollars*), 1928

Richard Burton, actor (*Cleopatra*), 1925

Claude Rains, actor (*The Wolfman*), 1889

John David Thompson, Canadian prime minister, 1845

Daily Oddity
Area codes were based on rotary phones, and areas with the largest populations received area codes that took the shortest time to dial (e.g., New York is 212).

NOVEMBER 11
50 days until next year

In a Days
Lest we forget, it's "Remembrance Day."

In the News
1880: Australian outlaw Ned Kelly was hanged.

1918: An armistice agreement was reached on the 11th hour of the 11th day of the 11th month, ending WWI.

1926: Route 66 from Chicago to California was opened.

1930: Einstein received a patent for his co-invention, the Einstein refrigerator.

1967: Canadian Clinton Shaw set the world distance record for rollerskating, 7885 km.

1980: Group of Seven member A.Y. Jackson's painting *Algoma Lake* sold for $210,000.

1992: The Church of England allowed women to become priests.

2004: Yasser Arafat, chairman of the Palestine Liberation Organization, died.

2008: Archaeologists in Egypt uncovered a 4300-year-old pyramid.

2008: The 7th severed foot inside a running shoe washed up off the coast of BC.

Scorpio
You are intelligent and a proponent for the greater good who may disregard your own needs.
2, 9, 22

#1 Song
2000: "With Arms Wide Open" by Creed

Birth Friends Forever
Trey Smith, actor (*The Pursuit of Happyness*), 1992

Jesse F. Keeler, Canadian musician (Death from Above 1979), 1976

Leonardo DiCaprio, actor (*Titanic*), 1974

Adam Beach, Canadian actor (*Flags of Our Fathers*), 1972

Calista Flockhart, actress (*Brothers & Sisters*), 1964

Demi Moore, actress (*Ghost*), 1962

Stanley Tucci, actor (*The Devil Wears Prada*), 1960

Stephen Lewis, Canadian politician, 1937

Harry Lumley, Canadian hockey player, 1926

Jonathan Winters, comedian, 1925

Kurt Vonnegut Jr., author (*Slaughterhouse-Five*), 1922

Alice Girard, Canadian nurse, 1907

Daily Oddity
750,000 Canadians served in WWI; 60,661 did not return home.

NOVEMBER 12
49 days until next year

In a Days
It's "National Indian Pudding Day." Or, if you're PC, it's "National Native American Pudding Day."

In the News
1847: Chloroform was first used as an anaesthetic.

1931: Maple Leaf Gardens opened.

1933: The Loch Ness Monster was first photographed.

1938: Vancouver's Lions Gate Bridge opened.

1939: Canadian surgeon Norman Bethune died.

1940: Canada banned the importation of comic books.

1951: The National Ballet of Canada held its first performance.

1956: The Canada Council was founded.

1981: The Canadarm was launched.

1984: The Canadarm was used in the first space salvage mission.

1991: June Rowlands was elected the first female mayor of Toronto.

1995: Canadian astronaut Chris Hadfield blasted off into space.

1998: Daimler-Benz merged with Chrysler.

Scorpio
You are an organized individual who loves to help others; however, you suffer from insecurity.
3, 12, 21

#1 Song
1966: "Poor Side of Town" by Johnny Rivers

Birth Friends Forever
Anne Hathaway, actress (*Get Smart*), 1982

Ryan Gosling, Canadian actor (*The Notebook*), 1980

Mark Hunter, Canadian hockey player, 1962

Megan Mullally, actress (*Will & Grace*), 1958

Neil Young, Canadian musician, 1945

Booker T. Jones, musician (Booker T and the MGs), 1944

Wallace Shawn, actor (*Gossip Girl*), 1943

Michel Audet, Canadian politician, 1940

Denis DeJordy, Canadian hockey player, 1938

Grace Kelly, actress/Princess of Monaco, 1929

Jean Papineau-Couture, Canadian composer, 1916

DeWitt Wallace, co-founder of *Reader's Digest*, 1889

Daily Oddity
The police act of driving unwanted characters to the city limits and abandoning them is known as a "starlight tour."

NOVEMBER 13
48 days until next year

In a Days
Shut up and celebrate "World Kindness Day."
If you don't know where you are, celebrate "National Geography Awareness Day."

In the News
1673: The beaver was first suggested as Canada's national emblem.

1775: American Revolutionary forces attacked Montréal.

1887: Bloody Sunday riots broke out in London.

1976: Edmonton's Citadel Theatre opened.

1979: The first private radio station (CJCD) in the NWT went on the air.

1984: Pierre Trudeau received the Albert Einstein Peace Prize.

1985: Canadian impressionist André-Philippe Gagnon appeared on *The Tonight Show*.

1990: Montréal invested $15 million to save the Expos.

1998: Michel Trudeau, son of Pierre Trudeau, died in an avalanche.

2003: The Canadian dollar closed at $0.7695 USD, a 10-year high.

Scorpio
You are a realistic observer who may isolate yourself from others.
4, 13, 22

#1 Song
2000: "Independent Women" by Destiny's Child

Birth Friends Forever
François-Louis Tremblay, Canadian short-track speed skater, 1980

Gerard Butler, actor (*300*), 1969

Jimmy Kimmel, talk-show host, 1967

Wayne Parker, Canadian musician (Glass Tiger) 1960

Whoopi Goldberg, actress (*Sister Act*), 1955

Chris Noth, actor (*Law & Order*), 1954

Gilbert Perreault, Canadian hockey player, 1950

Joe Mantegna, actor (*Criminal Minds*), 1947

Daniel Pilon, Canadian actor (*Ryan's Hope*), 1940

Garry Marshall, director (*Pretty Woman*), 1934

Richard Mulligan, actor (*Soap*), 1932

John MacIntosh Lyle, Canadian architect, 1872

Robert Louis Stevenson, writer (*Treasure Island*), 1850

Daily Oddity
The beaver has been the national emblem of Canada since 1975.

NOVEMBER 14
47 days until next year

In a Days
If you're uptight, celebrate "Loosen up, Lighten up Day."
Who wants 6-week-old leftovers? It's "National Clean out your Refrigerator Day."

In the News

1533: Spanish conquistadors arrived in Peru.

1606: Canada's Marc Lescarbot wrote and produced North America's first drama, *Neptune's Theatre*.

1835: Canada's first insane asylum opened in Saint John, NB.

1849: After a mob burned down the Montréal Parliament buildings, Toronto became the new seat of the Union government.

1922: BBC radio went on the air.

1950: Alberta junior farmer Ricky Sharpe won the world wheat championship with his submission of Marquis Wheat.

1964: Canada's Gordie Howe scored his 627th NHL goal.

1989: CP Rail trains began going caboose-less.

1991: Ontario sold the SkyDome to a group of 8 companies for $280 million in cash.

Scorpio
You are a perceptive individual who contributes to the greater good; however, you tend to ignore your own feelings.
6, 9, 16

#1 Song
1973: "Keep On Truckin'" by Eddie Kendricks

Birth Friends Forever

Travis Barker, musician (Blink-182), 1975

Lori Dupuis, Canadian female hockey player, 1972

Patrick Warburton, actor (*Seinfeld*), 1964

Rev Run, rapper (Run-D.M.C.), 1964

Yanni, composer, 1954

Charles, Prince of Wales, 1948

Murray Oliver, Canadian hockey player, 1937

McLean Stevenson, actor (*M*A*S*H*), 1927

Frederick Banting, Canadian co-discoverer of insulin, 1891

Claude Monet, painter, 1840

Johann van Beethoven, father of Ludwig van Beethoven, 1740

Leopold Mozart, father of Wolfgang Amadeus Mozart, 1719

Daily Oddity
New technology and mounting safety concerns led to the demise of the train caboose.

NOVEMBER 15
46 days until next year

In a Days
If you're a crazy loner writing your manifesto, celebrate "I Love To Write Day."
If you're a zesty recluse, celebrate "National Spicy Hermit Day."

In the News
1880: Canadian rower Ned Hanlan won the World Single Sculls Rowing Championship in England.

1926: NBC radio went on the air.

1948: Louis St. Laurent became prime minister of Canada.

1960: Canada declared that D.H. Lawrence's novel *Lady Chatterley's Lover* was not obscene under the Criminal Code.

1985: A package from the Unabomber (Ted Kaczynski) exploded, injuring a University of Michigan professor.

1993: NHL referees went on strike.

1996: Céline Dion's album *Falling Into You* was certified multiplatinum.

2004: The U.S. Securities and Exchange Commission filed a civil fraud lawsuit against Canadian newspaper magnate Conrad Black.

Scorpio
You are an empathic humanitarian who doesn't always listen to the opinions of others.
6, 14, 15

#1 Song
1993: "I'd Do Anything for Love (But I Won't Do That)" by Meat Loaf

Birth Friends Forever
Yannick Tremblay, Canadian hockey player, 1975

Chad Kroeger, Canadian singer (Nickelback), 1974

Jonny Lee Miller, actor (*Hackers*), 1972

Ol' Dirty Bastard, rapper, 1968

"Macho Man" Randy Savage, pro wrestler, 1952

Sam Waterston, actor (*Law & Order*), 1940

Petula Clark, singer, 1932

Ed Asner, actor (*Elf*), 1929

Joseph Wapner, TV judge, 1919

Gordon Churchill, Canadian lawyer, 1898

Georgia O'Keeffe, painter, 1887

Joseph Quesnel, Canadian composer, 1746

Daily Oddity
According to the biography *Dancing on the Edge*, Conrad Black was allegedly expelled from Upper Canada College for selling stolen exams.

NOVEMBER 16
45 days until next year

In a Days
I won't stand for the "International Day of Tolerance."
Pick me! Pick me! It's "National Adoption Day."
Don't come undone, it's only "Button Day."

In the News
1849: Russian writer Fyodor Dostoevsky (*Crime & Punishment*) was sentenced to death for anti-government activities; his sentence was later reduced to hard labour.

1857: William Hall became the first Canadian sailor, the first African Canadian and the first Nova Scotian to win the Victoria Cross.

1869: Louis Riel invited Manitoba settlers and Métis to meet at Fort Garry to form a provisional government.

1885: Canadian folk hero and leader of the Métis, Louis Riel, was executed for treason in Regina.

1938: LSD was first produced.

1983: Margaret Trudeau filed for divorce from PM Pierre Trudeau.

2003: The Edmonton Eskimos defeated the Montréal Alouettes 34–22 in the 91st Grey Cup.

2004: U.S. President George W. Bush announced that he would visit Canada on November 30 for the first time since becoming president in 2001.

Scorpio
You are an inquisitive and progressive individual who tends to ignore the ideas of others.
7, 9, 36

#1 Song
1988: "Bad Medicine" by Bon Jovi

Birth Friends Forever
Allison Crowe, Canadian singer, 1981
Maggie Gyllenhaal, actress (*The Dark Knight*), 1977
Lisa Bonet, actress (*The Cosby Show*), 1967
Dean McDermott, Canadian actor (*Tori & Dean*), 1966
Diana Krall, Canadian jazz singer, 1964
Marg Helgenberger, actress (*CSI: Crime Scene Investigation*), 1958
Pierre Larouche, Canadian hockey player, 1955
David Leisure, actor (*Empty Nest*), 1950
John Swartzwelder, television writer (*The Simpsons*), 1950
Don Loney, Canadian football player, 1923
Burgess Meredith, actor (*Rocky*), 1908

Daily Oddity
Louis Riel Day is a statutory holiday in Manitoba, established on September 26, 2007, and celebrated in February.

NOVEMBER 17
44 days until next year

In a Days
If you are a counterfeiter, enjoy "Homemade Bread Day."
Get lost! It's "Take a Hike Day."

In the News
1558: Elizabeth I ascended to the throne of England.

1603: Explorer Walter Raleigh was put on trial for treason.

1623: Canada's first highway, connecting Lower and Upper Québec, was built.

1771: Fifteen-year-old Mozart's opera *Ascanio in Alba* premiered.

1840: Canadian James Evans invented a 9-character Cree and Inuit alphabet.

1950: At the age of 15, Tenzin Gyatso became the 14th Dalai Lama.

1968: Al Balding and George Knudson became the first Canadians to win the World Cup Golf Tournament.

1970: The computer mouse was patented.

2008: The world's oldest polar bear died at the Assiniboine Park Zoo in Winnipeg, a month shy of her 42nd birthday.

Scorpio
You are an analytical and rational individual who can also be too critical.
8, 17, 26

#1 Song
1944: "I'll Walk Alone" by Dinah Shore

Birth Friends Forever
Rachel McAdams, Canadian actress (*The Notebook*), 1978

Sophie Marceau, actress (*Braveheart*), 1966

Daisy Fuentes, model, 1966

Randy Black, Canadian musician (Annihilator), 1963

RuPaul, drag queen, 1960

Dennis Maruk, Canadian hockey player, 1955

Stephen Root, actor (*Office Space*), 1951

Lorne Michaels, Canadian creator of *SNL*, 1944

Danny DeVito, actor (*Taxi*), 1944

Martin Scorsese, director (*The Departed*), 1942

Gordon Lightfoot, Canadian singer, 1938

Rock Hudson, actor (*Pillow Talk*), 1925

Frank Calder, Canadian president of the NHL, 1877

Pierre Gaultier, Canadian explorer, 1685

Daily Oddity
The Hawaiian alphabet only has 12 letters.

NOVEMBER 18
43 days until next year

In a Days
Sorry, Goofy, it's "Mickey Mouse Day."
Sorry, rotary phone, it's "Push-button Phone Day."
Put an apple on your child's head and take aim. It's "William Tell Day."

In the News
1883: Standard time zones, the brainchild of Canadian inventor Sanford Fleming, were implemented

1929: An earthquake near Cape Breton triggered a tsunami that killed 27 Newfoundlanders.

1931: The highest Canadian windspeed was recorded at 200 km/h.

1936: *The Globe & Mail* was founded.

1963: The first push-button telephone went into service.

1978: Over 900 followers of cult leader Jim Jones died when they drank cyanide-laced Kool-Aid.

1980: Founder of the Toronto Maple Leafs, Conn Smythe, died.

1984: The Winnipeg Blue Bombers won the Grey Cup.

1992: RCMP seized 4323 kg of cocaine worth $2.7 billion.

2008: Eva Aariak became the new premier of Nunavut.

Scorpio
You are an empathic and reliable individual who can become overwhelmed by your emotions.
9, 11, 17

#1 Song
1990: "Love Takes Time" by Mariah Carey

Birth Friends Forever
Chloë Sevigny, actress (*Big Love*), 1974
Owen Wilson, actor (*Zoolander*), 1968
Jocelyn Lemieux, Canadian hockey player, 1967
Elizabeth Perkins, actress (*Weeds*), 1960
Warren Moon, football player, 1956
Alan Moore, comic book author (*Watchmen*), 1953
Kevin Nealon, actor (*Weeds*), 1953
Linda Evans, actress (*Dynasty*), 1942
Margaret Atwood, Canadian author (*The Blind Assassin*), 1939
Alan Shepard, astronaut, 1923
Jean Paul Lemieux, Canadian painter, 1904

Daily Oddity
On average, women speak 25,000 words a day, while men speak only 12,000.

NOVEMBER 19
42 days until next year

In a Days
I wish you nothing but the worst. It's "Have a Bad Day Day."

In the News
- **1863**: Abraham Lincoln delivered his *Gettysburg Address*.
- **1959**: Ford discontinued the Edsel.
- **1963**: Gordie Howe scored his 545th goal.
- **1969**: Football (soccer) star Pelé scored his 1000th goal.
- **1983**: Canadian Bruce Hood officiated over his 1000th NHL game.
- **1990**: Singing duo Milli Vanilli were stripped of their Grammy when it was discovered that it wasn't their vocals on their album.
- **1995**: The Baltimore Stallions won the Grey Cup.
- **1997**: A woman in Iowa gave birth to septuplets.
- **1998**: Vincent van Gogh's *Portrait of the Artist Without Beard* sold for US$71.5 million.
- **2004**: The CRTC approved CHUM's purchase of Internet provider Craig Media.

Scorpio
You're an energetic and clear-sighted individual who can feel drained at times.
1, 10, 19

#1 Song
1989: "Blame it on the Rain" by Milli Vanilli

Birth Friends Forever
McCaughey septuplets, world's first surviving septuplets, 1997
Daria Werbowy, Canadian model, 1983
Chandra Crawford, Canadian skier, 1983
Matt Dusk, Canadian jazz singer, 1978
Sandrine Holt, Canadian actress (*The L Word*), 1972
Jodie Foster, actress (*The Brave One*), 1962
Meg Ryan, actress (*When Harry Met Sally*), 1961
Dennis Hull, Canadian hockey player, 1944
Calvin Klein, fashion designer, 1942
Larry King, talk-show host, 1933
Indira Gandhi, prime minister of India, 1917
Tommy Dorsey, bandleader, 1905

Daily Oddity
The Huron believed that Oki, the soul of the sky, controlled the weather.

NOVEMBER 20
41 days until next year

In a Days
Baptize your computer. It's "Name your PC Day."

In the News
1820: An 80-tonne sperm whale attacked a whaling ship off the coast of South America; the event inspired *Moby Dick*.

1903: Moose Jaw, SK, was incorporated.

1945: The Nuremberg Trials against 24 Nazi war criminals began.

1946: Oil drilling commenced in Leduc, AB; wells pumped 3500 barrels a day.

1947: Queen Elizabeth II married Prince Philip.

1985: Microsoft Windows 1.0 was released.

1989: The roof of Montréal's Olympic Stadium was torn off during a windstorm.

1992: A fire destroyed parts of Windsor Castle.

2008: A fiery meteorite streaked across western Canada skies. The event was witnessed by thousands of people in Alberta, Saskatchewan and Manitoba.

Scorpio
You are a rational and perceptive individual who regularly sabotages yourself.
2, 11, 20

#1 Song
1998: "Doo Wop (That Thing)" by Lauryn Hill

Birth Friends Forever
Jason Thompson, Canadian actor (*General Hospital*), 1976

John MacLean, Canadian hockey player, 1964

Bo Derek, actress (*10*), 1956

Nanette Workman, Canadian singer, 1945

Joe Biden, U.S. vice president, 1942

Richard Dawson, game-show host, 1932

Robert F. Kennedy, politician, 1925

Alistair Cooke, journalist, 1908

Chester Gould, creator of *Dick Tracy*, 1900

James Bertram Collip, Canadian biochemist, 1892

Edwin Hubble, astronomer, 1889

Wilfrid Laurier, Canadian prime minister, 1841

Daily Oddity
In 1946, Toronto hat maker Sammy Taft agreed to give Chicago Black Hawk forward Alex Kaleta a free hat if he could score 3 goals in a single game. Kaleta scored the first "hat trick" and got his hat.

NOVEMBER 21
40 days until next year

In a Days
Well, hello "World Hello Day."
Where's the remote? It's "World Television Day."

In the News
1783: The first hot-air balloon flight took place.

1784: The new Province of New Brunswick was proclaimed.

1791: Napoleon Bonaparte was appointed commander-in-chief of the French Republic armies.

1877: Thomas Edison unveiled his phonograph.

1921: King George V proclaimed Canada's coat of arms and designated red and white as the country's official colours.

1942: The Alaska Highway was completed.

1980: Over 80 people died when the MGM Grand Hotel in Las Vegas caught fire.

1988: Brian Mulroney was re-elected prime minister of Canada.

2000: Canada launched its most powerful COMSAT, *Anik F1*.

2004: The Toronto Argonauts won the Grey Cup.

Scorpio
You are an empathetic and tenacious individual who often suppresses your own needs.
3, 12, 21

#1 Song
1984: "Wake Me Up Before You Go-Go" by Wham!

Birth Friends Forever
Jena Malone, actress (*Donnie Darko*), 1984

Alex Tanguay, Canadian hockey player, 1979

Ken Griffey Jr., baseball player, 1969

Björk, singer, 1965

Nicollette Sheridan, actress (*Desperate Housewives*), 1963

Goldie Hawn, actress (*The First Wives Club*), 1945

Harold Ramis, actor (*Ghostbusters*), 1944

Dr. John, musician, 1940

Tom Gayford, Canadian equestrian, 1928

Foster Hewitt, Canadian radio announcer, 1902

Samuel Cunard, Canadian shipping magnate, 1787

Voltaire, philosopher, 1694

Daily Oddity
The notoriously short Napoleon Bonaparte was actually 5'6". During his autopsy, his height was not converted to Standard English measurements.

NOVEMBER 22
39 days until next year

In a Days
If you reside on a different astral plane, you should celebrate "International Aura Awareness Day."

In the News
1594: Explorer Martin Frobisher died.

1718: Blackbeard the pirate was killed.

1859: Charles Darwin's *The Origin of Species* was released.

1922: The tomb of Tutankhamun was opened.

1963: U.S. President John F. Kennedy was assassinated.

1968: The Beatles *White Album* was released.

1981: The Edmonton Eskimos won the Grey Cup.

1983: According to Statistics Canada, the country's population reached 25 million.

1986: Wayne Gretzky scored his 500th goal.

1995: The first full-length computer-animated movie, *Toy Story*, was released.

2003: Edmonton hosted the Heritage Classic, the first regular-season NHL game to be played outdoors.

Sagittarius
You are a curious and incisive individual who often imposes your ideas on others.
4, 13, 22

#1 Song
1976: "Tonight's the Night" by Rod Stewart

Birth Friends Forever
Scarlett Johansson, actress (*He's Just Not That Into You*), 1984

David Pelletier, Canadian figure skater, 1974

Mark Ruffalo, actor (*Zodiac*), 1967

Boris Becker, tennis player, 1967

Jamie Lee Curtis, actress (*Freaky Friday*), 1958

Lawrence Gowan, Canadian singer (Styx), 1956

Yvan Cournoyer, Canadian hockey player, 1943

Jacques Laperrière, Canadian hockey player, 1941

Terry Gilliam, director (*Brazil*), 1940

Irene Macdonald, Canadian diver, 1933

Arthur Hiller, Canadian director (*Love Story*), 1923

Rodney Dangerfield, comedian, 1921

Raymond Collishaw, Canadian ace pilot, 1893

Daily Oddity
The first outdoor NHL game was an exhibition game held in Las Vegas in 1991.

NOVEMBER 23
38 days until next year

In a Days
Why, thank you, it's "You're Welcome-giving Day."

In the News
1815: Canada's first streetlights went into operation along Montréal streets.

1889: The first jukebox was unveiled.

1936: *Life* magazine was first published.

1946: The Toronto Argonauts won the Grey Cup.

1975: The Edmonton Eskimos won the Grey Cup.

1976: Apneist (freediver) Jacques Mayol became the first person to swim to a depth of 100 m without any assistance from additional breathing apparatus.

1980: The Edmonton Eskimos won the Grey Cup.

1988: Wayne Gretzky scored his 600th goal.

1990: The first all-woman expedition to the South Pole set off on their journey.

2008: After a 14-year wait, Guns N' Roses released their album *Chinese Democracy*.

Sagittarius
You are a perceptive and courageous individual whose ambitions may be perceived as being too radical.
3, 15, 42

#1 Song
1983: "All Night Long (All Night)" by Lionel Richie

Birth Friends Forever
Miley Cyrus, singer, 1992

Colby Armstrong, Canadian hockey player, 1982

Myriam Boileau, Canadian diver, 1977

Jonathan Seet, Canadian singer, 1969

Bill Bissett, Canadian painter, 1939

Michael Gough, actor (*Batman*), 1913

Victor Jory, Canadian actor (*The Shadow*), 1902

Robert McClure, Canadian missionary, 1900

Harpo Marx, comedian (Marx Brothers), 1888

Boris Karloff, actor (*Frankenstein*), 1887

Billy the Kid, outlaw, 1859

William Jack, Canadian mathematician, 1817

Daily Oddity
According to the ancient Egyptians, to bring good luck when you see a new moon, you should bow to it 3 times: once for Osiris (the Father), once for Isis (the Mother) and once for Horus (the Son).

NOVEMBER 24
37 days until next year

In a Days
As long as it's appropriate outside the boudoir, "Celebrate Your Unique Talent Day."

In the News
1890: The Cape Breton Railway opened.

1905: The CNR reached Edmonton.

1922: Edmonton outlawed swearing in public.

1951: The Ottawa Rough Riders won the Grey Cup.

1956: The Edmonton Eskimos won the Grey Cup.

1963: JFK's assassin, Lee Harvey Oswald, was shot and killed by Jack Ruby.

1966: New York City experienced its smoggiest day in history.

1971: Hijacker D.B. Cooper stole $200,000 from an airplane before parachuting into a severe thunderstorm; neither Cooper nor the money was ever recovered.

1985: The BC Lions won the Grey Cup.

1996: The Toronto Argonauts won the Grey Cup.

2008: A U.S. meteorite hunter offered a $10,000 reward for a piece of the meteorite that fell over western Canada on November 20.

Sagittarius
You are an inquisitive and independent person who often hides your inner emotions.
6, 15, 24

#1 Song
2003: "Baby Boy" by Beyoncé

Birth Friends Forever
Meredith Henderson, Canadian actress (*Queer as Folk*), 1983

Karine Vanasse, Canadian actress (*Killer Wave*), 1983

Katherine Heigl, actress (*Grey's Anatomy*), 1978

Christian Laflamme, Canadian hockey player, 1976

Keith Primeau, Canadian hockey player, 1971

Todd Brooker, Canadian skier, 1959

Spider Robinson, Canadian sci-fi author (*The Free Lunch*), 1948

Billy Connolly, comedian, 1942

Pete Best, musician (The Beatles), 1941

Eric Wilson, Canadian children's author (*Terror in Winnipeg*), 1940

William F. Buckley Jr., author, 1925

Lucky Luciano, gangster, 1897

Florence Wyle, Canadian artist, 1881

Scott Joplin, composer, 1868

Adam Shortt, Canadian historian, 1859

Daily Oddity
The safest age to be is 10 years old.

NOVEMBER 25
36 days until next year

In a Days
Don't forget to spend, spend, spend. It's "Shopping Reminder Day."

In the News
1867: Alfred Nobel patented dynamite.

1885: Banff National Park in Alberta was established.

1947: The "Hollywood Ten" were blacklisted from Hollywood under suspicion of communism.

1950: The Toronto Argonauts won the Grey Cup.

1963: JFK was laid to rest at Arlington Cemetery.

1976: The Band played their last concert, which became the Martin Scorsese documentary *The Last Waltz*.

1984: Thirty-six musicians formed Band Aid and recorded "Do They Know It's Christmas?"—a benefit song for Ethiopia.

1989: An earthquake measuring 6.0 on the Richter scale hit eastern Canada.

1990: The Winnipeg Blue Bombers won the Grey Cup.

2007: The Saskatchewan Roughriders won the Grey Cup.

Sagittarius
You are a capable and progressive individual; however, you are intolerant of other people's ideas.
6, 15, 24

#1 Song
1970: "I Think I Love You" by The Partridge Family

Birth Friends Forever
Christina Applegate, actress (*Samantha Who?*), 1971

Jacqueline and Jill Hennessy, Canadian actresses, 1968

Tim Armstrong, singer (Rancid), 1966

Holly Cole, Canadian jazz singer, 1963

Gilbert Delorme, Canadian hockey player, 1962

John F. Kennedy Jr., publisher, 1960

John Larroquette, actor (*Night Court*), 1947

Ricardo Montalbán, actor (*Fantasy Island*), 1920

Augusto Pinochet, dictator, 1915

Joe DiMaggio, baseball player, 1914

Eddie Shore, Canadian hockey player, 1902

Andrew Carnegie, industrialist, 1835

Daily Oddity
Shoplifters primarily steal between 3 PM and 6 PM on Fridays and Sundays.

NOVEMBER 26
35 days until next year

In a Days
Thanks for giving us reality TV. It's "Thanksgiving" in the U.S. I'll be at the bar celebrating "Tie One on Day."

In the News

1476: Vlad the Impaler became ruler of Wallachia, Romania, for the 3rd time.

1789: A national Thanksgiving was observed in the U.S.

1917: The National Hockey League was formed.

1941: The 4th Thursday in November was established as Thanksgiving in the U.S.

1977: An alien named "Vrillon" delivered a message of peace over a British TV station.

1983: 6800 gold bars were stolen from Heathrow Airport.

1984: Guy Lafleur announced his retirement from hockey.

1991: Canada's Manon Rhéaume became the first woman to play on a junior A hockey team.

2003: The Concorde made its final flight.

2008: Over 160 people were killed in a terrorist attack in Mumbai, India.

Sagittarius
You are a vigorous and focused individual who often neglects your emotions.
8, 17, 26

#1 Song
1991: "Set Adrift on Memory Bliss" by P.M. Dawn

Birth Friends Forever

Chris Hughes, co-founder of *Facebook*, 1983

Gina Kingsbury, Canadian hockey player, 1981

Patrice Lauzon, Canadian figure skater, 1975

Chris Osgood, Canadian hockey player, 1972

Tina Turner, singer, 1939

Rich Little, Canadian impersonator, 1938

Robert Goulet, Canadian singer, 1933

Ernie Coombs, Mr. Dressup, 1927

Charles M. Schulz, cartoonist (*Peanuts*), 1922

Bat Masterson, gunfighter, 1853

John Harvard, founder of Harvard University, 1607

Daily Oddity
The first five NHL teams were the Montréal Canadiens, the Montréal Wanderers, the Ottawa Senators, the Québec Bulldogs and the Toronto Arenas.

NOVEMBER 27
34 days until next year

In a Days
I'm always anxious on "Pins and Needle Day."

In the News

1924: The first Macy's Thanksgiving Day Parade was held.

1934: Bank robber Baby Face Nelson was killed by the FBI.

1960: Gordie Howe scored his 1000th point.

1961: Gordie Howe played his 1000th game.

1978: A disgruntled former city supervisor assassinated San Francisco mayor George Moscone and openly gay city supervisor Harvey Milk.

1989: Marred by charges of child abuse, the Mount Cashel Orphanage for Boys in St. John's, NL, was closed.

2001: The first hydrogen atmosphere was discovered on an extrasolar (beyond the solar system) planet.

2005: The first partial human face transplant took place.

2006: The House of Commons recognized the Québécois as a nation within Canada.

Sagittarius
You are an independent seeker of truth who can be oversensitive.
9, 18, 27

#1 Song
1986: "You Give Love a Bad Name" by Bon Jovi

Birth Friends Forever

Alison Pill, Canadian actress (*Milk*), 1985

Chad Kilger, Canadian hockey player, 1976

Patricia Zentilli, Canadian actress (*New Waterford Girl*), 1970

Garry Valk, Canadian hockey player, 1967

Caroline Kennedy, journalist, 1957

Bill Nye, the Science Guy, 1955

Pierre Mondou, Canadian hockey player, 1955

Sheila Copps, Canadian politician, 1952

Jimi Hendrix, guitarist, 1942

Eddie Rabbitt, singer, 1941

Bruce Lee, actor (*Enter the Dragon*), 1940

L. Sprague de Camp, sci-fi author (*A Gun For Dinosaur*), 1907

Daily Oddity
Expect love, peace and prosperity if you dream of cantaloupe.

NOVEMBER 28
33 days until next year

In a Days
Head down to the Nothing Store. It's "Buy Nothing Day."
Don't buy anything, just listen to their sales pitch. It's "National Salesperson Day."
Wash your hands before you celebrate "Flossing Day."

In the News
1814: The first newspaper was printed with an automatic press.

1893: Women in New Zealand got the vote.

1907: Canadian-raised producer Louis B. Mayer opened his first movie theatre.

1907: Canada's first dial telephones were used at the Sydney Mines.

1939: Canadian inventor of basketball, James Naismith, died.

1975: Soap opera *As the World Turns* aired its final live episode.

1979: Billy Smith became the first NHL goaltender to score a goal.

1992: CBC's *The Fifth Estate* won the Emmy for International Documentary of the Year.

2005: Representatives from 190 nations gathered in Montréal for a climate change conference.

2008: A piece of the meteorite that fell on November 20 was discovered in Lone Rock, SK.

Sagittarius
You are an analytical observer who tends to isolate yourself.
1, 10, 19

#1 Song
1994: "On Bended Knee" by Boyz II Men

Birth Friends Forever
Marc-Andre Fleury, Canadian hockey player, 1984

Chamillionaire, rapper, 1979

Anna Nicole Smith, model and sex symbol, 1967

Jon Stewart, TV host (*The Daily Show*), 1962

Ed Harris, actor (*Pollock*), 1950

Paul Shaffer, Canadian bandleader, 1949

Randy Newman, composer, 1943

Ray Perkins, Canadian singer (The Crew-Cuts), 1932

Carlyle Clare Agar, Canadian pilot, 1901

Albert Henry George Grey, donor of the Grey Cup, 1851

William Blake, poet, 1757

Noël Levasseur, Canadian sculptor, 1680

Daily Oddity
Empty cans tied to the back of a wedding car ward off evil spirits.

NOVEMBER 29
32 days until next year

In a Days
Say hello to your toaster. It's "Electronic Greeting Day."

In the News

1830: The November Uprising, a rebellion against Russian rule, began in Poland.

1910: The traffic-light system was patented.

1922: The tomb of Tutankhamun was opened to the public.

1963: A Trans-Canada Airlines DC-8 carrying 118 passengers crashed near Montréal just after take-off; no one survived.

1964: Canadian actor Lorne Greene (*Bonanza*) had a number-one hit with his song "Ringo."

1965: Canada launched the *Alouette 2* satellite.

1972: The first commercially successful video game, Pong, was released.

1983: Kanchan Stott became the first woman to run across Canada; it took her 207 days.

2004: Tommy Douglas was voted "The Greatest Canadian."

2007: A 7.4-magnitude earthquake occurred in the Caribbean Sea.

Sagittarius
You are an energetic and perceptive individual who sometimes expects too much from others.
2, 12, 21

#1 Song
1964: "Ringo" by Lorne Greene

Birth Friends Forever

Tanner Glass, Canadian hockey player, 1983

Anna Faris, actress (*Scary Movie*), 1976

Jonathan Knight, singer (New Kids on the Block), 1968

Don Cheadle, actor (*Boogie Nights*), 1964

Howie Mandel, Canadian TV host (*Deal or No Deal*), 1955

Stan Rogers, Canadian musician, 1949

Denny Doherty, Canadian singer (The Mamas and the Papas), 1940

Diane Ladd, actress (*28 Days*), 1932

Vin Scully, baseball announcer, 1927

John Tully, Canadian oceanographer, 1906

C.S. Lewis, author (*The Chronicles of Narnia*), 1898

Louisa May Alcott, author (*Little Women*), 1831

Daily Oddity
Canadian $20 bills are usually in circulation for approximately 2.2 years.

NOVEMBER 30
31 days until next year

In a Days
Call in sick so you can enjoy "Stay Home Because You're Well Day."

In the News
1886: The Folies Bergère opened in Paris.

1936: London's Crystal Palace was destroyed by fire.

1940: Lucille Ball married Desi Arnaz.

1954: A sleeping woman was hit by a meteorite.

1989: Serial killer Aileen Wuornos claimed her first victim.

1992: Canadian writer Michael Ondaatje won the Governor General's Award for his novel *The English Patient*.

1995: Operation Desert Storm ended.

2000: Canada's Marc Garneau returned to space for the 3rd time.

2002: Dennis Fentie became the premier of Yukon Territory.

2004: Ken Jennings' 74-game *Jeopardy!* winning streak ended.

2005: A Montréal judge overturned the 14 conditions imposed on convicted Canadian serial killer Karla Homolka.

Sagittarius
You are an active person with great clarity; however, you are too direct at times.
3, 12, 21

#1 Song
1969: "Na Na Hey Hey Kiss Him Goodbye" by Steam

Birth Friends Forever
Elisha Cuthbert, Canadian actress (*24*), 1982

Jason Pominville, Canadian hockey player, 1982

Clay Aiken, singer, 1978

Mike LeClerc, Canadian hockey player, 1976

Ben Stiller, actor (*Tropic Thunder*), 1965

Colin Mochrie, Canadian comedian (*Whose Line Is It, Anyway?*), 1957

Billy Idol, musician, 1955

Ridley Scott, director (*Bladerunner*), 1937

Henry Taube, Canadian chemist, 1915

Lucy Maud Montgomery, Canadian author (*Anne of Green Gables*), 1874

Winston Churchill, British prime minister, 1874

John McCrae, Canadian soldier/poet ("In Flanders Field"), 1872

Henry Birks, Canadian jeweller, 1840

Mark Twain, author (*Tom Sawyer*), 1835

Daily Oddity
Ken Jennings lost when he answered "FedEx" instead of "H&R Block."

DECEMBER 1
30 days until next year

In a Days
Go to the front of the bus. It's "Rosa Parks Day."
Use a condom. It's "World AIDS Day."

In the News
1891: Canadian James Naismith invented basketball.

1913: Ford introduced the first moving assembly line.

1922: New Brunswick drivers began driving on the right-hand side of the road.

1955: African American Rosa Parks refused to give her bus seat to a white man.

1981: The AIDS virus was officially recognized.

1982: Barney Clark received the first permanent artificial heart.

1988: Benazir Bhutto became prime minister of Pakistan and the first woman elected to lead a Muslim country.

1990: Canada banned leaded gas.

1994: Canadian politician Lucien Bouchard was stricken with flesh-eating bacteria.

2008: Canada's Liberal, NDP and Bloc Québécois parties formed a coalition government in hope of ousting the Conservative minority government with a "vote of no confidence."

Sagittarius
You are an exuberant trailblazer who may be perceived as being too extreme.
1, 10, 19

#1 Song
1991: "Black or White" by Michael Jackson

Birth Friends Forever
Sarah Silverman, comedian, 1970
Larry Walker, Canadian baseball player, 1966
Sam Reid, Canadian musician (Glass Tiger), 1963
Nathalie Lambert, Canadian short-track speed skater, 1963
Carol Alt, supermodel, 1960
Bette Midler, actress (*Beaches*), 1945
Richard Pryor, comedian, 1940
Lee Trevino, golfer, 1939
Woody Allen, director (*Annie Hall*), 1935
Lou Rawls, singer, 1933
Len Norris, Canadian editorial cartoonist, 1913
Alexander Wilson, Canadian athlete, 1905
Marie Tussaud, creator of wax sculptures, 1761

Daily Oddity
The Canadian government opened a medical marijuana grow-op in an abandoned mine in Flin Flon, MB.

DECEMBER 2
29 days until next year

In a Days
Batter yourself up and hop into the deep fryer. It's "National Fritters Day."

In the News
1907: Canadian boxer Tommy Burns retained the world heavyweight boxing title.

1933: Newfoundland gave up its status as a self-governing dominion.

1939: NYC's La Guardia Airport opened.

1942: The first self-sustaining nuclear chain reaction, part of the Manhattan Project, was detonated.

1949: British Parliament gave Canada the power to make changes to the BNA Act.

1961: Fidel Castro declared that Cuba would adopt communism.

1971: The United Arab Emirates was formed.

1995: Goaltender Patrick Roy resigned from the Montréal Canadiens.

2000: Same-sex couples in Canada gained full benefits and obligations save for marriage under the Modernization of Benefits and Obligations Act.

2001: American energy company Enron filed for bankruptcy.

Sagittarius
You are a charismatic and driven individual who is dualistic in nature.
2, 11, 20

#1 Song
1974: "Kung Fu Fighting" by Carl Douglas

Birth Friends Forever
Cassie Steele, Canadian actress (*Degrassi: TNG*), 1989

Britney Spears, singer, 1981

Nelly Furtado, Canadian singer, 1978

Monica Seles, tennis player, 1973

Lucy Liu, actress (*Charlie's Angels*), 1968

Ron Sutter, Canadian hockey player, 1963

Stone Phillips, TV journalist, 1954

Francis Fox, Canadian politician, 1939

Bill McCreary, Canadian NHL referee, 1934

Louis-Marcel Raymond, Canadian botanist, 1915

Ray Walston, actor (*My Favourite Martian*), 1914

Charles Ringling, circus ringmaster, 1863

Daily Oddity
At 5'7" and 162 lbs, Canadian boxer Tommy Burns was the smallest heavyweight champion ever.

DECEMBER 3
28 days until next year

In a Days
Don't park in their parking spots. It's "International Day of Disabled Persons."

In the News
1921: The Canadian Badminton Association was founded.

1960: Annette Toft of Denmark became Canada's 2-millionth immigrant since the end of WWII.

1960: The Edmonton International Airport opened.

1967: The first human heart transplant took place.

1976: Reggae singer Bob Marley was shot twice in an assassination attempt; he performed 2 days later.

1979: Eleven Who fans in Ohio were killed during a stampede for concert seats.

1984: More than 3800 people in Bhopal, India, were killed when methyl isocyanate leaked from a pesticide plant.

1997: Over 120 countries, excluding the U.S., China and Russia, met in Ottawa and signed a treaty prohibiting the deployment of anti-personnel landmines.

2008: Bratz dolls were removed from store shelves after Mattel won a court injunction against manufacturer MGA Entertainment.

Sagittarius
You are a clear-sighted and analytical individual who is also single-minded at times.
3, 21, 30

#1 Song
1989: "We Didn't Start the Fire" by Billy Joel

Birth Friends Forever
Rainbow Sun Francks, Canadian actor (*Stargate Atlantis*), 1979

Keegan Connor Tracy, Canadian actress (*White Noise*), 1971

Brendan Fraser, Canadian actor (*The Mummy*), 1968

Katarina Witt, figure skater, 1965

Julianne Moore, actress (*Blindness*), 1960

Daryl Hannah, actress (*Splash*), 1960

Ozzy Osbourne, singer, 1948

Yves Trudeau, Canadian sculptor, 1930

Andy Williams, singer, 1927

Eli Mandel, Canadian poet, 1922

William Otter, Canadian soldier, 1843

Daily Oddity
The term "housewarming" comes from the practice of using the embers from your old home to start a fire in your new home.

DECEMBER 4
27 days until next year

In a Days
Roll 'em if you got 'em. It's "National Dice Day."
Don't take all the credit. It's "Extraordinary Work Team Recognition Day."

In the News

1881: The *Los Angeles Times* was first published.

1884: Calgary's town council held their first meeting.

1902: Prohibition went into effect in Ontario.

1909: The first Grey Cup game was held.

1952: Over 12,000 Britons died when a combination of cold fog and air pollution descended upon London.

1954: The first Burger King opened.

1971: A fan with a flare gun set Switzerland's Montreux Casino on fire during a Frank Zappa concert.

1973: Except for police, all wiretapping and electronic surveillance was outlawed in Canada.

1996: Canadian country music legend Wilf Carter died at the age of 91.

2006: A giant squid was caught off the coast of Tokyo.

Sagittarius
You have an active mind and are a technical expert; however, you often act without regard.
4, 13, 22

#1 Song
1995: "One Sweet Day" by Mariah Carey & Boyz II Men

Birth Friends Forever

Kristina Groves, Canadian speed skater, 1976

Tyra Banks, model, 1973

Jassen Cullimore, Canadian hockey player, 1972

Jay-Z, rapper, 1969

Marisa Tomei, actress (*The Wrestler*), 1964

Rick Middleton, Canadian hockey player, 1953

Jeff Bridges, actor (*The Big Lebowski*), 1949

Roberta Bondar, Canadian astronaut, 1945

Anna McGarrigle, Canadian singer, 1944

Max Baer Jr., actor (*The Beverly Hillbillies*), 1937

Victor French, actor (*Highway to Heaven*), 1934

Deanna Durbin, Canadian actress (*Christmas Holiday*), 1921

Crazy Horse, Sioux chief, 1840

Daily Oddity
In the first Grey Cup match, the University of Toronto defeated the Toronto Parkdale Canoe Club 26–6.

DECEMBER 5
26 days until next year

In a Days
If you like looking like a raisin, celebrate "Bathtub Party Day."
If you like working for free, celebrate "International Volunteer Day."

In the News
1890: Canadian strongman Louis Cyr lifted 222 kg with one finger.

1892: John Thompson became Canada's 4th prime minister.

1893: The world's first electric car was unveiled in Toronto.

1902: Guglielmo Marconi sent the first legible wireless telegraph signal from Glace Bay, NS, to Cornwall, England.

1933: Prohibition ended in the U.S.

1970: The Stanley Cup, Conn Smythe Trophy and Bill Masterson Trophy were all stolen from the NHL Hall of Fame in Toronto; all 3 were later recovered.

1976: Four Canadian women were chosen as Rhodes Scholars.

1983: The Hells Angels arrived in Québec to do battle with rival biker gang the Rock Machine.

2008: The death toll of Canadian soldiers in Afghanistan reached 100.

Sagittarius
You are an imaginative and original individual who sometimes alienates those around you.
4, 5, 23

#1 Song
2004: "Drop It Like It's Hot" by Snoop Dogg, featuring Pharrell

Birth Friends Forever
Frankie Muniz, actor (*Malcolm in the Middle*), 1985

Shalom Harlow, Canadian model, 1973

Kevin Haller, Canadian hockey player, 1970

Margaret Cho, comedian, 1968

Johnny Rzeznik, singer (Goo Goo Dolls), 1965

Andy Kim, Canadian singer/songwriter, 1952

Serge Chapleau, Canadian artist, 1945

Little Richard, singer, 1932

Walt Disney, animation magnate, 1901

Fritz Lang, director (*Metropolis*), 1890

Arthur Currie, Canadian military general, 1875

George Armstrong Custer, military general, 1839

Daily Oddity
It is believed that the Sun has enough energy to last another 5 billion years.

DECEMBER 6
25 days until next year

In a Days
Dig a hole to celebrate "Miners' Day."
Hock some jewellery. It's "National Pawnbrokers Day."

In the News
1768: The *Encyclopedia Britannica* was first published.

1880: *The Edmonton Bulletin* was first published.

1917: More than 1900 people died and half the city destroyed when a freighter carrying munitions exploded in the Halifax harbour.

1921: Canadian women voted in their first federal election.

1969: Meredith Hunter was stabbed by Hells Angels who were serving as security during a Rolling Stones concert.

1989: Fourteen women were gunned down at the École Polytechnique in Montréal (the Montréal Massacre).

1990: The Ottawa Senators returned to the NHL after a 34-year hiatus.

1995: Canada's Joni Mitchell was honoured with the Billboard Century Award.

2001: The province of Newfoundland was renamed Newfoundland and Labrador.

Sagittarius
You are a highly developed, objective individual who can sometimes be too naïve.
6, 15, 24

#1 Song
1980: "Lady" by Kenny Rogers

Birth Friends Forever
Nick Stajduhar, Canadian hockey player, 1974

Torri Higginson, Canadian actress (*Stargate Atlantis*), 1969

Judd Aptow, director (*Knocked Up*), 1967

Steven Wright, comedian, 1955

Lawrence Cannon, Canadian politician, 1947

George Beurling, Canadian WWII ace pilot, 1921

Irv Robbins, Canadian co-founder of Baskin-Robbins, 1917

Baby Face Nelson, bank robber, 1908

York Wilson, Canadian painter, 1907

Agnes Moorehead, actress (*Bewitched*), 1900

Ira Gershwin, lyricist, 1896

Susanna Moodie, Canadian author (*Roughing It in the Bush*), 1803

Daily Oddity
At their first time at the ballots, Canadian women elected Agnes McPhail to the House of Commons.

DECEMBER 7
24 days until next year

In a Days
Don't accidentally get it confused with pink insulation. It's "National Cotton Candy Day."

In the News
1827: Canada's first steam engine went into operation in Stellarton, NS.

1907: Christmas seals were sold for the first time to fight tuberculosis.

1918: An earthquake stopped the Vancouver Block clock on Granville Street.

1941: The Japanese carried out a sneak attack on U.S. forces stationed at Pearl Harbor, Hawaii.

1941: Canada declared war on Japan.

1963: Instant replay was used for the first time in a football game.

1977: Gordie Howe scored his 1000th career goal.

1982: Canadian world record track and field star Harry Jerome died.

1995: BC became the first province to pass regulations for car manufacturers to provide less-polluting vehicles.

2008: The first NFL game was played north of the border in Toronto.

Sagittarius
You are an unconventional person who is attracted to the unusual; however, you isolate your emotions.
6, 16, 36

#1 Song
1942: "White Christmas" by Bing Crosby

Birth Friends Forever
Brent Johnson, Canadian football player, 1976

Nicole Appleton, Canadian singer, 1974

Larry Bird, basketball player, 1956

Tom Waits, singer, 1949

Garry Unger, Canadian hockey player, 1947

Harry Chapin, singer, 1942

Gerry Cheevers, Canadian hockey player, 1940

Ellen Burstyn, actress (*The Exorcist*), 1932

Noam Chomsky, linguist, 1928

Jean Carignan, French Canadian fiddler, 1916

Margaret Carse, Canadian dancer, 1916

Max Braithwaite, Canadian author (*All the Way Home*), 1911

Daily Oddity
Winnipeg, Québec City and Saskatoon are the only Canadian cities guaranteed to always have a white Christmas.

DECEMBER 8
23 days until next year

In a Days
As long as you didn't purchase them from a hippie, celebrate "National Brownie Day."

In the News
1869: The Red River Rebellion began.

1869: Timothy Eaton founded Eaton's department store.

1915: Canadian soldier John McCrae's poem "In Flanders Fields" was first published.

1941: The U.S. declared war on Japan.

1953: John Diefenbaker married Olive Palmer.

1980: John Lennon was shot and killed by Mark David Chapman.

1987: Canadian mobster Frank Cotroni was sentenced to 8 years in prison.

2003: Twenty-six Canadian soldiers, including four deceased, received U.S. Bronze Stars for their work in Afghanistan.

2008: Marc Mayer was appointed the director of the National Gallery of Canada.

Sagittarius
You are an ambitious and enthusiastic individual who can sometimes be unfocused.
8, 17, 26

#1 Song
1998: "I'm Your Angel" by R. Kelly & Céline Dion

Birth Friends Forever
Drew Doughty, Canadian hockey player, 1989

Haley Wickenheiser, Canadian hockey player, 1978

Dominic Monaghan, actor (*Lost*), 1976

Sinéad O'Connor, singer, 1966

Teri Hatcher, actress (*Desperate Housewives*), 1964

Kim Basinger, actress (*Batman*), 1953

Jim Morrison, singer (The Doors), 1943

Red Berenson, Canadian hockey player, 1939

David Carradine, actor (*Kung-Fu*), 1936

Flip Wilson, comedian, 1933

Sammy Davis Jr., singer, 1925

Andy Russell, Canadian actor (*The Canadian Cowboy*), 1915

Diego Rivera, painter, 1886

Mary, Queen of Scots, 1542

Daily Oddity
The first Eaton's store opened at Yonge and Queen in Toronto and offered a "Satisfaction Guaranteed" refund policy.

DECEMBER 9
22 days until next year

In a Days
If your Willie is weary, celebrate "Weary Willie Day."

In the News
1755: Canada's first post office opened in Halifax.

1851: The first North American YMCA opened in Montréal.

1941: In the wake of Pearl Harbour, BC closed Japanese Canadian schools and newspapers.

1960: The first episode of Britain's *Coronation Street* was broadcast.

1965: A fireball crashed in Pittsburgh; 40 years later, NASA said the object was a reentering Russian satellite.

1973: The first episode of *The Royal Canadian Air Farce* aired on CBC Radio.

1979: Smallpox was declared eradicated,

2001: Astronaut Chris Hadfield became the first Canadian to perform a space walk.

2001: CTV purchased *The Globe and Mail*.

2008: Illinois governor Rod Blagojevich was arrested for trying to auction off the U.S. Senate seat left vacant by newly elected President Barack Obama.

Sagittarius
You are an idealistic educator who sometimes suffers from jealousy.
9, 18, 27

#1 Song
1990: "Because I Love You (The Postman Song)" by Stevie B

Birth Friends Forever
Ryder Hesjedal, Canadian cyclist, 1980

Sebastian Spence, Canadian actor (*First Wave*), 1969

Dave Hilton Jr., Canadian boxer, 1963

Felicity Huffman, actress (*Desperate Housewives*), 1962

Donny Osmond, singer, 1957

John Malkovich, actor (*Being John Malkovich*), 1953

Rick Danko, Canadian musician (The Band), 1943

Pit Martin, Canadian hockey player, 1943

Beau Bridges, actor (*Stargate Atlantis*), 1941

Christopher Pratt, Canadian painter, 1935

Judi Dench, actress (*Casino Royale*), 1934

Redd Foxx, comedian, 1922

Kirk Douglas, actor (*Spartacus*), 1916

Emmett Kelly, circus clown, 1898

John Milton, poet (*Paradise Lost*), 1608

Daily Oddity
In 2007, the Canada Post website received 45,000 emails to Santa Claus.

DECEMBER 10
21 days until next year

In a Days
If you're a human and love having rights, celebrate "Human Rights Day."

In the News
1901: The first Nobel Prizes were awarded.

1906: Theodore Roosevelt became the first American to win a Nobel Prize.

1927: The *Grand Ole Opry* debuted on the radio.

1948: The UN adopted the Universal Declaration of Human Rights.

1955: *Mighty Mouse* debuted.

1968: A 300-million-yen robbery was executed in Tokyo; the money was never recovered.

1984: The Montréal Expos traded Gary Carter to the New York Mets.

1985: Steve MacLean was named Canada's 2nd astronaut.

1986: Canadian John Polanyi received the Nobel Peace Prize in Physics.

2003: Joe Handley became premier of the Northwest Territories.

2008: Police in BC and Winnipeg pulled all Tasers purchased before 2006 from use, pending a safety study.

Sagittarius
You are a progressive individual and a keen observer who may be too driven. 1, 10, 19

#1 Song
2006: "Irreplaceable" by Beyoncé

Birth Friends Forever
Massari, Canadian singer, 1980

Emmanuelle Chriqui, Canadian actress (*Entourage*), 1977

Meg White, musician (The White Stripes), 1974

Rob Blake, Canadian hockey player, 1969

Stephanie Morgenstern, Canadian actress (*Flashpoint*), 1965

Bobby Flay, television chef, 1964

Kenneth Branagh, actor (*Hamlet*), 1960

Michael Clarke Duncan, actor (*The Green Mile*), 1957

John Colicos, Canadian actor (*Star Trek*), 1928

Emily Dickinson, poet, 1830

Eugene O'Keefe, Canadian brewmaster, 1827

Daily Oddity
Border collies are considered the smartest dogs, while Afghan hounds are considered the least intelligent.

DECEMBER 11
20 days until next year

In a Days
If it is the year 2009, "Chappy Chanukah."

If you're a mountain goat or mountain folk, celebrate "International Mountain Day."

In the News
1911: Alberta brought in Canada's first Motor Vehicles Act, which set speed limits in rural and urban areas.

1919: A Labrador retriever saved 60 passengers and 32 crewmembers of a sinking ship off the coast of Newfoundland.

1931: British Parliament passed the Statute of Westminster, which gave the Dominion of Canada and the Dominion of Newfoundland their independence from Britain.

1941: The U.S. declared war on Germany and Italy.

1946: The United Nations International Children's Emergency Fund (UNICEF) was established.

1948: Newfoundland premier Joey Smallwood signed an agreement allowing Newfoundland to enter Confederation and become Canada's 10th province.

1962: Canada held its last judicial hanging.

2008: U.S. businessman Bernard Madoff was arrested and charged with securities fraud in a billion-dollar Ponzi (pyramid) scheme.

Sagittarius
You are an empathic and vigorous individual who can be too self-indulgent.
2, 12, 20

#1 Song
1986: "The Way It Is" by Bruce Hornsby & the Range

Birth Friends Forever
Mos Def, actor (*Be Kind Rewind*), 1973

Carolyn Waldo, Canadian synchronized swimmer, 1964

Michel Courtemanche, Canadian comedian, 1964

Nikki Sixx, musician (Mötley Crüe), 1958

Tony Gabriel, Canadian football player, 1948

Teri Garr, actress (*Friends*), 1944

Brenda Lee, singer, 1944

Elmer Vasko, Canadian hockey player, 1935

Pierre Pilote, Canadian hockey player, 1931

John A. Larson, Canadian inventor of the lie detector, 1892

Fiorello La Guardia, New York City mayor, 1882

John Labatt, Irish Canadian brewmaster, 1838

Daily Oddity
Under Alberta's Motor Vehicles Act of 1911, only boys over the age of 16 were allowed to drive, while only girls over the age of 18 were allowed to drive.

DECEMBER 12
19 days until next year

In a Days
Turn your green thumb red. It's "National Poinsettia Day."

In the News

1894: Canadian prime minister John Thompson died while still in office.

1901: Marconi transmitted the letter "S" over a radio signal from Signal Hill, NL, to England.

1942: A hundred people died in fire at a hostel in St. John's, NL.

1970: Roy Spencer, the father of Toronto Maple Leaf Brian Spencer, was shot and killed by police after forcing a Prince George, BC, TV station off the air at gunpoint for not carrying the Maple Leafs vs. Blackhawks game.

1981: Wayne Gretzky scored his 50th goal in 39 games.

1984: "Happy Hour" was abolished in bars throughout Ontario.

1985: Over 250 people died when an Arrow Air flight crashed near Gander, NL.

1996: Lise Thibault became the first female and first disabled person to be appointed lieutenant-governor of Québec.

2003: Paul Martin was sworn in as Canada's 21st prime minister.

Sagittarius
You are a born communicator with a sense for social justice; however, you force your beliefs onto others.
3, 12, 21

#1 Song
1978: "You Don't Bring Me Flowers" by Barbra Streisand & Neil Diamond

Birth Friends Forever

Daniel Magder, Canadian actor (*X-Men*), 1991

Colin White, Canadian hockey player, 1977

Jennifer Connelly, actress (*Hulk*), 1970

Robert Lepage, Canadian playwright, 1957

Herb Dhaliwal, Canadian politician, 1952

Billy Smith, Canadian hockey player, 1950

Bill Nighy, actor (*Underworld*), 1949

Dionne Warwick, singer, 1940

Connie Francis, singer, 1938

Bob Barker, game-show host, 1923

Frank Sinatra, singer, 1915

Huck Welch, Canadian football player, 1907

Edward G. Robinson, actor (*The Ten Commandments*), 1893

Daily Oddity
Alternative names for the poinsettia plant are the Mexican flame leaf, the Christmas star and the winter rose.

DECEMBER 13
18 days until next year

In a Days
Use some glue or enjoy some gelatin. It's "Day of the Horse."

In the News
1941: Hungary and Romania declared war on the U.S.

1979: Canadian PM Joe Clark was defeated in the House of Commons by a "vote of no confidence"; a federal election was called for February 18, 1980.

1983: Wayne Gretzky scored his 300th goal.

1990: The Canadian Senate approved the 7% Goods and Services Tax.

2000: Al Gore gave his concession speech following the Florida recount, which declared George W. Bush U.S. president.

2006: The Chinese river dolphin (*baiji*) was declared extinct.

2007: The Mitchell Report was released, listing 89 baseball players presumed to have used steroids and human growth hormone.

2008: Canada unveiled a $3.5-billion aid package for struggling auto manufacturers GM, Ford and Chrysler.

Sagittarius
You are a brisk, optimistic individual who can't help but interfere with other people's business.
4, 13, 22

#1 Song
1961: "The Lion Sleeps Tonight" by The Tokens

Birth Friends Forever
Taylor Swift, country singer, 1989
Laurence Leboeuf, Canadian actress (*The Secret*), 1985
Tom DeLonge, musician (Blink-182), 1975
Marie-Odile Raymond, Canadian cross-country skier, 1973
Jamie Foxx, actor (*Ray*), 1967
Morris Day, singer (The Time), 1957
Bob Gainey, Canadian hockey player, 1953
Ted Nugent, musician, 1948
Ferguson Jenkins, Canadian baseball player, 1943
Christopher Plummer, Canadian actor (*The Sound of Music*), 1929
Dick Van Dyke, actor (*Mary Poppins*), 1925
Emily Carr, Canadian artist, 1871
Mary Todd Lincoln, U.S. first lady, 1818

Daily Oddity
Canadian artist Emily Carr used to push her pet monkey, Woo, around in a baby carriage.

DECEMBER 14
17 days until next year

In a Days
Fling your poop. It's "Monkey Day."

In the News
1542: Princess Mary Stuart became Queen Mary I of Scotland.

1903: The Wright Brothers made their first flight attempt.

1911: Roald Amundsen became the first person to reach the South Pole.

1916: Québec banned women from entering the legal profession.

1939: The Soviet Union was expelled from the League of Nations.

1947: The National Association for Stock Car Auto Racing (NASCAR) was founded.

1972: Eugene Cernan became the last person to walk on the moon.

1982: Canada's Marcel Dionne scored his 500th NHL goal.

2003: President George W. Bush announced that Iraqi President Saddam Hussein had been captured.

2008: During a press conference, an Iraqi journalist threw his shoes at President George W. Bush; he missed both times.

Sagittarius
You are an imaginative and energetic individual who is often perceived as intimidating.
6, 16, 37

#1 Song
2001: "U Got It Bad" by Usher

Birth Friends Forever
Vanessa Hudgens, actress (*High School Musical 3*), 1988

Emilie Heymans, Canadian diver, 1981

Kim St-Pierre, Canadian hockey player, 1978

Tomasz Radzinski, Canadian soccer player, 1973

Bill Ranford, Canadian hockey player, 1966

Spider Stacy, singer (The Pogues), 1958

Steven MacLean, Canadian astronaut, 1954

Patty Duke, actress (*The Patty Duke Show*), 1946

Lee Remick, actress (*The Omen*), 1935

Don Hewitt, creator of *60 Minutes*, 1922

Deanna Durbin, Canadian actress (*Three Smart Girls*), 1921

Nostradamus, astrologer, 1503

Daily Oddity
Thursday is the best day to get a haircut.

DECEMBER 15
16 days until next year

In a Days
Warm up your mini branding iron. It's "Cat Herders Day."

In the News
1891: Canadian James Naismith introduced the first version of basketball.

1902: Using Marconi's radio system, Canada's governor general said "Hello" to King Edward VII.

1939: *Gone with the Wind* premiered.

1964: The House of Commons voted in favour of adopting a new flag design for Canada.

1969: Red River Community College opened in Winnipeg.

1973: Canadian Sandy Hawley became the first jockey to win 500 races in one year.

1979: Canadians Chris Haney and Scott Abbott created *Trivial Pursuit*.

1993: Canadian synchronized swimmer Sylvie Fréchette received her gold medal from the Barcelona Olympics after it had initially been awarded to an American because of a judge's error.

2001: The Leaning Tower of Pisa reopened after 11 years.

2008: Subzero temperatures crippled many parts of Canada.

Sagittarius
You are a forward-thinking and practical individual; however, you are impatient.
6, 15, 24

#1 Song
1974: "Cat's in the Cradle" by Harry Chapin

Birth Friends Forever
Brendan Fletcher, Canadian actor (*Supernatural*), 1981

Eric Young, Canadian pro wrestler, 1979

Michael Shanks, Canadian actor (*Stargate SG-1*), 1970

Chantal Petitclerc, Canadian wheelchair racer, 1969

Mario Marois, Canadian hockey player, 1957

Don Johnson, actor (*Miami Vice*), 1949

Dave Clark, singer (The Dave Clark Five), 1942

Tim Conway, actor (*The Apple Dumpling Gang*), 1933

Alan Freed, radio DJ, 1921

Roger Gaudry, Canadian chemist, 1913

Nero, Roman emperor, 37

Daily Oddity
Scruples, Balderdash, Mind Trap and *Pictionary* are all board games invented by Canadians.

DECEMBER 16
15 days until next year

In a Days
Break out the steel wool. It's "National Anything Covered in Chocolate Day."

In the News
1707: Mount Fuji erupted for the last recorded time.

1773: The Boston Tea Party occurred.

1948: The Winnipeg Symphony Orchestra first performed.

1949: Automobile manufacturer Saab was founded.

1950: Canadian hockey players Jean Béliveau and Bernie Geoffrion played their first NHL game.

1985: On the order of John Gotti, mafiosi Paul Castellano and Thomas Bilotti were shot dead in New York.

1992: Ottawa, New Brunswick and PEI agreed to build a 13 km bridge to the mainland, later known as the Confederation Bridge.

1994: Canadian singer Céline Dion married her manager, René Angélil.

2002: Canada agreed to limit its greenhouse gas emissions with the signing of the Kyoto Accord.

Sagittarius
You are an intelligent and meticulous individual who tends to isolate yourself from others.
6, 15, 24

#1 Song
2001: "How You Remind Me" by Nickelback

Birth Friends Forever
Éric Bélanger, Canadian hockey player, 1977

Benjamin Kowalewicz, Canadian musician (Billy Talent), 1975

Jonathan Scarfe, Canadian actor (*ER*), 1975

Donovan Bailey, Canadian sprinter, 1967

Benjamin Bratt, actor (*The Cleaner*), 1963

André-Philippe Gagnon, Canadian impressionist, 1960

Billy Gibbons, musician (ZZ Top), 1949

Philip K. Dick, author (*A Scanner Darkly*), 1928

Arthur C. Clarke, author (*2001: A Space Odyssey*), 1917

George Ignatieff, Canadian diplomat, 1913

Jane Austen, author (*Pride and Prejudice*), 1775

Ludwig van Beethoven, composer, 1770

Daily Oddity
The ancient Greeks only celebrated the birthdays of adult males, even after death.

DECEMBER 17
14 days until next year

In a Days
Smoke a cigar in celebration of "Clean Air Day."
Attempt to fly. It's "Wright Brothers Day."

In the News
1822: Canadian cartographer Peter Fidler died.

1903: The Wright Brothers first flew.

1921: Canada's beaver design for the nickel was unveiled.

1953: CBUT, Vancouver's first TV station, premiered.

1964: The Senate approved the new national flag of Canada.

1969: Bank of Canada announced it would replace the picture of Queen Elizabeth II with former PMs on the $5, $10, $50 and $100 bills.

1969: The U.S. Air Force concluded its study of UFOs, stating they are nothing but hoaxes created for publicity.

1983: Six people were killed when the IRA bombed London's Harrods department store.

1992: Canadian PM Brian Mulroney signed the North American Free Trade Accord.

2003: One hundred years after the Wright Brothers, Flight 11P of SpaceShipOne made its first supersonic flight.

Sagittarius
You are a vital and resolute individual who is often resentful of others.
8, 17, 26

#1 Song
1953: "Rags to Riches" by Tony Bennett

Birth Friends Forever
Neil Sanderson, Canadian musician (Three Days Grace), 1978

Éric Bédard, Canadian short-track speed skater, 1976

Milla Jovovich, actress (*The Fifth Element*), 1975

Giovanni Ribisi, actor (*Boiler Room*), 1974

Chuck Liddell, UFC fighter, 1969

Paul Tracy, Canadian racecar driver, 1968

Vincent Damphousse, Canadian hockey player, 1967

Craig Berube, Canadian hockey player, 1965

Bill Pullman, actor (*Independence Day*), 1953

Eugene Levy, Canadian actor (*SCTV*), 1946

Kenneth E. Iverson, Canadian computer scientist, 1920

William Lyon Mackenzie King, 10th Canadian prime minister, 1874

Daily Oddity
In Canada, $50 bills are in circulation for 2.3 years, while $100 bills last for 2 years.

DECEMBER 18
13 days until next year

In a Days
If you wish to celebrate "Wear a Plunger on your Head Day," please make sure it hasn't been recently used.

In the News

1912: The fossilized remains Piltdown Man were uncovered, but were later revealed to be a hoax.

1950: The first Canadian troops landed in Korea.

1954: Montréal Canadien Maurice Richard scored his 400th goal.

1991: Canadian singer Céline Dion signed a $10 million contract with Sony Music.

1993: Grace Hartman, the first Canadian woman to lead a national union (CUPE), died at the age of 75.

1996: Ebonics (African American Vernacular English) was officially declared a language.

1997: The Nova Scotia government apologized for the 1992 Westray methane mine explosion in Plymouth, NS, that killed 26 miners.

2008: Snow fell in Malibu, CA.

2008: Severe winter weather crippled Detroit and many parts of Ontario.

Sagittarius
You are a focused and resourceful individual who can be too focused on one task.
9, 18, 27

#1 Song
1965: "Turn! Turn! Turn!" by The Byrds

Birth Friends Forever
Christina Aguilera, singer, 1980

Katie Holmes, actress (*Batman Begins*), 1978

Trish Stratus, Canadian pro wrestler, 1975

Stone Cold Steve Austin, pro wrestler, 1964

Brad Pitt, actor (*The Curious Case of Benjamin Button*), 1963

Brian Orser, Canadian figure skater, 1961

Leonard Maltin, film critic, 1950

Steven Spielberg, director (*E.T.*), 1946

Jean Pronovost, Canadian hockey player, 1945

Keith Richards, musician (The Rolling Stones), 1943

Bramwell Morrison, Canadian musician (Sharon, Lois & Bram), 1940

Ty Cobb, baseball player, 1886

Joseph Stalin, Soviet dictator, 1878

Daily Oddity
Seasons are caused by the axial tilt of the Earth.

DECEMBER 19
12 days until next year

In a Days
Crawl underneath your Great Dane. It's "Underdog Day."

In the News
1813: James McGill died, leaving behind funding to found McGill University.

1917: The first 2 NHL games were played.

1924: The world's last Rolls-Royce Silver Ghost was sold.

1941: Adolf Hitler became the supreme commander-in-chief of the German army.

1977: In protest of apartheid in South Africa, Canada ended all commercial relations with the country.

1983: The original FIFA World Cup trophy was stolen.

1984: Wayne Gretzky scored his 1000th point.

1984: Scotty Bowman became the NHL's top winning coach.

1997: The most financially successful movie in history, *Titanic*, was released in theatres.

2008: The U.S. announced its $17-million bailout package for car manufacturers.

Sagittarius
You are an original and independent person who may be combative at times.
1, 10, 19

#1 Song
1994: "Here Comes the Hotstepper" by Ini Kamoze

Birth Friends Forever
Paulina Gretzky, daughter of Wayne Gretzky, 1988

Matt Stajan, Canadian hockey player, 1983

Jake Gyllenhaal, actor (*Brokeback Mountain*), 1980

Alyssa Milano, actress (*Charmed*), 1972

Warren Sapp, football player, 1972

Criss Angel, illusionist, 1967

Jennifer Beals, actress (*Flashdance*), 1963

Robert Urich, actor (*Spencer for Hire*), 1946

Zalman Yanovsky, Canadian musician (The Lovin' Spoonful), 1944

Cicely Tyson, actress (*Roots*), 1933

Doug Harvey, Canadian hockey player, 1924

Édith Piaf, singer, 1915

Daily Oddity
The film *Titanic* was not only directed by Canadian director James Cameron, but Canadian singer Céline Dion also provided the theme song.

DECEMBER 20
11 days until next year

In a Days
Tag! You're it. It's "Games Day."

In the News

1817: The Bank of Montréal opened.

1891: Canadian strongman Louis Cyr held his own against the pull of 4 horses.

1955: Cardiff became the capital of Wales.

1972: Canada banned whaling on the East Coast because of dwindling whale numbers.

1974: Canadian Parliament increased the number of seats in the House of Commons from 264 to 282.

1982: For the 3rd straight year, Wayne Gretzky won Canada's Male Athlete of the Year Award.

1991: The Ottawa Senators and the Tampa Bay Lightning were granted membership into the NHL.

1995: NATO forces began their peacekeeping mission in Bosnia.

1996: Apple Computer Inc. merged with NeXT, precursor to Mac OS X.

2007: Queen Elizabeth II became the UK's oldest monarch.

Sagittarius
You are a perceptive leader who often becomes too driven.
2, 11, 20

#1 Song
1993: "Hero" by Mariah Carey

Birth Friends Forever

JoJo, singer, 1990

Jonah Hill, actor (*Superbad*), 1983

Saukrates, Canadian rapper, 1977

Cory Stillman, Canadian hockey player, 1973

Nicole DeBoer, Canadian actress (*The Dead Zone*), 1970

Travis Green, Canadian hockey player, 1970

Chris Robinson, singer (Black Crowes), 1966

Ray Coburn, Canadian musician (Honeymoon Suite) 1962

Nalo Hopkinson, Canadian writer (*The Salt Roads*), 1960

Billy Bragg, singer, 1957

Peter Criss, musician (Kiss), 1945

John Hillerman, actor (*Magnum, P.I.*), 1932

Judy LaMarsh, Canadian politician, 1924

Harvey Firestone, tire magnate, 1868

Daily Oddity
Four-year-olds believe in Santa more than children of any other age.

DECEMBER 21
10 days until next year

In a Days
Bah! It's "Humbug Day."
Break out the syllables. It's "National Haiku Poetry Day."

In the News
1620: The *Mayflower* landed at Plymouth, MA.

1883: The Royal Canadian Dragoons and the Royal Canadian Regiment were formed.

1913: The world's first crossword puzzle was published.

1945: U.S. general George S. Patton died.

1963: The Canadian Weather Service received the first picture via satellite transmission.

1966: Canada passed the Medicare Act, effective July 1, 1968.

1967: The first heart transplant recipient died, 18 days after surgery.

1968: *Apollo 8*, the first manned mission to the moon, was launched.

1995: Palestine took control of the city of Bethlehem.

2004: Same-sex marriage was legalized in Newfoundland and Labrador.

Sagittarius
You are an innovative visionary who can be too self-confident.
3, 12, 21

#1 Song
1987: "Faith" by George Michael

Birth Friends Forever
Kiefer Sutherland, Canadian actor (*24*), 1966

Joey Kocur, Canadian hockey player, 1964

Ray Romano, comedian, 1957

Chris Evert, tennis player, 1954

Samuel L. Jackson, actor (*Pulp Fiction*), 1948

Frank Zappa, musician, 1940

Lloyd Axworthy, Canadian politician, 1939

Jane Fonda, actress (*On Golden Pond*), 1937

Phil Donahue, talk-show host, 1935

Edward Schreyer, premier of Manitoba, 1935

Jean Gascon, Canadian opera director, 1920

Frank Patrick, Canadian hockey player, 1885

Daily Oddity
Some believe that Christ was not born in the winter but in the spring or fall, when shepherds would leave their flocks outside to sleep.

DECEMBER 22
9 days until next year

In a Days
Put on your longjohns and take your SAD medication. It's "Winter Solstice."

In the News

1849: The execution of author Fyodor Dostoevsky (*Crime and Punishment*) was cancelled at the last minute.

1956: Colo, the first gorilla bred in captivity, was born.

1967: Pierre Trudeau made his famous statement: "There is no place for the state in the bedrooms of the nation."

1972: Canadian singer Joni Mitchell received a gold record for her album *For the Roses*.

1973: Pierre Berton made his famous statement, "A Canadian is somebody who knows how to make love in a canoe."

1974: Canada's Phil Esposito scored his 500th NHL goal.

1984: Bernhard Goetz shot 4 men on a NYC subway.

1987: Canada won the first-ever gold medal at the annual Izvestia hockey tournament.

2001: A passenger on American Airlines Flight 63 was arrested after attempting to ignite explosives hidden in his shoe.

Capricorn
You are a methodical and practical individual who can be intolerant of other people's point of view.
4, 22, 31

#1 Song
1980: "(Just Like) Starting Over" by John Lennon

Birth Friends Forever

Jordin Sparks, *American Idol* winner, 1989

Steve Kariya, Canadian hockey player, 1977

Caroline Olivier, Canadian freestyle skier, 1971

Pat Mastroianni, Canadian actor (*Degrassi*), 1971

Myriam Bédard, Canadian biathlete, 1969

Ralph Fiennes, actor (*The English Patient*), 1962

Ian Turnbull, Canadian hockey player, 1953

Maurice and Robin Gibb, musicians (The Bee Gees), 1949

Diane Sawyer, television journalist, 1945

Lucien Bouchard, Canadian politician, 1938

Lady Bird Johnson, U.S. first lady, 1912

Daily Oddity
Most Christmas trees are cut down when they are 10 years old.

DECEMBER 23
8 days until next year

In a Days
It's a Christmas gift to the atheists. It's "Festivus."

In the News

1869: Louis Riel became president of the National Committee of Métis.

1938: A coelacanth, a long-thought-extinct relative of the lungfish, was discovered in South Africa.

1947: The transistor was first demonstrated.

1954: The first human kidney transplant was performed.

1958: Tokyo Tower, the world's highest self-supporting iron tower, was dedicated.

1966: The Royal Canadian Mint announced that dimes and quarters would be minted from nickel instead of silver.

1977: After protests from vending-machine operators, the Canadian mint postponed minting smaller pennies.

1983: Jeanne Sauvé became the first female Canadian governor general.

1986: *The Voyager* became the first aircraft to fly non-stop around the world.

2007: Canadian jazz pianist Oscar Peterson died.

Capricorn
You are a decisive leader who may be perceived as too authoritarian.
4, 23, 30

#1 Song
1952: "I Saw Mommy Kissing Santa Claus" by Jimmy Boyd

Birth Friends Forever

Esthero, Canadian singer, 1978

Estella Warren, Canadian model, 1978

Corey Haim, Canadian actor (*The Two Coreys*), 1971

Catriona LeMay Doan, Canadian speed skater, 1970

Eddie Vedder, singer (Pearl Jam), 1964

Dan Bigras, Canadian singer, 1957

Susan Lucci, actress (*All My Children*), 1946

Harry Shearer, voice actor (*The Simpsons*), 1943

Robert Labine, Canadian politician, 1940

Chet Baker, jazz trumpeter, 1929

Guy Beaulne, Canadian theatre director, 1921

Yousuf Karsh, Canadian photographer, 1908

Daily Oddity
The "X" in "Xmas" is actually an ancient Greek abbreviation for "Christ."

DECEMBER 24
7 days until next year

In a Days
It's too late to pretend to be nice. It's "Christmas Eve."

In the News

1781: Canada's first Christmas tree was erected at Fort Sorel, Québec.

1906: Canadian Reginald Fessenden sent the world's first radio broadcast, which also featured the first broadcast of music.

1914: The WWI "Christmas truce" between the Germans and the British went into effect.

1939: Pope Pius XII made a Christmas Eve appeal for peace during WWII.

1948: Canada officially recognized the state of Israel.

1955: North American Aerospace Defense Command (NORAD) began tracking Santa's progress on Christmas Eve.

1974: Canadian singer Joni Mitchell went Christmas carolling with James Taylor, Carly Simon and Linda Ronstadt.

1989: Canada's House of Commons approved the North American Free Trade Agreement (NAFTA).

2003: Canada placed a partial ban on U.S. beef following a case of mad cow disease in Washington State.

Capricorn
You are an astute and rational individual who sometimes can be too self-absorbed.
6, 14, 24

#1 Song
2005: "Run It!" by Chris Brown

Birth Friends Forever

Ryan Seacrest, TV host, 1974

Ricky Martin, singer, 1971

Steve Smith, Canadian actor (*The Red Green Show*), 1945

Lemmy, singer (Motörhead), 1945

Bill Crothers, Canadian runner, 1940

Mary Higgins Clark, author (*Where Are the Children?*), 1927

Paul Buissonneau, Canadian theatre director, 1926

Ava Gardner, actress (*The Barefoot Contessa*), 1922

Howard Hughes, director/aviator/inventor, 1905

Joey Smallwood, premier of Newfoundland, 1900

Johnny Gruelle, creator of Raggedy Ann, 1880

Émile Nelligan, Canadian poet, 1879

Daily Oddity
Santa must travel 112 km per second to deliver all the toys on Christmas Eve.

DECEMBER 25
6 days until next year

In a Days
Where are the presents? It's "Christmas Day!"
I simpy ove no "No 'L' Day."

In the News

7–2 BC: The Virgin Mary gave birth to a son in Bethlehem.

1223: Francis of Assisi organized the first Nativity scene.

1535: Jacques Cartier and his crew celebrated the first recorded Canadian Christmas.

1643: Christmas Island, an Australian territory, was founded.

1818: The first performance of "Silent Night" was held.

1855: Members of the Royal Canadian Rifles used field hockey sticks and a lacrosse ball to play the first-ever game of ice hockey.

1914: German and British troops called a ceasefire in honour of Christmas.

1974: A man strapped with explosives and claiming to be the Messiah drove his Chevy Impala through the gates of the White House.

1990: The first successful trial run of the World Wide Web occurred.

2008: The first Canada-wide white Christmas in over 30 years occurred.

Capricorn
You are an idealistic bringer of the greater good; however, you may be too much of a perfectionist.
6, 15, 24

#1 Song
1970: "My Sweet Lord" by George Harrison

Birth Friends Forever

Alexandre Trudeau, son of Pierre Trudeau, 1973

Dido, singer, 1971

Justin Trudeau, son of Pierre Trudeau, 1971

Stu Barnes, Canadian hockey player, 1970

Jon Kimura Parker, Canadian pianist, 1959

Rickey Henderson, baseball player, 1958

Alannah Myles, Canadian singer, 1955

Annie Lennox, singer, 1954

Jimmy Buffett, singer, 1946

Rod Serling, creator of *The Twilight Zone*, 1924

Gerhard Herzberg, Canadian physicist, 1904

Humphrey Bogart, actor (*Casablanca*), 1899

Isaac Newton, physicist, 1642

Daily Oddity
The 12 days of Christmas begin today and last until Epiphany, January 6.

DECEMBER 26
5 days until next year

In a Days
Knock someone out. It's "Boxing Day."
If you celebrate "Kwanzaa," it starts today.
Ahhh, maaan, I can't believe it's "National Whiner's Day."
Suck it! It's "Candy Cane Day."

In the News
1871: William Gilbert and Arthur Sullivan teamed up for the first time.

1898: The Curies isolated radium.

1919: Babe Ruth was sold to the New York Yankees.

1925: Turkey adopted the Gregorian calendar.

1933: FM radio was patented.

1966: The first Kwanzaa was celebrated.

1982: *Time* magazine's "Man of the Year" was the PC (personal computer).

1986: The world's population allegedly hit 5 billion.

1991: The USSR was dissolved.

1998: Strong winds knocked out power throughout the UK.

2004: Hundreds of thousands died when a 9.0-magnitude earthquake created a tsunami, which ravaged Thailand, Malaysia and Indonesia.

2005: A gang shootout on Toronto's Yonge St. claimed the life of a 15-year-old female bystander.

Capricorn
You are an objective and resourceful individual who tends to neglect the help of others.
10, 19, 28

#1 Song
2005: "Don't Forget About Us" by Mariah Carey

Birth Friends Forever
Jared Leto, actor (*Fight Club*), 1971
Lars Ulrich, musician (Metallica), 1963
Ozzie Smith, baseball player, 1954
John Walsh, TV host (*America's Most Wanted*), 1945
Phil Spector, music producer, 1940
Ronnie Prophet, Canadian singer, 1937
Norm Ullman, Canadian hockey player, 1935
Arnold Spohr, Canadian choreographer, 1927
Steve Allen, talk-show host, 1921
Richard Widmark, actor (*The Alamo*), 1914
Henry Miller, author (*Tropic of Cancer*), 1891
Jean-Baptiste Lagimodière, Canadian fur trader, 1778

Daily Oddity
More people appear to have died on Boxing Day than on any other day.

DECEMBER 27
4 days until next year

In a Days
Have an impromptu family reunion. It's "Visit the Zoo Day."

In the News
1831: Charles Darwin set sail aboard the HMS *Beagle*.

1845: Ether was used as an anesthetic for the first time.

1869: Canadian folk hero Louis Riel was elected president of the provisional government of Rupert's Land and the North West.

1945: The World Bank was formed.

1972: Former Prime Minister Lester B. Pearson died at the age of 75.

1978: Spain became a democracy.

1981: Wayne Gretzky set the record for the fastest 100 points scored in NHL history.

2004: Canada donated $4 million to the Indian Ocean earthquake relief effort.

2007: Pakistan's first female prime minister, Benazir Bhutto, was assassinated.

Capricorn
You are a perceptive and kind person; however, you disregard your own self-interests.
11, 32, 44

#1 Song
1989: "Another Day in Paradise" by Phil Collins

Birth Friends Forever
Hayley Williams, singer (Paramore), 1988

Paul Stastny, Canadian hockey player, 1985

Fernando Pisani, Canadian hockey player, 1976

Chyna, pro wrestler, 1969

Arthur Kent, Canadian TV journalist, 1953

Jay Hill, Canadian politician, 1952

Mickey Redmond, Canadian hockey player, 1947

Elizabeth Smart, Canadian poet, 1913

Marlene Dietrich, actress (*Touch of Evil*), 1901

Alfred Edwin McKay, Canadian WWI ace pilot, 1892

Cyrus S. Eaton, Canadian financier, 1883

Mackenzie Bowell, Canada's 5th prime minister, 1823

Daily Oddity
New Year's Around the World: South American families fill a life-sized male effigy with items that have bad memories attached to them and light it on fire at midnight; people in Spain eat 12 grapes for each stroke of the clock; Brazilians wear all-white clothing; children in Greece leave their shoes by the fire in the hope that St. Basil will fill them with gifts.

DECEMBER 28
3 days until next year

In a Days
If you are a male child born in Bethlehem around the same time as Christ, be warned, it's "Childermas: The Massacre of the Innocents."

In the News
1065: Westminster Abbey was consecrated.

1612: Galileo Galilei became the first to observe the planet Neptune.

1795: Upper Canada Governor John Graves Simcoe commenced the construction of what would become Toronto's Yonge Street.

1908: Over 75,000 died in an earthquake in Sicily.

1929: Former WWI pilot Wilfred Wop May flew the first airmail to Aklavik, NWT.

1944: Canada's Maurice Richard became the first NHL player to score 8 points in one game.

1981: America's first test-tube baby was born.

1989: Thirteen people died when a 5.6-magnitude earthquake hit New South Wales, Australia.

2000: After 128 years in business, American retail giant Montgomery Ward announced it was going out of business.

Capricorn
You are an inspirational and profound individual who tends to wear yourself too thin.
10, 19, 28

#1 Song
1975: "Saturday Night" by The Bay City Rollers

Birth Friends Forever
Sienna Miller, actress (*Factory Girl*), 1981

Elizabeth Jordan Carr, test-tube baby, 1981

John Legend, singer, 1978

Raymond Bourque, Canadian hockey player, 1960

Denzel Washington, actor (*Glory*), 1954

Maggie Smith, actress (*Harry Potter* series), 1934

Terry Sawchuk, Canadian hockey player, 1929

Moe Koffman, Canadian musician, 1928

Stan Lee, comic book legend, 1922

Woodrow Wilson, U.S. president, 1856

Calixa Lavallée, Canadian composer of "O Canada," 1842

John Molson, Canadian brewmaster, 1763

Daily Oddity
The top 2 New Year's resolutions are losing weight and quitting smoking.

DECEMBER 29
2 days until next year

In a Days
Be it an alarm clock or a maternal clock, it's "Tick Tock Day."

In the News
1635: Québec banned blasphemy.

1813: A British-led Canadian militia set fire to Buffalo, NY.

1890: Over 200 men, women and children of the Lakota Sioux were killed in the Wounded Knee Massacre.

1967: Canada abolished the death penalty.

1989: Canada became the first country to ban smoking on all domestic airlines.

1989: Associated Press named Wayne Gretzky the "Male Athlete of the Decade."

1997: Racecar driver Jacques Villeneuve was voted Canada's "Male Athlete of the Year."

1997: To prevent the spread of influenza, 1.25 million chickens were slaughtered in Hong Kong.

2004: The USDA announced that Canada was a "minimal-risk region" for BSE, following a case of mad cow disease in Alberta; as well, Canadian beef importation would resume on March 7, 2005.

Capricorn
You are a multitalented and tenacious individual who tends to put other people's desires before your own.
11, 20, 29

#1 Song
1973: "Time in a Bottle" by Jim Croce

Birth Friends Forever
Mekhi Phifer, actor (*8 Mile*), 1974

Jude Law, actor (*Alfie*), 1972

Ashleigh Banfield, Canadian journalist, 1967

Andy Wachowski, co-director (*The Matrix*), 1967

Dexter Holland, singer (The Offspring), 1965

Lisa Savijarvi, Canadian alpine skier, 1963

Georges Thurston, Canadian singer, 1951

Ted Danson, actor (*Cheers*), 1947

Rick Danko, Canadian musician (The Band), 1942

Jon Voight, actor (*Deliverance*), 1938

Mary Tyler Moore, actress (*Mary Tyler Moore Show*), 1936

Charles Goodyear, tire magnate, 1800

Daily Oddity
The English translation of the New Year's phrase "Auld Lang Syne" is "As Time Goes By."

DECEMBER 30
1 day until next year

In a Days
Gather round your artificial Christmas tree and celebrate "Falling Needles Family Fest Day."

In the News

1870: Manitoba held its first provincial election.

1909: Gold was discovered in Porcupine, ON.

1924: Astronomer Edwin Hubble announced the existence of other galaxies.

1953: The first colour television went on sale for US$1175.

1965: Ferdinand Marcos became president of the Phillipines.

1977: Serial killer Ted Bundy escaped from his jail cell for the 2nd time.

1981: Wayne Gretzky scored 50 goals in 39 games.

1988: The Canadian Senate approved the Canada-U.S. Free Trade Agreement.

1995: The UK experienced its coldest ever temperature, −27°C.

2003: Canadian Governor General Adrienne Clarkson met with Canadian troops stationed in Afghanistan.

2006: Former Iraqi president Saddam Hussein was hanged.

Capricorn
You are a focused and down-to-earth individual who is easily irritated.
12, 21, 30

#1 Song
1979: "Please Don't Go" by K.C. & the Sunshine Band

Birth Friends Forever
LeBron James, basketball player, 1984

Kristin Kreuk, Canadian actress (*Smallville*), 1982

Tiger Woods, golfer, 1975

Carl Ouellet, Canadian pro wrestler, 1967

Michelle Douglas, Canadian activist, 1963

Douglas Coupland, Canadian author (*Generation X*), 1961

Tracey Ullman, comedian, 1959

Matt Lauer, TV journalist, 1957

Jeff Lynne, musician (ELO), 1947

Patti Smith, singer, 1946

Davy Jones, singer (The Monkees), 1945

Bo Diddley, musician, 1928

William Aberhart, Canadian politician, 1878

Stephen Leacock, Canadian humorist, 1869

Rudyard Kipling, author (*The Jungle Book*), 1865

Daily Oddity
In the Middle Ages New Year's Day was March 25.

DECEMBER 31
0 days until next year

In a Days
Hurry up! It's "Make Up Your Mind Day."
Pardon me, but it's "No Interruptions Day."
Apply cold-sore medication and pucker up. It's "New Year's Eve."

In the News
1638: A lunar eclipse sent Huron Natives into a panic.
1857: Ottawa was chosen as Canada's capital.
1904: The first New Year's Eve celebration was held in Times Square.
1923: BBC broadcasted the chimes of Big Ben over the radio for the first time.
1929: Canadian bandleader Guy Lombardo played "Auld Lang Syne" to usher in the New Year for the first time.
1955: GM became the first American corporation to make over $1 billion in a year.
1960: The British farthing was discontinued.
1999: The Y2K Bug threatened to wipe out all computer systems.
2004: Taipei 101, the world's tallest skyscraper at 509 m, opened.
2008: Because of the slowing of the Earth's rotation, an extra second was added to the last day of 2008.

Capricorn
You are a rational and resourceful individual who becomes impatient when you are impeded.
4, 13, 22

#1 Song
1896: "A Hot Time in the Old Town" by Dan Quinn

Birth Friends Forever
Joe McIntyre, singer (New Kids on the Block), 1972
Gerry Dee, Canadian actor (*Trailer Park Boys*), 1968
Nicholas Sparks, author (*The Notebook*), 1965
Val Kilmer, actor (*The Doors*), 1959
George Thorogood, musician, 1951
René Robert, Canadian hockey player, 1948
Burton Cummings, Canadian singer (The Guess Who), 1947
John Denver, singer, 1943
Ben Kingsley, actor (*Gandhi*), 1943
Anthony Hopkins, actor (*Silence of the Lambs*), 1937
Elizabeth Arden, Canadian cosmetics magnate, 1878
Jacques Cartier, French explorer of Canada, 1491

Daily Oddity
Wearing red underwear on New Year's Eve will bring new love in the coming year.

ABOUT THE AUTHOR

Shane Sellar

Born in Winnipeg, Manitoba, Shane Sellar always had a fascination with the strange and unusual, leading him to the worlds of comic books, film, pulp art, early sci-fi publications and most recently, trivia books. Thanks to this ever-expanding knowledge of ancient and useless things, he is very popular with the over-80 crowd.

Shane is lead reporter at *The Community Voice* newspaper—a job that relies on the collection of facts, figures and dates all day long. He continues to write as The Vidiot, a sardonic film review column now found in *BeatRoute* magazine. Shane lives in Spruce Grove, Alberta, with his fiancée.

MORE TRIVIA FROM BLUE BIKE BOOKS...

WEIRD CANADIAN WEATHER
Catastrophes, Ice Storms, Floods, Tornadoes, Hurricanes and Tsunamis
by A.H. Jackson
This book covers everything from prairie chinooks to the different types of snow crystals, flash floods, ice storms, droughts and everything in between. It includes statistics such as the warmest lake waters in Canada and where exactly the most rain fell in just one hour.
$14.95 • ISBN: 978-1-897278-39-0 • 5.25" x 8.25" • 224 pages

BOOK OF BABIES
Parent's Guide to Tradition, Trivia and Curious Facts
by Lisa Wojna
Babies are life's little miracles. Everything about them—from conception to birth and beyond—is fascinating. *Book of Babies* includes intriguing scientific facts, strange stories, famous stars and their "celebu-spawn" and cultural practices across the globe.
$14.95 • ISBN: 978-1-897278-53-6 • 5.25" x 8.25" • 224 pages

CANADIAN BABY NAMES
by Carla MacKay
Naming your child is one of the biggest decisions of early parenting because whatever name you choose becomes the identity of your baby for life. *Canadian Baby Names* helps parents get a handle on what's in a name and highlights the interesting history behind the most popular names in Canada throughout the 20th and 21st centuries.
$18.95 • ISBN: 978-1-897278-55-0 • 5.25" x 8.25" • 344 pages

BRIDE'S BOOK OF TRADITIONS, TRIVIA & CURIOUS FACTS
by Rachel Conard and Lisa Wojna
Around the world, unique traditions and observances are connected to the marriage ceremony. This fun and fascinating book recounts many of the more distinctive facts associated with getting hitched.
$14.95 • ISBN: 978-1-897278-51-2 • 5.25" x 8.25" • 224 pages

WHAT IS CANADA?
The Ultimate Canadian Quiz Book
by Dan de Figueiredo
Test your knowledge on Canadian quotes, emblems, holidays, history, words, language, sports, geography, science, arts, entertainment, literature, crime and First Nations.
$18.95 • ISBN: 978-1-897278-50-5 • 5.25" x 8.25" • 392 pages

Available from your local bookseller or by contacting the distributor,
Lone Pine Publishing
1-800-661-9017
www.lonepinepublishing.com